William Crozier, Peter Henderson

How the Farm Pays

The Experiences of Forty Years of Successful Farming and Gardening

William Crozier, Peter Henderson

How the Farm Pays

The Experiences of Forty Years of Successful Farming and Gardening

ISBN/EAN: 9783337076207

Printed in Europe, USA, Canada, Australia, Japan

Cover: Foto ©ninafisch / pixelio.de

More available books at **www.hansebooks.com**

HOW THE FARM PAYS.

THE EXPERIENCES OF FORTY YEARS

OF

SUCCESSFUL

FARMING AND GARDENING

BY THE AUTHORS,

WILLIAM CROZIER

AND

PETER HENDERSON.

NEW YORK:
PETER HENDERSON & CO., 35 & 37 CORTLANDT ST.
1884.

CONTENTS.

	PAGE.
INTRODUCTION	7 and 8

CHAPTER I.

TRAINING FOR THE BUSINESS OF FARMING—AGRICULTURAL COLLEGE EDUCATION—SELECTION OF SOILS—USE OF MANURE—FARM ROADS—DRAINING...................................9 to 25

CHAPTER II.

MANURES AND THE MODES OF APPLICATION—SPECIAL FERTILIZERS—GREEN MANURING—FERTILIZING BY FEEDING.....26 to 37

CHAPTER III.

PLOWING, HARROWING AND CULTIVATING—PLOWS—HARROWS—CULTIVATORS—ROLLING LAND—ROLLERS—USE OF THE FEET IN SOWING AND PLANTING.........................38 to 51

CHAPTER IV.

ROTATION OF CROPS—CORN—POTATOES—POTATO DISEASES—SWEET POTATOES—ROOTS—WHEAT—OATS—BARLEY—RYE—BEANS—BUCKWHEAT.................................52 to 84

CHAPTER V.

CROPS FOR SOILING AND FODDER—RYE—LUCERN OR ALFALFA—MILLET—PEAS AND OATS—FODDER CORN—FEEDING SOILING CROPS—ABORTION IN COWS AND ITS CAUSES—ERGOTS...85 to 109

CHAPTER VI.

GRASS AND ITS MANAGEMENT—VARIETIES OF GRASSES—MIXED GRASSES FOR PASTURE AND HAY......................110 to 133

CHAPTER VII.

CUTTING AND CURING OF HAY—CLOVER HAY—ENSILAGE—ENSILAGE COMPARED WITH ROOTS.....................134 to 145

CHAPTER VIII.

LIVE STOCK OF THE FARM—VARIETIES OF CATTLE—RECORDS OF JERSEY COWS—RECORDS OF GUERNSEY COWS—CATTLE FOR BEEF—POINTS OF PURE BRED CATTLE—THE BEST COWS FOR THE DAIRY—FEED AND CARE FOR MILK AND BUTTER—YOUNG CATTLE AND THEIR CARE—MANAGEMENT OF THE DAIRY—FARM HORSES—SHEEP—SWINE—FARM BUILDINGS—FENCES—REARING AND KEEPING POULTRY—DOGS FOR THE FARM—USEFUL TABLES FOR THE FARM............146 to 250

CHAPTER IX.

PESTS OF THE FARM—DESTRUCTIVE ANIMALS—INSECT PESTS—PARASITES—PESTS OF THE CROPS—INJURIOUS INSECTS—REMEDIES—VEGETABLE PESTS......................251 to 274

CHAPTER X.

FARM MACHINERY—PLOWS—HARROWS—CULTIVATORS—MOWERS AND REAPERS—HAYING MACHINERY—FODDER CUTTERS—CORN HUSKERS AND SHELLERS—CARTS—STEAM ENGINES..275 to 300

CHAPTER XI.

PAGE.

FARM CULTURE OF VEGETABLES AND FRUITS—CABBAGE—CELERY—THE WHITE PLUME CELERY—SWEET CORN—CUCUMBERS FOR PICKLES—MELONS AS A MARKET CROP—ONIONS....301 to 360

CHAPTER XII.

CULTURE OF PRINCIPAL SMALL FRUIT CROPS—STRAWBERRIES—BLACKBERRIES—RASPBERRIES—CURRANTS—GOOSEBERRIES—GRAPES—ORCHARD FRUITS........................361 to 379

INDEX...381 to 400

INTRODUCTION.

It is doubtful if any book on agriculture has ever been written in this country of which the writers have had opportunities for such extensive and varied experience as have the authors of this work. WILLIAM CROZIER is, perhaps, now better known than any other farmer on this continent, principally from the fact that for the past twenty years the exhibition of his fine stock and other farm products has enabled him to take more prizes than any other working farmer in the country, and that to-day the dairy and farm at Northport, L. I., on which these products have been raised, are models worthy of imitation by the tens of thousands engaged in farming who have failed to make it the profitable business that it has been, and still continues to be, to Mr. Crozier. The co-author, PETER HENDERSON, the senior member of our firm, although not a farmer, has long been considered, as is well known, an authority on all matters relating to practical garden work. His book, *Gardening for Profit*, now in the hands of probably 100,000 readers, has shown how to make gardening pay. In the present work Mr. Henderson tells in plain words the manner of growing such *Vegetables* and *Fruits* as can best be made profitable on the farm, besides interchanging with Mr. Crozier his opinions on such operations of the farm as his long practice in cultivating the soil enables him to do.

Mr. Crozier and Mr. Henderson have had the project in contemplation of getting up a work on American farming for the past ten years; but both being engaged in the active work of their large operations on the farm and garden, it is doubtful if they would ever have got together to accomplish it, unless the idea had been conceived of getting the work up in conversational form, the words as spoken being taken down by a stenographer. This simplified the work of book making greatly, and it is believed that given in this way it has been made plainer and more interesting to the reader than if written in the usual manner. The benefit of this plan is derived from the fact that the answer often suggests a question, just such as the reader would be likely to ask, but with no one at his elbow to answer. It is here answered to the satisfaction of the questioner, or if not, the question is repeated till the subject has been made clear.

The illustrations given in the work are believed to represent the best standard types of their several kinds that we possess up to this date, the object in all cases being to give such as are the best and the most practical and economical for the farmer's purposes.

PETER HENDERSON & CO.,
Publishers.

35 & 37 CORTLANDT ST.,
NEW YORK.

CHAPTER I.

TRAINING FOR THE BUSINESS OF FARMING.

QUESTION. What, in your opinion, Mr. Crozier, are the chances of making a farm pay, if the owner is unable to superintend it himself, and has to rely on the knowledge of hired superintendence? This is a question that has been asked me scores of times each season, in regard to the business of market gardening, and my unvarying reply has been, that the chances for success are all against the person undertaking such a business under such conditions.

ANSWER. I am inundated with the same sort of inquiries, and am glad to have an opportunity of making a general reply. I entirely coincide with your opinion, that no man should attempt farming, or gardening, in the hope of making it a profitable business, unless he is willing and able to take hold with his own hands and employ his own brains in the work. I have known of many who have made large investments in farming and stock raising, but have never known one instance where the owner who failed to take an active part in the work ever made it a success. It is unreasonable to expect it. If you or I took it into our heads to engage in the dry goods or grocery business, and put our hands in our pockets and trusted entirely to the knowledge, honesty and energy of a hired manager to run the business, it is certain that these pockets would soon be empty if their supply was dependent upon the profits. But the educated city merchant, doctor, lawyer or parson is apt to look upon the tillers of the soil as a slow, ignorant, unlettered class, destitute of business capacities, and often deludes himself with the belief that his want of knowledge of rural affairs will be more than compensated by his advantages of education or business experience, when he concludes to engage in farming. This delusion draws hundreds from the city to the farm, to their ruin, every year. The only true way for a man who has previously been engaged in other business, and who wishes to become a farmer, is to get the privilege of taking active hold of the work, under the instruction of some farmer who has made the business a success. Twelve months thus spent with energy and application, would give him a knowledge from which a reasonable chance of success might be expected, always provided he has the elements of success within himself. But this advice is only applicable to young men. It would be folly for men of middle age or past it to make the attempt. In this connection I may cite a very marked case, and one which gives me a very pleasing remembrance. Dr. Shann, of York, England, wrote to me some twelve years ago, asking me to take his son, a young man of twenty-one, who had just completed a college course at Cambridge. I agreed to his proposal, and the young fellow duly appeared one morning, very unlike the ideal farmer indeed, dressed in the latest fashion and cane in hand. I much feared to look at him, that he would not be a success at the plow; but after allowing him to prospect around for a few days, I told him that the contract between his father and me required that he should take hold and obey orders the same as my ordinary hired men. He at once went down to the village, rigged himself out with a pair of overalls, flannel shirt and strong boots, and announced himself ready. His first initiation to work was assisting to wash a herd of Berkshire pigs shoulder to shoulder with a rough Irishman. From this point I saw that he was made of the right stuff, and placed him during the year and a half that he was with me through all the grades of our work. He was so energetic and trustworthy, that after he had been with me a year, I entrusted him to take a lot of cattle, sheep and swine to the State Fair at Atlanta, Ga., with permission to sell all if he deemed the price sufficient. This he did to my entire satisfaction. While there he saw a farm which his father purchased and stocked for him, and to-day he is one of the most successful farmers, perhaps, in Georgia.

(Mr. H.) I have always some five or six such men in my employment who have come to learn the finer parts of Horticulture. They come to us at a younger age than would be suitable for the heavier work of the farm, usually from fifteen to sixteen, and I select all by the merit of their letters of application, for I hold, that with the advantages of education which our school system affords, if a boy at sixteen has not had ambition enough to be able to write intelligently at that age, the chances are that he is not likely to become an intelligent workman; and for an apprentice we want nothing else, as we can get all the hewers of wood and drawers of water we want, at our doors; but brains are not so easily obtained. But with all our care in selecting, not more than one in ten ever attains to any prominence, and such usually develop superiority from the first. About ten years ago I received an application from a boy living in one of the suburbs of New York. He said that he was sixteen, and his letter was so terse and to the point that I told him to call. When he made his appearance he looked so small and slight that I told him I thought our work would be too heavy for him. He begged to be allowed to try. He was started at $3.00 per week, but before he was twenty years of age, his energy, intelligence and untiring industry made his services so valuable, that I paid him a salary of $1,200 per year, which was more than I paid my foreman, a man of forty, who had been at the business for twenty years. But I could not keep the young man even at that. He had saved money enough to start on his own account, and is now on the straight road to fortune. But there are few similar cases in my experience of over twenty years with such youths. I have only had one other instance of the kind, but many of them have made fairly successful business men, and scores of graduates from our establishment are now engaged in the florist and market garden business in all parts of the country.

Q. What is your opinion of the value of agricultural colleges, Mr. Henderson, as training schools in the branches of farming or gardening?

A. I am afraid my opinion is too pronounced on this subject to be agreeable to the directors of some of these institutions. That they might be made the very best mediums for such a purpose I have not the least doubt, if the directors would only be convinced that the superintendents, to be successful, must have an actual practical working experience varied and extended enough to make them masters of the subject. But thus far I have good reason to believe that few of them have such men. The great trouble is that they fritter away the time of the students on abstruse and practically useless theoretical studies, wasting life in attempting to get at the often doubtful causes for the attainment of important results in the so-called science of agriculture; which, after all, with all the help of Liebig, and other such men, is almost entirely ignored by the farmers and gardeners who are the kings in those industries to-day both in Europe and America.

I will here repeat the views I expressed in the *Rural New Yorker* in May, 1883, in a discussion of this question.

"The longer I live, the less I believe in the value attached to the so-called science of agriculture. I believe that a fairly educated youth would have far better chances for success in life if the four or six years spent under the different professors of an agricultural college (as they are generally conducted) were spent in actual work of ten hours a day in a well conducted farm or garden. The work might not be so pleasant, and his manners might not have the polish that friction with scholastic minds might give, but he would be better fitted for the battle of life.

"There is awful humbug about many parts of the so-called Science of Agriculture. The 'Agricultural Chemist' analyzes the soil and finds that it contains, or does not contain, certain elements which must be withheld, or put in, in fertilizing. He analyzes cabbage, corn, potatoes, wheat, turnips, oranges, lettuce, strawberries, roses and a score of other genera of plants, and makes a special formula of a fertilizer for each. Every intelligent, practical farmer, with ten years' experience, knows that this is utter nonsense; and yet, in not a few of our agricultural colleges, these special fertilizers, for special purposes, are religiously adopted. If, in the schools for instruction in agriculture, the lessons were given in the field, instead of, as now, in the college, we might then look for different results.

"When a boy, I was a pupil in a country school in Scotland. It was the time when Captain Berkley, and other sprigs of the English aristocracy, made the science of pugilism fashionable, and many of the sons of the better class of British yeomen took lessons in the 'science.' One of these, one day, landed at Edinburgh as a pupil at our country school. He was an aggressive fellow and a great blower, and in a few days he succeeded in making most of us stand in fear and awe of his wonderful 'science.' But one day another new boy came, a blacksmith's son, who had occasionally taken a hand with the sledge-hammer, a quiet, retiring lad, whom the bully thought a good subject to force a quarrel upon. It was accepted quicker than he anticipated. In a few minutes the young blacksmith had given him a thorough thrashing. He blubbered and admitted he was whipped, but said the fight had not been a fair one, for '*that boy had not fought according to science.*' Maybe he had not, but he came out victor, nevertheless. It is true that the graduates of West Point proved some of the best generals during the late war, but it must not be forgotten that the training there is but the rehearsing of actual war, except the bloodshed—practical work, all of it—call it science, if you please. 'The tree is known by its fruits,' and if ever the day comes that the graduates of our agricultural colleges become the leaders—the generals in agriculture and horticulture—then the advocates of these institutions will be justified in glorifying themselves; but while the representative farmers come (as they almost exclusively now do) from the ranks of the hard-handed workers in old mother earth, the agricultural community will look with doubtful approval on the agricultural colleges, as now conducted, as a means of instruction."

Q. From your business as a breeder of fancy stock, Mr. Crozier, you must have had many opportunities of judging whether the hundreds of gentlemen farmers, as they are called, make their ventures pay in money in the long run?

A. I do not, of my own knowledge, recall a single instance where such men have ever got their original investments back, although many of them, having competent overseers, are handling their fancy stock in a manner which, if energetically followed up as a business, ought to pay them nearly as well as we farmers who have to make our living by it. But there is another element that compensates, outside of any money return, and that is that it is a healthful recreation, a safety-valve, so to speak, from the perplexities of business with which the merchant or professional man is visited. A well known New York gentleman at the head of one of the largest corporations there, in speaking with me the other day about this matter, said that his original investment in fancy stock on his farm and gardens was upwards of $100,000, and that it cost him to maintain them nearly $40,000 annually; but he said that the recreation he enjoyed from such an investment, which he could well afford, in all probability would add ten years to his life. The advantage gained by men of wealth in indulging in such an occupation, instead of in paintings or other works of art, is, that before they can view their treasures, they must get out into the open air and sunshine, which is a valuable factor to take into account along with the pleasures of the pursuit.

THE SOIL.

(Mr. H.) I suppose you will agree with me in believing that the first subject, and by all odds the most important factor, of success in farming, is the soil. This must ever be, other things being equal, the fundamental element of success. While in Europe a few years ago, on an extended tour in Great Britain and the Continent, I observed that although the lands in all these regions had been cultivated probably for five hundred years, wherever the soil was naturally fertile there were found good farm buildings, good fences, horses, wagons and harness, everything to indicate prosperity. On the other hand, wherever a poor, sterile soil predominated, there were found farm buildings, fences and cattle that indicated poverty. As well may a stage coach attempt to compete with a locomotive, as a farmer owning poor and sterile land with the owner of a rich, fertile soil, if they sell their products in the same market. It is a delusive belief, that manuring or tillage, no matter how good, will ever bring a poor, thin soil into *permanent* fertility, unless the application of manure is yearly continued; for no ordinary amount of manuring or cultivation will maintain the fertility of any soil over two years, as it will then either have been taken up by the crops growing on it, or else have been washed down below the depth at which the roots penetrate. It requires some extent of practical experience to know what is a good soil. I well remember a blunder that I made in my early experience in this matter. My partner and I, when we started business in Jersey City, N. J., had both been regularly bred as horticulturists, partly in Europe and partly here, and yet on our first purchase of lands for market garden purposes in Hudson County, N. J.—which borders on New York City—we made a mistake in our selection, and no amount of the highest culture, although that is now thirty years ago, has ever been able to bring the soil into what would be termed even second-rate condition. The error we made was in selecting a soil apparently good, but which was underlaid by a stratum of clay ten inches below the surface; and to-day, with all our draining and subsoiling and every known means of culture, it is impossible for us to raise crops as good as those half a mile away where the subsoil is of porous sand. I mention this to show the importance of selecting, whenever practicable, a suitable soil for all operations, whether of the farm or of the garden; for had it not been by an accident of circumstance, that our lands became valuable from their proximity to the city, our unfortunate purchase would have ruined us. Now, Mr. Crozier, with these preliminary remarks in relation to soil, let me ask: What are the general characteristics of the soil here on your farm, on which you have been so successful in raising the various root and other crops?

A. It is a sandy loam in some places and gravelly loam in others; the sandy loam runs from ten to fifteen inches in depth, and the subsoil is a mixture of loam and sand. The gravelly soil is about ten inches in depth, with a subsoil which runs into a fine sand, similar to that which the sandy loam overlies.

Q. Have you ever had any experience with adhesive soils overlying clay, and what has been your success with such soils, and with what crops?

A. I have had good success with oats, rye, barley and turnips; but for mangels, carrots, or other deep-rooted root crops, the lighter soil is preferable.

Q. If the subsoil is perfectly free from water, I presume you will agree with me in believing that the more level the land is, the better?

A. In this climate I would say yes.

Q. Why not in any climate?

A. Because in Europe, for instance, they have a wetter climate, with less sunshine than we have here, and crops such as oats, barley and wheat could be better harvested on ridge lands than on level surfaces.

Q. Yes, I am aware of the greater moisture of the European climate, although we have more rain in the year here; but my question related more to the choice of lands that are level, such as some of the prairies; or rolling, as in districts of Pennsylvania, New York and Ohio—I mean, if the soil is of equal fertility, which would you consider preferable—a slightly rolling, or a level soil?

A. I should prefer the level soil—that is, always providing the water passes away freely. It depends, however, upon the purpose for which the farm is wanted. If for general farming purposes, then, I should say by all means the level land would be best; but if the farm is used for pasturing or grazing, rolling land would be preferable, because cattle will always do better on the slope of hills than they will do on flats.

Q. Do you know the reason of their doing better, or is your opinion simply derived from observation and general practice?

A. I think that there is more change of herbage, and it is sweeter and finer, on the hill-sides, than in the flat lands, where it is too rich.

Q. In that you are probably correct; and this, too, you consider would be true of almost every other crop, as well as grasses?

A. Yes; sorghum grown on a hill-side will produce from the same amount of juice one-third more sugar than if grown on bottom lands, and the same principle will be found to be carried through nearly all kinds of vegetation. Melons and grapes that have been planted on rolling ground are always richer in flavor, because they contain more sugar than those on the bottom land.

Q. What has been your experience with land composed of peat or vegetable mold?

A. I have always considered it to be the best land for root crops. You can grow a larger quantity of roots such as mangels, beets, turnips or potatoes on such land, with less labor and less manure, than on any other soil; provided always that the subsoil is free from water.

Q. Have you ever experienced any difficulty in breaking up land of this kind for crops grown the first season?

A. Yes; on two occasions in my experience in breaking up land of this character, even when thoroughly turned, there was some acidity in the soil that destroyed the roots. Lime would have counteracted all that trouble, if thoroughly mixed with the soil at the rate of fifty to three hundred bushels per acre; for market gardens or other lands where it can be afforded, the larger quantity would be preferable.

Q. Do not swamp lands vary very much in character; and should their treatment not be in accordance with this variation?

A. These lands do vary; some consist wholly of peat or vegetable matter, and some have a large proportion of sand in them. The former kind is much improved by the addition of sand or gravel; the latter kind is benefited by a mixture of clay.

Q. Would you consider lime indispensable if sand, or gravel, or clay could be had?

A. Yes, I should say by all means to put on lime, no matter how little of it; the clay or loam can be better dispensed with.

(Mr. H.) I have had only one experience in my life with a swamp of that kind, and, probably for want of using the means you now advise, I failed completely the first year. I had turned up the swamp land in the fall, thoroughly drained it, and thought it was in perfect condition for a crop. I planted the first crop with cabbages, but failed completely; I turned it up again and planted it with celery, which was equally a failure, although I had used nearly twenty-five tons per acre of manure for each crop. To all appearances there was nothing in the handling or condition of the soil that would indicate any element injurious to vegetation.

Q. What depth of soil was it?

A. It was probably three feet deep, overlying a fine white sand. The next season, and for some years after, by heavy manuring, but still without lime, we had good crops, although from my past experience on other lands, and from what you say about the effect of lime when first used for swamp land, I have no doubt it would have greatly helped such a soil. I had an opportunity of examining the soil of Florida last winter, which I believe is very nearly identical with that of Vineland, N. J., and was astonished to see the fertility which land apparently little else but sand contained. This goes to confirm the opinion that I have long held about soils, that their mechanical condition—that is, the ease with which roots can push deeply into them—has much to do in producing good crops when great depth of that soil exists.

In your opinion, Mr. Crozier, which is best fitted to retain barnyard manure—an adhesive soil with a clayey bottom, a loam with a sandy or gravelly bottom, or well drained swamp land with a sandy bottom?

A. A heavy land with a clay subsoil will retain manure twice as long as any other soil. But it would depend altogether on what purpose the land was used for. If for permanent grass, there is no land will retain manure so long as stiff soils with clayey subsoils. I have known it to be kept forty years without being plowed, by applying an occasional top dressing of either barn-yard manure or a compost made of loam and lime. The best loam for such purposes is that taken from fence rows, because it contains rich fibrous sod.

Q. About what quantity of such a compost would you consider a good top dressing per acre?

A. About twenty two-horse wagon loads.

Q. How much stable manure would you advise for a dressing on such land?

A. About ten wagon loads. I would say, however, that stable manure should not be put on unless over a year old or composted and worked up fine, as coarse manure is not suitable for permanent grass lands.

Q. What season of the year do you consider the best for putting on top dressing for permanent grass lands?

A. I think the fall is the best time. If put on in the fall it protects the roots of the grass from freezing and thawing, acting as a mulch, and also by freezing it is made fine for the harrow in the spring to work it into the roots of the grasses.

Q. What harrow do you use for such a purpose?

A. I use the square iron-tooth harrow or diamond chain harrow, which latter is now coming into use among some of our best farmers in this country. The common sloping tooth harrow does this work very well, and so does that useful new implement, the Acme harrow.

Q. On sandy loam lands, what do you consider the most profitable way to apply barn-yard manure for general crops?

A. I have found in my experience that the best way is to plow the land, spread the manure broadcast, harrow it, and plow again two or three inches deep. The nearer the top of the ground we keep the manure, so long as it is covered, the more benefit the crops will receive from it, and the manure of course will always work downwards, from the rains. The general practice of farmers in the United States is to spread the manure, and then plow it under.

(Mr. H.) Your practice in this respect is certainly good and is entirely new to me; it shows the benefit of a personal interchange of ideas on these subjects. I am satisfied that your plan of harrowing the manure on the surface before plowing it in lightly, as just described, must be of great benefit, although in my thirty-five years' experience as a market gardener, and living in a section where there are scores of others, many of whom have had a practice as extended as mine, I have never yet seen it done. It is obvious that no matter how well manure may be rotted, still when spread on the land it will form hard lumps, less or more, unless broken up by the harrow as you describe, while the disintegration of other particles by the harrow will leave it just in the condition necessary for the food of plants.

Is there any guide, Mr. Crozier, by which inexperienced men, without any one to help them, can determine what is the best soil for general farm work?

A. If the farm is to be selected on lands where there has been general cultivation, the best test to determine the value of such lands is to closely examine and compare the crops growing on lands adjacent. If under ordinary culture you see these lands producing good crops of corn, wheat or potatoes, it is reasonable to suppose, if on the same level, that the land in question will, in all probability, be of similar quality.

Q. But suppose the farm has to be selected in a region where there is nothing but timber or the natural grasses to guide? What then would be your advice?

A. Under such circumstances I would take a spade and dig in different parts of the farm and find out what the soils and subsoils are composed of, and what they would be best adapted for. The timber and native grasses growing on such lands would not always help to decide as to the quality of the land. There would be no safety in judging from such indications, as we find sometimes heavy timber growing on lands not well fitted for farm operations, and even some lands on which the natural grasses seem to be poor, will under proper cultivation produce excellent crops. So that in such cases, if there are no cultivated crops growing in the vicinity, the only thing is an examination of the soil by digging into it with a spade. For this reason, it will be advisable, if a disinterested and capable practical farmer can be found, for any one about to invest five or ten thousand dollars in a farm, to employ such a man to guide him in the choice of the soil. Of course the object for which the farm is wanted must be stated to the expert, whether it be wanted for grazing purposes only, or for rotation of crops, or for what is known as mixed farming, which combines stock raising and general tillage. If the selection be a good one it is reasonable to expect fair success with ordinary industry, while if it is bad, failure and ruin will in all probability be the result.

(Mr. H.) I have scores come to me in the course of every season for advice in this matter of soils, but in most instances the advice is asked too late. Many persons have been unfortunate enough to buy or rent land that they had been led to believe was excellent, but only "run down." In my opinion, this wide-spread notion of "exhausted lands" is, to a great extent, a fallacy, and that the greater part of the lands said to have been exhausted never were good; and no power on earth short of spreading a good soil over them, half a foot thick, would ever make them good. In a recent visit to the South, I met a man who had gone down four years ago, and had bought an "exhausted farm." With Northern energy and Northern capital he hoped to restore it to what he had been told it had previously been— a fertile farm. A large expenditure and the hard work of several years had failed to give a crop of corn that paid for the labor. I could see no stalk that had been more than five feet high, and many of them less than that. The poor, yellow soil in no place exceeded four inches in depth, and was underlaid by a hard pan of clay. The labor put upon such a soil will never pay. Millions of acres of lands are purchased annually which are of but little more use for farming purposes than the same area in a barren wilderness. Then, it may be asked, How is a farmer to select his soil? First, he should never buy a farm without personal examination—never take the seller's word about it; he may honestly believe that what he asserts is true, or he may know it to be false; but in either case if you are deceived you suffer. Make the examination thorough; observe the surroundings, and if the district is settled and cropped. Examine with care the condition of crops on the farm and those upon land adjoining it. If the crops are sickly looking and weak—if the corn-stalks, instead of being seven or eight feet in height, are but two or three—you had better lose your time and expenses and get home again, than take the farm as a gift. If there are no crops growing, the character of the soil will be indicated by its appearance. A good soil is usually of dark brown color; the subsoil, lying immediately under the top soil, should be of a porous nature, and it is usually, in first-rate soils, of a yellowish, sandy loam. A gravelly subsoil is often found underlying soils of good quality, but this is not so common. A subsoil of blue or yellow clay, such as might be used for brick making and that is impervious to water, when near the surface, is a certain indication of a poor quality of soil for either farming or gardening. As an illustration of the value of different soils for market garden purposes, there are men in our immediate neighborhood who pay $100 per acre annual rent, and who, in the past ten or twelve years, have made snug little fortunes upon eight or nine acres in cultivation. Not more than half a mile away there are others paying less than half that amount in rent, who have in the same time been struggling to make both ends meet. Though equally industrious, and having as good a knowledge of the business, their failure has resulted simply from the difference in the character of the soil. In the one case the land would be cheaper at $100 per acre annual rent than the other would be if it could be had for nothing.

(Mr. C.) A farm suited for mixed farming is safer than when the farm is devoted, as in some cases, to growing exclusively one crop—safer because you are not thus compelled to carry all your eggs in one basket. If the season is wet and cold, the grass crop will respond to it, although your corn crop may fail, and *vice ver. a.* Stock raising, in connection with tillage, compels the raising of root and forage crops, some of which will always prove profitable under proper management, no matter how the seasons or the markets vary. It also has the advantage of allowing the farmer to keep the most of his hands during the entire year. In the vicinity of towns or villages, summer boarding houses, or hotels, the growing of the finer vegetables or fruits, in addition to the regular farm crops, will always prove profitable. A single acre of fruit or vegetables, when sold direct to the consumer, will often yield more profit than an entire farm of one hundred acres. But you, Mr. Henderson, who have had such ample experience in these subjects, will append to this work brief and plain instructions of how to do it.

Q. You are aware of the fact, I suppose, Mr. Crozier, that it is currently believed in the Southern States, and probably in other parts of the country, that lands are exhausted almost irreparably by the continued growing of tobacco or other exhaustive crops on them. I would like to hear what is your opinion on this matter. To give you my own opinion in advance, I believe it is a fallacy to a great extent.

A. I should say that continual planting of one crop on the same soil will impoverish it until it becomes worthless.

Q. Do you mean permanently worthless?

A. No.

Q. That is just the point I wish to make—that the injury to the land is only temporary.

A. Yes; and by judicious cropping with grasses or clovers the land may again be brought up to its former fertility. The reason for the popular opinion in this matter, and which I believe has led to a great deal of unnecessary loss, is that when such lands are first broken up, they will produce good crops with very little or no manure, because the plants have the roots of the grasses, leaves or other organic matter to feed upon, but when this supply of plant food is exhausted, without a corresponding amount of manure being again applied, the land is robbed of nearly all the fertility which it had, in the first two or three years after being broken. That I think is the true cause of this wide-spread belief that has allowed thousands of acres of land to lie waste.

FARM ROADS.

(Mr. C.) In selecting a farm, it is of vital importance to see that the roads leading from it to the depot or market are in such condition, or can be made so, as to be easily used by loaded wagons. Many a fine farm is rendered completely worthless when the approaches to it are intercepted by steep hills or other obstructions to the hauling of heavy loads. It is also worth noting that many difficult roads that are carried over hills could have been carried around them on a level, without increasing their length and of course greatly increasing their usefulness. Nearness to a depot, town or city of course vastly enhances the value to the cultivator, not only for the advantage of selling his products and getting manure, but also when hired help is used; the facilities for getting such are better, besides the price paid is usually higher the farther you get away from populous centres. It is bad enough when harvest hands strike or abscond when you are near a city, but it is disheartening in the extreme when they do so when you are five or six miles from a depot, and perhaps twenty miles from a town. A word here as a caution. If you engage new hands from any hiring mart in New York or other large city, do not trust to have them meet you at depot to go home. From the moment you hire them keep possession of them, or the chances are five to one that you will never see them again. Another thing: if you want two men, it will be best to hire three, for the chances are more than equal that one of the three will either prove worthless or run away.

DRAINAGE.

The following short essay on draining is embodied in Peter Henderson's work, "Garden and Farm Topics." We give it here, as it is of general character. Although it refers more particularly to areas of small extent, when used for market garden purposes, it will be found to apply equally to larger areas. The broad fact may, however, be asserted, that the expense of draining farm lands would in many cases exceed the cost of land equally good that required no draining; and of course it is to the interest of the farmer to assure himself that the farm he wishes to purchase does not require to be drained artificially, but whenever, by any unfortunate circumstance, possession is had of lands requiring draining, the cultivation had better be abandoned, rather than attempt to till it if water is held stagnant in the soil. Certain conditions of land might, however, be utilized for pasturage without underdraining, provided that open ditches were made to allow the surplus water to pass off, but of course, as all cultivators well know, even for pasturage no fertile crop can be obtained if stagnant water remains on the soil.

Draining is one of the most important operations in horticulture. No matter how fertile the normal condition of the soil, no matter how abundantly it is fertilized, no matter how carefully and thoroughly it is tilled, if water remain in it at the depth to which roots penetrate, all labor will be in vain; for no satisfactory result can ever be attained until the water is drained off. The subject is one of such importance that we cannot give it full attention here, and to such as require to operate on a large scale, works specially devoted to the subject should be consulted, or a draining engineer employed. Soils having a gravelly or sandy subsoil ten or twenty inches below the top soil do not usually need draining; but in all soils underlaid by clay or hard pan, draining is indispensable, unless in cases where there is a slope of two to three feet in a hundred; and even in such cases draining is beneficial if the subsoil is clay.

In soils having a clay or hard pan subsoil, drains should be made three feet deep and not more than twenty feet apart. If stones are plenty, they may be profitably used to fill up the drains, say to a depth of twelve or fifteen inches, either placed so as to form a "rubble" drain, if the stones are round, or built with an orifice at the bottom, if the stones are flat. In either case, care must be used to cover the stones carefully up with inverted sods, or some material that will prevent the soil being washed through the stones and choking up the drain.

Drain tiles, when they can be obtained at a reasonable price, are the best material for draining. The round tile is generally used. If the drain has a hard bottom they can be placed directly on it when leveled to the proper grade ; but if the ground is soft and spongy, a board must be laid in the bottom, on which to place the tiles. It is often a very troublesome matter to get the few drain tiles necessary for a small garden, and in such cases an excellent and cheap substitute can be had by using one of boards. Care must be taken that the boards are not nailed together too closely, else they might swell so as to prevent the water passing into the drain to be carried off. These drains are usually set with a flat side down, but they will keep clear better if put with a point down, though it is more trouble to lay them. Drains made in this way will last twenty years or more.

Of course, in draining, the greater the fall that can be got, the better, though, if the grading is carefully done by a competent engineer, a very slight fall will suffice. Some of the trunk or main sewers in our cities have only a grade of one foot in a thousand.

The following details of the method of the construction of drains may be found useful:

CONSTRUCTION OF DRAINS.

In draining land, there are two things to be decided: the first is if the land requires to be drained; and the second, the best kind of drains to be put in. An easy way of deciding the first is to notice if water will stand in a hole, two feet deep, for a week, at any time of the year. If it does, the land requires drainage. There are several kinds of drains. One kind, that is often very useful, is a perpendicular drain. This is used for draining hollows that cannot easily be freed from water any other way, because of the depth of the necessary cutting. A pit is dug down to sand or gravel, and is filled with large stone up to the surface, which is raised by filling in the earth dug out of the pit—of course keeping the surface soil on the top. Two things are gained by this: the ground is freed from water, and the surface of the hollow is raised. In pastures where there is no other water, a pump may be put in such a hollow.

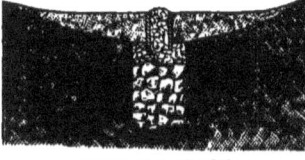
DRAIN IN A HOLLOW.

Where there is plenty of stone or coarse gravel on the land, drains may be made very cheaply by filling in with these materials to within a foot of the surface. Some stone drains, well made, are better than tile drains, because the stone is imperishable; but if a stone drain is not well made, it will soon be useless; and so will a tile drain, more particularly if the tiles are not thoroughly burned, so as to ring when struck. The best stone drain is made of flat, narrow stones, bedded firmly at each side of the ditch, and covered by broad, flat stone, stretching across; rough stone may be put on the top of these.

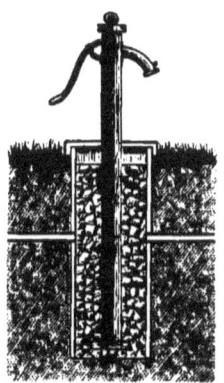
DRAIN WITH PUMP.

Where only round stone is to be found, a special way of placing them must be used. (This is shown very plainly in the accompanying illustrations.) In making drains of gravel, all that is necessary is to dig the ditch as if tile was to be put in—that is, thirty inches or three feet deep; eighteen inches wide at the top, and four or six inches wide at the bottom—and fill in the gravel eighteen inches. Stone or gravel drains are better for very wet lands and for swamp meadows than tiles, for the reasons that they carry more water, are not so easily choked, as there are many channels, and will not get

FLAT STONE DRAIN.

stopped by the settling of the soft ground, as with tile; for a tile that settles in a soft place, stops and ruins the whole drain. Where tiles are used in soft ground, they should always be laid upon hemlock boards, as this timber is almost imperishable in such a place, or any other where it is always wet. Sometimes cheap drains of wood may be very useful for wet ground. Such drains are generally made triangular, of three boards, nailed edge to edge. A better way is to put the cover on top of the drain tube crosswise, cutting the lumber into short pieces; this gives more openings for the water to flow into the pipes, and also makes them stronger. Where roads cross a drain of this kind, it is safer to make them in this way, and also to lay a plank upon the drain to distribute the pressure. Every precaution should be taken to have the work of draining done right, because it is costly, and is a difficult and particular work, and, if one little blunder is made, everything may be spoiled; for a

ROUND STONE DRAINS.

drain is like a chain which has a link broken, and even worse; for if one part of a drain is out of order, the whole drain may be useless, while part of a broken chain may be as good as ever. For this reason,

WOODEN DRAIN.

when one is about to lay out considerable money in a job of draining, it would always be safe to have the advice and assistance of an expert, whose experience might and would often be of great value.

Observation wells are necessary to be made about every quarter of a mile in a drain. This is a small well or deep box, let down two feet below the drain, and into which one drain discharges, while another takes the water. These are necessary in every main drain, where the smaller drains enter. Their purpose is to catch sediment which would otherwise obstruct the drains, and also to watch the working of the drain occasionally, to observe if it is in good order. When sediment gathers in these wells, it is easy to clean them out. This should be done before it is really necessary, or it will be apt to be left until too late.

Every complete set of drains should be laid out on a systematic plan. The courses of the drains should be marked by permanent posts set in the fences; the lines of the observation wells should be marked by other posts, so that the exact spot where each drain begins and ends, and where each well is placed, may be found without trouble. The wells should be covered with flat stones, a foot beneath the surface, so that the cover may not be disturbed. As complete drainage costs about $50 an acre, it is wise to take every possible precaution against any waste of this money, to the smallest extent.

CHAPTER II.

MANURES AND THEIR MODES OF APPLICATION.

("Manures and Their Modes of Application" is the title of an essay published by Peter Henderson in 1882. Like all his other essays, this was written more to meet the wants of the horticulturist, than the agriculturist, but the necessities of both are so near alike that we here give it entire, following which will be the remarks of Mr. Henderson and Mr. Crozier on such portions of the essay as may seem to require modification.)

THE subject of manures is one of the greatest importance to every operator in the soil, whether farmer, market gardener, florist, or such as cultivate only for their own use, for under few conditions can crops be long grown without the use of fertilizers. Although I have already given general instructions about fertilizers in all my works on gardening, yet I find, from the number of inquiries received from even such as have my works, that the matter has not been there treated sufficiently in detail to meet the wants of the varied conditions under which the necessity for the use of fertilizers arises. The comparative value of manures must be regulated by the cost. If rotted stable manure, whether from horses or cows, can be delivered on the ground at $3 per ton, it is about as valuable, for fertilizing purposes, as Peruvian guano at $65 per ton, or pure bone dust at $40 per ton. It is better than either of these, or any other concentrated fertilizer, from the fact of its mechanical action on the land—that is, its effect, from its light, porous nature, in aërating and pulverizing the soil. Guano, bone dust, or other fine commercial fertilizers, act only as such, without in any way assisting to improve what may be called the physical condition of the soil.

All experienced cultivators know that the first year that land is broken up from sod, if proper culture has been given, by thorough plowing and harrowing (provided the land is drained artificially or naturally, so as to be free from water, and relieve it from "sourness"), the land is in better condition for any crop than land that has been continuously cropped without a rest. The market gardeners in the vicinity of New York are now so well convinced of this, that when twenty acres are under cultivation, at least five acres are continually kept in grain, clover or grass, to be broken up successively, every second or third year, so as to get the land in the condition that nothing else but rotted, pulverized sod will accomplish. This is done in cases where land is as valuable as $500 per acre, experience having proved that with one-quarter of the land "resting under grass more profit can be got than if the whole were under culture.

When the rotation, by placing a portion of the land under grass, cannot be done, then it is absolutely necessary to use stable manure, at least to some extent, if the best results are desired, for continuous cropping of the soil. Where concentrated fertilizers only are used, they will not continue to give satisfactory results after the grass roots or other organic matter have passed from the soil, all of which will usually be entirely gone by the third or fourth year after breaking up. I have long held the opinion, that the idea of lands having been permanently exhausted by tobacco or other crops, is a fallacy. What gives rise to this belief, I think, is the fact that, when lands are first broken up from the forest or meadow lands, for three or four years the organic matter in the soil, the roots of grasses, leaves, etc., not only serves to feed the crops, but it keeps the soil in a better state of pulverization, or what might be called aërated condition, than when, in the course of cropping for a few years, it has passed away. Stable manure best supplies this want; but on farm lands away from towns, it is not often that enough can be obtained to have any appreciable effect on the soil, and hence artificial fertilizers are resorted to, which often fail, not from any fault in themselves, but from the fact that, exerting little mechanical influence on the land, it becomes compacted or sodden, the air cannot get to the roots, and hence failure or partial failure of crop.

Thus we see that to have the best results from commercial fertilizers, it is of great importance to have the land "rested" by a crop of grain or grass every three or four years.

The best known fertilizers of commerce are Peruvian guano and bone dust, though there are numbers of others, such as fish guano, dry blood fertilizer, blood and bone fertilizer, with the various brands of superphosphates, all of more or less value for fertilizing purposes. It is useless to go over the list, and we will confine ourselves to the relative merits of pure Peruvian guano and pure bone dust. Guano, at $65 per ton, we consider relatively equal in value to bone dust at $40 per ton, for in the lower priced article we find we have to increase the quantity to produce the same result. Whatever kind of concentrated fertilizer is used, we find it well repays the labor to prepare it in the following manner before it is used on the land:

To every bushel of guano or bone dust add three bushels of either leaf mould (from the woods), well pulverized dry muck, sweepings from a paved street, stable manure so rotted as to be like pulverized muck, or, if neither of these can be obtained, any loamy soil will do;

but in every case the material to mix the fertilizers with must be fairly dry and never in a condition of mud; the meaning of the operation being, that the material used is to act as a temporary absorbent for the fertilizer. The compost must be thoroughly mixed, and if guano is used, it being sometimes lumpy, it must be broken up to dust before being mixed with the absorbent.

The main object of this operation is for the better separation and division of the fertilizer, so that when applied to the soil it can be more readily distributed. Our experiments have repeatedly shown that this method of using concentrated fertilizers materially increases their value, probably twenty per cent. The mixing should be done a few months previous to spring, and it should, after being mixed, be packed away in barrels, and kept in some dry shed or cellar until wanted for use. Thus mixed, it is particularly beneficial on lawns or other grass lands. The quantity of concentrated fertilizer to be used is often perplexing to beginners. We give the following as the best rules we know, all derived from our own practice in growing fruits, flowers and vegetables.

Taking guano as a basis, we would recommend for all vegetable or fruit crops, if earliness and good quality are desired, the use of not less than 1,200 pounds per acre (an acre contains 4,840 square yards, and cultivators for private use can easily estimate from this the quantity they require for any area), mixed with two tons of either of the materials before recommended. Of bone dust about one ton per acre should be used, mixed with three tons of soil or the other materials named.

For market garden vegetable crops, in the vicinity of New York, this quantity of guano or bone dust is harrowed in after twenty-five or thirty tons of stable manure have first been plowed in; so that the actual cost of manuring each acre is not less than $100, and often $150.

When fertilizers are used alone, without being mixed with the absorbent, they should be sown on the soil after plowing or digging, about thick enough to just color the surface, or about as thick as sand or sawdust is sown on a floor, and then thoroughly harrowed in, if plowed, or, if dug, chopped in with a rake. This quantity is used broadcast by sowing on the ground after plowing, and deeply and thoroughly harrowing in, or, if in small gardens, forked in lightly with the prongs of a garden fork or long-toothed steel rake. When applied in hills or drills, from 100 to 300 pounds should be used to the acre, according to the distance of these apart, mixing with soil, etc., as already directed.

When well rotted stable manure is procurable at a cost not to exceed $3 per ton, delivered on the ground, whether from horses or cows, it is preferable to any concentrated fertilizer. Rotted stable manure, to produce full crops, should be spread on the ground not less than three inches thick (our market gardeners use from fifty to seventy-five tons of well rotted stable manure per acre when no concentrated fertilizer is used), and should be thoroughly mixed with the soil by plowing or spading. The refuse hops from breweries form an excellent fertilizer, at least one-half more valuable, bulk for bulk, than stable manure. Other excellent fertilizers are obtained from the scrapings or shavings from horn or whalebone manufactories. The best way to make these quickly available is to compost them with hot manure, in the proportion of one ton of refuse horn or whalebone with fifteen tons of manure. The heated manure extracts the oil, which is intermingled with the whole.

The manure from the chicken or pigeon house is very valuable, and when composted as directed for bone dust and guano, has at least one-third their value. Castor oil pomace is also valuable in about the same proportion.

Poudrette is the name given to a commercial fertilizer, the composition of which is night soil, and dried swamp muck or charcoal dust as an absorbent. It is sold at about $12 to $15 per ton, and at that price may be equal in value, if too much of the absorbing material is not used, to bone dust at $40 per ton.

In my early experience as a market gardener, I used large quantities of night soil for vegetable crops with the very best results. It was mixed with stable manure at the rate of about one ton of night soil to fifteen tons of stable manure, and put on the land, so mixed, at the rate of twenty-five tons per acre. In the absence of stable manure, dry soil, charcoal dust, sawdust, or any material that will absorb it, will do. Thus mixed, if equal quantities of each have been used, ten tons may be used per acre, if plowed in; if sowed on top, to be harrowed in, say five tons.

Salt has little or no value as a fertilizer, except as a medium of absorbing moisture; for experience shows that soils impregnated by saline matter are no more fertile than those inland, out of the reach of such an atmosphere.

Muck is the name given to a deposit usually largely composed of vegetable matter, found in swamps or in hollows in forest lands. Of itself it has usually but little fertilizing property, but from its porous nature, when dry, it is one of the best materials to use to mix with other manures as an absorbent. It can be used to great advantage if dug out in winter and piled up in narrow ridges, so that it can be partly dried and "sweetened" in summer. Thus dry, if mixed with stable manure, or, better yet, thrown in layers three or four inches thick in the cattle or hog yard, where it can be trodden down and amalgamated with the manure, the value of the manure thus treated will be nearly doubled.

In reply to questions that I receive by the hundred each season, asking whether or not it is worth while to use the so-called special fertilizers claimed to be suited to the wants of particular plants, such as the "Potato Fertilizer," "Cabbage Fertilizer," "Strawberry Fertilizer," "Rose Fertilizer," etc., I can only give this general answer, that while these manures may suit the plants they are claimed to be "special" for, I have no doubt that either one would suit equally well for the others, or, if all were mixed together, the mixture would be found to answer the purpose for each kind of crop, just as well as if kept separate and applied to the crop it was named for. These hair-splitting distinctions are not recognized to be of any value by one practical farmer or gardener in every hundred; for a little experience soon shows that pure bone dust or well rotted stable manure answers for *all* crops alike, no matter what they are. These special fertilizers for special crops are gradually increasing in number, so that some dealers now offer fifty kinds, different brands being offered for plants belonging to the same family. There is an ignorant assumption in this, and any cultivator of ordinary intelligence cannot fail to see that the motive in so doing is to strike as broad a swath as possible, so that a larger number of customers may be reached.

One of my neighbors called the other day, and informed me that his lettuce crop, in his green-house, was failing, and asked me what I thought of the lettuce fertilizer that was offered in a circular that contained some fifty other "specials." An inquiry developed the fact, that he had been keeping his lettuce crop at a night temperature of sixty-five degrees in January, so that there was just about as much chance of the special lettuce fertilizer helping the crop, as there would be of giving health to a man by feeding him beef-steak in the last stages of consumption. I merely mention this incident to show how, and in what manner, the sellers of these special fertilizers obtain customers.

Q. Have you had any experience, Mr. Crozier, with these so-called special fertilizers to which I refer in the preceding article, and if so, what opinion do you hold in regard to them? I noticed in looking at your crop of fodder corn, which you showed me yesterday, and which you said was sown about five weeks ago, that the portion whereon you had used the special corn fertilizer, pure and simple, has had to lower its flag to that portion of the field which was manured with stable manure at a cost but little more per acre, the latter already towering over a foot above that part of the field on which you used the "special" fertilizer, and the difference being so marked as to appear like separate sowings.

A. In several experiments that I have carefully made, with a view to ascertain if there was any foundation for the claims now so commonly made for special fertilizers, in no single instance have I found any verification of these claims. For example, I have tried them on potatoes, corn, rye, barley, mangels and turnips, applying a special kind of manure on each, at the same time using one of the specials on all the crops with the same results as obtained from each of the different specials. I have no doubt that had I mixed them all together, and applied the mixture to each special crop, the results would in all probability have been the same. The only difference is that we pay two or three dollars per ton more when we get the special name. These special fertilizers for special crops may do very well for gentlemen farmers, who can afford to play at the business; but we, who have to make our bread and butter from the soil, had better let them alone. One of the best fertilizers, compared with its cost, I have ever tried, was sent me last season under the name of "rotten bone," price $16 per ton. I was solicited to try it by a gentleman who was placing this article on the market and who made very strong claims for it. I wrote him, saying that if his manure was what he stated it to be, he might send me two or three tons. He sent me three tons, which I applied, and the results, as I write (July 10th), on mangels, potatoes, turnips and fodder corn, seem to indicate that it was a more valuable fertilizer than any that I have yet used. It was put on broadcast, and harrowed in thoroughly with the Acme harrow, at the rate of 1,500 pounds per acre, which at $16 per ton you will see was an exceedingly cheap fertilizer. Whether it will hold out for the following season I cannot tell, but will give it a further trial.

Q. Into what shape was it broken up?

A. It came in pieces about the size of peas, and contained a kind of greasy substance that, when taking it in your hand, would leave a mark.

Q. Is that article in commerce, or was it only by a special chance that you got it?

A. I think it is in commerce, as I had recently a letter from the party from whom I got it asking how it had turned out, as he had more to dispose of. I do not know whether it is a part of the refuse from glue factories or not, but I have reason to believe that it is.

(Mr. H.) You are correct in this, as I had a sample of a similar substance, although it came to me without name from some glue manufactory in Massachusetts. I gave it a thorough trial on grass as a top dressing about the first of June. I examined the result about thirty days after and the grass had developed to double the length on the area where I had tried it. To make the test comparative I sowed pure bone dust along-side of it, and found that there was no apparent difference between the one and other, except that this cost $16 per ton and bone dust costs $45. If it can be bought at $16 per ton and can be obtained in sufficient quantities, it will no doubt be of great value wherever fertilizers are needed.

How do you explain the beneficial results of this bone fertilizer as compared with special fertilizers?

(Mr. C.) In this way. A poor soil mostly needs three substances—nitrogen, potash and phosphoric acid. But few soils are so poor as to need all these. Potash is very abundant in nature, and it is phosphoric acid that is usually most deficient. A special fertilizer contains all these three substances and some others. If the soil only needs one, a farmer who buys a special fertilizer pays for more than he needs. If he needs only phosphoric acid he can get that in this cheap bone manure. It is evident that my soil needs phosphoric acid and shows it by the effect of this bone, which is pretty nearly all phosphate of lime. Then, you see, for $12 I get 1,500 lbs. of this fertilizer, which I need, while for as much special fertilizer I should pay $37.50 and pay money for what I do not want. There are glue factories all over the country, the refuse of which is most valuable, and farmers should by no means neglect the opportunity of availing themselves of it.

I am so impressed with its value as a fertilizer that I intend at once ordering forty tons of it, and will apply it as a top dressing on my grass lands the coming spring, at the rate of about 1,000 pounds per acre.

(Mr. H.) In my article on manures, Mr. Crozier, I made no allusion to lime or marl, which I have always held to have no fertilizing properties of themselves, except inasmuch as they act to correct the acidity of the soil, or to lighten heavy soils, or to give adhesiveness to soils that are too light. In fact, I believe they are beneficial for their mechanical effects on almost every soil, unless such as are impregnated with oyster shell deposit, which is found on lands lying along the sea coast, and in some cases for a considerable distance inland. On such soils there is no benefit to be derived from the application of lime, as there is usually sufficient of it supplied by the disintegration of the shell deposit.

(Mr. C.) I would agree with you so far in saying that I have never found any fertilizing properties when lime was applied to such crops as mangels or potatoes, but on cereals, particularly wheat or oats, I have found an application of 100 bushels per acre of pure stone lime, when composted with double the amount of loam, to be one of the most valuable fertilizers for such crops.

Q. In what manner do you apply it?

A. It should be sown broadcast after plowing, and then harrowed in—not plowed under—but kept as near the top of the soil as possible. By this means I have received ten bushels of wheat per acre more than by using horse manure put on at the rate of eight cords, which is equal to twenty tons, to the acre.

(Mr. H.) I would like to remark, just here, in regard to gas lime, that it is useless and injurious to any crop until the noxious gases in it have been expelled by long exposure to the air. As this is a matter of years, it would be well for farmers to decline the very liberal offers of gas companies, made for the purpose of getting rid of what is a nuisance to them.

Q. In my article on manures, Mr. Crozier, you took exception—and I think with some reason—to my suggestions about using muck by spreading it in layers in the open cattle or hog yard. Will you state what has been your experience with dried muck or other similar absorbents?

A. My practice with such absorbents has been to use them for bedding in the cow stables and box stalls in quantity sufficient to absorb all the urine, which I consider to be more valuable than the solid manure. I cart this mixed manure direct from the cow stables and sheds to the compost heap in the field, which in the spring of the year is thoroughly turned over and broken up fine and made ready to be spread on the land after plowing, when, as I have before said, it is harrowed and then plowed in lightly. So much am I impressed with the necessity of heavy manuring, that, contrary to the usual practice of farmers in my neighborhood, I not only use all the straw and hay my own farm produces, but buy besides an amount nearly equal to what I produce. The result is, and I trust I may say so without any feeling of egotism, that my crops pay me, acre for acre, much better than any of my neighbors who do not follow this same practice.

(Mr. H.) I entirely agree with you in your opinion that farming without sufficient manuring can never be made so profitable as when manure is freely applied. I have had no experience whatever in farming, strictly speaking, but as is well known, I have had large experience as a market gardener in the vicinity of New York, and I have found that when any man was foolish enough to attempt to cultivate ten acres with only a supply of manure enough for five, he rarely made money. I have no doubt whatever that the same rule is equally applicable, when the farmer attempts to cultivate 100 acres while only able to procure fertilizers enough for fifty.

(Mr. C.) Many farmers think and believe they have not the means to improve their lands or manure them liberally; but I say we nearly all have the means, to some extent, for in our many idle hours we could gather sods from the roadside and leaves from the woods and put them in heaps until needed for bedding for cattle (over the absorbent material of course is placed a heavy bed of straw), and these when composted and turned over a few times would make the most valuable of manures for the average crops of the farm. If it were not rich enough for certain crops, a mixture of bone or guano at the rate of 100 to 200 lbs. per acre would make it one of the very best fertilizers, as, from the nature of such a compost, its value will be retained in the land for years.

Q. Plaster is by some considered a valuable fertilizer. What experience have you had with it?

A. I have used plaster to some extent. It is one of those fertilizers which have a remarkable effect upon some soils, while in other places it has no effect at all. Where the soils are benefited by it, it is of course advisable to use it. Its greatest effect is upon clover, and where clover is used as a means of improving land, plaster is indispensable. It is one of the cheapest of all fertilizers, and should by all means be used where it is beneficial; this of course is to be proved by a test. It is sown on clover grass or corn when the plants are young.

Q. In the foregoing article I have said salt has little value as a fertilizer excepting so far as it absorbs moisture, in the vicinity of the ocean, where perhaps sufficient salt is brought on to the land by the sea fogs and rains. What has been your experience in this direction?

A. I have been in the habit of using 600 lbs. to the acre on my mangel crop, and find it useful, and indeed necessary. I know wheat growers who use it on this crop for the purpose of preventing rust, stiffening the straw and improving the appearance and quality of the grain, which I know it does. How it does this I don't pretend to explain. I only mention the facts in my experience.

(Mr. H.) I know market gardeners in inland districts use salt liberally upon asparagus, thinking it useful for that crop. The rule as to quantity is to put on as much as will give the ground the appearance of a sanded floor. I might say incidentally that salt is an excellent means of clearing gravel walks of grass and weeds, as when liberally used it is fatal to all sorts of vegetation.

Q. I believe you have used wood ashes very freely as a fertilizer. What results have you observed from their use on different crops?

A. I have used wood ashes very freely. But it is necessary to mention that the wood ashes that are in the market have been leached for making potash, and of course are different from unleached or fresh ashes. As these cannot be purchased to any extent, I refer only to the leached ashes which are brought to market in boat loads or car loads. I have used these on grass lands, with great benefit, at the rate of fifty to one hundred bushels to the acre. As the ashes stay in the soil for many years, it is best in my opinion to put them on grass, and when the sod is broken up, the other crops get the benefit from them. I think they are a valuable fertilizer for farmers who are able to procure them at a reasonable price. In boat or car loads near the City of New York, they sell for eighteen to twenty cents a bushel.

(Mr. H.) I am sure you are right. But I would go a little further, and say that as wood ashes contain all the substance of the wood, which of course is a vegetable product that has been taken from the mineral part of the soil, everything contained in them is of course necessary to a growing plant and therefore there is no waste whatever in them. Every part of them is valuable and they are necessarily useful for any or all crops. I don't know of any plant or crop to which they would not be useful. The question often comes up, if coal ashes are not also useful. But coal is a mineral and not a vegetable, and coal ashes do not therefore contain valuable fertilizing property to any considerable extent. I consider their only use to be mechanical, in loosening heavy soils, and in compacting light soils.

GREEN MANURING.

(Mr. C.) The practice of growing crops for the purpose of plowing them under to fertilize the soil, is one that can often be turned to very great advantage. When a farmer has unfortunately become possessed of a poor farm, there is no better way of cheaply improving it than this. To procure an adequate supply of manure is rarely possible, and at the best is a very costly process. But a crop that may be easily grown in a few weeks, and then turned under, may furnish to the soil as much fertilizing matter as eight or ten tons of manure; and the process may often be repeated two or three times in one year. For instance, if land is plowed in October and sown to rye, the rye may be turned under in May or June, and corn may be planted. This will be in full growth early in August, when it may also be turned under, furnishing ten or twelve tons more of valuable matter. In turning under so tall a crop as corn or rye the plow should be run across the rows, and a heavy chain looped from the plow beam, just ahead of the standard, to the land side end of the inner whiffletree. This loop drags in the furrow, so as to catch the falling corn or rye, and pulls it down and into the furrow so that the soil covers it. To prevent the disturbance of the green manure by the harrow after this, the ground should be rolled after the plowing, and then harrowed with the smoothing or brush harrow, or worked with the

Acme harrow. It may then be sown with rye, and with clover in the spring; and after the clover has been cut for hay, and the second crop plowed in, the land may be brought under a regular course of rotation as described in Chapter IV. Buckwheat is frequently used for this purpose, and is very valuable, as the seed costs but little, and a crop may be sown in May and plowed in early in July, when a second crop may be sown, and this plowed in, and the ground fitted for a crop of rye as before mentioned. When buckwheat is thus used, it will be advisable to give a dressing of lime on the ground after the second crop is plowed under, as this will decompose the green matter and greatly help the growth of the rye.

Clover is a very valuable green manuring crop, and especially the large variety known as the mammoth or pea vine clover, which often makes a stem four or five feet long, and on poor soils produces considerably more herbage than the common red kind. But as a soil that will produce a sufficient yield of clover, to be of much value for plowing in, is past the stage when it will be profitable to grow crops solely for manurial purposes, clover is of more value for maintaining land in good condition than for starting a course of improvement. Growing clover, however, to be plowed under instead of manure, may be made of the utmost value for the fertilizing of hilly land, or for fields that are distant from the homestead, and which cannot be conveniently supplied with manure from the barn-yard on this account. The late Hon. George Geddes, whose recent early death is to be much regretted for the loss of an accomplished and successful farmer, practiced this method for many years on his farm with entire success. He sowed the most distant fields with clover along with wheat; the clover gave a crop of hay the next year; it was then dressed liberally with plaster, and the next year was plowed under after being pastured, and wheat again sowed. In this way, after fifty years of cultivation by his father and himself, the land was kept sufficiently rich to yield thirty-five or forty bushels of wheat to the acre one year, give a large yield of hay the second year, pasture the third year and wheat again the fourth year, and so on. Perhaps no better instance than this can be given of the value of this kind of manuring for preserving the fertility of the land.

FERTILIZING LAND BY FEEDING.

Another method of restoring a farm to a good condition, or of keeping it fertile, is by feeding stock. This may be made very profitable in skillful hands. Thousands of farmers in Pennsylvania, New Jersey, New York and Ohio, and even further west, where the land is not as rich as it once was, and where farmers are learning the value of manure and the advantage of good farming, practice a regular system of feeding animals to feed their land. They make hay, grow corn, roots, wheat, rye, potatoes, and make butter; sell the grain, potatoes and butter, and feed hay, corn fodder, roots and straw, and even purchase feeding stuffs, and buy lean stock in the early fall to consume all these. The cattle or sheep are turned on to the stubbles and pastures as long as there is good feeding. They are then fed during the winter on dry feed, and as they become fat and fit for market are turned off, so that by the spring they are all disposed of. A steer weighing 1,200 lbs. and costing $40, is thus made to weigh 1,600 lbs. and sell for $80, or even more; because there is not only the increased weight made for the profit, but the increased value of a fat animal for every pound of its weight over the value of a thin and unsalable one. The feed is thus disposed of at a good price, and there is a profit besides to pay for the labor. In addition, there is a large quantity of manure, which is worth much more than common barnyard manure because of the high feeding of the cattle. In a similar way the owner of poor land may buy cattle, and all the fodder and grain, and feed them, and make an equal profit as the farmers above mentioned; because they charge the animals with the feed at market price. There is then the manure left to go upon the land and increase the next year's crop, which makes less purchased food necessary. As the land improves, and the crops increase in yield, the profits of the business are larger. In a few years it will be unnecessary to buy fodder, and the income from the farm will then be more satisfactory, because the expenses will be lessened considerably. In my long experience with different farms, and some of them very poor when I went onto them, I have found this practice very successful. But cows are more profitable to keep than fat stock, where there is a good market for milk, and the owner can make an extra good article of butter.

CHAPTER III.

PLOWING, HARROWING AND CULTIVATING.

Q. As you and your men, Mr. Crozier, have had almost a monopoly of the prizes given for plowing offered by the different fairs in the vicinity of New York within the past ten years, will you please state what kind of a plow you consider the best fitted for general farm work?

A. I used the Scotch plows up to 1876, and always with the best results, preferring them up to that time to all makes of American plows that I had tried. It was with these plows that we did the work in competition for the prizes offered by the different fairs. All our competitors used plows of American manufacture. At the trial at Mineola, Queens Co., L. I., in 1872, where there was over $300 offered in prizes, we had upwards of thirty competitors, all of whom used American plows. In this test every prize offered was taken by us with the Scotch plow.

Q. Are Scotch plows in anything like general use amongst the farmers in the United States?

A. No. I have imported about fifty plows for different farmers. I think that is about all there are in use.

Q. If they have shown such superiority as at the fair at Mineola, how do you account for their not being more generally in use?

A. One objection is their cost, and their great weight also is an objection against them among those unaccustomed to handling them.

Q. Do you still use the Scotch plow?

A. No; I use an American steel plow which is made a good deal after the pattern of the Scotch plow, but of lighter weight. I find this plow is more convenient for handling in turning in small fields; but were I operating on long stretches of prairie land I would by all means use the Scotch plow, because there, on long lines, the turning would be no objection, and its advantage is that in laying the furrow in a clean, compact, unbroken strip at an angle of about forty-five degrees, thus turning the sod completely down, the sod decomposes much better than if portions of it were irregularly turned and broken into fragments, as is the case, less or more, with the usual American plow, with its bulging mold-board. The great improvement made in American plows since 1876, in the shape of the mold-boards, is obviating this difficulty largely, and I am now using these steel plows exclusively.

Q. Given the best plow for the work and a soil of usual depth, what is the depth and width of a furrow you make with the plow you now use?

A. I first square up the field, and mark out with four poles a straight line; the first and second furrows are plowed very lightly; the third furrow is run a little deeper, and the fourth is run the depth

ROLAND CHILLED PLOW.

I intend to plow. This is to prevent making a high ridge in the centre, and to bring the field to a level finish. I plow for corn seven inches deep by nine inches wide; for oats, six by eight inches, and for potatoes or root crops, nine by ten inches.

Q. My plan is somewhat different from yours. I open a double furrow first to the full depth. Then I plow the soil back again, and close the furrow, and then go on with the plowing. In this way every part of the land is plowed to the full depth, which for some crops is very important. Why do you make any distinction between the depth you plow for oats and for corn? I can understand why you make a distinction between grain crops and root crops; but why do you make a distinction between oats and corn?

A. Oats have rather a tufted root and do not go down into the soil, while corn will go down deeper, and it is necessary to give it plenty of root space. In sowing oats, I find that the nearer the top of the ground I can get them, the better.

Q. I think you have said that in soils similar to yours, where you have twelve or fifteen inches depth of top soil, with a sandy or gravelly subsoil, there is no necessity for subsoiling?

A. It would be useless to subsoil on such lands as we have here. On sandy or gravelly loam I do not think there is any benefit in it at all. I think it is rather an injury as far as my experience has gone.

Q. But in all cases where you have adhesive soils with stiff bottoms, would you not think it an advantage, where time will admit?

SUBSOIL PLOW.

A. By all means in such cases subsoil what you can do thoroughly; it is better to cultivate one acre right than to undertake ten and leave such important work half done. The same amount of seed will be required, the same amount of plowing, harrowing, cultivating and harvesting must be done, and if subsoiling is left undone the crop will be of little value on land having clay or hard gravel subsoils unless it is stirred deep enough to allow the water to pass through. I used the subsoil plow, which follows in the furrow after the ordinary plow, loosening and stirring the subsoil to a depth of ten or twelve inches. In heavy subsoils two horses are necessary.

Q. When in Scotland some years ago I saw that steam plowing was quite common. Do you know what has been the experience with it in this country?

A. At first sight, it seems that in this country of machinery and steam engines, steam plowing would be found of the widest use, if not a necessity; but the fact that to-day, I believe, not one steam plow is working in this country, shows there must be some obstacles which cannot be got over. Several have been used in different localities— in Pennsylvania, Louisiana, California, Dakota and Minnesota—but all seem to have failed of success. I think there are several reasons for these failures: their cost is considerably greater here than it is

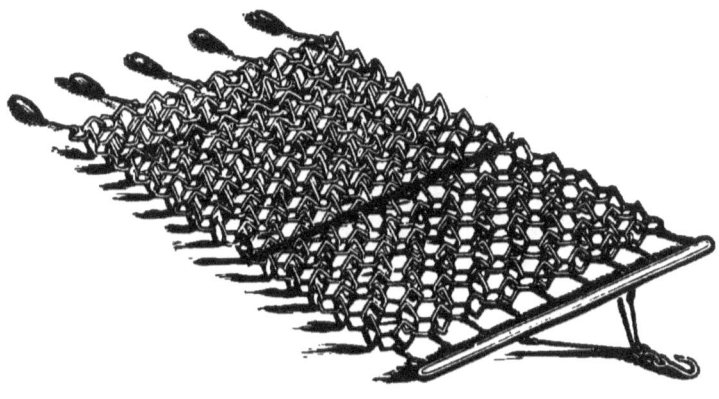

CHAIN HARROW.

abroad; engineers' wages are higher; coal is dearer; but worst of all for the steam plow, is the fact that we plow only for two or three months in a year, and then the costly machine rusts in idleness or must be well cared for at great expense; so that, in fact, the first cost operates to restrict their purchase, and the great cost of operating prevents them from being worked economically by those who have tried them.

Q. After plowing comes the harrowing. Please describe your method.

A. In my experience with help, I have found ten men competent to plow where I have been able to get one competent to harrow; not that there is any more skill required in harrowing than in plowing, but from the fact that it is not so easy for the eye of the master to detect bad work in harrowing, and consequently men indolent or careless can run over the surface so that it may appear to be well done when it is not. For this reason, it is all-important to have a full examination made of the work, for harrowing has everything to do with the welfare of the crop—to have the soil thoroughly disintegrated and pulverized. This harrowing should penetrate to a depth of five or six inches, in order that the soil may be thoroughly and deeply worked.

Q. You take pretty strong ground in regard to harrowing. Give me your ideas of what is good work and bad work in harrowing?

A. Let us take a newly plowed field; the soil is mostly in lumps, small and large. A poor workman runs a harrow over the surface

ACME HARROW.

and smooths it and makes it fine; it looks well, but it is bad work; it is bad because when one sows seed on such ground it works down under the fine surface and among the lumps and clods, where it may sprout, but soon dies because the soil is too loose and open and is filled with air spaces. A good workman makes his harrow teeth work down in the soil among the lumps at the bottom, and breaks these up, or brings them to the surface, and so works the fine, pulverized soil down where the seed will lie in it, and sprout and grow perfectly because the soil is fine and compact around it. This is good work. It may not look so smooth to the eye, but it is better for the crop.

Q. But this rough surface would not be suitable for seed; then I presume the use of a roller would be necessary?

A. Yes—then the roller is used, followed again by the chain harrow, so that the surface may be made level and smooth for the seed.

Q. Is the chain harrow you have referred to in speaking of manures in general use?

A. It is slowly coming into use as people become acquainted with it. Our local blacksmith here has made for my sales alone over sixty within the past two years. They weigh about 300 lbs. They are eight feet long and five feet wide, and the diamond-shaped chain link five by five inches. The harrow is made of the best wrought iron, and costs $40 finished and ready for the field.

Q. What harrow as a pulverizer do you consider the best?

A. I have heretofore used the imported Scotch harrow, which I had found to be the best; but this season a trial of the American harrow known as the Acme leads me to believe that it will supersede the Scotch as a pulverizer or leveler, for it is the best implement I have ever used for these purposes.

(Mr. H.) I am pleased to agree with you in this matter. After a thorough trial this season with this harrow, I find it to be the best implement I have ever used for the purpose of pulverizing and leveling the soil. It is not only a harrow, but under certain conditions of the soil it is to all intents and purposes a gang of small plows; or, in other words, in a soft or light soil you can plow the ground just as thoroughly for six feet wide as you can do it with the ordinary plow eight inches. The great value of this implement induces us to use more space for a description of it, and its uses, than will be probably given to any other implement in this work. Upon this account I would like to give the views of a well known farmer, whose experience with this implement has been longer than mine, and who is a high authority upon such subjects. This is Henry Stewart, of Hackensack, N. J., who, after using the harrow for six or seven years, says: "After plowing, the soil is worked over with the Acme harrow and is thoroughly broken up; the furrows are leveled; the whole soil to the depth of four inches at least is disturbed as though a series of small propeller screws passed through it; it is thoroughly mingled; the upper portion, which has been exposed to the air, is turned under and buried, and the whole soil is loosened up, broken and made mellow. This is the only implement, so far as I know, that does this necessary work, and with this the best preparation for crops is easily possible. That is to say, that the full effects desired cannot be obtained by, or through, any other one implement than this; because it does all that a plow could do, and it does all that the harrow can do to pulverize the soil, but it does what no mere harrow can possibly do in the way of turning over the soil and presenting a fresh surface to the atmosphere, and it does all that a cultivator can do, without the objectionable effects of that implement; and lastly, it does all that a roller can do in the way of pulverizing cloddy soil, without the objectionable effects of that implement in packing the soil so closely that the air cannot penetrate it."

Q. You make a distinction between what you would call leveling the soil and smoothing it, do you not?

A. Yes. For instance, the Acme harrow levels and pulverizes the soil, while the Chain harrow smooths the surface.

Q. When you say that you harrow your manure after spreading it on the land (which I believe is an excellent plan, and one that was entirely new to me), what harrow do you use for that purpose?

A. I would by all means use the Acme or a similar harrow, as for that purpose we require to mix in part with the soil. The great advantage of the Acme harrow for working up the manure, would be that you can regulate the depth of the teeth at will.

(Mr. H.) In my experience among our market gardeners, where the pulverization of the soil is as perfect as we can get it for the reception of small seeds, I have used for the past two years a smoothing harrow known as the Disc harrow, which consists of some sixty sharp discs placed on revolving shafts, so as to cut the soil to a depth of three inches by one inch in width, which fines and levels the ground as completely as can be done with a steel rake in the hands of an expert workman, but whether such an implement would answer the purpose as well for the requirements of a farm as the Chain or Acme harrow I am not able to say.

THE DISC HARROW.

(Mr. C.) One great advantage of the Acme harrow over all others is the disposition of the teeth, which are so placed that on sod that has been plowed it cuts and pulverizes it, without dragging it to the surface. The present season I turned down a piece of sod on which I sowed mangels and planted potatoes. The thoroughness of the cultivation by the use of this implement was such, that I was enabled to work the land up in ridges—which is my usual practice with such crops—as easily as if it had been stubble land.

Q. What do you deem a proper day's work for plowing for a man and team?

A. One acre on sod land and one acre and one-fourth on stubble.

Q. What area should a man and a pair of horses harrow in a day, to do it properly, with the Acme or other harrow?

A. From four to five acres, to do it thoroughly.

Q. Of course you are aware that about twice that area is harrowed when done in the ordinary way?

A. Yes, and even more. But I consider that such labor thoroughly done is the best investment the farmer can make. My experience of thirty years has been varied and extensive, and every succeeding year only impresses the more strongly upon me the fact, that to get good crops you must have thorough pulverization of the soil.

Q. Of course you use the various kinds of cultivators for the various crops. What implement do you at present use for cultivating corn?

A. Cultivators are now so varied and improving every year, that it is hard to say that any particular one is the best. There are many

PLANET, JR., CULTIVATOR AND HORSE HOE.

patterns more or less valuable. My rule in all such things, when purchasing at an implement or a seed warehouse, is to ask what tool is in largest demand for a certain purpose, and I usually find that the public in the long run finds out which is the best article, and that the article most in demand is the one usually having the most merit. At present I have found that the cultivator known as the Planet, Jr., Horse Hoe, does the best work in this way, and as it is mostly used in this vicinity, public opinion bears me out in mine.

(Mr. H.) I agree with you in that entirely, and as a seedsman I can well endorse it; for whenever a customer asks for any particular tool, the answer I make to him (unless I have certain knowledge myself of the subject), is to go and ask the clerk having charge of that department to select for him the kind that is in most general demand, and as a rule it will be such as is the best. However, I may state that I have used for nearly twenty-five years a simple form of cultivator —which any blacksmith can make—known as the Harrow-tooth Cultivator. It is merely a triangular harrow having from twelve to sixteen teeth, which we use to stir up the soil almost immediately after a crop has been sown or planted, and this we continue to do once a week or so, between the rows, until it may become necessary to use (in particular crops) a cultivator to work deeper, such as the Planet, Jr. But the use of this Harrow-tooth cultivator is of great importance in checking the first growth of weeds, and as it is light and easily worked, a vast amount of labor can be saved by using it often enough, so that the weeds will never be allowed to be seen.

Q. Do you make much use of the roller on your farm, Mr. Crozier?

A. I used it on all crops and particularly on my pastures early in the spring. I thoroughly believe in the practice which you so persistently advocate, of firming the soil for all seeds and plants. You, in your limited areas in market gardening, can afford to do this with the feet, which probably there answers the purpose of firming the

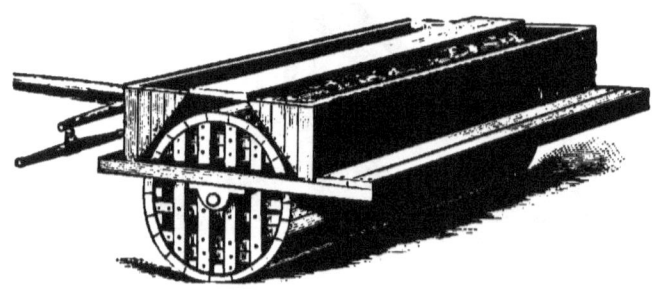

A FIELD ROLLER.

seeds or plants better than the roller, but on a farm that, of course, would be impracticable; but, whatever method is used, the principle should never be neglected, of compacting the earth around newly sown or planted crops, especially in hot, dry weather, and particularly so on loose and porous soils.

While you, as a gardener, advocate the use of the feet to firm the soil, in sowing and planting, I, as a farmer, advocate the use of the roller. The object in both is the same; and I am satisfied beyond any shadow of a doubt, that millions and millions of dollars are annually lost to the farming community, through a want of the knowledge of the vast importance of firming the soil over the seed. This is particularly the case with buckwheat, turnips and other crops that are sown from the month of July until September, as at such seasons we very often have long-continued droughts, and the soil is like a hot ash heap, and to expect germination from small seeds when sown in such soils, without being firmed against the entrance of the hot air, is just about as useless as if we threw them in the fire.

(Mr. H.) I consider this subject of so great importance, that I think we should take the liberty to again print here the article which I read before the National Association of Nurserymen held at Cleveland, O., in June of 1879, entitled "The Use of the Feet in Sowing and Planting." I have written a great deal on horticultural subjects in the last twenty years, but I think (and I say this advisedly) that the value of this article to the horticultural and agricultural community is more than the whole I have ever written, put together, and I have great satisfaction in knowing that thousands of men have thanked me for impressing so strongly the necessity for this work. This article has been reprinted in thousands of newspapers in the past four years, but if it, or some other similar advice on the necessity of firming the soil after sowing, was ever placed before the eyes of the farming community and acted upon, thousands would be saved from mourning the loss of wasted seed, manure and labor; for in a country vast as ours, a new crop of inexperienced men are annually engaging in farming and gardening. In no European work on farming or gardening that I have ever seen, has the importance of what we have so strongly argued for been referred to, probably for the reason that in the cooler and more humid atmosphere of most European countries the necessity is not so great.

THE USE OF THE FEET IN SOWING AND PLANTING.

[Read before the National Association of Nurserymen held at Cleveland, O., in June, 1879.]

It may be useless to throw out any suggestions in relation to horticultural operations to such a body of practical men as is now before me. Yet I candidly admit that, although I have been extensively engaged in gardening operations for over a quarter of a century, I did not fully realize, until a few years ago, the full importance of how indispensable it was to use the feet in the operations of sowing and planting.

For some years past I have, in writing on gardening matters, insisted upon the great importance of "firming" the soil over the seeds after sowing, especially when the soil is dry, or likely to become so. I know of no operation of more importance in either the farm or garden, and I trust that what I am about to say will be read and remembered by every one not yet aware of the vast importance of the practice. I say "vast importance," for the loss to the agricultural and horticultural community, from the habit of loosely sowing seeds or planting plants in hot and dry soils, is of a magnitude which few will believe, until they have witnessed it; and it is a loss all the more to be regretted, when we know that by "firming" the soil around the seed or plant, there is, in most cases, a certain preventive.

Particularly in the sowing of seeds, I consider the matter of such vast importance, that it cannot be too often or too strongly told; for the loss to the agricultural and horticultural community, by the neglect of the simple operation of firming the soil around the seed, must amount to many millions annually. For the mischief done is not confined only to the less important garden operations, but even corn, cotton, wheat, turnips and other important crops of the farm, often fail, in hot and dry soils, by being sown without being firmed sufficiently to prevent the dry air shriveling or drying the seeds. Of course, the use of the feet is impracticable in firming seeds on the farm, but a heavy roller, applied after sowing, is an absolute necessity under certain conditions of the soil, to ensure perfect germination. From the middle of April to nearly the end of May of this year, in many sections of the country, there was little or no rain. Such was particularly the case in the vicinity of New York City, where we have hundreds of market gardeners, who cultivate thousands of acres of cabbage, cauliflower and celery, but the "dry spring" has played sad havoc with their seed-beds. Celery is not one-fourth of a crop, and cabbage and cauliflower hardly half, and this failure is due to no other cause than that they persist in sowing their seeds without even taking the precaution to firm the soil by rolling.

We sow annually about four acres of celery, cabbage and cauliflower plants, which produce probably five millions in number, and which we never fail to sell mostly in our immediate neighborhood, to the market gardeners, who have, many of them, even better facilities than we have for raising these plants, if they would only do as we do, firm the seed after sowing, which is done thus:

After plowing, harrowing and leveling the land smoothly, lines are drawn by the "marker," which makes a furrow about two inches deep and a foot apart; after the man who sows the seed follows another, who, with the ball of the right foot, presses down his full weight on every inch of soil in the drill where the seed has been sown; the rows are then lightly leveled longitudinally with the rake, a light roller is passed over them, and the operation is done.

By this method our crop has never once failed, and what is true of celery and cabbage seed is nearly true of all other seeds requiring to be sown during the late spring or summer months.

On July 2d of 1874, as an experiment, I sowed twelve rows of sweet corn and twelve rows of beets, treading in, after sowing, every alternate row of each. In both cases, those trod in came up in four days, while those unfirmed remained twelve days before starting, and would not then have germinated had not rain fallen, for the soil was dry as dust when the seed was sown.

The result was, that the seeds that had been trodden in grew freely from the start, and matured their crops to a marketable condition by fall; while the rows unfirmed did not mature, as they were not only eight days later in germinating, but the plants were also, to some extent, enfeebled by being partially dried in the loose, dry soil.

This experiment was a most useful one, for it proved that a corn crop, sown in the vicinity of New York as late as July 2d, could be made to produce "roasting ears" in October, when they never fail to sell freely at high rates, but the crop would not mature unless the seed germinated at once, and which would never be certain at that dry and hot season, unless by this method.

The same season, in August, I treated seeds of turnips and spinach in the same way. Those trod in germinated at once and made an excellent crop, while those unfirmed germinated feebly, and were eventually nearly all burned out by a continuance of dry, hot air penetrating through the loose soil to the tender rootlets.

I beg to caution the inexperienced, however, by no means to tread or roll in seed if the ground is *not dry*. The soil may often be in a suitable condition to sow, and yet may be too damp to be trodden upon or rolled. In such cases these operations may not be necessary at all, for if rainy weather ensue, the seeds will germinate of course; but if there is any likelihood of a continued drought, the treading or rolling may be done a week or more after the seed has been sown, if there is any reason to believe that it may suffer from the dry, hot air. Another very important advantage gained by treading in the seed is, that when we have crops of beets, celery, turnips, spinach, or anything else that is sown in rows, the seeds to form the crop come up at once; while the seeds of the weeds, that are just as liable to perish by the heat as are those of the crop, are retarded. Such of the weed seeds as lie in the space between the rows when the soil is loose, will not germinate as quickly as those of the crop sown; and hence we can cultivate between the rows before the weeds germinate at all.

Of course, this rule of treading in or firming seeds after sowing must not be blindly followed. Very early in spring or late in fall, when the soil is damp and there is no danger from heated, dry air, there is no necessity for doing so.

Now, if firming the soil around seed, to protect it from the influence of a dry and hot atmosphere, is a necessity, it is obvious that it is more so in the case of plants whose rootlets are even more sensitive to such influence than the dormant seed.

Experienced professional horticulturists, however, are less likely to neglect this than to neglect in the case of seeds, for the damage from such neglect is easier to be seen, and hence better understood by the practical nurseryman; but with the inexperienced amateur the case is different. When he receives his package of trees or plants from the nurseryman, he handles them as if they were glass, every broken twig or root calls forth a complaint, and he proceeds to plant them, gingerly straightening out each root and sifting the soil around them, but he would no more stamp down that soil than he would stamp on the soil of his mother's grave. So the plant, in nine cases out of ten, is left loose and waggling; the dry air penetrates through the soil to its roots; the winds shake it; it shrivels up and fails to grow; and then come the anathemas on the head of the unfortunate nurseryman, who is charged with selling him dead trees or plants.

About a month ago I sent a package of a dozen roses by mail to a lady in Savannah. She wrote me a woful story last week, saying that, though the roses had arrived seemingly all right, they had all died but one, and what was very singular, she said, the one that lived was the one that Mr. Jones had stepped on, and which she had thought sure was crushed to death, for Mr. Jones weighs 200 lbs. Now, though I do not advise any gentleman of 200 lbs. putting his brogan on the top of a tender rose plant, as a practice conducive to its health, yet, if Mrs. Jones could have allowed her weighty lord to press the soil against the root of each of her dozen roses, I much doubt if she would now have to mourn their loss.

It has often been a wonder to many of us, who have been workers in the soil for a generation, how some of the simplest methods of culture have not been practiced until we were nearly done with life's work.

There are few of us but have had such experience; personally, I must say that I never pass through a year but I am confounded to find that some operation can not only be quicker done, but better done, than we have been in the habit of doing it.

These improvements loom up from various causes, but mainly from suggestions thrown out by our employees in charge of special departments, a system which we do all in our power to encourage.

As a proof of the value of such improvements which have led to simplifying our operations, I will state the fact that though my area of greenhouse surface is now more than double that which it was in 1870, and the land used in our florist's business is one-third more, the number of hands employed is less now than in 1870, and yet, at the same time, the quality of our stock is infinitely better now than then.

Whether it is the higher price of labor in this country, that forces us into labor-saving expedients, or the interchange of opinions from the greater number of nationalities centering here, that gives us broader views of culture, I am not prepared to state; but that America is now selling nearly all the products of the greenhouse, garden, nursery and farm lower than is done in Europe, admits of no question; and if my homely suggestions in this matter of firming the soil around newly planted seeds or plants will in any degree assist us in still holding to the front, I shall be gratified.

CHAPTER IV.

ROTATION OF CROPS.

Q. When we begin cultivation of land that has not been previously cropped, whether in the natural meadow or in brush or woodland, the first operation is to get the land in condition for tillage. Will you please state, Mr. Crozier, what has been your plan of operating on lands of this kind?

A. My method has been to prepare the land for the plow (if brush land) by first removing the brush by the use of brush scythes or brush hooks and burning it on the land. If there are many roots, I put three horses abreast on a heavy plow and turn the soil eight or nine inches deep; I then spread on manure according to the necessities of the land; harrow it in thoroughly; mark both ways with a plow, three and a half feet, ready for corn. I plant my corn in hills, cover it with a hoe, and run a heavy roller over the whole surface. As soon as the young corn appears I keep the cultivators moving through it both ways until the corn gets too high to cultivate. I do not hill it up, as I prefer flat culture for this crop.

Q. On such land how much manure per acre do you use?

A. It would be difficult to name a specific quantity, as so much would depend upon the necessities of the soil—upon how much leaf mould there might be on it. I would say, however, that in my operations here on such soils I have used about twenty-five two-horse loads to the acre. I have actually produced (by measurement of a committee from the New York Farmers' Club) 240 bushels of ears of corn, per acre, from virgin soil. Continuing my method of culture: in the fall, after the corn is taken off the field, the land is again thoroughly plowed and left through the winter. In the spring it is harrowed and plowed again and sowed with oats and peas, sowing part in oats, and part in oats and peas mixed, which we use as a soiling crop. The third year I plant with roots and fodder corn, thoroughly manured. The fourth year, seed down to grass with oats.

Q. What variety of corn was it you refer to as producing 240 bushels of ears to the acre?

A. It was a large yellow flint corn. The ears were twelve rowed and very long, and filled out to the end, and the cob was small. Although there is a good deal in the variety, yet there is a good deal, too, in the character of the soil and the cultivation. Probably the well known variety, King Phillip, or any other good kind, suited to this northern locality, would have done as well under the same circumstances. But it is an all-important matter, that a farmer should choose a suitable variety of seed for his climate. For instance, the corn crop this season (1883) in Michigan and Wisconsin has generally failed, because the most of the seed planted was brought from Kansas and Nebraska, where the season is much longer than in the north, and more time is required for corn to ripen. Had they got their seed from any other northern locality they would probably have been safe. Just now there are a number of very promising new varieties of corn making their appearance. It would be wise for farmers to test these judiciously in a small way at first, that their adaptation to special climates may be tested. Among these might be mentioned the two excellent kinds, Golden Beauty and Chester County Mammoth, but with the proviso that these should only be planted where there are at least 100 days of safe growing season.

CHESTER COUNTY MAMMOTH.

GOLDEN BEAUTY.

Q. This mode of culture you describe, Mr. Crozier, is the one you followed on your farm here. For what purpose was your farming land intended?

A. It was intended for a dairy and stock farm, and the preparations to the fourth year were simply laying a broad foundation for my future work. The fifth year corn, wheat, rye, oats, peas, mangels and turnips were my general crops.

Q. Having detailed your method of laying the foundation, as you term it, will you now describe your system of growing root crops, beginning with potatoes?

A. My plan of growing potatoes is to plow, and manure broadcast at the rate of ten or twelve loads per acre, as I never lose sight of what is to come after, and roll the ground well before furrowing. The ground can never be furrowed so well when it is loose as when it is made firm by the use of the roller, and my practice has always been, no matter what length the rows, they must be straight and of even width. When the furrows are marked out three feet apart, I also manure at the rate of five loads per acre in the furrows. I plant the largest potatoes cut lengthwise in two parts, dropped fifteen inches apart in the rows, and cover with the plow about four inches, and before the sprouts come through the ground harrow with the chain harrow or with a light sloping tooth harrow, the object being to break the crust to a depth of an inch or two and to destroy the weeds in the embryo state. The after cultivation is done with the hoe and cultivator. In gathering, plow out with the double furrow plow, pick up, put in pits or the cellar. The largest of the potatoes are marketed if the price is good. If it is not, they are fed to the stock with the small ones.

Q. At what price do you consider they should be sold rather than fed to the stock?

A. Forty cents per bushel. If less than that, it would pay better to feed them to cattle or hogs. In fact, it has always been my practice to feed everything raised on the farm, unless the market price was such as would justify disposing of it at a fair profit.

Q. Have you ever had any trouble, in feeding potatoes to cows, from the danger of their choking, and if so how do you guard against that danger? I remember when a boy of many a good cow being choked by potatoes.

A. To prevent any possibility of choking I run the potatoes through my "pulper" or root cutter, but cattle occasionally get choked with apples and potatoes which they pick up out-doors. In such cases there is no other remedy but the probang—a flexible instrument with a

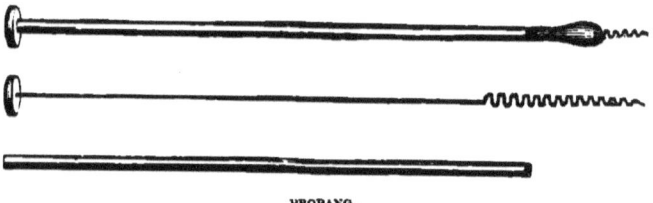

PROBANG.

corkscrew in the lower end, to bring up the potato or apple, if it will come—if not, it must be shoved down into the stomach. A method which has been used when the obstacle cannot be removed by the probang, is to crush the root in the throat by a sharp blow of a mallet, a block of wood being held on the other side. This has saved animals which would have been lost without it. (The probang, shown in the illustration, consists of a flexible tube, which is pushed down the throat until it meets the obstacle, when, if this cannot be pushed down, the flexible rod with the corkscrew at the end is pushed down the tube, and the obstacle is then caught and drawn up.)

Q. I presume, of course, you are thoroughly familiar with the endless discussions that have been in the papers for the last twenty years on the question of what kinds of potatoes we should use for seed—whether they should be small or large, whether cut or in single eyes, or cut in halves. What has been your practice and the result of it?

A. I have always practiced, with the exception of experiments, to choose the largest potatoes, and cut from the top end through to the butt, straight, making two pieces of each, thus giving the seed ample substance. In my experience in cutting to single eyes I have never had much success in getting a full crop.

(Mr. H.) Although I have grown but few potatoes, I think my general experience in horticulture will warrant me in saying that the result of the practice of cutting the potatoes to single eyes, or even two eyes, unless a good portion of what may be called the nutritious substance of the potato is left, can never be good, because this substance of the potato is absolutely necessary to sustain the bud or eye until it starts. Experiments with beans and peas that have been attacked by the weevil, where the whole or portions of this pabulum of the seed has been eaten out, have shown so clearly, by frequent and careful trials, that when the pabulum of the seed is completely exhausted, the seed germ will not start at all, and that when it is partially exhausted it will start feebly, and make a weak plant. This undoubtedly must be true of the tuber of the potato as well as the seed of the pea or bean. Nature provides this substance for the germ or bud to feed on until it is able to take care of itself, and if you rob it of its sustenance you must pay the penalty. I know well that it is often the custom when new potatoes are introduced to cut them up into single eyes, in the hope of producing a larger crop from the costly seed; but I doubt very much if any additional weight of crop will be gained, and undoubtedly the vitality of the roots will be weakened for future products, if wanted for that purpose, which, with new potatoes, is generally the case; as of course when purchased at two or three dollars per pound, as in the case of the Early Rose, men do not plant such potatoes to eat the first year. I remember very well, when the Early Rose variety was introduced, that I purchased a tuber weighing five ounces.

In April I cut this five-ounce potato in two pieces, so that each surface would present the greatest number of eyes. I then placed them on a shelf, keeping them entirely dry until the cut part had healed over, when they were placed on soil on the bench of the greenhouse. The shoots soon began to start from the eyes, the temperature of the greenhouse averaging, perhaps, seventy-five degrees.

As soon as the shoots got to be three or four inches in length, they were cut off about one-fourth of an inch from the surface of the potato, or far enough from the surface so as not to injure the dormant eyes that were yet to start. The slips were then placed in the propagating house, and shaded and watered until rooted in the usual way. They were then potted in small pots, in ordinary soil, and started to grow in the same temperature in which the potato had been placed. As the season advanced, shoots in great numbers were thrown out by the potato, which, in turn, were submitted to the same process of rooting. As the first shoots grew to lengths of five or six inches the tops were cut from these and used as cuttings, so that by the end of May this small potato of five ounces had given me nearly 150 plants, every one of which was equal to a "set" made from a tuber. These were planted out on the first week in June, in land very ill suited for the growth of the potato, and the crop, when dug, weighed exactly 450 pounds, or an increase of about 1,800 fold. It may be asked if this process is of any practical value, or whether it will pay. It is not claimed that there is any use in the practice when potatoes are sold at ordinary rates; but, when they are sold at the rates even yet paid for new varieties, there is no doubt of its utility. For instance: one pound of potatoes so grown will easily produce 500 plants, making 500 hills, which, with ordinary culture, will give three pounds per hill or 1,500 pounds. The process of rooting the slips is neither difficult nor costly, and can be done in a common hot-bed. The ordinary hot-bed sash, four by six feet, will hold 600 plants, if placed in the soil of the hot-bed just as lettuce or cabbage plants are planted out, and treated much in the same way by careful shading and watering until the cuttings have rooted. These, as they grow, make other cuttings from the top, as before described. Without resorting to the glass propagation at all, a potato crop may be doubled or trebled in quantity by "slipping" the shoots, and planting them out at once in the field, if there is a continuance of rainy weather for two or three days at the time. This should be done in June. The thinning out of shoots from the regular planting will do no injury to the plants. It is not claimed that the growing of potatoes in this way is new; in fact, it may be doubted if there is much new in agriculture; processes that are suggested to us by circumstances to-day may have been practiced by others centuries ago, and if published to the world at all have long since been forgotten; but there is little doubt that this practice of growing potatoes from cuttings will be new to many who will read this book, though the principles involved, and, perhaps, the practice followed, have been long known to many farmers and gardeners of experience.

Although this system of propagating the potato may be of very little use to the farmer in a general way, when there is plenty of seed, yet whenever he invests at the rate of one or two dollars per pound for new varieties it will be worth his while to try it, and he may be assured that if properly done it will give good results.

POTATO DISEASES AND INSECTS.

(Mr. H.) The potato disease which has frequently been so disastrous in Ireland and parts of Scotland has never been devastating here. There is but little doubt that it is a parasitical fungus of some kind, for which all remedies are useless when the crop is attacked. Like all diseases of this kind, the only help we have is prevention. As far as experiments have gone, they have shown that potatoes are always less liable to attacks of disease or rot if planted in new land broken up from the sod, or at least that which has not been long in cultivation. Another enemy to this crop is the well known striped potato beetle. Fortunately, for this pest we have a certain remedy in the use of Paris green, which may be put on either by dusting while the dew is on the leaves in the morning, or after a rain, or else in a liquid form of one ounce of Paris green to ten gallons of water. But whichever way it is applied, it should be begun at the very first appearance of the beetles. If they once get a foothold, they increase so rapidly that often the crop is destroyed before the remedy can be of any avail. Paris green being a deadly poison, it is absolutely necessary that fields on which potatoes are growing should be protected from cattle. It is sometimes supposed that danger might arise from the use of the Paris green affecting the potato tubers. There need be no fear of this, as the tubers do not in any way absorb it.

The disease known as the potato rot is a vegetable parasite which grows within the substance of the plant, and affects the leaves, stems and tubers, as is well known. Some part of its life history is known; and while all is not known, yet enough has been learned to give us some indications of how it may be prevented, for as to cure when once the plants have been attacked, there is and can be none, because of the impossibility of applying any remedy. The parasitic plant, a species of fungus, propagates itself by means of spores, which are the seed. The spores mature in the leaves and stems, as well as the tubers. To prevent its further spread by infection of the ground, as far as we can we should gather the vines and leaves when the crop is dug and burn them. Also cook and feed the affected tubers to pigs and preserve only sound ones for next year's seed. This will help us as far, probably, as we have learned how to go. I have heard that it prevents the spread of the disease in the stored potatoes to sprinkle them freely and thoroughly with air-slaked lime, but I have no personal experience of that. From my experience with the fumes of sulphur in destroying mildew and all other parasitic life, I am of opinion that sulphur burned in places where potatoes are kept would arrest the spread of disease.

The simplest method of applying the sulphur fumes is to sprinkle flowers of sulphur on sheets of paper, roll these up and burn them so as to keep a continuous supply of the fumes to saturate the air of the cellar for four or five days. This is a cheap and simple application which I think would be effective. It would be useless to apply sulphur in any other way, as it must be volatilized by heat.

SWEET POTATOES.

Although sweet potatoes can hardly be called a crop for the farm in the neighborhood of New York, yet in the Southern States it is one of the leading farm products, and it is even grown successfully as far north as New Jersey. The plants are raised in hot-beds from so-called "seed" sweet potatoes, which are usually of small size, but must be sound. These are placed in hot-beds any time during the month of April. After the hot-bed has been made in the usual way—that is, one and one-half or two feet deep of horse manure—a layer of sand or sandy loam is thrown over it to the depth of four or five inches and the seed potatoes placed on this close together. As soon as the shoots begin to appear, a layer of an inch of sand is thrown over them. The shoots quickly sprout through the sand, and by the middle or end of May, in the latitude of New Jersey, they are in condition to be set out in the open ground. In Southern New Jersey and further south, these beds are not covered with glass, but with a light covering of straw or coarse hay, to retain the warmth. This is removed when the plants appear. In sections of the country where sweet potatoes are grown even to a small extent, there are generally men who make a business of growing the plants, which are often to be bought as low as one dollar per 1,000, and it will be found better for the grower to purchase than to raise them himself, if he has not the proper convenience of sashes and hot-beds. The plants are set out in rows three or four feet distant, and about two feet apart in the rows, using a good shovelful of well rotted manure, mixed in, for each hill. They are always planted in light, sandy soil, heavy soils being entirely uncongenial to the nature of the root. As they advance in growth the rows are hilled up with the plow in the same manner as ordinary potatoes, care being taken, however, to prevent the shoots, as they hang over, from rooting in the sand. This is done by running along the rows occasionally under them with the hand to break the young roots and keep them from striking into the soil. If this is not done, it would divert the growth from the main root, and the tubers would be small and nearly worthless. In the Northern States sweet potatoes must always be used previous to December, unless they can be kept in a warm place. The ordinary cellar, which is suitable for the common potato, will quickly rot the sweet potato. In the Southern States they are kept in pits in the open ground in much the same way as we keep ordinary potatoes North; but the temperature of the sand is of course much higher in Florida and other extreme Southern States than it is North. Most of the sweet potatoes that find their way to our Northern markets in the winter and spring months are grown in Georgia, South Carolina and other Southern States. They are preserved in the South by storing them in houses specially built for that purpose. The potatoes are packed in boxes not more than eighteen inches deep, which are placed in tiers one above the other, leaving spaces between for ventilation. But in extreme cold weather it is necessary that the apartment should be heated in some way so that the temperature at no time is allowed to fall below fifty degrees. There is no necessity for packing anything around them, as, if the heat in the apartment is sufficient, they will keep by the air circulating around them among the shelves or boxes in which they are placed. Probably the best temperature at which sweet potatoes can be kept in winter is sixty degrees.

ROOTS FOR FEEDING.

(Mr. H.) The most important of all the root crops used for feeding are mangels and turnips. These have been largely grown in Europe for more than thirty years, and considering how well the American climate and soil are adapted for their culture, it is surprising that so little attention has hitherto been given to them in this country. It is more particularly surprising when we consider our special necessities, arising out of our long, dry summers, which diminish the yield of the hay and other fodder crops; as well as our long winter feeding season, in which some succulent fodder, such as roots, is so useful to feed with the hay and other dry provender. Mangels, which are the most valuable of all roots for this purpose, may be grown in any part of the American Continent upon any fairly good farm land, if only the necessary care is given in their cultivation. The soil best adapted for them is a loose, friable loam, with a dry,

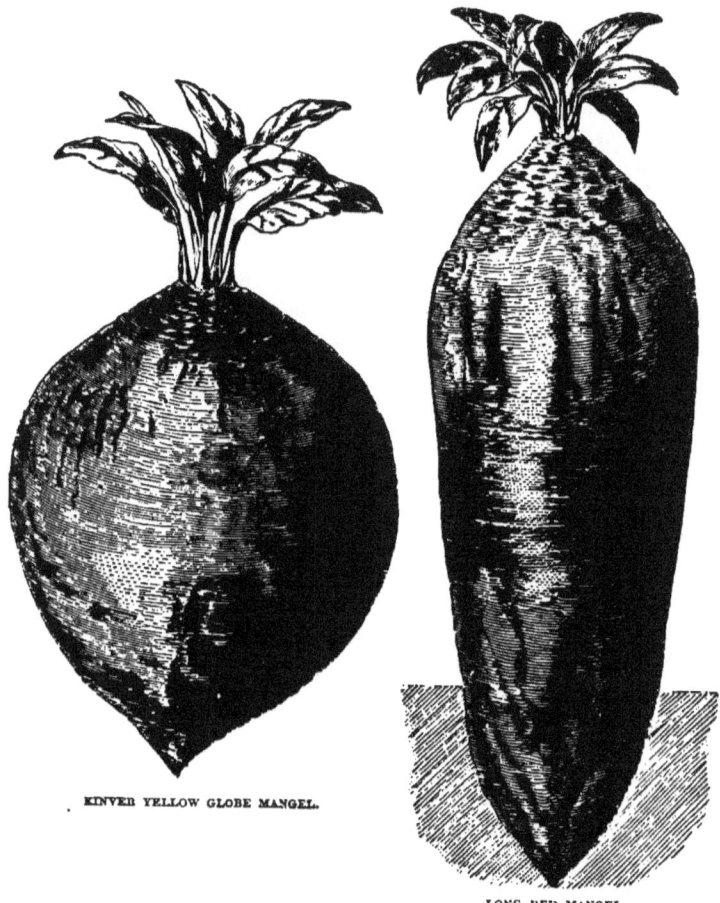

KINVER YELLOW GLOBE MANGEL.

LONG RED MANGEL.

loose subsoil, as deep culture is indispensable. The soil should be plowed if necessary to the depth of ten inches, or the land should be broken to that depth by following the plow with a subsoiler.

In all soils, excepting sufficiently deep, rich new land, well rotted manure or compost should be used at the rate of twelve to twenty tons per acre, spread upon the surface before plowing and covered in with the plow. In place of this, but all the better with it, 300 to 500 pounds per acre of superphosphate, or Peruvian guano, should be applied by sowing on the surface after plowing, and harrowing it in. Immediately after this, the soil should be well smoothed by the smoothing harrow and roller. The seed is sown in drills, by means of a seed drill, the Planet or any other of an equally good kind, twenty-four inches apart in light soils, and thirty inches in strong, rich land, the plants being thinned to nine inches apart in the former case and twelve in the latter. This is what is termed flat culture.

Some farmers, however, practice the ridge system, and as this is your method, Mr. Crozier, please describe it, and say how you produce the enormous crops which I have seen in your fields?

(Mr. C.) After thoroughly plowing, harrowing and smoothing the land, I strike out furrows with the double mold-board plow (if this is not obtainable, any plow that will make such a furrow will do), thirty inches apart. The furrow is six to seven inches deep. These furrows are then half filled with compost (see chapter on Manures) or stable manure, thoroughly decomposed, or, if yet rough and unrotted, it is pressed down in the rows with the feet. After the manure has been placed in the furrows, the plow is run on each side, so as to cover in the manure, and to raise a ridge as high as the furrow was deep. These ridges are leveled with a roller or chain harrow, about two or three inches, which widens the ridge, so as to permit the seed sower to work on it. Where stable manure is scarce, I use

SEED DRILL FOR ROOT CROPS.

superphosphate, or bone dust, sown in the furrows at the rate of about 300 pounds to the acre, keeping the ridge over the furrows not so high as over the manure. About six to eight pounds of seed are used to the acre, sown with the seed drill. If sown by hand, fully double that quantity will be required. The plants are thinned to twelve or fourteen inches apart, the land is well cultivated, and kept loose and free from weeds.

This system of culture, both for mangels and turnips, requires more labor, but is a saving in manure. The best time for sowing, in the latitude of New York, is from May 1st to the 15th; but this time may be extended up to June 1st. The time to sow is from eight to ten days *before* corn is usually planted. The varieties most used are Long Red, and the Golden Tankard and Kinver Globe, which are both yellow kinds. The average yield of mangels is thirty tons or over per acre; this is equal to 1,000 bushels. I consider the

GOLDEN TANKARD MANGEL.

average value of mangels, for feeding stock, to be $4 per ton, or $120 per acre, at the least. Two tons per acre of hay would be only worth $30. The seed, manure and cultivation of a crop of mangels, at the utmost, need not exceed $80 per acre, even where the manure is purchased at a high price. The crop for feeding purposes is therefore a profitable one, even under these circumstances.

TURNIPS.

The culture of turnips differs in no respect from that of mangels, except as to the time of sowing—the Swedish turnip, or Ruta Baga, sown, in this latitude, from May 25th to June 25th; the Yellow Aberdeen, or strap-leaved kinds, from July 1st to the middle of August.

TURNIPS. 63

The distance apart may be the same as for mangels, but both varieties may be sown a month later; that is, the Ruta Bagas may be sown from June 25th to July 25th, and the strap-leaved kinds from the middle of August to the middle of September. In this case the plants should stand, both in the rows and between plants, one-third closer. The best kinds are American Ruta Baga and Purple-top Swede, of the strap-leaved kinds, Red-top and Yellow Aberdeen. Perhaps the best of all turnips, after the Swedes, is the White Cow-

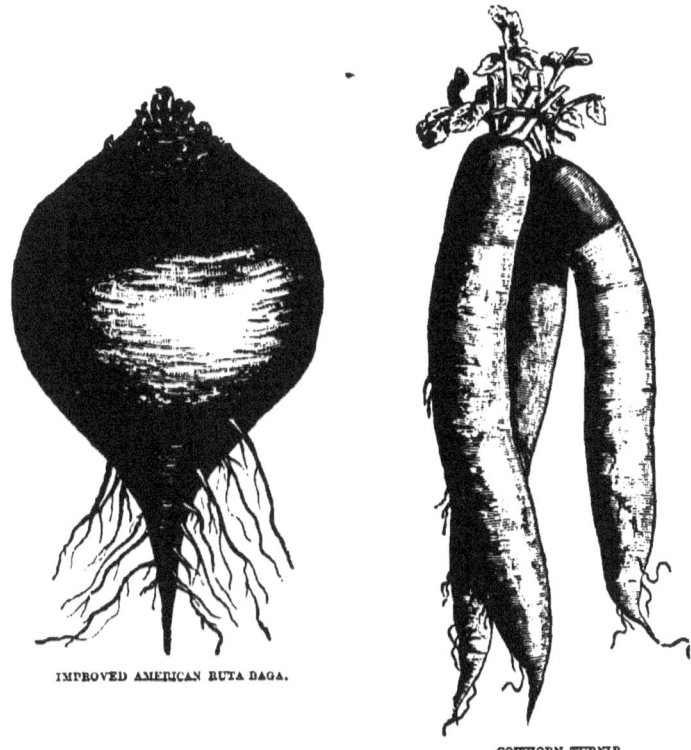

IMPROVED AMERICAN RUTA BAGA.

COWHORN TURNIP.

horn, a long, thin root, but very sweet and tender, and unexcelled for cows, as it grows very quickly and may be sown in September. I value Ruta Bagas, as compared with hay at $15 per ton, at $5 per ton; an average crop of twenty-five tons per acre is thus worth $125. Strap-leaved and Yellow Aberdeen or Cowhorn turnips are worth $3.50 per ton, or, with a yield of thirty-five tons per acre, $122.50. If the expense of culture is half the whole value, the crop is still very profitable. Turnips may be sown upon a barley, oats or rye stubble, or even after potatoes.

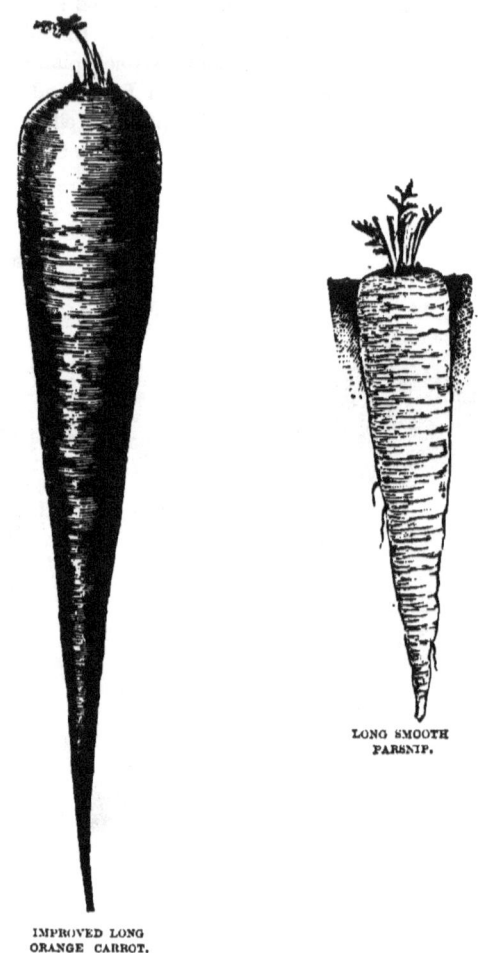

LONG SMOOTH PARSNIP.

IMPROVED LONG ORANGE CARROT.

CARROTS AND PARSNIPS.

The culture of these two roots is precisely the same. Parsnips, however, are hardy, and can be left in the ground all the winter, so that, if required for use in the spring, they may be gathered then, when it is found convenient to do so. This root is an excellent one for dairy cows, and is extensively grown in the islands of Jersey and Guernsey for this purpose.

Carrots are chiefly grown for horses, but I consider them inferior to Ruta Bagas for that purpose. Carrots require a similar soil and the same preparation as for mangels. In a previously well manured corn stubble, enough fertilizing material will be left to manure a good crop of carrots or parsnips. Twenty tons of carrots per acre have been grown on land in this condition, without using any manure. The seed is sown any time in May; if sown with a drill, about four pounds are used to the acre. The rows should be two feet apart, and the plants thinned out to five or six inches. An average crop is fifteen tons, or 700 bushels by measure, of the Long Orange. This variety is the one usually grown for farm purposes.

HARVESTING AND STORING ROOTS.

(Mr. H.) The simple and cheap method of preserving roots in pits in the open ground is better than any other. I will briefly describe our plan, which I have practiced with all kinds of market garden roots for twenty-five years. Mangels in this section of the country are dug up toward the end of October, or just after our first slight frost; they are then temporarily secured from severe frosts by placing them in convenient oblong heaps, say three feet high by six feet wide, and are covered with three or four inches of soil, which will be sufficient protection for three or four weeks after lifting; by that time, say the end of November, they may be stowed away in their permanent winter quarters. For turnips and carrots there is less necessity for the temporary pitting, as they are much hardier roots, and may be left in the ground until the time necessary for permanent pitting, if time will not permit of securing them temporarily. The advantage of this temporary pitting is, that it enables them to be quickly secured at a season when work is usually pressing, and allows their permanent pitting to be extended into a comparatively cold season. This is found to be of the utmost importance in preserving all kinds of roots; the same rules regulating the preservation in winter apply as in spring sowing. While in this section of the country it must be done not later than the end of November, in some of the Southern States the time may be extended a month later, while in the places where the thermometer does not fall lower than twenty-five degrees *above* zero, there is no need to dig up any of these roots at all, as that.

degree of temperature would not injure them. The permanent pit is made as follows:

A piece of ground is chosen where no water will stand in winter. If not naturally drained, provision must be made to carry off the water. The pit is then dug four feet deep and six feet wide, and of any length required. The roots are then evenly packed in sections of about four feet wide, *across* the pit, and only to the height of the ground level. Between the sections a space of half a foot is left, which is filled up with soil level to the top. This gives a section of roots four feet deep and wide, and four feet long, each section divided from the next by six inches of soil, forming a series of small pits, holding from six to twelve barrels of roots, one of which can be taken out without disturbing the next, which is separated from it by six inches of soil.

(Mr. C.) Scotch farmers have a method of keeping roots in long pits which I have used here for many years. A dry spot is selected,

ROOT PIT UNFINISHED.

where no water will stand in winter; a space is marked out six feet in width, and of any length required; this bed is excavated ten to twelve inches deep, and the soil is thrown out on the bank. The

MANNER OF COVERING THE PIT.

roots are built up evenly to a sharp point about five or six feet in height, so that they form almost an equal-sided triangle, six feet on the sides. This heap of roots is covered with four inches of straw and the earth is banked over the whole about one foot in thickness.

This covering of earth and straw is sufficient to keep out any cold that is not much below zero. In colder or warmer sections judgment must be used to increase or lessen the covering. In providing against an excessive cold, the covering of straw is to be increased, and not the earth, as the straw is really the non-conductor. Vents or chimneys, made by a three-inch drain-pipe, or anything of similar size, are placed every six or seven feet along the top of the pit, resting on the roots, so that the moisture and heat may escape. In extreme cold weather these vents or chimneys should be closed up, as the cold might be severe enough to get down to the roots. Pits so constructed rarely fail to preserve roots perfectly until late in spring, and are in every respect preferable to root cellars; for, no matter how cold the weather may be, they are easily got at; the ends once opened, the soil forms a frozen arch over the pit. Hundreds of tons of mangels, etc., may be put in a long pit of this kind.

There are two or three points that you make, Mr. Henderson, that I think might be improved upon. When you state that in the absence of stable manure, bone dust, superphosphate or guano should be applied at the rate of three to five hundred pounds per acre, I would say that in my practice I have found in recent years that 1,000 pounds of any of these fertilizers is not too much. Again, when you speak of digging the mangels up I think you advise unnecessary labor, as mangels can be pulled up without trouble, our practice being as follows: One man takes two rows. Having a sharp knife in the right hand, he catches hold of the top of the root with the other and pulls it up from the ground, cuts the top off and lets the root drop into the furrow at his right hand, the top being dropped to the left. By this means two men have taken up forty cart loads per day, each cart holding thirty-two bushels of sixty pounds per bushel. With reference to your system of preserving in winter, I can give you no better evidence of its practical value than by showing you to-day (11th of July) sound roots that were placed in my root pits last fall, grown somewhat, to be sure, but still in good condition to feed to hogs.

Q. In this article nothing has been said about thinning the plants of mangels, turnips or carrots. Will you please state, Mr. Crozier, what is your method of thinning the crop in the drills?

A. I use a ten-inch draw hoe. The man standing partly sideways, shoves his hoe from him, and then drawing it back cuts out the width required, thus leaving the plants in small bunches ten inches apart. It is an operation that is done very rapidly. Two men by this method can thin or single out an acre per day. In a few days the plants left will again straighten up. We leave the thinnings in the rows, of course, which in a short time make the very best vegetable manure by being stirred and worked by the cultivator. For mangels it is necessary to thin to single plants by hand afterwards. Turnips are thinned in the same manner, but hand thinning is not necessary if the hoeing is well done. Carrots are thinned exactly the same way, but with what is known as the carrot hoe, which is not over half the width of that used for mangels or turnips. From the nature of the carrot, it is not so easily singled out to one plant as turnips, and it is necessary to run over the rows with the hands after the hoe, to thin out so as to leave the crop standing about five inches apart between the plants. I observed, Mr. Henderson, also, that in your remarks on root crops you have neglected to impress the necessity of firming the soil after sowing, which in our practice, in addition to the roller following the drill, we follow after with a heavy two-horse iron roller eighteen inches in diameter, which covers three rows at a time.

WHEAT CULTURE.

Q. The method of raising wheat, I presume, is so well known, that comparatively little can be said about it. In a work of this kind, however, it is necessary to touch on all subjects connected with the

SMOOTHING AND BRUSH HARROW.

farm, and this of course with the others. Is wheat much grown on Long Island and vicinity?

A. Yes, I think there is as much wheat grown on Long Island as corn. When wheat is to follow corn my method of culture is as follows: The land being plowed about the middle of September, the manure is spread, thoroughly harrowed in, and wheat sown broadcast at the rate of one and one-half to two bushels to the acre. It is then plowed under about three inches deep with a light one-horse plow. If seeded to grass the surface is rolled before the grass seed is sown, and harrowed with a chain harrow or brush harrow. The brush harrow, as it is well understood, is an improvised harrow made by the farmer, consisting of branches about ten or twelve feet long, which are driven into holes bored in a piece of scantling ten feet long and attached in the usual way to the whiffletree. The harrow shown above answers as a smoothing, leveling and brush harrow, and is convenient, cheap and useful for many purposes, and is a good substitute, sometimes, for the roller.

I have put on as high as eight cords or twenty-four tons per acre. Of course the object of this heavy manuring, as has been referred to, is not so much for the wheat crop, as it would cost more than the product, but it is for the after crop of grass.

If this manure had to be purchased in the vicinity of New York it would cost $72 per acre, which of course is more than double what the wheat crop would sell for, but it will be understood that the crop of wheat is never expected to pay for the manure. It is the after crop of grass that we are laying the foundation for, and here is where the profit of this heavy manuring comes in. The straw from the wheat we consider about pays for the labor of sowing and harvesting the crop. It will be understood that this heavy manuring for a wheat crop that is to be succeeded by grass, is only on fields where oats or corn have been grown the year previous. If a root crop had been grown the previous year, which is our usual custom, there would be no necessity for manuring, as the heavy manuring used for the root crop is ample to carry a crop of wheat and grass for succeeding years.

(Mr. H.) This work of spreading manure is a slow and laborious one. There is an excellent machine made for this purpose which saves the greater part of this labor. It breaks up and scatters the manure, no matter how coarse it is, and spreads it much more evenly than it could be done by hand, and with great rapidity. I think the invention of this machine is a very valuable aid to our agriculture. It will spread from five loads up to twenty loads per acre, and forty loads is an easy day's work.

Q. Is it not the custom generally amongst wheat growers on a large scale on the prairies or in the extensive wheat lands of California to use the wheat drills, instead of sowing broadcast, as you advise?

A. Yes. They do not care so much for the grass there. The wheat crop is what they are after. They sow whatever crop they can market to best advantage, and that is wheat. But we are working under different circumstances.

Q. Why cannot the drill be followed by grass as well as when sown broadcast?

A. For the reason that the drill leaves a furrow after it which the grass seed drops into, leaving a clear space of five or six inches between the rows of grass, which would be too wide. By plowing the seed wheat under we get an even surface for the grass.

Q. Then you mean to say that by drilling, you could not get as heavy and even a crop of grass as by sowing the wheat broadcast, plowing it under and sowing the grass seed after in the usual way?

A. We could not. By plowing in the seed we get a uniform surface over the wheat, and having this smooth surface for the grass seed, we get a much better stand.

KEMP'S MANURE SPREADER.

Q. When following corn with wheat at about what date do you begin to plow?

A. We commence cutting our corn about the 1st of September and clear it off the field, placing it in shocks, either on an adjacent grass lot, or by the fences, so as to get the land clear for sowing the wheat, which we generally put in from the 15th to the 20th of September.

Q. This is your experience with the wheat crop following corn. Does it differ in any way when the wheat follows potatoes?

A. Yes. The potato land having been thoroughly manured in the spring, and well cultivated by the use of the cultivators and plow, I do not manure for the wheat crop. The land is usually in such good condition that it does not need additional manure for the wheat; with too much manure wheat grows rank and weak, and is apt to fall down and lodge, and the crop is then injured.

Q. Do you make any difference in the time of sowing wheat following potatoes and that following corn?

A. After potatoes we get it in about the 10th of September, and we thus get a stronger stand or I would say "braird," for the protection of the roots in winter. This word "braird" is very significant and useful; it means the young growth of any crop from seed.

Q. I notice that after sowing the wheat, when you brush harrow in the grass seed, you do not make any mention of using the roller after?

A. It is not necessary, except occasionally when it is very dry; the rains usually at that season being sufficient to wash down the seed, and compact the soil so as to cause germination. If we have any reason, however, to apprehend a continuation of dry weather, then, as in all other such cases, the roller is applied.

Q. It is not possible, I presume, for you to get a wheat crop after mangels or turnips without plowing too late?

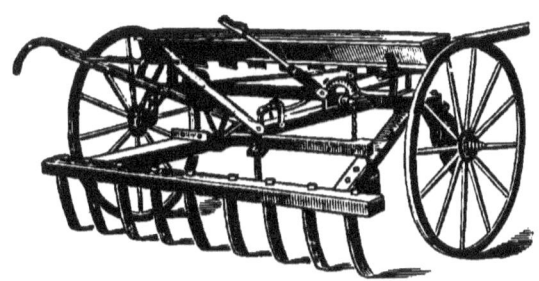

TRAVIS WHEAT CULTIVATOR.

A. The best wheat crop I ever raised—I do not at present exactly remember the number of bushels, but I think it was over fifty per acre—was put in between the mangel rows in the autumn before the mangels had been taken off the ground. The wheat was sown and put in with the cultivator about the 20th of September, and the quality of the crop was so good that it was all engaged by a New York seed firm for seed. When the mangels were pulled the tops were left on the wheat. Early in the spring I put on a large iron harrow, harrowed both ways and sowed with lucern, rolled it both ways, so that the land was thoroughly firmed.

Q. In sowing the wheat between the rows of mangels in the fall, as you state having done, was it possible to get a uniform crop over the surface? I can understand how it might be evenly distributed between the rows, but on the rows directly were there not spaces left?

A. Yes. I have counted as many as sixty spears from one grain which had spread or "stooled," and I am of the opinion that we can raise more wheat in that way than by any other process; that is, by cultivation. The cultivation of wheat, in trials, clearly shows this, and if I were making wheat my general crop, I would by all means sow in drills seven to nine inches apart, and cultivate it; but grass being my staple crop, I have no occasion to do so.

Q. You say you sowed the wheat on the mangels about the 20th of Sept. At what date, do you remember, were the mangels harvested?

A. I think about the usual time, the middle of November, or perhaps it might have been the end of November. Any time before frost will serve for harvesting mangels, and we generally leave that until the last work in the fields.

Q. Was there no injury done to the wheat by the leaves of the mangels shading it?

A. I rather think it improved it, as the shade for the "braird" seemed to be a protection until strong enough to take care of itself. As the season advanced, as you are aware, the leaves of the mangels withered, and shaded less, so that by the time they were ready to take off, the young wheat plants were relieved of the shade, and in pulling up the mangels just enough soil came up with them to make a nice top dressing for the wheat. The tops of the mangels also were spread as a mulch over the wheat.

Q. How late have you ever sown your wheat in the fall in the vicinity of New York?

A. I sowed a piece of wheat the latter end of December of last year.

Q. What advantage was there in sowing it at a date when there could be no germination until spring?

A. My reason for sowing it at that season was that I was slack of work and the ground was in good condition, and I wanted to topdress the piece of land that I sowed, as it was in the centre of a twenty-two-acre lot seeded down with grass on both sides, and I wished to make the whole field uniform.

Q. What was the result of this late sowing?

A. It lay dormant until early spring, but when the weather opened, it, of course, was ready for germination long before I could have prepared the ground for spring wheat, and the result of the crop is that to-day (12th July) it is nearly ready to cut, being only about ten days later than that sown at the usual time. It is not what we would call a good crop, nor yet a poor one, but, I think, will be a fair yield.

Q. But if it had not been for the peculiar circumstances of the case—that you wished to get a uniform field of grass—you would not have sown the wheat at that late date, in preference to spring sowing, would you?

A. No; it was simply a matter of convenience.

Q. Under what conditions do you usually sow your wheat in the spring?

A. I seldom ever sow spring wheat; it does not pay in this vicinity. The straw is too weak, which is one of the great difficulties in wheat raising.

Q. In what sections of the country, do you know, is spring wheat grown with success?

A. It is grown to a great extent in Canada, to some extent in Wisconsin, Michigan and northern Iowa, and wholly in Minnesota, and further north and west—the conditions necessary to success being a low temperature at its first stages of growth.

Q. When wheat is sown in the spring is it usual to sow grass with it?

A. Yes; just in the same manner as in the fall.

Q. I think I heard you drop the remark that you pastured your wheat in the spring (after it had well started to grow) with sheep. What was the advantage of that?

A. The object in that is to take off all the old weather-beaten leaves and to feed it down as close as we possibly could, and the treading of the sheep compacts the roots of the wheat, while their droppings serve as a top dressing for it. This of course can only be done on light soils; on wet or sticky clay land it would be an injury.

Q. At about what time, in your vicinity, do you turn on the sheep?

A. Just as soon as the frost or snow is gone, and allow them to remain until the end of April. Then we harrow with a light harrow so as to stir the surface, after which we roll thoroughly, being careful at that time, of course, that the land is dry enough, so that there may be no danger of dragging the roots of the wheat out of the ground.

Q. What, in your opinion, is the best stage of the wheat for harvesting?

A. I always cut my wheat a week ahead of most of my neighbors, and put it in shocks or "stooks," using a cap sheaf, as, in my experience, the grain by this process fills out in the shocks during that period of time. If let stand until ripe the grain shrinks. Wheat should always be cut before the grain becomes hard, and when you can easily crush it between the finger and thumb, or about the stage when the milk disappears, and the grain becomes firm, but not hard.

Q. Is it usual in your vicinity for wheat to be put up in stacks or placed in barns, or is it threshed in the field?

A. I put my wheat in stacks in the field or in barracks so as to "sweat" it. As soon as it is through the process of sweating, I thresh it. The threshing is done by two-horse tread power.

Q. On your high priced lands and limited areas, as compared with the Western and other wheat fields, how do you find wheat to pay as a farm crop?

A. It does not pay, because the manure and labor necessary cost too much, as we have to manure so heavily. But we sow wheat only to prepare for the after crop of grass. I raised last year forty bushels per acre, but the average in this section of the country is from twenty-five to thirty bushels. About $1.25 per bushel is a fair average price for this section, then the straw is worth about $15.00 per acre. I sell no straw, but buy all I can get in this neighborhood at a fair value to use as bedding for cattle.

Q. Are there any special varieties of wheat that you prefer to others?

A. I think that it was in 1876, when in Europe, I brought back with me six bushels of a variety called Champion wheat. This I think was in part the cause of my average of forty bushels per acre. The same wheat is now grown for miles around here. It weighed when I got it sixty-five pounds per bushel; last year it fell to sixty-one pounds, and this experience confirms me in the opinion that I have long held: that change of wheat, as well as any other seed, should be made annually, as it is a benefit to the crop.

Q. Would you make any preference in changing from Europe or to localities in the United States?

A. No; I would much rather get my seed wheat from Ohio or Pennsylvania than from Europe, if I could get it as pure, but more care is certainly taken in Britain to keep varieties pure and true, than we do in this country. The best farmers of England and Scotland are so careful when they grow for seed, that men are sent through the fields with shears to cut out all heads that are not considered to be true and genuine. By this precaution a uniformity is secured that cannot be obtained in any other way.

(Mr. H.) I can well understand the necessity of that. In our business as seedsmen we have seeds grown in different sections of the country, and we find it necessary to have men devoted especially to the purpose of examining the crops—particular care being taken with crops such as peas, that are more liable to degenerate from the true types—to see that all "rogues," as they are called, or such plants as are of a different variety, are weeded out.

Q. Under this head of Rotation of Crops, I will ask the question, Mr. Crozier, whether in your section, or the vicinity of New York, it is ever the practice to let one wheat crop follow another?

A. No; it would not be advisable to follow such crops as wheat or corn year after year on the same land, and wheat particularly being a great feeder, the land would soon be exhausted. Another reason is, and it is true of a great many other crops, that when one of the same kind is continuously sown there is far more danger of injury by insects or blight, as it seems to be a law of nature that special plants are subject to the ravages of special insects or diseases, and the best way to get relief from their attacks is to change the crop as radically as possible from one kind to another; thus I would follow after a wheat crop with grass, or if that is not used, I would succeed it with beans, peas or some such cultivated crop.

Q. Have you had any trouble with diseases such as rust or smut, or from insects on wheat?

A. No; but where such trouble is apprehended, the best preventive I know is to soak the seed in strong brine for ten to twelve hours, after which air-slaked lime should be mixed through it in quantity sufficient to dry the seed. The midge occasionally attacks wheat when sown in the fall, but not much in our section. I have understood that in western New York its ravages have been so great that farmers have been compelled to give up growing wheat, and after two years, during which the growth of wheat was suspended, the midge has disappeared for twenty years afterwards. This proves, as you previously remarked, the benefit of rotation. In regard to rust and smut, these are not troublesome in this vicinity, and I attribute this exemption to proximity to the sea; for that reason I would advise in sections inland, where there is no saline atmosphere, if danger of rust is apprehended, to use from two to three hundred pounds of salt per acre, at time of the sowing.

(Mr. H.) I believe a very common and effective remedy is to steep the seed in a solution of four ounces of sulphate of copper in a gallon of water, this being enough for four bushels of seed.

Q. Although the army worm is not a special wheat insect, yet as that crop has suffered greatly from its ravages on Long Island, what has been your most effectual remedy in preventing its attacks?

A. I have found a sure and certain protection against it by plowing ditches eighteen inches wide, by about ten deep, around my wheat fields, and strewing lime in them to prevent the insect from crossing. To attain the same end, straw saturated with kerosene may be thrown in the ditches and ignited, but I do not consider that as good as lime, because after the straw is burned there is nothing then to prevent the worm crawling up on the other side of the ditch, while the lime, if carefully spread on so as to make an unbroken line, really is a true dead line against their further approach. The Western method in similar cases is to plow such a ditch, and as the insects gather in it to drag a log along it to crush them and loosen up the soil, the loose soil itself being a barrier.

Q. In your vicinity what other crops are attacked by the army worm, besides wheat?

A. It seems to give preference to oats and grass, corn and root crops being little injured by it.

OAT CULTURE.

Q. How do oats compare with wheat as a profitable crop?

A. It is a more profitable crop to me, as a stock raiser, than wheat. My method is to cut my oats while in the milky state, for the purpose of feeding dry in the form of hay. I have grown considerable oats on sod land that had been pastured some years previous. This I consider the best land for producing heavy oats, but it does not produce so good a crop of straw. Such land should be broken in the spring, as early as the ground will admit. It should be plowed to a depth of five inches, the sod being turned under at an angle of forty-five degrees. I think, if my soil was a clay, I would plow the sod in the fall.

Q. Is this plowing not shallower than the usual practice?

A. Yes; and the reason for it is that the land, having been pastured for years previous, has accumulated cow, horse and sheep manure, which I want as near the surface as possible; and there is the sod, besides, which is better than all. Oats is a crop that does not root deeply, forming a sort of shallow, tufted root.

Q. Why do you lay the sod over at an angle of forty-five degrees?

A. It then forms an angle or furrow into which the seed, when sown, falls, and works down in the space where the sods lap, and thus gets the benefit of the surface manure as well as of the decaying sod. The seed is sown at the rate of four bushels to the acre, and the land is then thoroughly harrowed and rolled. Oats should be sown as soon as the ground is dry enough to be worked.

Q. Is there not some danger of the harrow pulling up the sod?

A. There would be if it were harrowed crosswise; but the harrow is run lengthwise of the furrow, and in this manner draws the soil into the crevices between the sods without tearing them up, after which we follow with the roller. Of this crop I have taken off sixty-five bushels per acre, weighing thirty-eight pounds per bushel. The seed was imported potato oats. If marketed, the product would have brought fifty cents per bushel. After the oats had been harvested, which was about the middle of July, the ground was plowed, harrowed, and drills opened, three and one-half feet apart, for fodder corn. Manure was placed in these drills to the depth of three or four inches. Planted with White Southern Corn at the rate of two bushels to the acre, lightly covered, and cultivated with a one-horse cultivator once a week until about four feet high, no more labor being required until curing time. This late planted second crop is not so productive as the general fodder corn crop, which yields with me about eight tons of dry fodder per acre. Part of the same land where the oats were grown was used for late or fall cabbage, and Cowhorn and Aberdeen turnips. The cabbage was planted out in rows prepared in about the same manner as for the fodder corn. The rows were opened by the plow and a good fork full of manure which had been made through the summer was dropped two feet apart, and covered with a hoe. The plants being in the seed bed and strong, were well watered and lifted with a dung fork so as not to injure the roots. The work of planting the cabbage was done late in the afternoon. The hills were opened with the corner of a sharp hoe, the plant set in, some soil drawn over it with the hand, and then stamped or firmed with the heel of the boot. In a few days, when the cabbage had straightened up, the soil was drawn around the plants with the hoe. Once more hoeing, and running the plow through the furrows, was all the work they required. In harvesting the cabbage, a deep furrow or trench was plowed, the cabbage pulled by the roots and turned into the trenches as close as they could be packed together. (See article on Cabbage.) My manure being all consumed in that portion of the field where I had planted the fodder corn and cabbage, I had to resort to bone meal for the turnips, which, however, I consider the most valuable fertilizer for that crop. This is used in the drills at the rate of 300 lbs. the acre. Drills were opened with a two-horse plow to the depth of nine inches, the bone dust was sown on the back of the furrow and the next furrow covered it to a depth of two or three inches. The turnips were drilled in with a one-horse drill, taking two rows at a time, at the rate of two pounds of seed to the acre. The growth was so quick, that in two weeks we went through the field singling or thinning them. By "singling" is meant thinning to one plant. This crop I believe produced over thirty-five tons per acre, and left the ground in far better condition than it was when I commenced in the spring. The value of the turnip crop, if sold, would have been $3.50 per ton. Thus we see that on the ten acres with which I started in the spring by sowing a crop of oats, I obtained a net profit of more than $800, as shown by the table given, and this after counting the labor. It will be seen that I paid $1.00 per bushel for the imported potato oats, while the product was sold for fifty cents per bushel, but if I had not sown this imported seed, I would probably not have had more than half the yield per acre. Consequently it is evident that it was economy to use the high priced seed.

PRODUCT OF TEN ACRES.

Value of Oat Crop, 650 bushels.........	$325.00	
Oat Straw, 10 tons....................	150.00	
Fodder Corn, 5 acres, 40 tons..........	200.00	
Cabbage, 2½ acres.....................	175.00	
Turnips, 2½ acres, 87½ tons............	306.25	
		$1,156.25

EXPENSES.

Plowing, harrowing and rolling.........	$30.00	
Cost of oat seed for 10 acres............	40.00	
Harvesting and threshing oats..........	45.00	
Manure for fodder corn................	100.00	
Harvesting fodder corn................	12.00	
Seed.................................	8.00	
Manure for 2½ acres cabbage...........	50.00	
Planting, cultivating and harvesting.....	30.00	
Cabbage seed.........................	2.00	
Manuring for 2½ acres turnips..........	10.00	
Sowing, cultivating and harvesting......	25.00	
Interest on value of land...............	30.00	
		$382.00
Net profit.....................		774.25
		$1,156.25

Q. In this estimate you have made no charge for your own work and skill in superintendence. I presume, with your experience, if your services were hired to another man on a farm of 200 acres they would be worth at least $10 per day. Would it not be fair to charge something for the time you have spent in this superintendence, against this estimate?

A. No. The profit made on these crops represents the value of my time and work, and not only the value of my own work, but the increased value which my superintendence and direction gives to the work of my hired workmen. I consider it a great mistake when a farmer has half a dozen men employed on different parts of the farm to use his own time in manual labor, because it is only by proper direction and supervision that he can make the work of each man of the fullest value.

(Mr. H.) In relation to that matter of importing oats, Mr. Crozier, I had recently a conversation with Mr. Wm. Saunders, Superintendent of the Experimental Department of the Agricultural Bureau at Washington, in which he stated to me that he imported from Scotland for his experiments, I think, a variety known as Hopetoun oats, which averaged forty-four pounds per bushel. The first year after sowing, the product deteriorated to forty pounds per bushel; that product being sown the second year, deteriorated still further to thirty-five pounds per bushel, which again being sown was still further reduced to the normal condition of American oats of thirty pounds, or less, per bushel. These facts suggest the query whether it would not pay our farmers to import their seed oats, in order to get this improved quality and product. In my opinion there is no other way to do it; for no matter how carefully the selection of seed is made, deterioration will take place when a crop is grown under circumstances uncongenial to it, as is the case with oats in nearly all parts of the United States and other warm climates, the nature of the plant requiring a long season of growth, which can only be had in cool, moist localities. A life-time spent in the practical study of horticulture, which is near akin to agriculture, has forced me to the conclusion that there is no such thing as the acclimatization of plants. The maize of the American continent resists all attempts to bring the crop to maturity in the climate of Great Britain, while the oat gives comparatively abortive results when grown in our half-tropical summers. Don't you think it would pay to import seed oats from Britain, so as to gain an advantage in the weight and product the first season here?

A. Yes; I think it would. I think imported seed could be sown two seasons to advantage. I have had seed oats from Nova Scotia, where the weight runs from thirty-eight to forty pounds per bushel, and planted them side by side with oats which I raised myself, preparing the ground in the same manner for both, and the Nova Scotia oats produced from eight to ten bushels per acre more than the common oats. Whether it was from the larger size of the imported oats or the change of climate I am unable to say. Probably both causes had something to do with it; for there it is well proven that change of seed of almost any farm crop is advantageous. To sum up: imported seed oats, costing even as much as $2 per bushel, will add one-fifth or one-fourth to the product. Hence it will always be the most profitable to use such seed.

Q. Are oats ever affected with diseases?

A. In some unfavorable years oats are affected more or less with rust, but of late years smut has appeared very extensively in the oat crop, in some localities almost destroying it. Upon this account it is advisable to treat seed oats in the same way as has been recommended on a previous page for wheat.

BARLEY.

Q. Is barley grown to any extent in New York or adjacent States?
A. Not to a great extent.

Q. Have you had any experience with it on Long Island?

A. I have sowed barley several times, but did not find it to be a paying crop. The straw is not of much value for bedding on account of the beards, which are sometimes injurious when eaten, particularly by sheep. Its culture, however, is wholly a question of soil; it wants a deeper and heavier soil than oats, as the roots strike deeper. Barley is grown to a great extent in western New York, and some places further west, and in Canada, to supply brewers. In Europe it was formerly grown for food, but has not been much grown in the last ten years, since our wheat has come so largely into use. It yields from thirty-five to fifty bushels per acre, but seldom brings more than eighty or ninety cents per bushel. There are a few special points in its culture which require attention or a full crop cannot be grown. The soil must be in good condition, well plowed and harrowed, and clean; fall plowing, followed by a thorough working by the Acme harrow, or other cultivator, in the spring. The seed, at the rate of two to two and one-half bushels per acre, is sown as early as the ground is dry. In harvesting, the greatest care is necessary to avoid damage by rains, as this spoils the color of the grain and unfits it for the brewer's use, and seriously reduces its value. Barley is not bound in sheaves, but cured in the swath and lifted by broad wooden forks known as barley forks. This may be considered as one of those special crops fitted for special soils and circumstances only, and is only profitable when the crop can be perfectly well grown.

CULTURE OF RYE.

Q. In what way does the culture of rye differ from that of oats?

A. We can sow rye on our poorest land; but when grown on rich land it is a valuable crop, in some cases giving from thirty to thirty-five bushels per acre, which sells at from twenty-five to thirty cents per bushel less than wheat. The straw being valuable for various purposes, is shipped to the cities in large quantities. A great deal of rye is cut in the spring while green as our first soiling crop, the land being immediately plowed and prepared for corn. This year a farmer in my neighborhood cut off ten acres of rye, planted the ground in cucumbers for pickles and intends following with a wheat crop in the fall, thus placing three crops in the ground in one season, as the cucumbers only take up about three months, and will pay a profit of $100 per acre after all labor and expense has been paid. I have known the straw of matured rye to produce two tons per acre, which brought $20 per ton in New York City. In the neighborhood of paper mills rye straw brings from $25 to $30 per ton and is largely grown for this purpose. As a bread grain it is next to wheat in value, and perhaps really more nutritious. Rye is largely used by farmers to seed down with in the fall, and I think it is preferable to wheat for this purpose, when about one and one-half bushels of seed per acre is used, as it protects the young grass through the winter and matures earlier the following summer, being generally cut two weeks in advance of wheat, thus allowing the grass to have freer growth at a season of the year when it grows very rapidly, and also making good pasture in the fall. As a soiling crop it will be fully referred to in the chapter devoted to that subject.

THE CULTURE OF AMERICAN FIELD BEANS.

Q. What soil, in your opinion, Mr. Crozier, is best adapted to the American field bean? I use this distinction because of the fact that in every book, and in nearly every paper, where beans are referred to, it is the English bean that is mentioned, and not our bean, which is an entirely different plant. The English bean, as you are aware, is used for feeding horses only, while ours is wholly used for human food. The plant which bears the English bean has a single straight, stiff stem, which bears several short, thick pods, each containing four or five brown-skinned, hard, kidney-shaped, thick beans, as long and wide, but twice as thick, as our large white beans.

A. Light, gravelly soils, which can hardly be made available for any other crop, will give a fair yield of beans. They are a crop that we plant after all other work in the spring is done. The land is plowed, harrowed and furrowed out thirty inches apart, and about two bushels of beans sown to the acre, by hand or seed drill. When drilled, the seeds are dropped about eight inches apart; when planted by hand it is usual to put three or four together at eighteen inches apart in the rows. They do not require much manure, or they will grow too much to vines. We cover very lightly, never allowing them to be cultivated or hoed in damp weather. If worked in damp weather they will rust or "damp off"; but in dry weather weekly cultivation for the first month should be given. No more work is then required until the beans are ready to be harvested. The usual way is to pull them up by hand and stack them around a pole eight or nine feet high, which is stuck in the ground. In this way they may be left until taken to the barn and threshed and cleaned. Harvesting beans by hand is a slow work and may do very well for small plantations. But when they are grown largely, as they are in some localities, where forty or fifty acre fields of them are not unusual, a machine is used for gathering them. This ingenious invention, which is the work of a farmer in New York State, is shown in the accompanying engraving. It pulls the beans, shakes the soil from

BEAN HARVESTER.

the roots and leaves the beans in rows behind it. It is drawn by one horse, which walks between the rows. Two-horse machines are made, which pull two rows at once. Beans usually bring in market from $2 to $3 per bushel. I have taken forty bushels per acre off such land as above described. I may say, however, that there is considerable labor attendant upon the raising of this crop, both in the cultivating and threshing and cleaning for market, as, being used for human consumption, the sample requires to be perfect. But in the winter season, if they can be hand-picked at idle times, they are quite a profitable crop. There is always a good demand for the Marrowfat Bean. The "Pea Bean," as it is called, is smaller, but similar to the Marrowfat, is a better yielder and brings a better price, and is, in my opinion, more desirable. It is of recent introduction. There is also the Navy Bean, used for naval stores, and the Red Kidney Bean, which brings usually twice as much as the white beans in the market; but as the demand for this variety is limited, the market is easily overstocked. It is a matter of economy in threshing beans to save the straw and pods, which are nutritious fodder for sheep and are readily eaten by them.

BUCKWHEAT.

(Mr. C.) Buckwheat, although a grain of less importance than some of the others, yet takes its place among farm crops. It can be sown after barley, rye or oats are harvested, the ground being immediately plowed, harrowed and about three pecks of seed sowed to the acre, and the ground thoroughly rolled. This crop being grown at a season of the year when the ground is often dry for weeks, the rolling which we have before insisted upon in many places in this work is absolutely imperative, or the crop will fail to germinate. Buckwheat, though not a large producing crop, is often sown just to keep the land in use for a partial crop rather than to grow a crop of weeds. The straw is worth nothing but for litter; the grain, as is well known, is used largely for human consumption. It is also excellent food for fattening swine, and poultry prefer it to all other grains. A great many farmers plant largely of this crop to plow under as a green manure. I myself did so some twenty years ago on a twenty-acre lot where the crop had grown so strongly that I was forced to roll it before I could plow it under. I am of the opinion that it was an injury to the field, as it did not produce good crops for two or three years afterwards.

Q. In what way do you consider it to have been injurious?

A. Why, I do not know, I only marked the results; but I was so well satisfied with that experiment that I would not again risk another trial. Many, I am aware, claim it is a valuable crop for plowing under, and I may be wrong in my conclusions from one trial, but I think not.

(Mr. H.) I cannot see why your experience in this way should have been so contrary to the general view and practice. I don't know of any reason why any vegetable matter plowed into the soil could be other than useful.

(Mr. C.) Buckwheat is a rather peculiar crop, and requires particular care in harvesting and threshing it. It has the habit of bearing ripe and half-matured seed and blossoms and buds all at the same time. The seed, too, is held by a very slender stalk, which snaps very easily when it is dry; upon this account it is cut early in the day, when the dew is on it. For these reasons, the newly harvested grain is moist and needs thorough drying. When it is cut it is raked up in gavels, which are not bound in sheaves, but are set up on end singly to dry. When the straw is dry, the crop is drawn in and threshed directly from the field, and the grain must be at once winnowed from the chaff, or, being quite moist, the chaff will heat and spoil the grain. A dry, windy day is chosen for threshing. The cleaned grain also requires close watching to avoid heating in the bin, and it is usual to move it from one bin to another on a dry, windy day, or shovel it over, for the purpose of airing and drying it. Buckwheat is a sort of special crop, and as the flour is used chiefly in the winter, the grain is usually sold as soon as it is threshed. By doing this a higher price is secured and all the dangers of keeping it are avoided. There are four varieties of this grain: one is known in northern New England as Indian Wheat or Merino Buckwheat, a small, wrinkled, dark, inferior grain; the others are the Black, the Gray, and the newly introduced Silver Hull, the Black being inferior to the other two.

CHAPTER V.

CROPS FOR SOILING AND FODDER.

(Mr. C.) The first of these in importance as regards time, in my opinion, is rye, which we have just discussed in a preceding chapter. I have commenced cutting it by the 10th of May, and by cutting it while young, or say three feet high, if wanted to cut the second time in about three weeks, a fair feeding can be had, which will supply the wants of stock until lucern or clover or orchard grass is ready; or oats and peas, which are ready for soiling usually by the 20th of June. When the oats and peas become hard or dry, fodder corn which has been planted the first week in May will take their place, and by sowing at intervals of one or two weeks up to the 10th of August, will give a continuous supply until frost. These are the different kinds of crops used for soiling, named in the order in which they are ready to use for that purpose.

Q. I observe, Mr. Crozier, that you do not mention having used tares or vetches for soiling or fodder.

A. I have tried to grow vetches for two seasons. The first season I imported seed of the Gray Vetch from England and it was a complete failure. Well knowing that this is one of the best soiling crops in Europe, I purchased the second year twenty pounds of seed which was grown in the vicinity of Montreal, Canada. This was a variety of Black Vetch, or tare, and did better, but was not satisfactory; and hence, as far as my experience has gone, I have come to the conclusion that the vetch is not suited for our latitude, and I doubt much if it will be found suitable for any part of America, unless it be the extreme northern portion of Canada; or possibly in the Southern States, as a winter crop, for which the winter variety would undoubtedly be found useful to supply green forage or pasture. I have also tried to my complete satisfaction, and to my sorrow let me add, the Prickly Comfrey, which I consider one of the biggest frauds that ever was perpetrated on the agricultural community. Whether or not I had trained my cows by careful feeding to be somewhat of epicures, I do not know, but certain it is that they turned up their noses at the Prickly Comfrey and would have nothing to do with it.

As the question of fodder for soiling is now one of vast importance to the breeder of fine stock, to the dairyman, and last, but not least, to him who feeds his farm, we will endeavor to give as briefly as possible the methods of culture of all the kinds in use.

RYE.

Where this crop is intended for soiling early in the spring, it should be sown the latter part of August or early in September, on very rich land. The ground should be thoroughly plowed and harrowed, but it is better not to use much coarse manure, as it has a tendency to make the crop grow soft and rank. I sow for soiling two bushels of seed per acre, as the ground is not intended to be seeded down. This will be fit to commence cutting by the 10th of May, before it heads out, and can be cut, if desired, a second time, giving a fair crop. I think an acre of good heavy rye will feed twenty cows for one week at least, but great care must be taken not to give a full feed at first. My plan is to run it through the cutter and mix it with dry hay or good wheat straw also cut, as this prevents any injurious effect upon the bowels, it being just the season when animals are changing their coats, as every animal in perfect health does at this time. As a feed for milch cows it produces purer milk or fat than any other soiling plant I know of, when fed before the blossom is formed; if fed later it has been thought injurious to the butter, but I never feed it so late as that. Its earliness, coming in at that season between hay and grass, makes it very valuable. Rye may be sown in succession up to November, or December even, increasing the quantity of seed sown, as the time is later. The last sowing may be made any time before the ground is frozen, using four or five bushels per acre. In this case the seed does not sprout until spring, and makes a spring crop, but one that is sown much earlier than would be possible any other way.

LUCERN.

Q. You say that the next crop that you use for soiling, to follow after rye, is Lucern, or Alfalfa, as it is sometimes called. You gave me some data a few months ago, which I have used in a rather exhaustive article on that subject, which we will insert here, after you have briefly given your own method of culture.

(Mr. C.) The land selected for Lucern should be a rich, deep, sandy or gravelly loam, where there is no fear of water standing.

The land is plowed, then harrowed and rolled, early in the spring. Then I sow at the rate of sixteen pounds to the acre. It is sown broadcast and covered with the brush harrow as early in the spring as the ground will admit being worked. For a soiling crop I do not use any mixtures. I sometimes cut it early in the fall, getting a fair crop. I have even cut it the second time in the fall of the same season as sown, but that is a rare occurrence. The next season I have taken three or four cuttings from it. After reading the article that you have written on this subject I do not know that I can add anything to it.

CULTURE OF ALFALFA OR LUCERN (MEDICAGO SATIVA.)

[Written by Peter Henderson on his return from a trip to Florida in February, 1883.]

In a country so wide-spread and diversified as the United States, it is not to be wondered at that a crop that is valued in some localities is unknown in others.

But it is somewhat surprising that, in many of the Southern States, where the want of forage is so much felt, the culture of a plant so admirably adapted for their soil and climate has so long been neglected. In a visit to Florida, in February, 1883, I was impressed, as every Northern man must be, with the utter dearth of forage plants, and as a consequence, the hungry and meagre, starved looking cattle. To my inquiries everywhere, the same reply was given that no good grass or clover could be found to stand the heat and drought of their long summers. Fortunately, in alluding to the subject, while in the company of Mr. R. Bronson, of St. Augustine, Florida, he promptly showed a practical solution of the difficulty, by taking me to a patch of Alfalfa about twenty-five feet by one hundred, or only about the one-sixteenth part of an acre. From that little patch Mr. B. assured me that he had fed a cow during the summer months, getting as fine milk and butter as ever he got North; and further said that twice that area, or one-eighth part of an acre, would be ample to supply a cow with food during the entire season. The land used by Mr. Bronson for his experiment with Alfalfa was identical with the thousands of acres in his immediate vicinity, which was given over to the Blue Palmetto and scrubby pines, through which the goat-like cattle browse out a miserable existence. Mr. Bronson, though only an amateur, is a careful observer, and an enthusiastic student in everything that relates to agriculture. In the culture of Alfalfa for Florida and other Southern latitudes, he advises that the crop be sown early in the fall—early enough to attain a height of four or five inches before growth is arrested by cold weather, in Florida say from 1st to 15th of October.

The soil best suited for the growth of Alfalfa is that which is deep and sandy; hence the soil of Florida and many other portions of the cotton belt is eminently fitted. The plant makes a tap root with few laterals, and its roots are often found at a depth of six to eight feet, thus drawing food from depths entirely beyond the action of drought or heat. When Alfalfa is to be grown on a large scale, to get at the best results, the ground chosen should be high and level, or if not high, such as is entirely free from under water. Drainage must be as near perfect as possible—either naturally or artificially. This in fact is a primary necessity for *every* crop—unless it be such as is aquatic or sub-aquatic.

Deep plowing, thorough harrowing and leveling with that valuable implement, the "smoothing harrow," to get a smooth and level surface, are the next operations. This should be done in the Southern States from 1st to 20th October—or at such season in the fall as would be soon enough to ensure a growth of four or five inches before the season of growth stops. Draw out lines on the prepared land twenty inches apart (if for horse culture, but if for hand culture fourteen inches), and two or three inches deep. These lines are best made by what market gardeners call a "marker," which is made by nailing six tooth-shaped pickets six or eight inches long at the required distance apart to a three by four inch joist, to which a handle is attached—which makes the marker or drag. The first tooth is set against a garden line drawn tight across the field, the marker is dragged backwards by the workman, each tooth marking a line; thus the six teeth mark six lines, if the line is set each time; but it is best to place the end tooth of the marker in a line already made, so that in this way only five lines are marked at once, but it is quicker to do this than move the line. The lines being marked out, the seed is sown by hand or by seed-drill, at the rate of eight to twelve pounds per acre. After sowing—and this rule applies to all seeds, if sown by hand—the seed must be trodden in by walking on the lines, so as to press the seed down into the drills. After treading in, the ground must be leveled by raking with a wooden or steel rake along the lines lengthways—not across. That done, it would be advantageous to use a roller over the land, so as to smooth the surface and further firm the seed, but this is not indispensable. When seeds are drilled in by machine, the wheel presses down the soil on the seed, so that treading in with the feet is not necessary. After the seeds germinate so as to show the rows, which will be in from two to four weeks, according to the weather, the ground must be hoed between, and this is best done by some light wheel-hoe, if by hand, such as the "Planet, Jr." On light sandy soil, such as in Florida, a man could with ease run over two or

ALFALFA, OR LUCERN (MEDICAGO SATIVA).

three acres per day. The labor entailed in this method of sowing Alfalfa in drills is somewhat greater than when sown broadcast in the usual way of grasses and clover, but there is no question that it is by far the best and most profitable plan, for it must be remembered that the plant is a *hardy perennial*, and is good for a crop for eight to ten years. Moreover, the sowing in drills admits of the crop being easily fertilized, if it is found necessary to do so; as all that is necessary, is to sow bone dust, superphosphates, or other concentrated fertilizer between the rows, and then stir it into the soil by the use of the wheel-hoe. In the ground of Mr. Bronson, of St. Augustine, Florida, he found that the seed sown in the middle of October gave him a crop fit to cut in three months after sowing, and three heavy crops after, during the same year; and I have little doubt that in that climate and soil, so congenial to its growth, six heavy green crops could be cut annually, after the plant is fairly established, if a moderate amount of fertilizer was used, say 300 pounds of superphosphate or bone dust to the acre. Mr. William Crozier, of Northport, L. I., one of the best known farmers and stock breeders in the vicinity of New York, says that he has long considered Alfalfa one of the best forage crops. He uses it always to feed his milch cows and breeding ewes, particularly in preparing them for exhibition at fairs, where he is known to be a most successful competitor, and always takes along sufficient Alfalfa hay to feed them on while there. Mr. Crozier's system of culture is broadcast, and he uses some fifteen or sixteen pounds of seed to the acre, but his land is unusually clean and in a high state of cultivation, which enables him to adopt the broadcast plan; but on the average land it will be found that the plan of sowing in drills would be the best.

Mr. Crozier's crop, the second year, averaged eighteen tons green to the acre, and about six tons when dried as hay. For his section— the latitude of New York—he finds the best date of sowing is first week in May, and a good cutting can be had in September. The next season a full crop is obtained, when it is cut, if green, three or four times. If to be used for hay, it is cut in the condition of ordinary red clover in blossom; it then makes after that two green crops if cut; sometimes the last one instead of being cut is fed on the ground by sheep or cattle.

Mr. E. M. Sargent, Macon, Ga., writing to me under date March 6th, 1883, says: "I consider Alfalfa to be the most valuable forage plant that can be used in this section of the country—that is, the entire cotton belt, or north of it—if the land is sandy without a clay subsoil too near the surface. Planters are just beginning to find out its merits, and no poverty of stock will ever occur where Alfalfa is raised. In the summer of 1881, when everything else was parched here with heat and drought, this alone was prompt in its maturity for the mower. It should be cut for hay when in blossom, and can easily be cut three or four times here, wherever the land is in fairly good condition.

"Those who *do not* succeed with it, sow it broadcast and surrender it to the hogs early in the season. Those who do succeed sow in drills, eighteen inches apart, and cultivate early."

It will be seen that Mr. Sargent advises drills much wider than we recommend, which I presume is to admit the horse-hoe, but a quicker crop undoubtedly would be got at fourteen inches apart, and by use of the hand wheel-hoe, the work could be done on light soil nearly as quickly as by horse cultivator.

Alfalfa is extensively grown in Europe, particularly in France and Germany, where it is considered a valuable crop for rotation, and is classed by the French as one of the *Plantes Ameliorantes* (restorative crops); for in southern France wheat has been successfully raised after six or seven years of Alfalfa on ground which formerly had failed to give good crops of wheat. Although Alfalfa may be grown in cold latitudes as well as in warm, as the plant is entirely hardy, yet its value is not so marked in cold climates, where it finds competitors in Red Clover and the grasses; but in light soils, anywhere, particularly in warm climates, its deep-rooting properties make it comparatively independent of moisture; hence it is the forage plant *par excellence* for the Southern States; and when it is considered that immense sums are paid annually for baled hay, by the Southern to the Northern States, not only for the hay itself, but to freight it, the wonder is how long they will continue to do so, with the material at hand to produce a better article at probably one-fourth the cost.

At the date of our writing, thousands in Florida and other Southern States are engaged in the culture of oranges, and other fruits and vegetables, for the Northern markets—and while in specially favored locations success has attended these enterprises, yet it is doubtful if one in four makes it profitable; while, with the culture of this valuable forage plant, the vast sums paid for Northern hay would not only be saved, but the products of the dairy would assume an importance which now, among most farmers in the extreme Southern States, is altogether unknown.

Q. If you were confined to one of these two crops, Mr. Crozier, which would you prefer to grow in your latitude, clover or lucern ?

A. As a general crop I would use clover, because my land is better suited to it than it is to lucern.

(Mr. H.) That is just the reason I asked the question, because, from the nature of the roots of the plant, I should judge that it was more fitted to the sandy soils of Florida and other Southern States, than to most of the loamy or gravelly soils of our Northern States. The appearance that it presented to me growing in luxuriance at St. Augustine, indicated that on such a soil the roots must have penetrated to a great depth, or such vigorous growth could not have been shown. I should say that on such lands as at Vineland, N. J., or, in fact, anywhere where the soil is loose enough that you could push a walking stick down to the depth of two or three feet, would be the soil for lucern.

Q. Is there any peculiarity in the method of curing it for hay?

A. I think it is more easily cured than clover hay, for the reason that the stems are less succulent than those of clover.

Q. Is any preference given to it by cattle over clover, either in a dry or green state?

A. Cattle prefer lucern to any other crop I have ever fed, and I believe it to be as nutritious as any other; the only reason I do not use it exclusively is, that some portions of my land are not suited to its growth as well as to that of clover.

CLOVER AND GRASS.

Q. What is your method of culture for clover and grass mixed?

A. The ground is prepared in the fall of the year and sown to wheat or rye. In the spring we sow two bushels of orchard grass and twenty pounds of Mammoth Clover Seed, mixed, per acre. The wheat or rye being first well rolled in the spring, the mixture of clover and grass seed is then sown and the ground again rolled. In the fall a light cutting is made, which should not be taken off, but left on the ground to protect the roots from freezing through the winter.

Q. Then I understand that it is your practice never to cut the crop the first season of its growth, unless, as you say, a light cutting in the fall? What advantage is there in making that cutting in the fall?

A. It protects the roots of the grass and young clover through the winter from freezing and thawing. If it were taken off the field, it would leave the roots so exposed that the frost in some soils would throw them out.

Q. Would not the protection of the plant uncut be as good as the protection given by its being cut and left on the ground? I can understand where the advantage might be as a mulch if it could be distributed by the mower as to cover the whole surface of the ground evenly.

A. The mower will leave it level over the ground, and thus afford a useful protection for the roots. Besides, the cutting of the grass leaves the surface smooth and clear for the first spring cutting. Otherwise the dead grass, if uncut, would be in the way of the mower.

Q. As this matter is a very important one, I should further ask you to give as near the date as possible at which you cut and the height you cut, supposing the clover and grass to be one foot high?

A. I cut from the 1st to the 10th of October, and raise the machine fully four inches high, leaving, as I have before said, the crop on the ground as a mulch. The young shoots of the orchard grass and clover strike through it very early in the spring—so early that I had to begin cutting my general crop this year on the 9th of June, for hay. I could only use it for a soiling crop for about one week, as lucern lasted up until the time the clover was in blossom.

Q. What is the advantage of mixing the orchard grass in the clover for soiling?

A. The reason is that the orchard grass has the habit of growing in bunches, and the clover fills the vacant spaces and adds very much to the yield. Another reason, the orchard grass prevents the clover from falling down. A third reason, I know that cattle are fond of mixed foods. A still further reason, and the most important of all, is, that orchard grass and clover come into blossom at the best time for cutting.

PEAS AND OATS.

Another crop that I have used with great satisfaction for soiling is peas and oats, mixed. This is what some farmers call a "stolen" crop, because it is so quick in its growth and matures so early that it is slipped in between crops and is off in seven or eight weeks; and, besides, it cleans the land and prepares it for a crop of turnips or fodder corn. I plow, harrow and sow the peas about the end of March, and not later than the 15th of April, putting on three bushels of oats and two bushels of peas to the acre, sowing broadcast on the rough ground after plowing. The reason for sowing on the rough ground before harrowing is that it gets the seeds deeper, which is a necessity, particularly with the peas. I would mention here that it is difficult to harrow in peas, and would suggest the use of the Acme harrow to cover in this crop. After harrowing the ground is rolled in the usual manner, which answers the double purpose of firming it and smoothing it for harvesting. About the middle of June the crop is fit for feeding, and will last up to the 1st of July, when what is left is cut and dried in the same manner as hay, and put in the barn, or in stacks in the field, putting about eight or ten two-horse loads in a stack, where it remains for winter use. In the winter the fodder is carted to the barn, run through the cutter and mixed with such other feeds as will be hereafter stated.

Q. How does the weight of this crop compare with clover cut and dried at the same date?

A. I had a field of ten acres of peas and oats which produced forty tons of well cured fodder. Although the conditions were not so favorable, the weight of the peas and oats exceeded that of the average yield of clover fifty per cent. The land which I sowed with peas and oats was not so fertile as the clover land, because the former crop does not require so much manure, as the land is manured heavily, after the crop is harvested, for a succeeding crop of fodder corn or turnips.

Q. Then would you consider the hay of peas and oats is worth as much, ton for ton, as clover hay?

A. I consider it worth one-half more than clover, for, while clover hay is worth from $8 to $10 per ton, I would pay $15 per ton for hay of peas and oats. I prefer it for either cattle or horses. There is no other feed that you can give to a farm horse that will carry him through the spring better than peas and oats, as this fodder is exceedingly nutritious.

Q. Why, then, is a crop that is only three months in the ground and that can be grown on poor soil, and which you say is superior to clover hay, not more generally cultivated?

A. It is a crop that was almost unknown in this country until within a few years past, although I have been growing it here for twenty years; but you know how slowly the average farmer takes to a new crop, and further, it must be sown very early or it will not succeed so well, and farmers as a rule do not get their crops in early enough. I am glad, however, to say that the use of peas to mix with oats for this purpose is increasing very rapidly, and the crop will soon be popular. Last season the demand was far greater than could be supplied. Our climate has peculiar advantages for such a crop. It takes the place completely of the tare or vetch so much used in Europe, our dry, bright weather in July being peculiarly suited to cure and make of it a sweet hay crop. The varieties used are the Canada gray pea, and the black eye marrowfat for the second crop.

Q. What is the best stage for cutting peas and oats for hay?

A. I cut for hay while the grain of the oats is in the milky state; at that time the peas are just passing the blossom and in their best stage for cutting.

Q. Have you ever attempted the culture of the Southern Cow Pea?

A. I planted twelve bushels one season that were sent me by a friend in Charleston. From the way it had been spoken of in the agricultural journals I expected to have a good soiling crop from it, but when I came to feed it to my cows they snuffed and tossed it around, but would not eat it. When I found they would not touch it I plowed it under as a manure crop. I well knew the estimation in which it is held at the South and for that reason was all the more disappointed. Whatever the cause, it is certain that my cattle refused to eat it, and it may be that the Southern cattle not having so much choice of food have become accustomed to it, but, as far as my observation has gone, the appearance of the cattle in the South is not such as to show that this is a good fodder plant, as they bear no comparison with our Northern stock; and I would advise our Southern friends to compare, under fair tests, our forage of peas and oats with this Southern Cow Pea. But, as has been before stated, lucern is the best of all fodder crops for the southern part of the country.

MILLET.

Q. Have you made any trials of any of the millets?

A. I have used the German millet and do not like it very well. It is coarse and the seed is too hard to digest. I have grown a great deal of Hungarian millet, or "grass," as it is commonly called. It makes very good winter food when cut before the seed ripens. If cut when in bloom before it goes to seed Hungarian grass is an excellent crop. It, too, may be called a "stolen" crop, as it can be sown and cut in condition for hay six weeks after sowing, and may be sown after the hay or oat crop has been taken off, which is far better than to let the land go to weeds. No good farmer should suffer his land to grow weeds. For one reason, because of leaving it too long and stocking the soil with the seeds; for another, that he may grow a useful crop like this, or some other, just as well as a crop of weeds. I have known as much as four tons of dry hay to be taken off per acre from Hungarian grass, in six weeks from the time of sowing. No other crop will stand the heat so well as this. It is just here that I may raise my voice in warning against the common practice with farmers of going over too much land. One hundred acres judiciously tilled will bring a greater profit than 200 acres tilled in a slipshod way; for with this crop we are just speaking of, after a crop of oats, or wheat, or rye, has been taken from the ground, there is yet plenty of time. And it is just the time to plow and sow with it, because of all plants it luxuriates the best in hot weather, and may be grown on fairly good to the richest soil, but, of course, with corresponding results. Common millet differs from Hungarian grass only in the form of the head or panicle, which is looser and more open than the spike of Hungarian grass. The awns or beards of millet are softer than those of Hungarian grass, and on this account the millet is better liked by some farmers, who believe that Hungarian grass is injurious to horses, and with, perhaps, some reason, on account of its short, stiff, sharp awns. The amount of seed of either kind sown is a peck to half a bushel per acre. Another important fodder plant, to a limited extent, is Pearl Millet, which I tried several years ago; but as you, Mr. Henderson, have got some notoriety by your experiments with it at that time, and some blame too, I think if you have no scruples in the matter it would be well to give such information in regard to it as your experience enables you.

(Mr. H.) Pearl Millet is now well known all over the country, especially in the Southern States, where it goes by the common name of Cat Tail Millet. In 1878 I determined to give it a thorough trial, and prepared a piece of good ground, as if for a root crop, by manuring at the rate of twelve or fifteen tons to the acre, plowing deeply and harrowing. The seed was sown in drills twenty inches apart, at the rate of four to five pounds to the acre. The seed was sown about the middle of May. When the plants were up a cultivator was run through the rows, and the growth became so rapid that no further culture was necessary. The first cutting was made forty-five days after sowing; it was seven feet high and covered the whole ground. The crop, cut three inches above the ground, weighed, as cut, at the rate of thirty tons per acre; *dried*, six and one-half tons per acre of hay. The second growth, cut forty-five days from the time of the first cutting, was nine feet high, and weighed at the rate of fifty-five tons to the acre fresh, equal to eight tons dried. The last growth started rapidly, but the cool weather retarded it, so that the last cutting only weighed ten tons green, and one and one-half tons dried. The total yield was as follows: First cutting, in forty-five days, gave thirty tons green, or six and one-half tons dry; second cutting, in forty-five days, gave fifty-five tons green, or eight tons dry; third cutting, in forty-five days, gave ten tons green, or one and one-half tons dry; in all being ninety-five tons green fodder in 135 days, equal to sixteen tons of hay. These results, published at the time, gave rise to some severe criticism by persons who had failed to do as well with the crop as I had done. But it should be remembered that the conditions under which an experiment is made are essentially necessary to a successful repetition of it, and if these differ in any respect, and especially if they are inferior, failure is apt to result.

As 1 have had many inquiries as to the best manner of drying Pearl Millet for "hay," I would say that our crop was sown in a solid block, so that when cut it had to be removed from the land where it grew, and tied in sheaves, and hung up on an extemporized rail fence until cured. This plan of course would not answer on a large scale, as the crop is so enormous that such an expedient for drying would be too expensive both for labor and rails, and as it is too heavy and succulent to be dried like Timothy and Clover, on the ground where it is cut, it must be removed, for to attempt to dry it where it grows would destroy the second crop. Circumstances, of course, must in a great measure be a guide, but we would suggest, that when grown for the purpose of being dried, that it be sown in beds, say twelve feet wide, with alleys six feet between, where it may be dried; this, of course, would be a loss of one-third of the land for the first crop, but it would be little or no loss of crop in the second, for the millet would spread so as to fill up all the six feet of alley.

FODDER CORN.

Q. I believe, Mr. Crozier, you hold that one of the most valuable crops for soiling purposes is fodder corn. Please state what is your mode of culture and experience with this crop?

A. In my hands fodder corn has been such a successful crop that it seems useless for me to attempt to grow anything else of the same nature. I consider it to be above all others the most valuable for soiling purposes, on account of the great length of time we can feed it in its green state, from July until frost, and at the very time when in most cases grass and all other green feed is withered and dried. As this, in my estimation, is a crop of such vast importance, I will give in detail my method of culture, which is as follows: I have found that to obtain the best results with this crop the land should be plowed in the fall and left to the action of the frost all winter. About the middle of April I harrow and strike out furrows three and one-half feet apart. This is done with a home-made implement called a "furrow marker," which has two triangular teeth, and makes two furrows at once, six inches deep and ten wide, thus making a greater width of row than could possibly be done with the plow. (See illustration.) Manure is dropped in the furrows at the rate of twenty wagon loads of good compost to the acre. If manure cannot be had, the best artificial fertilizer that can be procured should be used instead, at the rate of

500 pounds per acre, sowed in the furrows. Two bushels of White Southern Corn is sown per acre, or a good handful to every step. I have found this variety to be the best for soiling. The work of spreading the manure in the furrows, sowing the corn and covering, should all follow each other in quick succession, so as to prevent the land or manure from drying up before the crop is in. The brush harrow with the brush taken out (shown on a previous page) is the best implement to be used to cover the grain lightly. I formerly covered with the plow, throwing a furrow up to each side of the drill; but I find that the lighter it is covered, the freer it is from rot or injury. After covering, it is rolled in the usual manner. In this section the first crop is sown about the last of May and others every two weeks in succession until the middle

FURROW MARKER FOR CORN.

of June, when I put in a larger quantity for drying for winter feed. It is cultivated once a week until it gets too large for a horse to pass through it, which will be with that sown in May about the first week in July, and for that sown in June, about the 1st of August. No more work is required until the corn is ready to cut and cure, which is from the 1st to the 15th of September, the corn at this time being tasseled out, and in the best stage for curing. I formerly cut with a mowing machine, taking two rows at a time; but of late years I have found that it is more expensive and entails more labor to gather it and shock it, after the machine, than when cut with corn hook and carried direct to the shock. Each man takes two rows at a time, carries his armful to the shock, which should be close by, plants it as straight on the end as possible, and so on until there is about 500 pounds in the shock. We then take a strong hemp rope, with an eye in one end, through which the other end is passed, and draw it tightly around the middle of the shock, and then tie or bind the top of the shock with a rye straw band, in such a way as best to shed the rains.

A letter to the Milwaukee *Sentinel* in June of 1883 says: "Hon. Geo. F. Lord, of Elgin, keeps 100 cows on 300 acres of land, and has not raised a pound of hay for years. The corn is sowed in drills three and one-half feet apart, and about the time it blossoms it is cut with a self-raking reaper, cutting one row at a time, the machine throwing it off in gavels. When sufficiently wilted it is bound and set in large stacks and allowed to cure standing on the ground until winter sets in, when it is hauled to the barn. He secures a yield of about seven tons of cured fodder to the acre, worth as much as the best hay. He is one of the most successful dairymen in Illinois."

In the latitude of New York, it will keep shocked in the open field through the winter until spring. If it is not convenient to leave it in the field after it is dried and cured, which is usually three or four weeks after it is shocked, it should be bound up in sheaves and carted to the barn, or stacked or put in sheds convenient to where it is to be used. My plan in feeding is to run it through the cutter worked by horse power, and mix it with cut hay, or peas and oats, and pulped or crushed roots, adding a little salt. We cut enough at one time to last for a week, unless the weather be warm, as the crushed roots would then naturally ferment. The roots when pulped or crushed are in the same condition as apples when they come from the cider press. In this state, they saturate the cut fodder better than when chopped up by the ordinary root cutter. A machine known as a "Root Pulper" is used almost exclusively for that purpose in Britain, but I think few of them are in use here. For cutting roots for a few cows, a useful cutter is made as follows: A heavy steel blade is made in the shape of a × and fitted to a strong handle; the roots are put in a feed box and chopped up with it very quickly. About twenty-five years ago when running a milk farm I steamed all the feed for the cattle, but it was mixed in the same way. I found some advantage in the saving of feed, and, in fact, continued steaming up to 1876. While visiting Europe and consulting with stock raisers there, I found they had abandoned steaming feed for their breeding animals, and on my return home I made the change from steaming to this mode of feeding, and have found it to be most beneficial, not only in the saving of labor, but the stock do much better. The calves are born stronger and healthier. The cows produce more butter, but not so much milk, as when fed on steamed feed.

Q. What is your estimate of the value for feeding purposes of Timothy hay or Orchard Grass hay as compared with fodder corn?

A. I consider fodder corn for feeding purposes to be more

valuable than Timothy, as the grass is too harsh for the animals, and I think that well cured fodder corn, with the mixtures heretofore mentioned, is equally as good, pound for pound, as Orchard Grass, or "peas and oats," or any other of the best hays.

Q. Why, then, if it is equally valuable, do you grow the hay grasses at all, as their weight is less than half, per acre, that of the fodder corn?

A. It would not be practicable to grow fodder corn exclusively upon the majority of farms. Growing the grasses is a necessity for the rotation of crops, and when once seeded down they will last for several years without any further cost, except that of a top dressing, which cost, of course, enters into the question, every time, when corn or other crops are grown, specially for fodder.

FEEDING SOILING CROPS.

Q. In feeding the green crops, Mr. Crozier, that you use for soiling, in what condition are they fed to the stock—are they fed fresh and green, as they are cut?

A. They are cut in the morning for feeding in the afternoon or next morning. I think it is better to let them wilt—they are not so apt to act unfavorably upon the bowels; and I find that cattle will eat their food with better appetite, and give more milk, when it is wilted, than when it is given fresh cut. When the fodder is cut, it is simply left on the ground until it is brought in for feeding.

Q. Would there be any danger of injury if too much of it were fed green to the stock?

A. It is very apt to bloat, or blow, as it is called, particularly if cut when wet. When too large a quantity is taken into the stomach, gases are evolved which cause death, if the animal is not relieved. It is always better, as a means of precaution, to mix with the green feed ten per cent. of cut hay or straw.

Q. Do you continue to use this mixture of cut hay or straw with such crops as you use for soiling throughout the entire season?

A. No; only until we get the bowels regulated, being careful not to make the change too quick from the mixture to the green feed.

Q. Then, when you are regularly under way with the soiling fodder, do you use that exclusively?

A. Yes; but we give in addition bran, and sometimes meal, according to the condition of the cattle. If they are in full milk we give both bran and meal, from seven to ten pounds per day to each, according to size of the cow. This is always mixed with some of the fodder cut. If they are coming into calving, we do not give anything but the soiling; but we are very cautious to commence light, and increase the feed gradually the first week, although I feed so much mangels and other roots, that the sudden change is not so much as it would be if hay or dry food alone were fed.

Q. When the cattle have become completely inured to the soiling do you give them as much feed as they can consume?

A. Yes; I give them all they will eat clean without leaving any.

Q. What is the indication when an animal has become "blown" by having had too much wet green feed?

A. The animal becomes restless, lies down and gets up and down again; breathes short and quick, indicating distress; her side is extended as high as her back, and sometimes higher than her backbone.

Q. In such cases is death inevitable if no remedy is used?

A. It is; but we fortunately have effective remedies. The quickest and best is, perhaps, the trochar and canula, which is driven into her

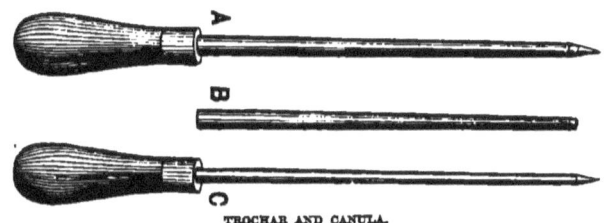

TROCHAR AND CANULA.

A—Ready for use.   B—Cover or Canula.   C—The Trochar, as it is withdrawn, leaving the cover in the wound.

left side, near the short rib. This instrument is made with a scabbard or cover, as shown in the accompanying cut; this is left in the wound until all the gas has escaped. It is then taken out, and the skin closes over the wound in the stomach, which, with the wound in the skin, soon heals, without any ill effect.

Q. When taken in time is the trochar certain to give relief?

A. Yes; immediately.

Q. Is there not danger of injuring the animal by use of it in inexperienced hands?

A. There is some danger, and I would not advise an inexperienced person to use it. A very simple and safe remedy is to saturate a horse blanket thoroughly with cold water, and throw it across the loins and back, and pour cold water over it. I have known this to give immediate relief.

Q. But in the hands of an experienced cattle man what remedy do you consider the best?

A. I always use the trochar myself, which I think affords the speediest and surest relief. Another remedy is to give brewer's yeast to the animal. It is a sure remedy if it can be had fresh. A quart of the yeast, given at once, acts as a purgative very quickly, and so relieves the animal. Another easy remedy is to put a short round stick, about two inches thick, crossways between the animal's jaws, in the manner of a bit, and fasten the ends to the horns, drawing it close up. This causes the cow to make efforts to relieve herself of it, holding up her head, and gives the gas a chance to escape. The trochar and canula, however, affords the most certain relief. The puncture is made at a spot half way between the last rib and the hip bone, on the left side, and a little below the line of the hip bone. The direction of the instrument should be downwards, so as to avoid injuring the kidney. The swelling is always the greatest just at this spot.

Q. To get at a right understanding of this important matter of soiling, please state at what season of the year you begin and your method of feeding it?

A. I begin to feed about the middle of May with rye, which, as has been stated before, is the first green feed. I feed about seven o'clock directly after milking in the morning, feeding a little at a time, until they seem satisfied. What is left is taken from before them and the mangers cleaned ready for the next feeding. They are fed again at noon and at four o'clock in the afternoon. At six o'clock they are milked, turned into the paddock for a night's rest, where they enjoy the fresh, cool air, and are free from the annoyance of flies. This process of soiling the cattle is continued until the middle of November, if frost and cold weather keep off so long; and very often later, as I often plant a few acres of late cabbage, and sometimes a portion of them do not head up, and are in that condition used for soiling, the same as any other green fodder. Field pumpkins are used late in the fall in the same manner, broken up with an axe, and fed to the cows once a day. The cabbage and the pumpkins then will carry us sometimes to the end of November, according to the season, but we generally make it a point to begin our regular winter feed about the middle of November, which is done in the following manner: Dried fodder corn, or hay made from oats and peas, orchard or other grasses is cut, and mixed with crushed roots, which have been run through the machine known as the "pulper" until they are of the consistence of apples ground for cider, enough being mixed to last a week at a time. The whole is mixed with a little salt (bone meal at times), bran and ground oats and corn, and lately I have used with great advantage a little cotton seed meal. There is nothing arbitrary in the quantities used of these, which we may call condiments, but the main articles, the cut hay and the crushed roots, are used about in the proportion of a cart load, or thirty bushels, of the roots, to a ton of the provender. It is then thrown in a heap on the barn floor and allowed to ferment enough to make it slightly warm, as I find it is a great advantage to give warm feed to milch cows in the winter. The quantity given to each cow of average size is a common bushel basket full twice a day, unless she is in full milk, when she is allowed a little more as may be thought necessary. At midday I give them hay after they have been watered in their stalls, the water being slightly warmed, as I find that if permitted to drink cold water, the change would make a loss of several pounds of milk per day with each cow. Practically this may be found difficult or inconvenient upon farms, which are not well provided with the facilities for warming the water. In such cases, however, it may be quite easy to take care that the water troughs are kept free from ice or snow in the winter season, and to give the cows only water that is fresh drawn from a well or a cistern. The troughs should be emptied as soon as the cattle are watered, by means of a hole in the bottom, stopped with a plug, and covers provided for them to prevent them becoming filled with snow. Well water is rarely colder than fifty or forty-five degrees, and this temperature is not injurious.

(Mr. H.) I have heard objections made to this practice of soiling by some persons, on account of the extra labor involved in it. I cannot see it in that light. I have been told, on the other hand, that this extra labor is by no means so great as some think it to be, especially when a well arranged system is practiced. For instance, take a farm where thirty cows are kept. Each feed amounts to forty pounds for each cow—that is, 1,200 pounds in all—which is a moderate load for one horse. A smart boy or a man takes a team and wagon to the field. A mowing machine is kept there. This I would say should be covered with a waterproof sheet when not in use. The horses are put to the mower and the fodder is cut. One, two or even three feeds ahead may be cut, to provide against rainy days. The load cut on the previous evening is loaded, and hauled to the barn. This is the work of an hour or perhaps more, but certainly not two. The wagon is drawn into the feeding passage and the load thrown off, or it may be put directly into the feeding racks, but it is preferable to have one or two feeds ahead in the barn. In this way half the time of a man might be taken up daily in getting the feed for thirty cows. The rest of his time may be profitably taken up in caring for them in other ways, and in caring for the manure. This will cost about three cents a day for each cow. The saving in manure will pay that, while the saving in the feed will pay even more. For smaller herds the cost in proportion is even less, as one horse and a boy will do all the work.

(Mr. C.) This view is undoubtedly correct and the description of the work is a fair one. In farming, all the work that can be done usefully adds to the profit, and no farmer should be afraid of soiling because it involves some little additional work, when this work pays so well for itself.

Q. How long do you continue to turn the cattle out at night?

A. On account of the danger of sudden cold storms coming up at night and of white frost on the grass, we do not usually leave them out later than the middle of September, to remain all night. We then change to feed morning and evening, and turn them out at midday, keeping them in the stables at night, as at that season of the year we always expect these sudden changes, in this northern latitude.

Q. Do you give them exercise in the severe weather?

A. I have had my animals in the stables three months at a time without ever letting them out of the stalls, for the reason that cows with calf are apt to be abused by the other cows, and if they are fresh in milk, the less exercise they have, the more milk they will produce, as they are more contented when in their stalls and at rest. It is a common practice with many farmers to let their cattle run about the stack yards all winter through. In the spring they are in a sad condition from poverty, and little can be expected from them the following summer. Many persons get the very mistaken idea that cows should have a chance to get out to lick themselves. This I think is a great injury to the animals and is one of the most fruitful sources of bad health, because they lick the hair off themselves, and of course swallow some of it. When it gets into the stomach it remains there, and impedes the free action of the bowels, sometimes gathering into hard balls and producing death. Instead of permitting the cow to lick herself or to be licked by her companions, I use a curry-comb and stiff brush, which are applied twice each day so vigorously as to remove all loose hair, and keep the pores of the skin open. If this is done a cow will never attempt to lick herself. This enables the constant perspiration from the skin to pass off in a proper manner, which greatly helps the health of the cow and indeed has a considerable effect upon the purity of the milk.

Q. Do not cows require a certain quantity of salt with their food?

A. I give a small handful of salt and fine bone meal mixed half and half, every morning, after their cribs are cleaned out. For the first few times a new comer does not like the bone meal; but as soon as she gets a taste of it she looks for it as regularly every morning as her feed. In the spring of the year the old practice was to bleed;

but instead of bleeding, which at times is a useless and injurious practice, especially when done without proper knowledge, I give salts and sulphur to cleanse and purify the blood. The proper quantity for a full-grown animal should be one-half pound of salts and two ounces of sulphur, which is made into three doses and a dose given every two days. In connection with this matter of allowing cows to run in the barn-yards, it is, in my opinion, one of the great causes of

ABORTION IN CATTLE.

I am constantly receiving letters inquiring as to the cause of this disease (for it has unmistakably shown itself to be a disease under certain conditions), and the permitting of cattle to run in the barn-yards, where they have the chance to push, butt and abuse each other, is, I am confident, in many cases, a frequent cause of the trouble; and once this disease gets into the herd, it is almost impossible to get rid of it until it has infected the entire stock. A farmer known to me had some twenty abortions amongst his fine herd of Jerseys this season, and only saved a few calves from cows that were on a distant farm. He told me that he had written to nearly every prominent breeder in the country to find out the cause, besides stating his case in several of the agricultural journals, but without getting any satisfactory reply. A letter received from him a few days ago stated that he had found that it was a heifer that he had purchased in the summer of 1882 that had brought this serious disease into his herd, entailing a loss of thousands of dollars. In my opinion, the probable cause was that the rest of his cows had set upon the stranger and gored her and hurt her, and in this manner caused her to abort. His yard, I think, is not more than 100 feet square, in which he kept thirty head of cattle. The yard was littered with salt or marsh hay, probably three feet deep. On this the herdsman would scatter the corn stalks or hay for the cattle, and the result was that the master cow would attack the one nearest her, and so on until all were bruised less or more. I believe this very improper manner of feeding has now been changed, and the animals are kept in box stalls.

Q. Abortion, I believe, Mr. Crozier, is generally supposed to be first brought about by mechanical means. How do you account for its being infectious?

A. It is probably caused by the taint or smell from the afterbirth, which always follows an abortion. The best preventive from infection from this odor is for the herdsman to promptly use his best judgment in relieving the cow from the placenta, being careful to bury all of it beyond possibility of odor arising. Thorough disinfection of the stable, by burning sulphur in it in some careful and safe manner, is also important, to destroy the germs of the disease. The infected cow should also be removed from the herd for several days. This disinfecting of stables will be found useful in all cases of epidemic diseases. For a stable of twenty cows one or two pounds would be required. Injections, three times a day, of a pint of blood warm water with ten drops of carbolic acid, should be given, for the purpose of cleansing the cow which has aborted. My own experience in this matter, I am happy to say, has never been such as to give me much annoyance, having been in the habit of taking suitable precautions. I am so confident that cows in a condition of pregnancy are abnormally sensitive to the foul odors from decomposing animal matter, that the slightest taint of it in our stables is at once hunted up and removed, and this is particularly the case with all the finer class of animals, such as Ayrshires, Jerseys or Holsteins, or any of the high bred or thorough-bred animals, as they are seemingly more sensitive to such impressions than the common stock. For this reason I consider it to be one of the most dangerous things for any stock breeder to permit the placenta, even from sound cows, in ordinary cases, or any other similar animal matter, to remain for a moment longer than is actually necessary to remove it. It should be at once removed and buried deep enough so that no odor can be emitted from it. Rats or mice, for this reason, should never be poisoned; the simplest remedy is plenty of cats. If rats are exceedingly troublesome the following plan is recommended: get a box trap and catch one; then paint it all over with gas tar, except the head, which must not be touched, putting as much tar upon the body as you can get to stick, and take it to its hole and let it run in. Care must be taken not to hurt the rat in any way, and not to get the tar into the eyes or mouth, as it must be able to run through all the holes in the yard. If half a dozen are caught and so treated, all the better chance of their being banished.

(Mr. H.) There is no doubt that this disease is exceedingly troublesome and occasions serious loss. It is not confined, either, to any one breed of cattle, although, perhaps, the Jerseys are the most subject to it, for cases occur quite numerously in dairies where only native cattle are kept. I am inclined to believe that, while you are correct as far as your experience goes, yet you do not go far enough in your explanation of this dangerous, and sometimes mysterious, disease. I have heard of cases in which the calves of a whole herd have been lost, when there has been no known mechanical cause for it. In these cases the abortion was emphatically a disease. In consulting a standard work on veterinary surgery, by the leading authority in the world (Prof. Geo. Fleming, whose work on Veterinary Obstetrics is a text book in the colleges), I find this disease has been a source of trouble for many years, especially in dairies, in many places the losses averaging seventeen, and even twenty-five, per cent. every year, until prevented. As any one who reads the leading agricultural papers may see, the losses (which, however, are not published in the majority of cases, for obvious reasons) among the higher classes of dairy cattle are exceedingly numerous, and, sometimes, are almost ruinous. It becomes, therefore, of serious importance to know something as to how this disease occurs and how to prevent its occurrence; for as to cure, any person can understand that that is out of the question, because the evil is, necessarily, past cure.

Prof. Fleming says this disease is either sporadic (or accidental) or epizootic (or communicated and contagious, or due to widespread causes operating over an extended space at the same time). The causes are external or internal. Of external causes he enumerates, atmospheric influences; irregular seasons; depressing effects of continuous bad weather; cold suddenly applied to the skin, as by a sudden cold storm in hot weather, or exposure to rain or sleet in the winter, or exposure to frosty nights after warm autumn days. The food and water often cause the trouble. Frosty herbage and very cold water, by suddenly chilling the stomach, affect the fœtus, and cause its death and premature expulsion. Indigestible food, or food that is too concentrated and disturbs the digestive organs and causes bloating or disorders of the blood, also endangers the fœtus. Foul water, which is charged with injurious germs of a fungoid character, is exceedingly dangerous. Some plants will produce the disease; common horse tails (*equisetum*), which is common in some pastures and meadows, and swamp sedges, are known to be dangerous. The leaves of red cedar (the *savin* of the druggists) surely produces it, and is used medicinally as the ergot of rye is. This fungus, when taken into the stomach in small quantities, produces violent contractions of the muscular fibre, and, when eaten in large quantities, is a deadly poison. Excessive muscular action, and blows and violent strains in moving in cramped positions, are also causes. Sudden excitement and alarm, as an attack by dogs, or by other cows, and anything which unduly excites the nerves, have been known to produce it. But contagion, produced by exposure to the virus from aborted cows, has been considered as the most frequent cause of this disease, which often runs through a whole herd, and even appears in others at some distance.

The internal causes enumerated are irregular feeding, either to excess, or in the opposite direction; constitutional predisposition;

natural organic weakness; disorders of the bowels; diarrhœa, constipation, and, especially, lung disorders, which cause convulsive coughs, or disturb the circulation, and produce congestion or anæmia.

The causes are thus very numerous, and are, no doubt, much more prevalent, in one form or another, than is generally supposed. For

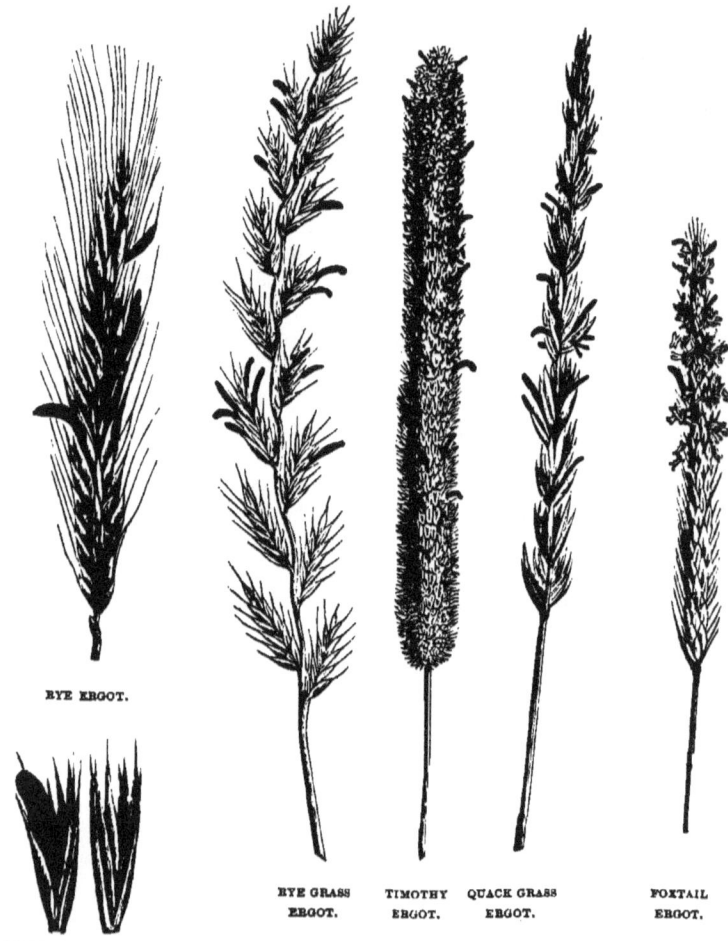

RYE ERGOT.

RYE ERGOT ENLARGED.

RYE GRASS ERGOT.   TIMOTHY ERGOT.   QUACK GRASS ERGOT.   FOXTAIL ERGOT.

instance, how often are cows suddenly chilled by exposure to snow or rain storms; cold drafts in the stable in severe weather, or other accidents, which too often happen in dairies where it is supposed the cows are treated with the utmost care; so much so, perhaps, as to unduly expose them to sudden changes, by making them more susceptible.

(Mr. C.) I know it is a common belief among the Scotch shepherds that feeding frozen turnips to ewes causes the loss of the lambs, and great care is taken to avoid it. In my dairy my plan of pulping the roots and mixing them with cut hay or fodder, and letting the heap ferment and heat a little, avoids this danger. It is quite certain that if greater precautions were taken, with a constant view of the always impending danger of this disease, its frequency would be very much lessened.

(Mr. H.) The danger of ergot in the grasses is one that is wholly overlooked, and yet it is extremely common. Rye is very much subject to this parasite (of which, on this account, it will be useful to give an illustration, that it may be recognized). This fungus is a sure provocative of this disease, as is well known. When the grain is threshed the spears of ergot are broken up, and either go out in the chaff, or remain to be ground up with the grain in the mill. In bolting the flour the ergot is separated with the bran, and rye bran is largely used as food for dairy cows. Then the grasses are very subject to ergot, especially the common quack grass, timothy, foxtail, and especially the rye grasses (see illustrations), and precautions in this respect are indispensable.

Then the prevalence of smut in the small grains, and especially in corn, of which not only the ear, but the tassel stalk and leaves, are infested, is a constant danger, because the effect of this fungus is precisely similar to that of ergot. I notice that Prof. Fleming, in his work above quoted, gives an instance in which eleven abortions in one herd were directly traced to the use of smut in corn.

In regard to its contagious character, your suggestion to completely destroy the discharged fœtus and membranes, and to thoroughly disinfect the stable by burning sulphur freely in it, I consider very valuable; and I would add, that the liberal use of lime to destroy the waste matter that should be safely buried, or the burning of it, would remove a constant danger. Further, the cow should be removed to a safe place by itself, and its manure destroyed or decomposed by lime until all danger of infection had passed away. And I think every owner of a valuable herd would be wise to carefully instruct his herdsmen upon these points and especially upon those which relate to the prevention of the trouble, for in this case prevention is the only remedy.

CHAPTER VI.

GRASS AND ITS MANAGEMENT.

(Mr. C.) There is probably no subject in which there is more interest taken by the farming community of the United States at the present time, than that of grass. There is but little doubt that the gravest blunders have been made, and are still being made, in the use of varieties that are entirely uncongenial to certain soils, and the continuance in use of the older sorts, through ignorance that there are better kinds, which would produce nearly one-third more than the varieties now commonly grown. The subject of grass in England is much better understood than with us, and experimental grounds have long been devoted to the purpose of ascertaining what varieties are best suited for the different soils. Here, however, we have already several such stations devoted to the same purpose, but they have not yet been long enough in use to definitely determine what varieties are best suited to the different sections. Of course here the task is a much more comprehensive one that it is in the limited area of Great Britain, as we have such wide variation of climate and soil, so that with the very best endeavors, it will take many years before we can hope to attain to that degree of perfection in this all-important matter that they have now reached in England. In addition to the official experimental stations, which are attempting this work in several sections of the country, wide-awake farmers have, by their own efforts, made great improvements in the selection of grasses suitable for permanent pasture or haying lands. The varieties of grasses named in the following pages are comparatively few, but they are such as in my long experience I have found of more or less merit. There are, no doubt, many other varieties that may yet be used, that may answer better than some of those named, but we can only anticipate in this matter. Heretofore the base grass, as it may be called, for hay crop in all the Northern States, has been Timothy; but experiments that have been carried on for a period of twenty years have led me to believe that

ORCHARD GRASS

is much better fitted to be the leading kind in mixtures, whether for pasture or for hay, or used alone or otherwise; and I place it far in advance, not only of Timothy, but of any other grass we have thus far in cultivation. Any one acquainted with the growth of roots will see at a glance, by the illustration, that it is a plant better fitted for permanency than any of the other varieties of grasses mentioned in this work. In addition to that it has a merit which I consider to be far above all the rest; this is the early date at which it is in a condition to be cut for hay, whether sown alone or in mixtures. It is found that it can be cut between two and three weeks before Timothy

ORCHARD GRASS.   MEADOW FOXTAIL.

is ready. The present season my whole crop was cut and in the barns about the 20th of June, at least twenty days before the other farmers in this vicinity had begun to cut their Timothy. The advantage of this earliness is not only that it gives three weeks longer for the aftermath to grow, but another reason, far more important, is, that at this date the white Ox-eye Daisy (*Chrysanthemum leucanthemum*), and other troublesome weeds, are not yet in a condition to seed, so that should any of them happen to be in the fields, they are destroyed by being cut before they have ripened their seeds. Any one riding along the railroads through Pennsylvania, New Jersey, New York or Connecticut, will understand the vast importance of this means of checking the white daisy, when it is seen that tens of thousands of acres have been given up to the possession of that worthless weed. It is in full seed at the time Timothy hay is cut, and its seed retains vitality for years. When this weed is mixed with the hay the mischief done is not only for the succeeding year, but it may be for half a dozen years after, as the seed, if plowed down into the ground, will remain for years, and will germinate when brought to the surface again by a subsequent plowing. So, then, we see, that if we are able to use Orchard Grass, which is not only equally as good, but better in many respects than Timothy, having in addition the valuable quality of being in fit condition to cut at a season before the devastating white daisy is in seed, we have accomplished something at which the farming community may well rejoice. There is an unfortunate matter connected with the name of this grass, however, which we shall endeavor as far as possible to set right. It is universally known with us as Orchard Grass, giving the impression to those unacquainted with it that it is only fitted for growing in the orchard or under partial shade. Although no other grass will do better under such circumstances, yet, like all other strong growing grasses, it will always produce a heavier crop if exposed to the bright and open sunshine.

Q. Have you ever in your practice, Mr. Crozier, used Orchard Grass without the admixture of clover or other grasses?

A. Very seldom. Believing in the great importance of having a variety of grasses, either for hay or for pasture, I make it a rule to include never less than five and sometimes as many as ten varieties of grass together, with a due proportion of Clover. The mixture which I sow after wheat in the fall or spring, for each acre of land, is composed of the following

VARIETIES OF GRASSES.

Orchard Grass,	Sweet Scented Vernal,
Meadow Foxtail,	Meadow Fescue,
Sheep Fescue,	English Rye Grass,
Rhode Island, or Creeping Bent,	Italian Rye Grass,
Hard Fescue,	Red Top.

(Engravings of these grasses will be found on the previous and succeeding pages.)

One-half of the bulk being in Orchard Grass, while the other half is made up of the other grasses mentioned. I vary the quantities in these mixtures according to the requirements of the soil, the quantity needed for average lands being, per acre, about five and one-half bushels, or seventy-five pounds. For rich, heavy lands from one-quarter to one-third less.

This is my favorite mixture for either mowing lands or pasture, whether sown in the fall or spring; to which is added, and sown in the spring always—as it is rather tender if sown in the fall in this latitude—ten pounds of Red or Mammoth Clover, which is also known under the different names of Peavine Clover, Broad Leaved Clover, and in England as Cow Grass. This variety is a great improvement on the ordinary Red Clover, and I would always advise it to be sown, for the best results. Another reason why it should always be sown separately is that its great weight makes it difficult to be kept properly mixed with the lighter grass seeds, and it is therefore better to sow it

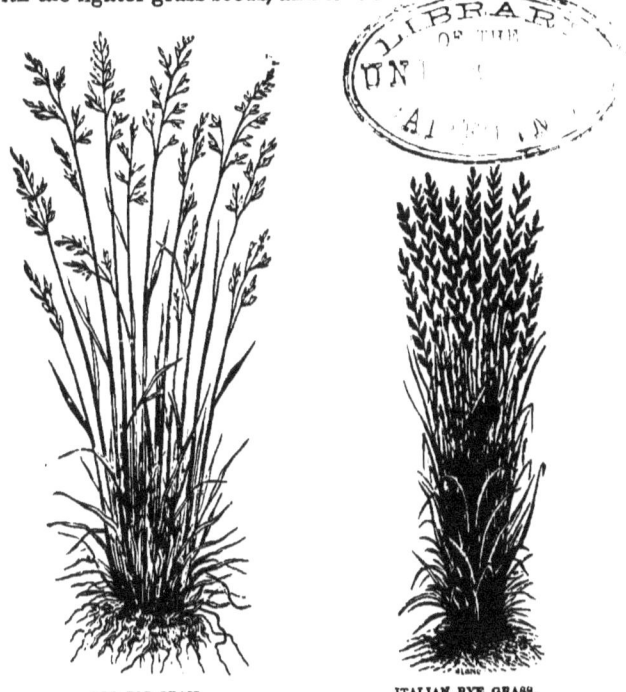

RED TOP GRASS. ITALIAN RYE GRASS.

alone in the usual way, over the grass seed, brush harrowing after sowing, and then rolling. This mixture as here given is much more expensive than that commonly used for seeding down either for hay or for pasture, the first cost being four or five times as much as that of the ordinary mixture. Thus far I have used the best grade of seed, costing from $20 to $25 per acre, but I am so well satisfied of its superiority, that if it cost me one-third more, I would still continue to use it, because it must be remembered that this investment is not for one year only, but if the land is properly treated there is no reason why permanent mowing land cannot be kept in good condition for twenty years, producing annually one-third more weight than the mixture in common use.

This quantity of grass seed is probably double as much as is usually sown per acre, but as in the quality, so in the quantity, I consider that the importance of the thicker seeding cannot be overestimated. Not only does it keep down the weeds, but what is of even greater importance, we get a thicker covering of the whole surface, so that in case of severe droughts, instead of the sun beating down on the bare soil, it is intercepted and shaded by the thickly growing plants. It paid me to use this mixture while I was renting land at $10 per acre even on a five years' lease.

SWEET VERNAL GRASS.   HARD FESCUE.   SHEEP FESCUE.

(Mr. H.) From what I have seen I can well attest the value of your opinion in this matter, as the hay-field which I saw you in process of cutting on the 9th of June is now, thirty days later, one foot in height, while grass lands on all sides of it, where the ordinary Timothy and Clover mixtures have been used, are only now being harvested, and the aftermath, let the weather be what it may, cannot be in the same condition as the field cut on the 9th of June now is, and probably never will be in that condition. The wonder to me is, why farmers, with the example that your land sets before them, do not learn that five acres treated by this method would produce certainly not less than as much as could be taken from twenty-five acres treated after the usual slipshod manner.

Q. Is it your practice to sow grass seed by hand or by machine?

A. I always sow grass seed and clovers by hand, using both hands and sowing crosswise, bearing in mind always to overlap at each turn. Then, after the field has been sown one way, I turn and sow the other way over the same ground, to prevent any chance of waste by unevenness.

Q. Is not a machine preferable in the hands of a novice, than to attempt the rather difficult process of distributing the grass seeds evenly by hand?

A. Probably it might. I have thus far done all the seeding on my farm myself, and I must say that I have little faith in sowing grass seed by machine. I have seen many instances where all the

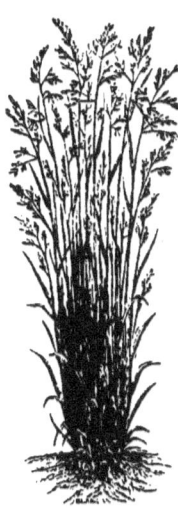

MAMMOTH CLOVER.   MEADOW FESCUE.

labor of the preparation of the land for the grass crop has been a failure by the uneven sowing of the machine.

Q. But if you were unable to do the sowing yourself, would you not prefer to have the work done by a machine rather than take the risk of having an inexperienced man do the sowing?

A. I would rather take the risk of allowing my best hired man to do the work. For sowing these seeds, however, a really good machine would be very useful, but so far I have not met with one which I would trust an unskilled workman to use.

Q. You are well aware, Mr. Crozier, that the great mass of the hay sold in the United States, particularly in the Northern States, is that produced from Timothy Grass?

A. Yes; twenty years ago it was the only grass I grew, until my observation while traveling in Europe taught me better, and I have since entirely abandoned it. I am so well satisfied with the results of these mixtures above mentioned, that I could not be induced to go back to growing Timothy. I believe that one of the greatest mistakes that the farming community is making to-day, is the almost universal one of growing Timothy as the base grass for haying lands and for pasture, instead of using Orchard Grass for that purpose. Mr. F. C. Havemeyer, who owns one of the most extensive and probably best appointed farms in New York State, after visiting me last summer, supplied himself this year with these grasses to be used for mowing lands and pasture, and I am certain he will be pleased with the result.

TIMOTHY AND CLOVER.

Timothy and Clover, however, is still the standard crop for mowing lands and for pasture in the great majority of farms in all sections of the Northern and Middle States; but, as I have before stated, I feel satisfied that this is a widespread error, and that those who will take the trouble to try the Orchard Grass, as a substitute for Timothy, are likely to continue its use. But the prejudice in favor of Timothy hay is so great in many sections, that it may be found that no other substitute will be received, and in such cases we can only advise, that to obtain the best results from Timothy and Clover, they should be sown on heavy, rich loam, or peaty soils, as these are the best. Upon dry, gravelly or sandy soils these grasses never give results worth the labor, unless with heavy manuring. When Timothy is sown with wheat in the fall, about eight to ten quarts is used per acre; or if sown alone, and not to be seeded with Clover in the spring, double that quantity should be used. When Clover is sown with it the most suitable kind is the Mammoth, at the rate of six quarts per acre, because it gives a full crop the first season of mowing. The Timothy, as is well known, does not give a full crop until its second year. This hay is still the favorite in the markets of our large cities; it is mainly so for the reason that the mixtures which are here given at length (having Orchard Grass as its base) are comparatively unknown. When it is known that the Orchard Grass mixture gives permanent mowing and pasture lands for a life-time, if fairly treated, and that Timothy and Clover requires renewal every three or four years— together with its other disadvantages of lateness of maturity and lightness of crop, compared with the other—the wonder will be that farmers are so slow to appreciate the difference. Already some of the wealthy owners of the best studs of horses in the country will use no other hay than what is sometimes called the "English mixture," believing it to be in all respects better. I have long ago discovered that it is more nutritious, pound for pound, to feed cattle and sheep, than Timothy hay.

I have been told by Mr. Henry Stewart, who has been quoted elsewhere in this book, that, when changing the feed of his cows from hay made from Orchard Grass, Clover and other mixed grasses to Timothy hay of good quality, the tri-weekly churning of butter fell off from 25 lbs. to 17 lbs., and no increase of grain food that could be safely given would restore the loss. Also that the same difference has occurred when changing from Orchard Grass to Timothy in pasture or soiling. I believe, in this case, Mr. Stewart used Orchard Grass alone to a large extent; and at the rate of four bushels of seed per acre, the cost of the seeding is reduced to about the same as that of Timothy and Clover. This example is one of the sowing of Orchard Grass alone, or nearly so; but the mixture of other grasses, as before described, will always give better results, because of the larger yield produced.

Timothy and Clover are so general in all the meadows, that one would suppose Timothy was the only grass that would succeed in our climate. In the East, Timothy is commonly called "Herd's Grass," a name which in Pennsylvania is given to Red Top. This formerly led to much confusion; but at present the name "Herd's Grass" is generally dropped. Timothy is especially unsuited to the too common method of treating grass lands. There are farmers who still, after taking a crop of hay, pasture the land, after grass has made a second growth. Timothy forms a bulbous swelling at the base of its stems, from which next year's growth will start, and is greatly injured by cattle trampling it and eating off the leaves that should protect the bulb during the winter, so that Timothy is a poor pasture grass. In this respect Orchard Grass is much more useful than Timothy. We never knew a farmer to fairly try Orchard Grass who was not so pleased with it that he did not continue its use. Yet, take the country through, it has made its way but slowly. It is preferable to Timothy to combine with Clover for hay, as the two are in perfection—that is, in blossom—at the same time, while as pasture grass it is vastly superior. Orchard Grass is, in fact, a true pasture grass, while Timothy is not. It at once recovers after it is closely cropped, and the earliness of its growth in spring is greatly in its favor. The chief, in fact, the only objection, that has been made to Orchard Grass, is its tendency to form tussocks or clumps, a trouble which may be overcome by thick seeding. Three bushels of clean seed to the acre, on rich land, and four bushels on lighter soil if alone, or two bushels if Clover is to be sown with it, will give a sufficiently thick growth to prevent the formation of stools.

BERMUDA GRASS.

This grass has long been considered the bane of the agriculturist in the Southern States. The slipshod culture too often in practice there made its presence among other crops the most troublesome of all weeds, but the necessity for fodder set the more advanced farmers to utilize this grass for that purpose. This is now being done in many sections with the most marked success. One difficulty, however, interposes: the seed rarely matures in our Southern States, and even some samples we have tested from Bermuda have failed to germinate. But Nature here compensates, as she always does, for her partial failures. The roots and stems of Bermuda grass root at every eye or joint, and when these are run through a hay or straw cutter, we thus have a "seed" that can be sown. These cuttings are sown on the newly plowed field, harrowed in and rolled, with a reasonable certainty of a good stand of grass. Such "seed" cannot well be made an article of merchandise, but may be transported to moderate distances, and for local use this plan is found to work very well. The Hon. Robert N. Gourdin, of Charleston, S. C., is experimenting on a large scale with this grass, and has every reason to be sanguine of great benefits to be derived from its culture in regions hitherto barren of forage for stock. But it is doubtful if it will ever be so satisfactory as the Alfalfa (Lucern), alluded to at length in this work as a forage crop for the Southern States.

It will no doubt be interesting to insert here some information given at our request by Mr. Gourdin in regard to Bermuda grass:

"Bermuda grass does not make seed with us. It propagates itself. It runs on the ground as a vine, having numerous joints, from each of which roots strike down and blades shoot up. It is propagated, artificially, by transplanting, and takes root readily. It should be transplanted in the fall and winter after rain, when there is moisture in the land. It matures and gives its first cutting, ordinarily, in June. Persons having most experience with Bermuda grass place the average yield of hay for ten years at four tons per acre per annum. This is a cautious and safe estimate of its productiveness. It grows on every kind of land here—wherever corn and cotton grows, and is their great enemy. On poor land Bermuda grass is stumpy and coarse; on rich land its growth is free, and its blades are long, tender and delicate. Properly cultivated in this latitude, animals prefer this grass and the hay made of it over all other varieties. I do not know how far north it grows, but I have observed it as far north as Petersburg and Richmond, Virginia, growing in the streets and vacant lots of these cities as it does in Charleston, and, apparently, with the same vigor."

CYNODON DACTYLON (BERMUDA GRASS).

A more recent account of this grass, given by Dr. Ravenal, of Charleston, S. C., states that the yield of Bermuda Grass for hay for two cuttings was equal to 5,100 pounds the first year after setting out and 9,004 pounds the fourth year. The cost of establishing a meadow is about $8 an acre; the hay is sold in bales at $20 to $25 per ton, and the sale is as easy as that of cotton, beef or any other farm product.*

---

* Since Bermuda Grass has become more widely cultivated in the South, it is found to produce seed, and the seed is now to be procured in the regular way.

OTHER SOUTHERN GRASSES.

The question of grasses and fodder crops for the Southern States is of the greatest importance. The changing character of the agriculture of the South necessarily draws attention to the rearing of live stock, and of course fodder and grass crops must follow. It has been

PANICUM SANGUINALE (CRAB GRASS).

supposed that the Southern climate is not favorable to grass and consequently few farmers venture to invest in live stock of any kind. But this idea is a great mistake. There is no other part of this continent where grasses—of the right kind—will flourish with greater luxuriance than in the South, and it is particularly desirable that attention should be called to this fact in this work, which is devoted to the subject of profitable farming all over this broad land. But there are an exceedingly great variety of grasses, and this large family of plants has its finest and most numerous representatives in the

South. The sorghums, millets, dourras, the panicums and others, all more or less closely related to the Millet family, luxuriate in the warm soil and bright sunshine of the Southern States. And attention is now being given to their culture in many localities. After Bermuda Grass, the common native grasses which spring up spontaneously when the fields are abandoned to them are found to have a special value for hay as well as pasture. One of the most valuable of these is that variety once thought to be the greatest pest of the cotton planter, known as

CRAB GRASS.

This is a species of *Panicum* well known in the Northern States by its purplish colored, spreading, finger-like panicle, and which appears late in the summer as a common weed in lawns and fields. But it attains a wonderful development in the South, even upon lands exhausted by continuous cotton growing. A case which happened a few years ago recently came to my knowledge. A Northern farmer went to Georgia in search for a cheap tract of land upon which to establish a farm. He found one covered with a luxuriant growth of this grass, which had been abandoned in despair by the owner, a cotton planter, and was offered to him at an exceedingly low price. He had seen baled hay from the North in car loads at nearly every station on his journey, and conceived the idea that this grass would make excellent hay and sell at a very profitable price. He purchased the farm, sent to a friend in New York to buy for him a couple of mowing machines and a hay press, and baled the crop, which that year amounted to over 300 tons, and far more than repaid his whole investment. This instance certainly carries a moral and a useful hint to Southern farmers, and those in the North who desire to find a field for enterprise in the sunny South.

DOOR-YARD AND BARN-YARD GRASSES.

Two other valuable native grasses are the common species of *Panicum* known as Door-yard, or Crow's Foot Grass, and Barn-yard, or Cock's Foot.* These are exceedingly common, and have a very vigorous growth. They will be easily recognized from the illustrations as also common in the North, appearing in flower late in the summer. They are both becoming valuable pasture grasses all over the South,

---

* This grass should not be confounded with Orchard Grass, previously referred to in this chapter, and also called Cock's Foot by English farmers.

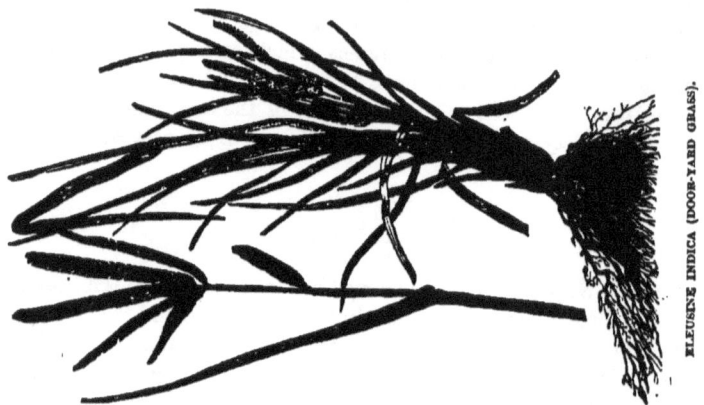

ELEUSINE INDICA (DOOR-YARD GRASS).

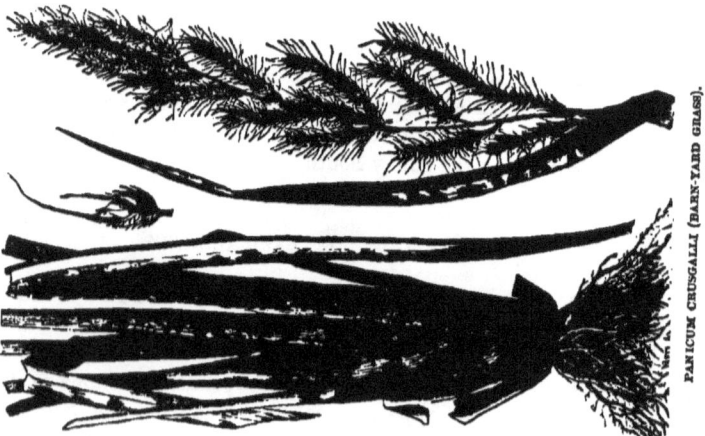

PANICUM CRUSGALLI (BARN-YARD GRASS).

from the Atlantic coasts of Carolina and Georgia to Texas, and the latter species is a very fine hay grass. It is beyond a doubt an excellent fodder crop in the North, yielding a very heavy cutting of rich and succulent and exceedingly sweet forage, that is eaten with avidity by cows. It thrives well in low, moist grounds, and may be found in such places having a rank and vigorous growth, which at times reaches to a height of five feet, its broad and long leaves adding

PANICUM JUMENTORUM (GUINEA GRASS).

very much to the weight of product. The seed is large and like Millet and highly nutritious, and might be usefully sown for a late fodder crop wherever common Millet is grown.

GUINEA GRASS.

Of late years much attention has been given to a very large variety of this genus, known by the common name of Guinea Grass. As it has been confounded with another popular fodder plant, to be next noticed, it is well to give the botanical name of it, *viz.*, *Panicum jumentorum*. It is a native of Africa, and was originally brought into Florida from the West Indies, and is rapidly coming into use all over the Southern States. It is a perennial and reaches a height of six to ten feet, with wide leaves, almost like corn blades, two feet long; but it is cut several times in the season, when at a height of two feet, for green fodder or for hay, or is pastured repeatedly until frost arrives, when the herbage is cut down to the ground. Its culture is

SORGHUM HALAPENSE (JOHNSON GRASS).

as follows: The root throws out a thick mat of stolons, like those of common Quack Grass, but much thicker. These are taken up and cut into pieces, each having a bud. The cuttings are set out in March or April in furrows, and covered with the next turn of the plow. The crop is ready for the first cutting in May, when it is very tender and sweet, and can be fed or cured for hay. Upon fairly good land it yields a cutting every six weeks until it is cut down by the frost, when the root remains in the ground safely and sprouts again the next season. Where the colder winters necessitate it, the crop is grown in drills, and when the herbage is cut down a furrow is thrown over the roots as a protection from the frost, the soil being leveled down with the harrow in the spring.

JOHNSON GRASS.

This species is known as *Sorghum halapense*, and is considered even more valuable than the one above mentioned. It is a perennial, and has long been the bugbear of the cotton planters, from the impossibility of eradicating it when it once gets a foothold in the soil. For a forage crop this is certainly a most excellent quality, especially when combined with its nutritive and agreeable feeding qualities and its abundant yield. The late Mr. Howard, of Atlanta, Ga., a careful and practical farmer and investigator, said of it, after an experience of forty years, that this grass was preferable to all others that could be grown in the South. Its analysis shows it to be more nutritious than even sweet corn fodder. Its seeds are as large as those of broom corn, and its leaves are long and tender. The stem reaches a height of six feet. Its perennial growth, and the firm hold it takes of the soil, in which it spreads with great rapidity, give it a high value for a fodder grass in the South.

JAPAN CLOVER.

This humble but useful plant also deserves some notice here. It is an imported variety of *Lespedeza*, a trefoil allied to the Clovers. It first appeared in 1849 near Charleston. The seeds are supposed to have been brought from Japan or China in some tea boxes. It rapidly spread into Georgia, where it was found soon after near Macon. In 1870 it appeared in Tennessee and now spreads from the Atlantic to the Mississippi. It is a low perennial plant, with a spreading habit, much like that of White Clover. It flourishes on the poorest soils, preventing washing by rains, and furnishing not only good grazing, but fertilizing the soil by the decay of its stubble, as Clover does, or by turning under as green manure. It is not a hardy plant and will not thrive further north than Virginia. For a sheep pasture it is scarcely excelled in value by any other forage plant.

The following extract from a report made by Mr. William Saunders, Superintendent of the grounds of the Agricultural Department, Washington, D. C., made on the Soils and Products of Florida, in compliance with an order from that Department made in 1883, will be found interesting and valuable in regard to this subject:

"One of the greatest wants in Florida is that of food for live stock. Northern grasses and clovers are of small value; they are not adapted to the climate. Lucern, or Alfalfa (*Medicago sativa*), has the reputation of succeeding well in warm climates, and would doubtless flourish in the rich bottom lands when once they are fitted for culture. This being a perennial, noted for a propensity to send its roots deep into the soil, would be almost as permanent a plant as the dwarf palmetto, and infinitely more useful. Lucern is one of the

LESPEDEZA STRIATA (JAPAN CLOVER).

most ancient of cultivated plants, and as a forage plant for dry, warm climates has always been held in high estimation. (For further information on this crop see page 87.)

"Among rapid growing grasses none excel the Italian Rye Grass, *Lolium italicum*. Seeds of this grass, sown in November, would produce a crop fit for cutting in April for hay. The winter season being also the dry season, would be so far unfavorable to continued growth, but the want of rain could be met by a proper selection of soil; the worst selection would be high and dry fields; the best, a thoroughly drained swamp. In an out-of-the-way corner to-day (15th February) I observed a small area covered with the Johnson Grass, *Sorghum halapense*, which had made over two feet of growth, and in good condition to cut for cattle food or for hay. This looked like an experimental plat, and it gave evidence of the value of this grass for this region of country. And I look upon the Johnson Grass as having greater prospective value than either of the plants before named. In Alabama and in others of the Southern States it is proving to be one of the best grasses for hay or for feeding in green state, that has so far been introduced to cultivation. This grass has long been known, but its persistent growth, and the difficulty of eradicating it from cultivated fields, caused it to be regarded as a nuisance. Its greatest fault is its greatest merit. A few days ago, in Polk County, in conversation with an Alabama farmer, I asked him what he found the most profitable crop to raise in that State. He promptly replied hay. To the further question as to what grasses he cultivated for this purpose, he answered, the Johnson Grass. He stated that he made three cuttings yearly, and from these his returns averaged five tons of hay from an acre. This is grown on good bottom land, and all the cultivation it receives is to plow it down once in two or three years, then give it a very thorough harrowing, and an increased growth ensues. A portion of the roots are thus destroyed, which prevents them from becoming too thickly matted, keeps up the fertility, and increases the growth. It would seem that a plant so well adapted to a warm, sunny climate will ultimately prove of great value all through this Southern country."

The best season for sowing Johnson Grass, in Florida or similar latitudes, would be October or November. It should be sown in the usual manner for grass seed, at the rate of two bushels per acre.

Q. As you are aware, Mr. Crozier, the question of grasses is one of such interest as to draw out several works on the subject, elaborate not only in their botanical descriptions, but also replete with chemical analyses and all other scientific data connected with the subject. Have you given such works any consideration, and if so what opinion do you hold as to their value?

A. As a working farmer, life has always appeared to me too short to dabble in these nice questions, and I am perfectly willing to leave it to such men who have the inclination and the time to fritter away on such subjects; but to the great mass of practical farmers, from their education and training, it is and always will be as a "sealed book." Whether it is that the pursuit of such knowledge prevents those engaged in it from getting at the real, practical operations of farming and gardening, I do not know; but there is no denying the broad fact, that the cases on record are very few (personally I know not nor never knew of one), where men who have tried to practice what they preached on these subjects have been successful. Whenever I see a man engaged in agricultural operations preparing himself by the chemical analyses of his soils and of his manures, I at once make up my mind that that man's chances for success are not as good as those of his unlettered contemporary, who probably does not know the meaning of the words. Still I would not discourage those who are engaged in these scientific pursuits, and who have the means to experiment, as the day may yet come when scientific farming and scientific gardening may give practical results.

Q. To return again to the subject of grasses—do you use the mixture previously mentioned on all portions of your farm?

A. No; on hillsides that are washed by the heavy rains I use Rhode Island Bent Grass, for the reason that it forms new roots and shoots from the joints, thus holding the soil and preventing its washing down. I find, also, that it affords excellent pasture for sheep. I sow it at the rate of three bushels to the acre (sometimes as much as four bushels, if the land is very steep), together with a mixture of two or three pounds of White Clover, as this is a low growing variety that sheep are very fond of. By this method I have protected and kept very steep hillsides from being washed by rains. The same mixture is excellent for sheep pasture for high wood lands, where the trees are not too close together.

Q. About what average weight of hay does the mixture which you advise for mowing produce?

A. From two and one-half to three tons per acre, though four tons is nothing unusual under high cultivation. Sometimes the second growth is cut for the purpose of feeding lambs or young calves. When not cut the sheep and young stock are turned onto it. When cut I have had it produce from one and one-half to two tons per acre; but always after a second cutting is made a top dressing of barnyard manure or bone meal should be put on, which stands in place of the droppings from the calves and sheep when the land is pastured.

Q. Is it not better, in laying land to permanent pasture or permanent hay, by sowing grass seed mixture by itself, to do so without sowing wheat or other grain?

A. Yes; and in fact it is the very best way to sow down to permanent grass, as the crop of wheat or rye takes away two-thirds of the manure the first year, besides checking the growth of the grass. It is a common idea that the grain is a fostering crop. This is a great mistake. Instead of fostering the grass it really robs it of its food, and the shade checks its growth. By carefully preparing the ground in August, and sowing the seed in the usual way, the young grass grows vigorously and rapidly, and a crop of hay can be taken the next year. In this preparation it is of the greatest importance that the soil be made very fine and very firm, not only to give a perfect bed for the small seeds, but to thoroughly compact the fine soil about them. In doing this work it must not be forgotten that it is intended to last for many years, and no expense or care that are necessary to secure perfection in it should be withheld. It has been previously recommended to sow the clover seed in the spring; this is not always necessary, as, if it is sown in August, the clover roots become strong enough to withstand the winter safely. It cannot be reiterated too often or too strongly, that the rolling of the soil after grass seeding is of the greatest necessity for success, particularly when done in August.

Q. When stock raising is the main object in view on the farm, would you advise the sowing of grains at all?

A. We gain many little advantages by sowing grain. We often get half the value of the manure used the first season, and we get the straw besides.

Q. When grass seed and clover are sown with a grain crop, is there any return from the grass the following summer or autumn?

A. There usually is not, but when sown alone there is.

Q. What is your usual time of sowing grass seeds alone without the grains?

A. The latter part of August. The next year it will give a fair crop of hay by the end of June or early in July, a crop always as heavy and often heavier than the ordinary crop from established Timothy lands. Timothy, in my experience, is the most exhaustive grass to land that we have. The first and second seasons it is as bad as a crop of wheat for exhausting the soil, and I find my neighbors can only run it three years, the last crop being very poor or hardly worth cutting. Weeds seem to take the place of Timothy, and especially if the summer previous has been dry, the small roots of the grass suffering from the sun beating down upon them, and the freezing and thawing of winter leaves the ground bare in many places; hence destruction of the roots and consequent failure of the crop.

Q. I would ask, however, Mr. Crozier, if Timothy and Clover, treated as liberally by top dressing with manure as you treat all your grass lands, would not continue much longer than the period you name?

A. My experience with it is that it would not. But in many localities, and even generally in the Central States, farmers do this with partial success. Their method is as follows: Timothy is sown with the wheat or rye in the fall; Clover is sown in the spring. A full crop of hay is taken next year, and a top dressing of fine manure is given as soon as the hay is taken off. This protects and feeds the roots, and the ground is soon covered and protected by a new growth. A second crop of hay is taken the next year, or perhaps two cuttings are made; the grass is pastured the year after, and the sod is turned under in the spring for corn. Corn is followed by oats, and oats by wheat, and this completes the rotation. This is very good practice for those farmers under their circumstances, and pays them well; all the better when it is well done. I am positive that no crop of Timothy will last well over three years, when the land must be reseeded. Every season I have scores of letters on this all-important subject to the farmer, asking me if there is any way of getting permanent mowing lands and pasture without this continuous trouble of plowing down and reseeding. I trust that what I have here advised in the grass mixture and method of culture will answer as a general reply to all such queries. I have explained my views far more fully and at length than can possibly be done in the necessarily limited compass of a letter, besides saving me many hours of valuable time, which at many seasons I can ill spare.

Q. I would like to refer again to the mixture of grass seeds which you prefer. This mixture will no doubt suit your manner of growing grass very well; but do I understand you to say that it is to be recommended under all circumstances?

A. I would not go so far as that. These seeds are very costly, and might not suit the circumstances of a great many farmers. There are some varieties which might be left out in many cases. For instance, Italian Rye Grass is not a perennial, and might be omitted, as it will run out the second year after sowing. The perennial Rye Grass would be sufficient without it. Rhode Island Bent is so nearly like Red Top, that both need not be sown, and the latter only used. So the Sheep's Fescue is useful chiefly where sheep are pastured, as it is a small variety, and serves chiefly to make up a succession of herbage. Sweet Vernal Grass might also be left out, as this grass is quite prevalent, and comes in naturally in almost all places. The quantities, too, might be reduced, and all the varieties retained. But certainly I would advise that not less than twenty-five pounds of seed altogether should be sown per acre, which is only half of the amount of seed I use. But for myself I prefer heavy seeding, and believe it is the cheapest in the end, because in sowing these mixed grasses it should not be forgotten that we are seeding once for twenty or thirty years or even more, if the soil is suitable for a permanent meadow.

CLOVER.

The culture of clover as a special crop is often found desirable both for hay, for seed and for plowing in as a preparation for wheat or corn. When thus grown it is sown on the wheat or rye in the spring as soon as the ground is in a fit condition, and may be harrowed in with the light sloping tooth harrow or the brush harrow, which not only covers in the seed but also greatly benefits the grain crop. The clover may be pastured in the fall if it has a rank growth, but otherwise it should be left on the ground and form a mulch during the winter. The next year it may be cut early for soiling or mown for hay in June; the after-growth will furnish a crop of seed and the next spring the sod with all the herbage may be plowed in for corn. A clover sod makes an excellent preparation for wheat. For this purpose the clover is plowed under in August; the ground is immediately rolled to compact it and in September a good harrowing will fit the soil finely for the wheat or rye. The clover hay is especially valuable for cows or sheep, but should never be fed to horses on account of its dustiness, which is provocative of the common disorder known as heaves. It requires slow curing in the cock, and should not be too rapidly or too much dried, or the leaves will be in great part broken off and lost.

BLUE GRASS.

The Blue Grass pastures of Kentucky, Missouri, West Virginia and parts of Ohio and Indiana, have a world-wide reputation. They offer examples of permanent grass lands equal to any in the world, which are a standing rebuke to those persons who declare that there can be no permanent pastures or meadows in our American climate. There are thousands of acres of these lands which have never been plowed, but which became covered with a natural growth of this grass as soon as the timber was cut off. As it has a spreading root, it soon takes possession of the soil and makes a thick sod. It is especially a pasture grass, and under the name of June Grass furnishes the pasture which makes such localities as Herkimer and Oneida Counties in New York so favorable for dairy purposes, and so productive of high flavored cheese and butter. The State of Iowa also affords similar instances. It thrives best on dry, rich, limestone lands, and if the grass is not eaten down in the summer it will afford a luxuriant pasture all through the winter in Southern districts, and until the ground is buried under the snow in the North. The Southern mountain region is peculiarly adapted in soil and climate to this

KENTUCKY BLUE GRASS (POA PRATENSIS).

grass. When sown alone two to three bushels of seed are required to the acre. It may be sown with wheat or rye in the fall. On account of its slow, weak growth at first, it is better to sow the seed with a grain crop.

RED TOP AND FOWL MEADOW GRASS.

These two grasses are specially adapted for low, wet lands. Reclaimed swamp meadows produce them in luxuriance. Elsewhere, and on dry ground, they afford fair pasture but a light hay, and are not to be recommended for such soils. But where the land lies low, and is subject to overflow, there are no other grasses so valuable as these, as they make a dense, tough sod, and afford good pasture, and also furnish a heavy yield of excellent hay. They are better mixed

FOWL MEADOW GRASS (POA SEROTINA.)

together, one and one-half bushels of each being sown early in August or in the spring, and on the soils referred to the seed must necessarily be sown alone.

CHAPTER VII.

THE CUTTING AND CURING OF HAY.

Q. You have already stated that you cut your hay of the Orchard Grass and other grass mixture from the 10th to the 20th of June. In what condition are the various grasses at that time?

A. The Orchard Grass and Clover are in full bloom, and the others are near to, or a little past that stage. In this condition the grasses are most valuable for stock. If allowed to stand until they seed, they are not only more dry and woody in texture, but they also exhaust the land to a great degree and weaken the roots. A large majority of our best farmers agree that hay and clover, and in fact all crops that are used for haying purposes, are best cut in that condition when they contain the largest percentage of saccharine matter, which is said to be when they are in full blossom.

This condition I believe to be better than if the seeds of the grasses were matured, as the juices are just in the state to be most palatable

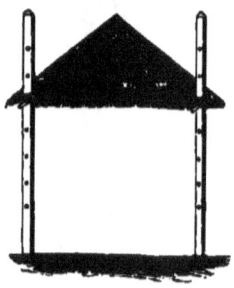

THATCHED BARRACK.

for feed. Of course all hay nowadays is cut by machine. Of these machines there are a large variety, which are popular in special localities; but I have always used the Buckeye, and consider it the best. After mowing, the hay is turned or tedded and raked into swaths, and then put into small cocks and left until the following day, when the cocks are turned over, and made anew, and left until the next day. The hay is then taken to the barn and put into the mow, about a peck of salt being scattered over each load, and trodden as firmly as can be done. The salt makes the hay palatable to the stock, and I believe tends to lessen the fermentation which always occurs in hay when it is put in the barn, and so prevents danger of mustiness. In this way the hay comes out as bright and green in the winter or spring as when put into the mow. Formerly, when I tilled very much more land than I do now, I had to stack most of the hay, which I consider the best way to keep it; that is, in round stacks, containing from ten to fifteen two-horse loads, placing it in the mows being only a matter of convenience. A stack, when prop-

FRAME FOR ROOF OF BARRACK.

erly headed, thatched and roped, will keep for several years. A very convenient way of stacking hay is under open sheds, commonly known as barracks. These are made of four heavy posts, set in the ground or framed together, and a movable, four-sided roof of boards or thatch. The roof can be raised or lowered and let down upon the hay, affording complete protection from the weather. In this country, where stacking is not much practiced, it is not always possible to find a workman or a farmer that can finish a stack so as to make it rain-proof.

BOARD ROOFED BARRACK.

Q. At what height do you cut your hay?

A. The height at which it should be cut depends somewhat on the moistness of the season. If the season is a wet one we can cut two inches from the ground; if the weather is very dry, from three to four inches.

Q. I observe that you top dress with manure after cutting your hay, particularly where it is cut short—the object in that, I presume, is to protect the roots of the grass from the sun, the manure acting as a mulch, as well as for its fertilizing properties, at that time of the year?

A. That is exactly the reason. Although the first heavy rains carry down the greater part of the fertilizing properties of the manure, the substance of it is left to act as a mulch until the aftermath grows sufficiently to protect itself.

CLOVER HAY.

Q. What is understood by the term "Clover Hay"?

A. When a piece of land is sown to wheat and grass in the fall, clover seed is sown the following spring, as soon as the frost is out of the ground, and the soil is sufficiently dry. The ground is then brush harrowed and rolled in the usual manner. The wheat is cut off in July. About September the young Clover is either fed off with sheep or young cattle—heavy animals, such as cows or horses, should never be permitted to go upon the field—or, if not fed off, it should be run over with the mowing machine, and cut three or four inches from the ground, and the cutting left on as a mulch. By June of the next year the clover is ready to cut for the first time. This cutting is made when the crop is in full blossom, and before a single head has turned brown. It is advisable then to give the clover a top dressing of manure or plaster, to hasten the growth of a second crop, which is cut in August. If the ground is rich two hay crops are thus taken.

Q. Is it any more trouble to cure clover hay than the ordinary grass hay?

A. Yes; clover having so much water in it, takes more time and care to cure it than hay. Clover should be cut when the weather is dry and the dew is off, and should be immediately put into cocks and cured in these cocks so as to preserve all the leaves, for if left in the usual way in the sun until it becomes dry, the leaves would get brittle, and in tedding or raking with the horse-rake would fall off. My plan of curing clover is to cut it when the dew is off, and about two hours afterwards rake it up into small cocks and leave it until the next day, when the cocks are turned with the fork and made over again, but larger. Here the clover sweats and heats or ferments and gets rid of a good deal of its moisture, and dries soft and tender, instead of brittle. The second day it is ready to be put in the mow or stack.

Q. Is there not more danger from wet weather in saving clover than in making grass hay?

A. Clover is a more leafy plant than grass, and lies more open and loosely in the swath or cock. It is upon this account that it is better to put it in cocks and cure it in that way, both because it is easily injured by over-drying and by exposure to the sun, and also by rain. To secure it against rain while in the cock, hay caps are found useful. These are squares of heavy brown cotton sheeting fifty-four inches wide, bound at the edges and having a loop at each corner. One of these is spread over a hay cock, and secured by pushing wooden pins through the loops into the hay. If these are taken care of as they should be, they will last a great many years.

HAY CAP.

Q. Is Clover ever sold in a green state in the market in our large cities?

A. At certain seasons there is a large demand for it; it is cut and tied in bundles, which brings from twenty to twenty-five cents each. It is thus given to city horses, not so much as a feed, but as a sort of tonic or alterative. A heavy crop of Clover in this way is often made very profitable, netting possibly four times as much per acre as when dried for hay. In the vicinity of Edinburgh, Scotland, there are fields of Clover which must produce not less than $500 per acre, when sold in this condition; because the farmers renting such fields pay the extraordinary price of fifty pounds sterling, or $250, per acre rent annually. The conditions under which Clover is grown in this way are peculiar. It is usually on land adjacent to the outlets of the sewage from the city, which is utilized by being put on the land in the fall and spring, and which gets it in such a condition of fertility that sometimes even in that cold climate six crops are cut in one season. I observed very recently that there was filed, in the office of the County Clerk, New York City, the certificate of incorporation of the National

Sewerage and Sewage Utilization Company. The capital stock is fixed at $3,000,000, divided into 36,000 shares. I heartily wish them as much success as has been gained at the City of Pullman, in Illinois, where this sewage is used to fertilize a farm of about 300 acres, with a profit of $8,000 last year, equal to ten per cent. of the whole cost. If the same conditions could be got here as in Scotland—and there is no reason why they should not—one-fourth more crop ought to be taken in our higher temperature. Wherever the soiling system is practiced we should have our barn-yard composts to put on the Clover fields in lieu of city sewerage. That is within every farmer's reach, and the cart or team should be used both ways, a load of Clover being brought to the barn and a load of manure taken back and spread on the land, repeating this continuously during the entire season. This system has other advantages as well. Cattle fed in their stalls in this manner will give double the quantity of milk, and it is of better quality than when they are driven to pasture. For, when driven to the fields by boys or dogs, they are often recklessly hurried, and as a general rule, in coming from the pasture, especially in the fly season, they will often make a fast run to the barns, and so injure the milk in the udder until it is nearly worthless. All this is avoided by the soiling system. If tied up in their stalls they do not require so much water, and their supply can be regulated more easily; while if let out to pasture, in our dry climate, where water is often scarce, they become heated in going to the tank or pond, and drink too much.

Q. Is there not sometimes a still later cutting made of the Clover?

A. A third cutting is very often made, but rarely for hay, as the seed is greatly more valuable. When the Clover is cut for seed, it is usual to make the second cutting earlier, so as to give ample time for the plants to make blossoms and mature seed by the fall. The Clover is then hard and woody and not of much value for hay, but it will often yield five bushels of seed to the acre; and as this is worth from $6 to $8 a bushel, and sometimes more, the gain is more than that from all the hay. The seed of Clover is contained in small pea or bean like hulls, and requires a particular method for separating it. The dried crop is threshed in the machine in the usual way and separated from the stems, and the chaff is afterwards hulled by a Clover huller some time during the winter. This is the end of the Clover, excepting upon strong, rich land it may last over the second year and yield the crop of seed the third year. Clover is a biennial upon light soils and poor lands, and cannot be depended upon after the second year, or for more than two crops of hay at the most; but on better and heavier soils it is a short perennial, and may live through the third or even into the fourth year, and give one or two crops each year. If the seeding has been liberal, and the Clover is manured, the yield is far more profitable. No greater mistakes are made in farming than short-sighted economy in the saving of seed. The tables given in many seedsmen's catalogues I consider to be one-third too little.

Q. You have alluded several times to the top dressing of grass lands. In what manner do you consider it best to be done, and what kinds and quantities of manures do you use for that purpose?

A. I would mention first the application of liquid manure, as the value of this is underrated, and it is too often wholly wasted. The best way of preparing liquid manure for such purpose I have found to be the following: Build a cistern in the barn-yard, at the lowest point, of such capacity as may be required, but be sure it be large enough, and run pipes made of boards, or sewer pipes, three or four inches diameter, into it, from the different buildings, where there may be any droppings from the cattle or hogs or sheep, so that all the drainage will flow into the cistern. In hauling this liquid manure to the fields, I use a large hogshead placed on two wheels. It is filled by means of a pump, and is driven to the field, a perforated pipe, such as is used for street sprinkling, and attached to the hogshead, is opened, and the horse is driven along at an easy walk, this being done always when other work is not pressing. This I find to be the best top dressing for meadow lands, if put on in the spring and fall, but not in the hot, dry weather. On land that has been pastured, and has become "hide-bound," as I call it, I usually take an iron or steel tooth harrow, and harrow it both ways thoroughly. The Acme Harrow is better still, and the cutters can be adjusted so as to loosen up the surface to whatever extent may be desired. After the ground has been harrowed in this manner, I re-seed with the grass mixture already mentioned, at the rate of two to three bushels per acre, according to the needs of the land. If the grass is thin, I put on more. If it is still thick, less. I then top dress with composted manure that has been turned over a few times and is worked up fine, after which I run over it with the brush harrow and then roll. The quantity of manure to be used depends in a great measure upon the condition of the land, although I might here say that there is very little likelihood of any farmer ever having manure enough to put it on to excess. I use all the way from five to twenty two-horse loads per acre, according to the condition of the land or the quantity of manure I have on hand. In the absence of barn-yard manure a compost of lime and loam, with the soils from the backs of fences, is excellent, or plaster at the rate of one ton per acre will answer. This I know is a good deal more plaster than is commonly used, but my principle, as you know, is to manure very liberally, because that is the surest way to make the farm pay. Bone meal at the rate of 300 to 500 pounds per acre, or hard wood ashes at the rate of 100 bushels to the acre, will all answer very well in lieu of barn manure. In all cases it is of great importance, in top dressing grass lands, whether for pasture or mowing, after the application of seed and manure has been made, to roll thoroughly. A failure to roll will entail a loss of all the labor, by evaporation and drying of seed, if the pasture has been re-seeded.

ENSILAGE.

Q. What is your opinion, Mr. Crozier, of the ensilage system?

A. I have some hesitation in expressing an opinion of any system that I have not had actual experience with, and I have had nothing to do with ensilage. My success in stock raising, by the methods I have pursued for the last twenty years, has, perhaps, made me a little prejudiced against innovations of this kind; but I can only form an opinion in a general way on the subject. I cannot understand why a green crop, which we know contains from ninety to ninety-five per cent. of water, preserved by the ensilage system, can be equal to the same fodder from which the water has been expelled by drying, and which, when mixed with roots, as we do it, contains all the elements of a complete food. It seems to me that this must certainly be a cheaper and better system than ensilage. I speak with hesitation, however, on this subject, never having had practice with it, and am willing to suspend my final opinion until the system has had a further trial. I know that many have claimed that it has been a great success with them. On the other hand, I know of several cases where it has been abandoned, and the system of feeding, such as we practice, has been again resorted to. A large and successful stock raiser, in the vicinity of Toronto, Canada, who had expended $3,000 on silos, which he had constructed in the very best possible manner, after a three years' trial, says that he has abandoned the system, and has fallen back to the old method of feeding with dry fodder and roots during the winter months. Still, in this case, there may have been some bad application of the system, which made its working unsatisfactory, and, as I have before said, until it has had years of comparative trial with other methods, no decided opinion should be expressed; because no one man's or half a dozen men's experience of such an important matter should be final. The whole claim of the ensilage system, as I understand it, is that it is used instead of fresh green feed, and it certainly would be a great advantage for cattle for that purpose, if we had not mangels to mix with the dry fodder. Like all widely diverging systems of agriculture that have their special adherents, the only safe decision can be arrived at by observation of the results. If we find that herds of cattle raised by the silo can be kept in as good condition as those raised by the fodder and root system, then it may take precedence, provided that it can be shown that the expense attending such system is less, but if no better results entails an increased cost, then it will not be likely to supersede the old method. To those who are interested in this matter the proceedings of The Ensilage Congress, published by the New York Plow Co., New York, will give full information. In the *Country Gentleman*, of March 17th, 1881, is the following article written by me, on the subject of ensilage, which will give my views at length. I also add the corroboration of that opinion by F. D. Curtis, in a letter in the *Country Gentleman* of same date.

ENSILAGE NOT SAFE FEED.

"I had a letter from a German farmer, who, in his youth, had to take a good deal of sauer kraut. He says he still takes a little now and then, but on a cold winter's day he wants solid food. When Dr. Bailey and others preach ensilage they will doubtless cause many who read the *Country Gentleman* to look in a few years on their deserted silos with feelings of sadness. The cow *will* eat ensilage. Certainly she will; but how much will it benefit her? How much fat will a 1,000-pound cow gain on seventy pounds of ensilage per day? How much solid food is there in this seventy pounds? Some of our learned friends say not more than six per cent. If this is so, then cattle will do well on air and water. If the gentleman had said that cattle would eat 200 pounds, then I would have more belief in the benefits they might derive from it. When the Doctor states that village farmers can keep a cow on one-fourth or one-half an acre of land, we know that this is so. The German and French peasants, living near large cities where land is worth from $400 to $500 per acre, raise truck for village and city markets. They make pits, and put all the tops of their vegetables in them, and cover them up with earth, and this they repeat with two or three crops in a season; but it comes out in the winter like tea leaves after they have been steeped (not so green as people in America say the ensilage comes out); but how long do they run their cattle on this? Only a short time, you will find. You will remember that the first case of pleuro-pneumonia ever heard of in America was traced to Dutch cattle. Ensilage, I am afraid, will eventually injure the constitutions and hence weaken the lungs of cattle. Cows, they tell us, do well on brewers' grains. How long do they do well? My opinion is often asked whether ensilage is being fed by the breeders on the Channel Islands or in England? I think not. John Bull generally is somewhat more of an old fogy in such things than we Americans are, and does not jump so quick at conclusions, and saves himself, in consequence, much loss from unwise experiment. I beg to say, be not tempted by this new plan of feeding, until time will tell its true worth. WM. CROZIER.

"*Northport, L. I.*"

MR. CROZIER ENDORSED.

" The silo discussion is getting interesting. It is natural for people who attempt new schemes to imagine them successful, or at least to be loth to admit that they are failures. I have been in this position myself, and hence am inclined to take the declarations of the advocates of silos with some allowance. The imagination of experimenters often paint their attempts with rosy hues; but stern reality after awhile changes the picture. I fail to see, as yet, the practical value of going to so much trouble and expense to preserve water (juice), and cannot comprehend how this water can be increased in nutritive value by being preserved, even though it may have an alcoholic smell. The difference between cornstalks kept in a silo, and cornstalks cured, is almost entirely a difference in the amount of water contained in them. The shrinkage in water makes a shrinkage in weight and bulk, but can make only a small reduction in the nutritive qualities. Admit that there is by curing a small loss in the nutrition, is it equal to the cost of the silos and the extra labor required to preserve the fodder in it? Mr. Bailey, who is an ingenious, if not an interested writer on silos, takes the ground that a silo is not as expensive as a barn, and urges the point that silos may do away with barns, as they upset the principles of science. This is quite a radical position, to say the least; but it loses its force when we consider that barns are not necessary for the preservation of cornstalks. They will keep better in stacks, which is the most economical, and, at the same time, one of the best methods of preserving this kind of forage. Silos without a granary or meal box will, in my judgment, make disappointment in the yield of good butter. Mr. Crozier's system of feeding is, as I know by frequent observation, a practical success. I have never been on a farm where cattle were always in any better condition and more productive in rich milk and good butter than his. His system of root

feeding seems to furnish just the necessary quantity of succulent food required for health and a large yield. Too much watery food, which is the kind the silo must necessarily supply, is not the natural food for cattle in cold weather. That the stalks are all eaten, when taken from a silo, is no more true than when cured and cut up. I have doubted the economy, after repeated trials, of cutting stalks at all for cattle, as so little is left by them uneaten. It certainly will not pay to go through with all the silo processes in order to get the butts of cornstalks eaten up. There is no particular value in bulk, so long as bulk does not add strength to the food, and when it is considered that bulk makes a great deal heavier and more laborious handling, I fail to appreciate how two tons of bulk in a silo can be any better than one ton in which the nutritive elements are condensed. In other words, I cannot see how the presence of a ton of water should enhance the value of cornstalks. In warm weather this juice takes the place of water for drink, but in winter so much is not required and must be hurtful. I must endorse Mr. Crozier in his distrust of the practical value of silos, and commend his outspoken convictions, although he seems to be pitted almost alone against them. Cornstalks are good food for cows, but so succulent in their nature that when dry they should be fed with something more substantial, or the animal will rapidly run down. Silo fodder is still more washy, unless the fermentation furnishes a stimulant which is at the same time victuals and drink. May be this is one of the scientific principles which silos upset, proving that fermented juice is not a stimulant, but food, and food proper for transformation into milk and butter. Verily these are days of progress, when alcohol becomes food, and tallow (Oleomargarine) is butter.   F. D. CURTIS.
"*Kirby Homestead, N. Y.*"

(Mr. H.) I notice, Mr. Crozier, on a careful reading of the report of the Ensilage Congress, held in New York last year, that nearly all the members present were enthusiastic advocates of the system, and according to the statements there made, there is but little doubt that it has proved of value to many. Still I would have been pleased to have seen it compared with the feeding by root crops pulped, as you term it, after your method, because that seems to me the turning point of the whole controversy, as it is certainly unfair to make a comparison against dry food, such as meal, bran, etc., when mixed with cut corn fodder, instead of comparing it with the corn fodder or hay mixed with an equal weight of pulped or crushed roots. In this connection I will quote from a communication published in the *Country Gentleman* for April, 1881:

ENSILAGE COMPARED WITH ROOTS.

Let it be admitted that forty tons of green fodder can be produced. Then, to be fair, let us admit that forty tons of mangels per acre can be grown with equal ease and at no more cost, when put in the pits, than that of the fodder preserved in the silo. Then we are ready to compare the actual value of these two crops for feeding to dairy cows. The following figures are taken from the report of the Connecticut Experiment Station, and will be found to be authentic:

COMPOSITION OF

	FODDER CORN.	MANGELS.	SUGAR BEETS.
Water..	85.70	88.0	81.5
Ash..	1.23	0.8	0.7
Albuminoids..	1.20	1.1	1.0
Crude Fibre..	4.95	0.9	1.3
Carbohydrates..	6.73	9.1	15.4
Fat..	0.18	0.1	0.1

The advantage is twenty-five per cent. in favor of the mangels, and in favor of the sugar beets nearly 100 per cent., as regards nutritive value. A butter maker, whose business depends on the quality of his product, will hesitate to use sour or alcoholic fodder in a condition of decomposition, when he can use perfectly fresh and well flavored food, such as mangels or beets. It may be objected that the crop of forty tons of roots is extravagant; but it is not, either as regards mangels or Lane's Sugar Beet. By planting in rows thirty inches apart, and eighteen inches in the rows, roots of eight pounds each can be grown with ease. I have had them to weigh fourteen to twenty-four pounds each, and have grown fodder corn at the rate of sixty tons to the acre, and know that neither of these large crops can be grown without high fertilizing, and that it is as easy to grow roots as corn, and as easy to harvest the one as the other. Roots of eight pounds each, eighteen inches apart, will yield forty-six tons per acre, and, with the advantage in point of nutritive value, will be equal to about sixty tons of corn fodder, which not one in a hundred will reach as easily as one in ten will reach forty-six tons of mangels. Now it seems to me that it is a useful thing to point out these facts, when there is danger of many persons' heads being turned in regard to this new idea, and especially when it cannot be tried without the sinking of a few hundred dollars in making a silo, and gathering stone to pile on top of it. What are those farmers to do, who, unfortunately, have no stone for this purpose, and find the market for it strong at $4 a load? They need not fret, however, if they cannot have their silo, because they can grow mangels and sugar beets—the large variety of Lane's Improved, and not the sugar beet which is small—and do as well, perhaps, with these, as they could with ensilage. Doubtless the new improvement is of great value in its place; but its place is by no means universal, and when the present excitement is cooled down, it will probably be found of very rare application; but root growing and feeding roots are of universal application. H. STEWART.

Bergen County, N. J.

CHAPTER VIII.

LIVE STOCK OF THE FARM.

Cattle.

I suppose that the question I am about to ask you, Mr. Crozier, has been propounded to you in the past twenty years hundreds of times—what, in your opinion, is the most profitable breed of cattle, at the present day, for the farmer engaged in dairying?

JERSEY CATTLE.

A. I think the Jersey (or as it is sometimes improperly called, "Alderney," a name commonly applied to both Jerseys and Guernseys), is the most profitable for butter making, though for milk a crossbred between the Short Horn and the Jersey is the best, or a cross-bred between the Ayrshire and Jersey, will produce rich milk and more of it than the thoroughbred Jersey. Some twenty years ago I kept a small herd of Short Horns, and another of Ayrshires, together with Jerseys. The demand for Jersey butter since then has increased so much that I sold out the Short Horns and Ayrshires, and confined myself exclusively to Jerseys. In my opinion, for the dairy farmer who has a large city for a market, such as New York, Philadelphia, Boston, Chicago, Cincinnati or St. Louis, within three or four hundred miles, Jerseys are more profitable to raise at the present time than any other breed. For selling milk in the villages or cities I should say the Ayrshires were the most profitable. They are easy keepers, hardy, and will produce from 4,000 to 6,000 pounds of milk in one season, the milk generally bringing from four to five cents per pound at retail. The Ayrshire milk is considered to be the most healthful for children. But when the object is a large quantity of milk, without regard to fineness of quality, then the Dutch, or as they are commonly called, Holstein, would be preferable. It is claimed for this breed that they are large producers of milk; but my objection to them is that they are hard keepers, and will consume nearly double the amount of food that an Ayrshire cow can be kept on. Or, at least, I would rather keep two Ayrshire cows than one Holstein. I have had Ayrshire cows to give sixty pounds of milk

JERSEY CATTLE.

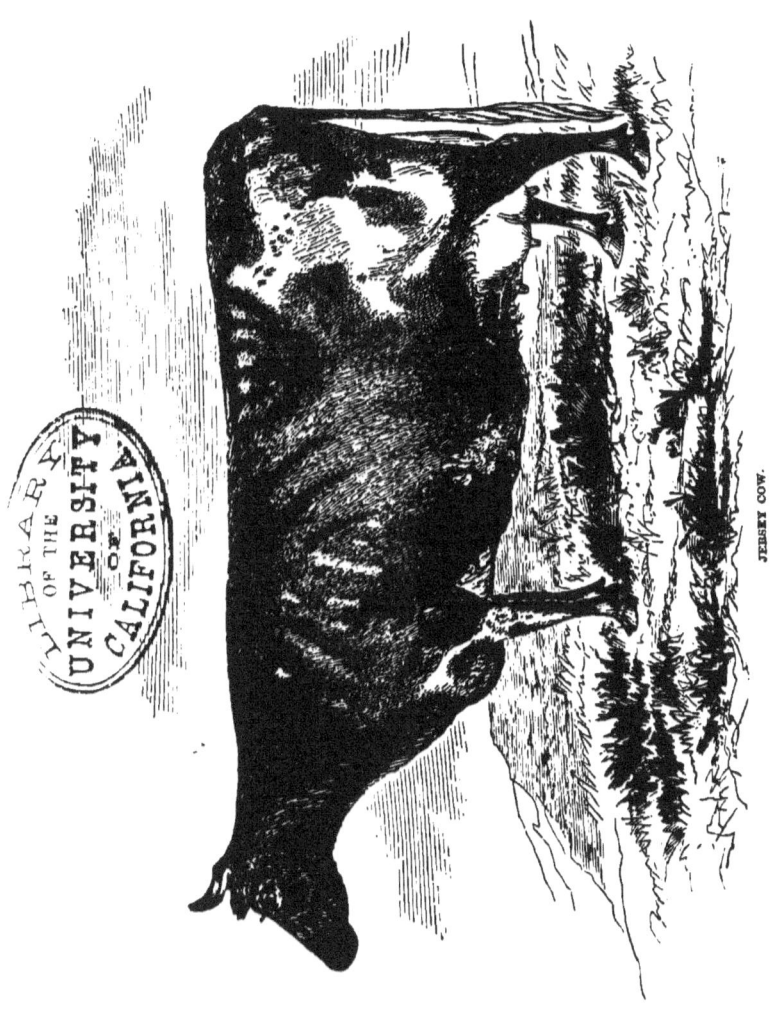

JERSEY COW.

per day when fresh, although it is claimed that the Holsteins have given, under the same conditions, eighty pounds. For this reason, the Holsteins being large milkers, are coming into demand somewhat, to supply cheese factories in the Western States, and will probably be the best cow for that purpose in the West, as the large amount of feed necessary to sustain them is not so great a consideration there as it is here with us. One great advantage of the Jersey cow, forty or fifty miles from a large city, is the cream, as cream can be sent that distance, and returns thirty-five cents per quart at least. I find that we get more butter from the Jersey milk than any other breed. The Jersey cow loves to be petted, and whatever kindness is shown her she gratefully returns in the pail; if used harshly there will be a great reduction in the quantities of milk and butter. She will milk the year round—at least that is my experience with them. I usually milk them within a month of the time of calving, which is of great value to those who have contracts to supply private families with butter the year around. I thus get a steady supply from these Jerseys, while other breeds do not hold to their milk so long, with the exception, perhaps, of the Ayrshires. For the purpose of stall feeding or soiling, they are just the cow that is wanted. Their calves are easily raised. In the last five years I have not lost over two per cent. Their bull calves, if not suited for breeding purposes, although they do not make so much weight as other breeds, when they are six or eight weeks old, make the best of veal. I have had calves that weighed, when two months old, 200 pounds, which brought eleven cents per pound when sold for veal. The Jersey cow, "Eurotas," produced in eleven months 778 pounds of butter, which sold for fifty cents a pound at the Fifth Avenue Hotel, New York. The Jersey cow, Mary Ann of St. Lambert's, 9,770, belonging to Mr. Valancey E. Fuller, Hamilton, Canada, was tested for thirty-one days, May 29th to June 28th (1883) inclusive, with the following results:

	MILK.	CREAM.	BUTTER, UNSALTED.	BUTTER, SALTED.
	LBS. OZ.	LBS. OZ.	LBS. OZ.	LBS. OZ.
1st week	291.0	74.9	22.8½	23.15
2d week	276.0	74.5	22.10	23.15
3d week	242.8	72.2	22.11½	24.0½
4th week	259.8	90.0	23.3	24.13
2 days	69.	22.12	6.7½	6.11
Total for 30 days			97.8½	103.6½
1 day	35.8	10.15	3.3½	3.6
Total for 31 days			100.12	106.12½

JERSEY CATTLE.

JERSEY BULL.

The following appeared in the *Breeder's Gazette*, July 5th, 1883:

BALTIMORE, Md., June 28th, 1883.

John G. Clark, Esq., President Maryland Breeders' Association:

SIR: In compliance with the request contained in your letter of the 13th ultimo, that we should assist in making a seven days' test of the Jersey cow, Value 2d, 6,844, owned by Messrs. Watts & Seth, of Baltimore, Md., we, the undersigned, would report as follows: That from Tuesday, the 19th of June, to Monday, June 25th, the product was 327 pounds of milk, from which twenty-five pounds, two and eleven-twelfths ounces of butter were produced.

Signed,
T. ALEX. SETH,
W. H. WEST,
A. M. FULFORD,
Committee.

This is the largest amount of butter from one cow, of any breed, that we have any authentic record of in this country. To further show what is done by a variety of cows of the Jersey breed we give the following, taken from the *Breeder's Gazette* of July 5th, 1883:

COWS THAT HAVE MADE FOURTEEN POUNDS AND OVER PER WEEK.

Eurotas, 2,454	22.07
Bomba, 10,330	21.11½
Valma Hoffman, 4,500	21.00
Pheadra, 2,561	19.14
Oak Leaf, 4,769	17.10
Gold Thread, 4,945	17.09
Mamie Coburn, 3,798	17.08
Welma, 5,942	17.08
Lass Edith, 6,290	17.00
Effie of Hillsdale, 1,521	16.15
Lida Mulin, 9,198	16.08
Lady Nina, 4,338	16.04
Lily of Maple Grove, 5,079	16.03
Grey Therese, 5,322	16.00
Myra 2d, 6,289	16.00
Lady Penn, 5,314	16.00
Pride of Corissande, 5,323	16.00
Emma Ganson, 6,283	16.00
Canto, 7,194	15.12
Lerna, 3,634	15.12

COWS THAT HAVE MADE FOURTEEN POUNDS AND OVER PER
WEEK.—(Continued.)

Myrtle 3d, 3,490	15.12
Niva, 7,523	15.08
Nymphea, 5,114	15.08
Zalma, 8,788	15.05
Crust, 1,775	15.00
Ideal, 11,842	14.12½
Maple Leaf, 4,768	14.12
Estrella, 2,831	14.12
Hartwick Belle, 7,722	14.08
Belle of Uwchland, 8,468	14.07
Marpetra, 10,284	14.06
Forsaken, 7,520	14.03½
Silver Sides, 3,857	14.03
Gilt 4th, 4,208	14.00
Canary Bird 2d, 4,264	14.00
Gilt Edge 2d, 4,420	14.00
Sasco Belle, 13,601	14.00
Bessie Bradford, 11,544	14.00
Spring Leaf, 5,796	14.00
Silver Bell, 4,313	14.00

A total of forty head.

These are records of extraordinary yields of butter, made by Jersey cows, under favorable conditions, and are above what can be expected from a general herd during the entire year. The record of my own herd of thirty cows, which I here submit, is far below any above given, but I flatter myself it will compare favorably with the yield of any herd for the same length of time, the extraordinary cases of special feeding or special animals being usually given for a day, a week or a month, and not for the year from the full herd. The record is for a herd of thirty cows for one year, commencing 1st of January, 1879:

	POUNDS.
January	693
February	635
March	1,031

(Here I sold off three cows.)

April	848
May	836
June	735
July	1,036
August	748
September	834
October	847
November	747
December	575
Butter sold	$4,823.50
Calves sold	4,711.00

EXPENSES.

Rent 40 acres	$500.00	
Pasture	200.00	
Cost of labor	800.00	
Salt for dairy and cows	26.00	
Expressage on butter	75.00	
Use of dairy fixtures	50.00	
Interest on value of stock	600.00	
		$2,251.00
Net profits on butter alone		$2,572.50
Value of calves sold		4,711.00
Total profits of the dairy alone		$7,283.50

I might say, in explanation of the seemingly small amount allowed for labor, that the work of the dairy was performed by my family of two daughters, and the care and feeding of the cattle was aided by my own labor and superintendence, which, if it had been hired, would probably have cost $1,000 more. The quantity of butter is taken from my account book; the expenses are estimated as nearly as possible, but are certainly not underestimated. No estimate is made for purchased food, as the value of the skimmed milk fed to pigs will amply offset that.

Q. According to this statement you show a profit, for a herd of thirty cows, to be over $7,000. As much of that is due to the high price received for the calves, and also to the high price, fifty cents a pound, received for the butter, what would be the probable profits derived from an ordinary working dairy?

A. In any common working dairy it is easily possible to make such a quality of butter as will sell for fifty cents a pound, if the proper care is taken in feeding and caring for the cows, and in managing the milk and the butter. It is only poor butter that is hard to sell; the highest quality is scarce, and there is a demand for more than is produced. Hence the profits on the butter from an ordinary dairy, stocked with good grade Jerseys or Ayrshires, should be as much, or very nearly as much, as from this herd. As regards the calves, it must be remembered that their high price is due to the large amount of capital invested in the cows. With cows of less value, the profits from the calves will of course be reduced in proportion. In other parts of this book we have tried to show the advantage of cultivating five acres well over twenty-five acres in a slipshod manner. Here too we would say, in choosing the cows for the dairy, it is better to have the best that can be procured, rather than waste good work and good feed upon inferior stock.

GUERNSEY CATTLE.

The Guernsey cow is larger than the Jersey, and is considered by some as equally profitable, her butter being as excellent in texture and flavor, and commanding as high a price in our cities. In my experience the Guernsey is in no way superior to the Jersey, nor do I think she is equal to the Jersey. I kept Guernseys for six or seven years, and they, like the Short Horns and Ayrshires, were sold to make room for Jerseys. I found they consumed more food than the Jerseys, which of course tends to reduce their value. These cattle come from an island near to, and in the same group, as the island of Jersey, and have been bred with much care. They are yellowish and reddish in color, with white intermixed, and are much liked by some persons who have tried them. Being larger bodied and stouter than the Jerseys, they make very fair beef when fatted, and when crossed upon common cows produce very good dairy cattle.

Considerable attention has been drawn of late to Guernsey cattle by the importations made by L. W. Ledyard, Esq., of Fernwood Farm, Cazenovia, N. Y. Mr. Ledyard has made several visits to the island of Guernsey, and has selected his stock with much judgment. The following records go to show that Mr. Ledyard made a fortunate selection, and that his best Guernseys are not surpassed in quantity and quality of butter product, except by a few of the best of the Jerseys. The cow, Countess of Fernwood, of which a portrait is here given, has the following record for seven days, ending November 28th, 1883, viz.: $303\frac{1}{2}$ pounds of milk and eighteen pounds, fifteen ounces of butter, equal to a pound of butter from sixteen pounds, or a little more than seven quarts, of milk. In the week ending December 11th, 1883, Countess of Fernwood's product was nineteen pounds, one ounce.

Of his herd Mr. Ledyard says: "I have another cow that will run over fifteen pounds in a week, and my impression is that the Guernseys will show as large tests as any other breed, and in time are quite likely to show phenomenal results, although I do not give these the importance usually accorded them."

Of Countess of Fernwood he states, that her milk set until sour, and all churned has shown three pounds, three ounces per day of unsalted butter, a product very nearly equalling that of the highest yet attained, and this without forcing, by which large products have been made from noted cows, with fatal results in some cases.

Of other Guernsey cows in this herd the following records are given:

TEST OF IMPORTED GUERNSEY COW, "LADY MAY," NO. 531.

DATE OF MILKING.	MILK.	DATE OF CHURNING.	BUTTER.
Dec. 11th, 1883.	34¼ lbs.	Dec. 14th.	2 lbs., 7½ oz.
Dec. 12th, "	35¼ "	Dec. 15th.	2 " 8 "
Dec. 13th, "	33½ "	Dec. 16th.	2 " 8½ "
Dec. 14th, "	35½ "	Dec. 17th.	2 " 8 "
Dec. 15th, "	33¼ "	Dec. 18th.	2 " 5 "
Dec. 16th, "	33½ "	Dec. 19th.	3 "
Dec. 17th, "	33¾ "	Dec. 20th.	3 " 1 "
7 even days.	239 lbs.		18 lbs., 6 oz.

Weather very variable, mercury falling suddenly below zero; she unfortunately took a little cold in her udder, which made it prudent to cut down her feed (which was not heavy), just as she was doing her full work. The butter was dry and not salted.

TEST OF "POLLY OF FERNWOOD," NO. 1,565, IMPORTED IN SEPT., 1883.

DATE OF MILKING.	MILK.	DATE OF CHURNING.	BUTTER, DRY, NOT SALTED.
Dec. 18th, 1883.	30 lbs.	Dec. 21st.	2 lbs., 12 oz.
Dec. 19th, "	30¼ "	Dec. 22d.	2 " 8½ "
Dec. 20th, "	31¾ "	Dec. 23d.	3 "
Dec. 21st, "	32½ "	Dec. 24th.	2 " 14 "
Dec. 22d, "	28¾ "	Dec. 26th.	2 " 4 "
Dec. 23d, "	30¼ "	Dec. 27th.	2 " 12 "
Dec. 24th, "	29½ "	Dec. 28th.	2 " 15 "
7 even days.	213 lbs.		19 lbs., 1½ oz.

Weather very variable and trying, mercury once eighteen below zero, and heavy gales.

MILKING RECORD OF FERNWOOD GUERNSEY HERD, DECEMBER 28TH, 1883, WEATHER VARYING AND VERY COLD.

11	Home bred and acclimated cows.
1	Two-year-old heifer.
8	Heifers with first calf, just out of quarantine after a very hard voyage.
5	Cows in same condition.
25	In all.

Average time since calving two months and twenty-five days; the heifers had calved in the fall; some of the older cows in milk a long time. Average weight of milk for an even twenty-four hours, seven-

GUERNSEY COW.

teen pounds, ten ounces. The milk of two or three went to their calves; that of two weighing twenty pounds, twelve ounces, and twenty-one pounds were put in a creamery for heifer tests; the remainder, 393 pounds, was set ten hours in a large, open, deep pan, and the cream made January 1st, 1884, twenty-two pounds of hard butter, so yellow as to need no color, the latter never being used on the farm. This is a pound from seventeen pounds, twelve ounces of milk, when the cream was not fully extracted. The sweet milk was left fully equal to ordinary normal milk. This system has since been changed to using two open pans of the same kind, one holding the milk fifteen and the other twenty-two hours; this gets the most high flavored cream for butter, and leaves a very rich milk for calves.

The thirteen newly imported Guernseys in the above list passed through the storm of August 29th, and were so hardly used by the rough sea that three fine cows died from injuries; all these were, and still are, thin.

This is a record, not of selected animals, but of every milking cow on the farm.

ALDERNEY CATTLE.

Although the cattle known by the name of Alderney are not of themselves of any importance to us, yet it may be well to notice them here, if only for the purpose of removing the quite common impression that this name relates as a synonym to the Jersey cattle. Alderney is the third of the Channel Islands in size, and is but a very insignificant spot, not much larger than a fair sized American farm, and smaller than some. But it possesses a race of cattle that were known as the Alderneys before the Jerseys were ever heard of. Forty or fifty years ago Alderneys were in demand in England for gentlemen's parks as ornamental animals, just as fawns and deer were tamed and kept in such places. These small, graceful cows furnished a small quantity of rich milk for the table, as well as made a pretty picture upon the lawn. As this class of cattle came into repute, Jersey was drawn upon for a supply, but the name Alderney was still retained, until the exportation from Jersey increased very much, and the Jersey cattle became improved in character, so as to make profitable stock for farms. The two races are entirely distinct, although they have some points in common, such as the graceful form, the fawn colors and their rich milk. But the Alderneys are smaller than the Jerseys, less numerous by far, and generally spotted white and fawn in color, while the Jerseys vary very much in their colors.

AYRSHIRE CATTLE.

The Ayrshire cow is probably most valuable for the special production of milk and cheese. In Edinburgh, Glasgow and other large cities of Scotland fresh milk brings six cents per quart, and skimmed milk and buttermilk half that price. In that climate there is no cow that does better, as they have produced as high as forty quarts of milk per day. They are very hardy and active in seeking their own provender. They mature early. The bullocks or steers make the very best of work cattle, and when slaughtered their beef is of average quality, but not equal to that of the Short Horns or Herefords. In the United States the Ayrshire cow fills a large place, being, from

AYRSHIRE COW.

her great milking qualities, valuable for milk dairies in the neighborhood of our large cities. They will give as high as 7,000 pounds of milk per year. The butter is rather pale, and to bring an average price must be colored. They are of hardy constitution, breeding from two years-old until twenty. They are in demand for the hills of Maine, Connecticut, New Hampshire and Pennsylvania, as they seem to thrive and do better in those sections than any other breed.

HOLSTEIN CATTLE.

The Holsteins, too, have their advocates, and within the last few years hundreds have been imported into this country, with the expectation that they will be suitable, from their great milking qualities, for some sections, particularly for the western country, to supply the numerous cheese factories that have been started there recently. They are of enormous size, and consume a large amount of feed; but they produce large quantities of milk, which is sold to these cheese factories for about two cents per quart. Some claims are made for them as butter cows; but they excel for the production of cheese, and in those sections of the country where feed is plentiful, they will no doubt prove to be very valuable. They are a very handsome breed, pure

HOLSTEIN COW.

black and white in color, and are much fancied on this account. This breed is claimed to make good beef. As to this I am unable to say, as I have had no experience with them for that purpose.

DEVON CATTLE.

The Devon cow is one of the hardiest of all improved breeds. In districts suitable for them the Devons will give a large yield of milk, and it is of excellent quality. It is believed to produce more and better butter than almost any other breed except the Jerseys or Guernseys. They are easily kept and are of gentle disposition. They are well suited for the rough hills of New England or the mountains of Pennsylvania, where they are also much used as working oxen, and preferred for that purpose above all other cattle. On new lands, or lands that are rough, they make the best team for plowing. They are easily trained and very intelligent, and I think superior for that purpose to any other breed. In Devonshire, England, it is claimed that when stall fed, this breed makes better beef than any other, and they have often carried off prizes at the Christmas shows when exhibited as beef cattle. Their long horns are a serious objection to them with Western cattle men, as being in the way of shipping them in the cars; but for farm grazing and feeding for beef they have some valuable points.

SCOTCH POLLED CATTLE.

This class of cattle includes the Galloway, and the Angus, or Aberdeen, breeds. They have been recently introduced from Scotland into this country. They are a beef animal, the cows having little reputation, even in Scotland, as milkers. They are of large size, black in color, of compact form and hornless. They are exceedingly easy keepers, mature early, and the beef is said to be of excellent quality. They are, perhaps, better suited for cold climates than any other breed. For this reason they are well adapted to Canada, or the extreme portions of our Northern States, where the finer breeds would be too tender. The demand for them in the West seems to be

SCOTCH POLLED COW.

taking the place of the Short Horns, and they are rapidly becoming popular there, on account of the absence of horns, and their special advantages and value for Western grazing. Recent single importations have numbered over 400 head.

There is another class of polled cattle which are excellent dairy stock. These are the Polled Norfolk. These are deep red in color, of good form, and, with the exception of the horns, very much like the Devons in appearance. They are fair dairy cattle, and, like all hornless cattle, quiet and docile in disposition. They have been recently introduced into this country, and are meeting with considerable favor with farmers who object to horns upon their cattle.

HEREFORD CATTLE.

The Herefords are the standard beef cattle of the County of Hereford, in England. These, and the Devons, are the two oldest breeds of domesticated cattle known to exist. I think it was probably fifty or sixty years ago that this breed was first introduced into this country, and there is hardly a section throughout New England, New York or Pennsylvania but you will find the mark of the Herefords among their herds. They have been bred so long, that where the bulls have been used among our native cows their progeny is marked with about the same color. All Herefords, without exception, have white faces; a brown, or dull red color, on the body, with a white stripe on the back; are compactly built, and have very little offal when they come to the shambles. In the past few years they have compared favorably with the Short Horns, weight for weight, in the carcass; but their beef is more valuable, as there is less waste in it, being mixed, with the fat evenly distributed throughout the carcass. When crossed with our native cows their progeny make

HEREFORD BULL.

useful animals for the milkman or dairyman, or for the farmer for grazing or stall feeding. As working oxen the steers are found to be remarkably gentle and docile, but slower than the Devons. For a few years past they have been extensively introduced into the West for stall feeding and grazing on the plains. They have become very popular there, since they have taken several first premiums at the fat cattle exhibitions.

SHORT HORN CATTLE.

This excellent breed of cattle, which used to stand first in the estimation of breeders in America, seems to have lost rank, and to be meeting with very close competition from the Hereford and the Scotch Polled cattle, which are rapidly taking their place in the West. A few years ago there was an enormous speculation in this breed of cattle, and $30,000 was actually paid for one single cow; but to-day the average price for a good pure bred Short Horn cow is

SHORT HORN COW.

about $200. It is claimed for them that there are families of good milkers in the breed, but, as far my experience goes, it takes two cows or mothers to raise one calf. I saw Dutchess 75th when in this country, and again at Lord Dunmore's in Scotland, when she was being prepared for the Christmas show of fat cattle. She had all the turnips, oil cake, peas and beans she could eat, and grew to such an enormous weight that, while standing up, she had to be put in slings, lest her limbs would give out; but after all this feeding and care, a Polled Angus cow led at nearly all the Christmas shows of beef cattle in London, the Herefords coming in second. I saw once a new importation of Short Horns, where the dams of the calves could not feed them, and Ayrshires were imported at the same time to supply this want. Originally the Short Horns were the best of dairy cattle, and were valued on that account as much as for beef. That they have so fallen off in the dairy by being bred solely for beef, and have fallen off as beef cattle by being bred too much for fat, shows how a splendid race of cattle may be destroyed by mismanagement. One family only of this breed, known as the Princess family, have now a reputation for milk and butter, although occasionally a few individual cows are found to be good milkers and butter makers. Some of the grade Short Horns are excellent dairy cows. Short Horns are not much used for oxen. They mature, when fed on rich feed, at an early age, but their beef is much better in quality at five or six years old, when they will dress from 1,400 to 1,500 pounds. The Texas

FAT SHORT HORN HEIFER.

cows have been much improved by the use of Short Horn bulls, and in fact, a large proportion of the Western cattle now show the Short Horn cross, which has much improved the native stock of the Western country.

SWISS CATTLE.

The Swiss cows I think a great acquisition to our dairy stock. Switzerland is a grand dairy country, and some of the Swiss cows have been bred with great care for many years. Some importations were made a few years ago, and the progeny of these, which have been kept pure, have been scattered considerably through New England, Pennsylvania and some other localities. There are several good sized herds and quite a number of smaller ones, which are gradually enlarging, and I think these cattle will soon be heard of more than they are now. They are something like the Ayrshire in form, but larger and heavier, of a yellow and red color spotted with white; are naturally quiet and docile and heavy milkers; some of them are said to yield two pounds and over of butter per day. It is claimed that one cow has given over 600 pounds in a year and 3,000 pounds in six years, all of which has sold for more than $1,500. Their native country is full of mountains and valleys, and consequently these cattle are hardy and active, and suitable to the rougher parts of this country.

TEXAS CATTLE.

The cattle of Texas and Florida are the descendants of the stock brought over from Spain by the early settlers of the Gulf regions. They are of no interest to the farmer of the Northern, Eastern or Middle States, and seem only to be fitted for a place on the Texan and other Western prairies, where they are still the leading breed used for beef purposes, but in all probability they are destined to become the basis for a greatly improved race of useful cattle, through crossing by the Short Horns, Herefords or other improved breeds.

The following are the distinctive "points" of the leading breeds:

JERSEY COW.

Purity of Breed.—A reputation for producing rich, yellow butter by the ancestors of both parents.

Head.—Small, fine and tapering.

Eye.—Full and lively.

Face.—Lean, muzzle often encircled with buff color, dished.

Horns.—Crumpled, short and fine.

Ears.—Small and orange colored within.

Neck.—Slender and tapering to the head.

Back.—Straight from withers to setting on of tail.

Chest.—Deep and nearly on the line with the belly.

Hide.—Thin, movable, but not too loose, well covered with soft hair and yellow in color.

Barrel.—Hooped and deep, well ribbed, with little space between the ribs and hips.

Tail.—Long and thin.

Legs.—Forelegs straight and fine; thighs full and long, close together when viewed from behind; hind legs short, bones fine, hocks small, not crossed in walking.

Color.—Creamy fawn, deeper fawn and squirrel gray, with white, occasionally, in patches.

Udder.—Well up behind; teats large and squarely placed, wide apart; good fore teats, with large milk veins running well forward; free from coarse hair.

Disposition.—Docile.

AYRSHIRE COW.

Breed.—As in the Jersey, purity of breed in both sire and dam.

Head.—Rather long and narrow.

Eye.—Not as full as the Jersey, placid, and not strikingly large.

Face.—Small; muzzle and nose variable in color.

Ear.—Small and fine; orange colored within.

Horns.—Tapering, with an upward and outward turn, and set wide apart.

Neck.—Medium length, clean in the throat and tapering to the head.

Chest.—Wide and round, the "wedge shape" of the animal, from the hind quarter forward, arising more from a thin, flat shoulder, than from any undue narrowness of chest.

Back.—Straight; loins wide; hips high.

Hide.—Soft and mellow, with soft and thick hair; woolly and mossy underneath.

Barrel.—Deep and round.

Tail.—Long and slim, and set well into the back.

Legs.—Delicate and fine in the bone, and well knit together at the joints.

Udder.—In this breed is most important, as the Ayrshires have been bred almost exclusively with reference to their milking qualities. Should be capacious but not fleshy, broad and square in front and show large behind; the teats should stand well apart, and be long, but not coarse.

Color.—Dark red, rich brown or mahogany, running into almost a black; sometimes broken, blotched and spotted with white.

Disposition.—Gentle and quiet.

HOLSTEIN COW.

Breed.—Purity of pedigree on both sides.

Head.—Small and long.

Eye.—Full.

Face.—Long and lean.

Horns.—Medium length, with upward turn.

Ears.—Large and yellow within.

Neck.—Slim.

Back.—Straight.

Chest.—Deep.
Hide.—Thin and soft.
Barrel.—Round and full.
Tail.—Medium length.
Legs.—Fore legs short; hind legs long and slender.
Color.—Black and white always; sometimes white stripe across middle of back.
Udder.—Large both rear and front.
Disposition.—Gentle; easy to handle.

DEVON COW.

Breed.—Purity on both sides.
Head.—Small, lean and bony.
Face.—Straight; muzzle fine; nostrils open.
Eye.—Prominent and clear; mild and gentle in its expression.
Ear.—Thin; medium size.
Horns.—Light, tapering, with waxy color toward extremity.
Neck.—Medium length; clean and well set upon the shoulders.
Back.—Loins and hips broad, and running on a line with setting of tail.
Chest.—Deep and round, carrying its fullness well back of the elbow, affording abundant internal room for the action of the heart and lungs.
Hide.—Soft and mellow, but not too fine, and covered with short, thick and fine hair.
Barrel.—Round and straight; ribs almost circular, and extending well back and springing nearly horizontally from the vertebræ, giving great capacity.
Tail.—At its junction level with the back; long; very slender in its cord, and finishing with a tassel of white hair.
Legs.—Not too short, and standing straight and square behind; bone small, sinews large and clean.
Color.—Deep red, always growing lighter around the muzzle.
Udder.—Should be capacious, free from long hair.
Disposition.—Gentle.

HEREFORD COW.

Breed.—As in all cases, purity in sire and dam.
Head.—Moderately small, with a good width of forehead, tapering to the muzzle.
Face.—White.

Eye.—Very small and cheerful in expression.

Horns.—Long and rather coarse, with outward and generally downward turn.

Neck.—Medium length and tapering finely to the head.

Back.—Loin and hips should be broad and level.

Chest.—Broad, round and deep, running well back, with springing fore rib, giving great interior capacity.

Hide.—Soft and loose, covered with long silky hair.

Barrel.—Round, reaches close up to hind-quarters.

Tail.—Large and full at its point of attachment, but fine in its cord.

Legs.—Straight, upright and firmly placed, and well apart.

Color.—Red or rich brown, sometimes darker, white on brisket and along the back.

Udder.—Broad, full, extending forward and well up behind.

Disposition.—Cheerful and lively.

SHORT HORN OR DURHAM COW.

Breed.—Should show unbroken descent on both sides from known animals entered in English herd book.

Head.—Small, lean and bony, tapering to the muzzle.

Face.—Somewhat long, the fleshy portion of the nose of delicate color.

Eye.—Prominent, bright and clear.

Horns.—Short, light in substance, waxy in color and evenly set on the head.

Ears.—Large and thin.

Neck.—Rather short than long, and tapering to the head; clean in the throat and full at the base.

Back.—Loin and hips should be broad, forming a straight and even line from the neck to setting on of tail, full behind the shoulder.

Chest.—Broad, deep, round and full back of the elbows.

Hide.—Soft under the touch, with soft mossy hair.

Tail.—Flat and broad at its root, but fine in its cord, and placed high up on the rump.

Legs.—Short, straight and standing square with the body.

Udder.—Should reach well forward, roomy behind, and teats wide apart and of good size.

Disposition.—Gentle.

In all breeds the points of the bull should as nearly resemble those of the cow as it is possible for the male to resemble the female, and especially so when milk or butter is the object.

THE BEST COW FOR THE DAIRY.

Q. Judging from the expressions of opinion advanced by you, Mr. Crozier, from your personal experience, and from the data that we have been able to gather on this important subject, as to what is the most profitable breed of cattle for dairy purposes, particularly for butter and cream, the conclusion to be arrived at is that the Jersey cow, as she stands to-day, is the breed *par excellence*. But may not fashion in this case, as in other things, have had something to do in giving the Jerseys so much prominence?

A. In my experience with the different breeds of cattle, I find none that will produce as much cream and butter in 365 days, and breed at the same time, as the Jersey cow—that is, if she is properly treated and taken care of. I have no doubt that if the Jersey cow has to rough it, that there are other breeds of coarser texture that would be found better adapted for taking care of themselves; but with proper care the Jersey, in my opinion, is by all odds the best breed we have for the production of cream and butter.

Q. But, as you know, there are comparatively few Jersey cows in the country, and, on account of their scarcity, are valued very highly, and are quite beyond the reach of the great mass of farmers, who could not possibly stock their farms with Jersey cattle. What, then, would you recommend to a farmer as the best dairy cow for general use—first for milk, next for butter?

A. That question opens up a wide subject, because it not only includes the selection of the cow, but the breeding and crossing of varieties, as well as the improvement of the native cows by the use of pure bred bulls. I will, therefore, give my ideas as fully as may be necessary on this very important question. As you say, there are not enough Jersey cows, nor, indeed, Ayrshires, or any other pure breed, to go around among our five million farmers. There are probably 40,000 Jersey cows only in the country, and perhaps half as many pure Ayrshires; and about 4,000 Holsteins. Devons, Polls, Herefords and Short Horns, I do not count as dairy cows. There are, perhaps, a few hundred Swiss cows. All these are in the hands of farmers who can afford to pay large prices for them. The great bulk of the dairy products of the country is from the native cows, made up of mixtures of Short Horns, Devons, Herefords and Ayrshires, which have been brought here by the first settlers and have been crossed and recrossed for 200 years until the traces of the original parents have been wholly lost, and we have a mixed sort which we call native. There is the best of blood at the bottom, and I believe the common native cows are susceptible of very great improvement if the same care should be given to them as has been given to what we call the pure breeds. During twenty years, or more, past, there has been a considerable mixture of Jersey and Ayrshire blood among the native stock, and traces of it are seen in almost every part of the country, more or less. So that the native cattle, as they are called, have a foundation upon which, by careful breeding, an excellent herd may be built up. And, in reply to your question, I should say, first, that a well selected herd of native cattle, showing a large trace of Ayrshire or Short Horn blood, would make the best cows for an ordinary working milk dairy. Next to these I would place cattle showing traces of Devon blood. And third, for the common butter dairy, I would select a herd of natives, having Jersey blood in them, of the best kind I could find, and then procure a good Jersey bull to improve them with. No farmer need complain or feel envious because he has not the means to purchase a herd of pure bred registered Jerseys. He can very easily procure a bull of first rate family record for butter production to improve his native stock with, and in a few years would possess a herd in all respects as good for yield of butter as a herd of pure bred cows.

The cost would be very soon repaid. If a farmer even borrowed $1,000 for the purchase of a two-year-old bull of good pedigree, he would get the money back again very quickly from a herd of twenty-five cows only. This is easily seen. The first year he would have twelve heifer calves and twelve the second year; the third year there would be eighteen heifer calves and twelve young half-bred cows. These young cows, with this breeding, would alone be worth all the bull cost, which would be only about $80 each. The fourth year there would be thirty young cows, easily worth $2,500, because no one who had them would sell them for that price. At the end of the fifth year the increase of the herd would number 100 cows, and if each one was worth only $10 more than a common cow, the bull would have been paid for. But after the third cross some of the cows, perhaps half of them, would produce butter enough to pay a good interest on $200 each. I think this answers your question as to the best cow for the dairy for the working farmer who is unable to procure the costly pure bred Jersey cows.

Several cases have come to my knowledge in which farmers have bought a well bred Jersey bull for $500 or more and crossed it upon their native cows, with the result, that in less than five years the extra product of butter, at thirty cents a pound, from the half and three-quarter bred cows, has alone, every year, repaid the whole cost of the bull in a herd of twenty cows and upwards. And the same result has been reached by using pure bred Ayrshire and Holstein cows in milk dairies and cheese dairies.

FEED AND CARE OF COWS FOR MILK AND BUTTER.

Q. You have given the results of the profit derived from your dairy product. Will you now state your mode of feeding and caring for milch cows, that give these results during the entire season, beginning at the 1st of January? Your answer may, in some respects, repeat information you have already given; but as the subject is all-important, and should be given in a consecutive manner, I think our readers will pardon any slight repetition in this matter.

A. As I have before stated, I was formerly a great believer in steamed feed for milch cows; but latterly I have changed to cutting corn stalks, hay or "oats and peas," and mixing this cut feed with bran, ground oats, pulped or crushed mangels and salt. Turnips I do not feed to milch cows, as they would flavor the butter, unless great care were used to feed the turnips immediately after the cows have been milked; and, as we find this would entail special trouble, we think it better not to feed turnips at all, as mangels answer every purpose. Besides, mangels give a heavier weight of crop from the ground. If, however, turnips, or any other food, has been used, that taints the cream, it will be neutralized to some extent by putting in a teaspoonful of saltpetre to every twenty quarts of milk.

I very often feed some ground cotton seed cake meal, as it enriches the milk, instead of, as formerly, feeding oil cake or linseed meal. The cotton seed meal is ground fine, and fed at the rate of two to four quarts per day. If the cow has gone a period of five or six months with calf, I reduce it to one quart. The regular feed—that is, the mixture of cut fodder, mangels, meal, etc.—is mixed in the barn, enough being cut to last a week at a time. About a bushel basketful is fed to each animal, morning and evening, and a little hay given in the middle of the day, after the cows have been watered. If the weather is very cold at that season I feed a little heavier, and sometimes mix a little hot water with it. The drinking water given to the cows should be slightly warmed, so as to make it as near blood heat as possible. This method of feeding is continued until the middle of May in this climate. If the cows are coming into calving I avoid feeding ground oats, by which I think I keep them in better condition. I also generally give them a few small doses of salts and sulphur just before calving time. About the middle of May green rye is ready to cut; this is run through the machine and mixed with the feed already named, which is the first process of soiling, being fed in small quantities at first, so as to gradually accustom them to the summer soiling. The rye is fed until clover comes in, which is followed by "oats and peas," lucern and fodder corn, lasting into November, when the feeding with dry fodder and roots is again begun. In feeding dry cows, I find it very profitable to cut up wheat straw and mix it with crushed turnips, giving about sixty pounds of turnips and twenty pounds of straw per day to two-year-old animals. The bulls are fed exactly as the milch cows. In addition to the matter of feed in the winter treatment, we consider it to be of the first importance to have the animals thoroughly curried and brushed, and the pores of the skin kept open. This is done every morning with each animal, and an abundance of clean straw is daily supplied for bedding. By this manner of liberal feeding, warm shelter and beds in winter, absolute cleanliness and careful watchfulness, I attribute not only exemption from abortion, milk fever and other similar troubles of the stock raiser, but have a certainty, from the products of the dairy, that the work is remunerated by a balance on the right side of the ledger.

YOUNG CATTLE.

Q. You have said nothing as yet, Mr. Crozier, of your manner of raising young stock. From the specimens I now see in your barns I would like to know the method by which you have raised them to such perfection. For it would certainly give great pleasure if every one interested in stock raising could see that herd of deer-like Jerseys, and I am persuaded that they would be convinced, as I am, that you practice as well, and I think a little better, than you preach.

A. I consider the primary reason for my success in raising young cattle to be, that the mothers are kept in the very best possible condition of health. This condition of health I believe is produced and continued only by the systematic method of feeding and care that has been here described and which I have practiced for years. Probably our mode of winter feeding has more to do with this than anything else. During the five years I have practiced this system, I have had sufficient evidence to prove that a higher degree of health and vigor is imparted to the animals than can be hoped for when the process of steaming the feed is followed. I had as fair success with the cows and calves when using the steamed feed as I could well expect, but since I have changed to my present system all the stock are more vigorous and healthier than ever before. While using the steamed feed we found that the average of milk during the twelve months was perhaps more than it is now, but I believe it stimulated the cows too much, and the effect was seen in the calves, which were not so strong and were more difficult to raise.

When the calf is dropped, our method is to take it at once from the cow and rub it dry with straw or a cloth. Many farmers think it necessary for the good of the cow that she should lick the calf dry. I do not think so. It is the natural way, no doubt, but a cow is a domesticated animal and we can do this work for her better than she can, and it is more cleanly. The calf is then taken to a box stall where it can be kept quiet and out of hearing of the cow. The milk is taken from the cow and given to the calf, it being necessary for a few times to give it the finger to suck, but it can very soon be taught to drink from the pail without this assistance. After about nine days the milk from the cow is changed to skimmed milk, which is mixed with oatmeal and ground flaxseed, boiled in water to a thin gruel, and a little salt; when this is added to the milk it will be about blood heat. My plan of taking the calf from the cow as soon as it is dropped is, I know, in opposition to the usual method, which allows the calf to suck its dam for a few days. But where this is done the change of taking the calf away injures both it and the dam. She gets acquainted with it, and when you take it away she becomes restless, and gets into a fever; and the same with the calf, looking for her mother. In addition to this, my plan of removing the calf at once trains the calf, so that when she becomes a cow she never looks for the calf, and does not fret and worry over it. This is quite important in a dairy. If the cow's udder becomes inflamed, we bathe it in hot water, as hot as the hand will bear, using a soft sponge, and afterwards taking a portion of the cow's milk and rubbing it gently, care being taken to dry off all milk clean from the udder, that none should be left to curd. This artificial means we believe to be safer and better than if the calf were allowed to nurse on the cow, as when it does not get milk freely from the cow, it will punch with its head so hard as to often ruin the cow for life. This, I believe, is the cause of so many quarters of the udder being lost. No use is ever made of the milk of the cow for the first nine days, except to feed the calf.

The calves are fed twice a day, about seven in the morning and the same hour at night. While young, great care is taken not to overfeed them, which will cause indigestion and this stops the growth of the calf at once. It also causes diarrhœa, which is the most fatal disease among young calves. Three quarts of milk is enough for one meal for a young calf, at first. The feed is gradually increased up to four quarts at a meal and the calf should not be permitted to drink too fast. A little care in these respects will ensure healthy calves. After a month, a little oatmeal and linseed meal may be given once a day, not more than an ounce to begin with, if it is not given with the milk; and some fine hay may also be supplied, of which the calf will soon begin to eat. The feed is carefully increased by degrees up to six or eight months. At this age some Jersey calves will breed and the sexes should be separated to prevent this. When putting calves to pasture, care is required to avoid gorging with wet grass, or chilling after overheating, by which that common, and always fatal, disease, "blackleg," may be caused. About May the yearlings are turned into a grass lot or paddock near to the barns, and are given a mash of bran, made into a drink, once a day. They are brought into the barns at night, and tied up and fed the same feed as that given to the cows, in due proportion. They are carded and brushed and treated generally the same as the cows, being handled all over, so that when they come to be cows they are docile, and need no training, or "breaking in," as it is called. Only the cow calves are thus reared. Only those bull calves are reared which are from the best milkers; these are always reserved for breeding purposes. It is our aim to improve the butter quality and quantity by this means, as certainly "like will beget like," and, if not at first, it always will at some time; and it is my opinion that this is the great point in breeding, for the reason that one bull will get fifty calves while a cow is producing one. I paid, in 1865, for a Jersey bull not two years old, $1,000, and my neighbors thought at that time I should have been put into an asylum, such a price for a Jersey never having been heard of; but it was the best investment I have ever made, as the produce proved to be of the highest standard.

Q. As you are thus particular in breeding, I presume you do not rear every calf that is dropped, as some may turn out to be inferior. What are the distinguishing points of the most promising calves?

A. When a calf is dropped an expert can tell at a glance whether it is likely to be a good cow or not. There are many points which altogether go to make up the general appearance, which strikes him at once. The head and neck are the most important of these; the head should be thin, long and fine; the ears fine and free from coarse hair; the eyes large; the face broad across the eyes; the neck is slender and tapers finely to the head; the hair is fine and silky; the legs fine and deer-like; but the udder marks are perhaps the most convincing along with all these. If the teats are well formed and are placed well apart and the skin of the future udder is loose, then the calf will have every promise of a good cow, and this promise rarely fails. On the contrary, a coarse, rough-haired calf with little apparent udder formation, will be apt to turn out a poor cow. This judgment of course comes by practice, but a close study of these points will rarely fail to lead to an accurate selection. All calves that do not come up to a proper standard, in this way, are at once destroyed, or vealed.

Q. Do you attach any importance to the so-called "escutcheon," as a mark of value

A. As the escutcheon, so-called, is considered by many persons to be of special importance, I have studied it very closely, but without discovering anything in it to form a judgment upon, excepting, perhaps, in this way, and to a limited extent, quality and character and marks are generally inherited together. If a calf has all the marks of her dam and sire, it is reasonable to suppose that it will inherit, with these marks, all the qualities and character as well. The escutcheon is one of these marks, just as the fine eye and face and slender tail and silky hair are, and will go just as far as one of these may go, and no farther. But I have been led to believe that if any person places all his reliance upon the escutcheon he will impose upon himself and cherish a delusion.

But, to return to our subject: my way of feeding is to rear the young animal up, never permitting it to run into fat; as once an animal is run into fat it has a tendency that way, and in the dairy we want milk and butter, and not fat in the carcass. The object in feeding skimmed milk is to be free from the butter or fat-forming substance, and we give larger quantities of the skimmed milk as soon as the young animal can digest it, to increase the capacity of the paunch, so that when grown to maturity they will consume and digest so much more feed, and hence produce larger quantities of milk; as a cow giving large quantities of milk requires a large amount of feed to supply it, and should have capacity to hold and digest a larger quantity. I had a Jersey calf which, at the age of five months, milked two quarts of good milk per day, and up to the age of fourteen months, when she was put to the bull, increased to four quarts per day. She is still in my possession, and has given me two calves, and has never been dry during the period of gestation. This was an unusual case, and was caused by the constant sucking of its companions. It shows, however, the natural inclination of this breed to milk production.

Q. Had it any weakening tendency on the animal?

A. No; I think not. This animal was in such a vigorous condition that it rather gave her a finer development than if she had not given milk until she came in at two years old. She is now four years old and carrying her third calf, and I cannot observe that she is in any way injured by it.

Q. You say the heifers are ready to breed at about fifteen months. Is it not an unusual thing to bring them in at that age?

A. In my experience in breeding Jerseys and Ayrshires, by bringing them into milk while young, I find that they make better cows, as it keeps them from running into fat or beef, and holds their milking qualities much better. I have known Jersey and Ayrshire heifers not to breed until twenty-eight and thirty months old, but they never proved to be good dairy cows, while Short Horns or Devons ought not to be bred until about two years old, because their uses nowadays are more for beef than for dairy purposes. My plan is to breed the Jerseys and Ayrshires while young, and on their second breeding to keep them back say three or four months, so as to make them hold out their milking qualities for a longer season.

Q. What is the highest price, to your knowledge, that has ever been paid for a Jersey?

A. I believe $10,000 each has been offered and refused for "Eurotas," "Bomba," and "Jersey Belle of Scituate." The two-year-old heifer, Khedive Princess, sold at the Cooper sale, May, 1883, for $5,150. Some twenty cows at the same sale averaged over $2,000 each, while the young bull, King of Ashantee, sold for $5,600. Since then a bull calf sold for $10,500.*

Q. What is the probability of a continuance of these high prices, Mr. Crozier? Are they occasioned by a craze of fashion, or is there an increase of popular demand for the Jerseys?

A. There is no doubt an increasing demand for Jersey cattle—a legitimate demand founded entirely on their great merits, which yearly are becoming more and more attested, and that, together with the great beauty of the animal, which brings into competition private gentlemen as purchasers, both at the auction sales and privately, will have the effect of keeping up present prices, until this demand is satisfied. At the present time I do not believe there is a Jersey cow for each county in the United States, and the number being thus limited, certainly the demand will continue. Fifteen years ago $250 or $300 would have been called an extravagant price for a Jersey cow and few buyers at that.

Q. The inference is, then, that as the character of this breed becomes known the price advances?

A. Wherever the Jersey cow plants her foot, there will soon be found a market for her, whether here in the East or in the South or the West. A few years ago she was slighted at our fairs by everybody, and called the "little scrag" and only considered fitted for

---

* Since the above was written a two-year-old bull has been sold by T. S. Cooper for $15,000.

gentlemen's lawns. But to-day every buyer who can obtain money to purchase a calf wants it, and while, but a few years ago, the highest price paid for the service of bulls was $5, to-day $250 is paid for some bulls and even as high as $500 for animals of special families.

Q. The cost of the Jersey to the average farmer in anything like a fair herd would of course be beyond his means at the present time, but would not the effect of a cross between a Jersey bull and an Ayrshire or other good cow, for instance, be found of great advantage?

A. I have known a great many instances where the breeder has crossed the Jersey bull and Ayrshire cow for the very purpose of getting the best family cows, and certainly the result has proved to be most satisfactory. Of course a herd in this way would cost very much less, as the Ayrshire cow has not any excessive value.

Q. What are the relative values of a pure Jersey cow and a pure Ayrshire of the same quality?

A. While the Jersey cow of pure breed and pedigree would now bring $1,500, the Ayrshire would bring only from $100 to $150. I paid in 1876, at the Highland Society's Exhibition, $500 for one, but since then the value of the Ayrshire has had a downward tendency, as she has not been appreciated by wealthy farmers as the Jersey has been, and so has not so high a market value.

Q. What is the result when the Jersey is crossed with our common, or, as sometimes called, native, cow?

A. I think it was in 1876 that an old farmer, upwards of seventy years of age, brought one of his cows to one of my Jersey bulls. The cow brought him a heifer calf which he raised and bred, and which in turn produced a calf when a little over two years old. Nothing remarkable was thought of the heifer until his wife (who had a lifetime experience in butter making) stated one morning that she had never had such a good churning of butter as she had had that morning. This sharpened the old gentleman's observation, and while turning the cows into the yard loose to be milked, as is the custom among our farmers here, he noticed that this heifer had a very large and richly colored udder. He went back to the house, and told the old lady that he guessed there must be something in Crozier's stock after all; that he thought the cause of her extraordinary yield of butter was in that heifer, and that to set the matter at rest she must begin and gather a week's milk by itself and churn it. It was done, and to the astonishment of the old gentleman, he had more butter from the one heifer a little over two years old than he had from all of his other three cows together. On the same day he came to my place and said he had come to take back what he had said about my stock, and that as long as he lived he would breed to no other bulls but the Jerseys. He now has several crosses of the Jerseys in his herd and you could not buy them for $100 each. I had an order from Texas asking if I could procure a car load of half breeds in this vicinity. I tried the old gentleman, but in vain, for although he had them he would not part with them. And this, which is by no means an exceptional case, tells the whole story. It is for wide-awake farmers to watch the changes of events in their business outside of their own farms, as well as inside of them, and to know what is going on around them, and when they see how some improvement can be made to seize upon it. A Jersey bull, at a cost of $200 or $250, would double the value of a herd of fifty cows in three years, at a cost of no more than $5 for each heifer calf reared. It is safe to say that each of these young cows would be worth $100 each, which is a return of $5,000 for the $250 in three years. This is one way in which the value of the Jersey breed can be made available to every farmer.

THE MANAGEMENT OF THE DAIRY.

The first great care in the management of the dairy is cleanliness. If the cows are kept in a filthy state, the milk will certainly become tainted less or more, and this taint will surely affect the cream and butter. Therefore I use every precaution to keep the cows clean and the stables free from taint or bad odors, and not only the stables, but the surroundings. Girls and boys make the best milkers, because their hands are small, and are less liable to hurt the cows; and it won't hurt any girl or boy to know how to milk, for if it is never necessary that they should do the work, they should always be able to know how it should be done and when it is well done. There are many ways of milking. Some clasp the teat with the whole hand and squeeze and pull at the same time; others use only the forefinger and thumb, with a sort of stripping motion. The first method is especially objectionable where the hand is large, as the fingers double in around the teat, and there is danger of pinching the teat with the finger nails. Stripping should rarely be practiced, excepting in cases where the teat is very small, or as a rest to the milker's wrist, occasionally. I once had a Swiss in my employ who, in milking, doubled up his thumb against the teat, placing his fingers around it, and I found he was much the easiest and best milker I ever had; and since then I have made my boys learn the same method. This way of milking is by far the best for men, because doubling the thumb in lessens the capacity of the hand, and the fingers reaching around the teat lap onto the thumb, and thus protect it from the finger nails. In milking with the whole hand the teat should not be pulled down, but squeezed from the top downwards, so as to force out the milk. The finger nails of milkers should be kept cut close. Every milker should wash and dry the hands before he begins, and no one should ever dip his fingers into the milk to moisten the teats. The milk stool should be about nine inches high and should have three legs. The best position for the milker is to place his head firmly against the side of the cow, between her thigh and flank, throwing one leg slightly behind and the other in front of her hind legs, so as to hold the pail firmly between the knees. In case the milker should happen to get hold of a kicking cow, this position will enable him to brace himself so as to prevent her from kicking the pail. Sometimes, however, we find vicious kickers, where it is necessary to use artificial means to break them of the habit. In such cases a good remedy is to tie a strap—such as a surcingle of a horse—tightly across the cow's back, and under her belly. In moving her leg forward to kick, the cow raises her back forward of the hip joint, and slightly expands the belly, and her back being particularly tender, if the strap is drawn tight, it hurts her to make this motion, and she soon desists. A very common

MILKING TUBE.

practice with kicking cows is to tie their hind legs together; but this should never be done, because in struggling to get loose they are apt to throw themselves. The strap applied in the manner described will be found effective.

I would say here that a great deal may be done to make cows quiet milkers and prevent them from kicking, by careful and gentle management when a heifer first comes in. A young heifer, newly calved, has generally a tender udder, and when it is full of milk, the act of milking is painful and she will often attempt to kick. This is the critical time; if she is beaten she will kick back, and, perhaps, become a confirmed kicker; but if gently soothed and treated with patience and kindness, as soon as the udder has lost its tenderness, she will never think of kicking.

I have known some of the most valuable animals to be ruined for life in breaking them from kicking. It is then that the previous training, before mentioned, is found to be of the greatest advantage.

Whipping or striking with the stools should never be allowed, as it only makes them worse. When cows are annoyed at milking by flies, it saves all trouble if a light sheet is thrown across the cow's back during the operation. In the case of sore or obstructed teats there is nothing I have found to give such quick relief as a silver tube made for that purpose. This instrument is simply a silver tube one-sixteenth of an inch in diameter and three inches long, and perforated near the top as shown in cut. It should be inserted in the teats and passed above the obstruction. The small slide is pushed up or down to shorten or lengthen the tube. I have also imported a milker which has been

COW MILKER.

recommended by the best dairymen in England and Scotland. I would not recommened this to be used constantly, but where the teats are sore it is of great value. Milking is done by my boys and men. Their hands must be washed clean, and if any filth gathers on the udder or teats of the cows, they are also washed and wiped dry with a clean towel. The milk is strained into cans twenty inches deep and eight inches in diameter, which are covered and carried immediately into the dairy, where the milk is strained in the winter time into a creamery which contains pans five feet long and twenty inches wide and about seven inches deep, thus giving a large surface for the cream. In cold winter weather we get the milk up to a temperature of sixty degrees by the simple process of placing a tin can filled with boiling water and corked tight, in the bottom of the creamery, the door of which is then shut. Judgment must be used to regulate the quantity of hot water, so as to keep as near as possible to the desired temperature; it will require nearly double the quantity of hot water to raise the temperature of the milk to sixty, when the thermometer marks ten *below* zero, than when it is ten *above* it. Over the milk or at the ends of these pans are ventilators, so that the bad air can pass off, but this we only practice for a few months in the winter time during the coldest weather. The remainder of the year the milk is set in a creamery holding six cans about twenty-four inches in depth and nine inches in diameter. These cans are covered with lids having chimneys or ventilators in the top. The cans are surrounded by cold spring water, which is left until the milk is cool. The water is then drawn off and fresh cold water and broken ice put in, to keep the milk down to as near forty-five degrees as possible.

Each setting is allowed to stand twelve hours, and the milk is then drawn off by a faucet placed in the bottom of the can, leaving the cream inside. The milk, being sweet, is fed to the calves as previously stated. A little salt is added to the cream, and it is put away in a cool room, where it remains until fully ripe, or a little sour, and is then churned, being at a temperature of about fifty-five degrees. I prefer to churn the cream a little soured, as I have found by different trials that when churned sweet, the butter is not so good. The churn we have had in use for several years is a small sized factory churn of the Blanchard make, having a capacity of eighty gallons of

BLANCHARD CHURN FOR A SMALL DAIRY.

cream. The churn is worked by pony power, and the churning usually requires about fifty minutes, although it could be done in half that time if hurried; but we find it is a mistake to work it too fast, as the butter would become oily. Before the churning is finished, two pails of brine made of salt and spring water (strong enough to float an egg) are thrown into the churn. This separates the butter from the buttermilk, and leaves it in kernels about the size of wheat grains. The pony revolves the churn a few times; then the buttermilk is drawn off, and either sent to market or is fed to the hogs. Several pails of water are then poured on the butter, until not a particle of buttermilk, or even the color of the milk, is left in the churn. The churning now being done, the Reed butter worker, which, thus far, I find to be the best, is scalded and cooled with ice-water, and the butter lifted from the churn onto it.

About one ounce of Eureka salt to the pound of butter is sifted over the whole surface, and about half an ounce of pulverized sugar to the pound added, and the whole thoroughly worked by the machine, about fifteen minutes being required for this process. The butter is

REED'S BUTTER WORKER.

next weighed into half-pound cakes, put into the butter press and stamped; the stamp showing the name of the farm, of the village, and my initials, to protect it in the market from imitations. These cakes are wrapped in fine muslin, put into the butter box, which is enclosed in a wooden box, and sent direct to the purchasers. In each of these outer wooden boxes are two compartments for ice, which in hot weather keeps the butter in good condition until it reaches its destination. This concludes my system of butter making, and I may say that I have yet to hear of one single complaint, although I have supplied some families for fifteen years without missing a week.

Q. I notice that you say that the temperature of the milk in the summer season is reduced to forty-five degrees, while in the winter season it is kept up to sixty. Why do you reduce the temperature in the summer time to forty-five?

A. Because at this temperature milk set in the deep pails we use will throw up all the cream in twelve hours, and while it is still sweet; if the milk was set at sixty degrees in the summer, it would sour before all the cream had risen. We also get the cream in the churn at a lower temperature than we otherwise could in the summer, for it is

BLANCHARD BUTTER WORKER.

necessary for the cream to go into the churn in the hot weather at no more than fifty-five degrees, as it quickly rises to sixty or sixty-two, which is the right temperature, or the butter would be too soft, unless a good deal of ice were used, and too much ice is not desirable. A point worth mentioning, too, that is secured by setting the milk at forty-five degrees, is that we get the skimmed milk sweet for the calves.

Q. Is your plan of mixing half an ounce of sugar for each pound of butter in general practice?

A. I think not; but it improves the butter, for certainly there is a waste of sugar in washing out the buttermilk. Years ago my method was to press out all the buttermilk we could in working it, and to absorb it with a sponge wrapped in a clean cloth, but since I have adopted the plan of washing out the buttermilk I replace the sugar in this way. Besides this, the sugar helps to preserve the butter.

Q. What is your opinion, Mr. Crozier, of the new Centrifugal Separator, as it is called?

A. I think it was in 1879 that we had it at the International Dairy Fair, in New York City, and I have no doubt that for those who supply cream to our large cities it is a very good machine, but where we sour the cream and make it fit for churning, I do not think that we can get as good butter or as much from the same quantity of cream. I do not think that we can make good butter to keep a week

SHIPPING BOX FOR BUTTER.

by that process, as the cream thus separated is not in the right condition for churning; for unless, after the separation is made, it is kept for the same length of time, there would be no advantage. For cheese factories, where the cream is taken off for butter and the sweet skimmed milk is used for cheese, it would be serviceable.

Q. One of the most common complaints of the dairy farmer is the trouble in getting help for the dairy. How do you manage this?

A. I have no trouble whatever, as it is all done within my own family. My two daughters have taken turns since they were fourteen years old in the dairy, month about. The thing is now so simple, that even a careful girl of that age is capable of doing the work without much exertion; the labor of dairying being so much eased and simplified by improved machinery and methods. Outside of the dairy there is a large boiler or kettle, which holds forty gallons of water, which is supplied from the waste of the creamery. The fire is made under this boiler the first thing in the morning, so that all the utensils are washed and scoured, and left on a table under a shed to air and sweeten. After the churn is emptied it is washed out, first with cold water, then thoroughly scalded and finally again washed with cold water. It is then wiped dry with perfectly clean towels. This matter of perfectly clean and sweet towels and wiping cloths is of too great importance to be neglected as it too often is. It is one of the great little things in the dairy. The butter worker and moulds are then thoroughly washed and cleaned in the same way, in readiness for the next churning, the work being so easily and quickly done that about four hours completes it all. The setting of the milk and the skimming and collecting of the cream does not occupy more than one hour each time, twice a day.

The dairy is a plain structure, twelve foot post and single roof. It consists of three rooms. No. 1 is for the creameries. No. 2 is the cold room for working the butter and preserving it. No. 3 is the ice room. Nos. 1 and 2 are finished with hard finish and painted. No. 1 is supplied with water from a faucet, which is fed from a tank into which it is pumped by a windmill. The average amount of butter from the dairy is about 200 lbs. per week, unless it is in the summer, when many of my city customers are away in the country, and for this reason I make it a point to have as many of my cows come in in the fall as possible. At convenient distance from the dairy the calf pens are placed. The skimmed milk being drawn from the creameries is mixed as previously stated with gruel made of oat meal and flaxseed meal, and taken direct to the calves. The calf pens or boxes are twenty-four by sixteen feet, and are littered with straw so that the calves have every chance to jump and play. After each meal their troughs are taken out and thoroughly cleaned; in this case, as in all others, cleanliness is imperative. If any milk is left by the calves, it is taken direct to the hogs, which, as is well known, are the scavengers of the cattle yard. The buttermilk when taken from the churn is put into a large cask or barrel, and mixed with bran in the summer season and fed to Berkshire hogs. I may state that in these loose boxes in which the calves are kept every precaution is taken to admit as much light and air as practicable, without allowing the sun to beat in upon them. The doors of these pens all around the building are supplied with four hinges, and each door is cut across the middle, so that the upper half can be opened and closed at will. The upper doors are left open at night to give plenty of ventilation, and in the day-time a thin gunny bagging is fastened across as a shade. The calves are protected from any sudden change or high wind by the lower doors being kept shut.

FARM HORSES.

Although an important animal for the farm, the horse is in most cases secondary to cattle; but, as with cattle, it is always best to have such breeds as will perform their work in the best manner. I have used several breeds of horses for farm work, notably the Clydesdales, which originated in Scotland, and which are used there almost exclusively. They are now becoming great favorites in the cities here for heavy draft horses. It has been objected to the Clydesdale that he is slow; but, after a trial of different breeds, I find that the Clyde horse can plow more acres in a week than any other breed I have used. In

CLYDESDALE HORSE.

1869 a premium was offered by the Queens County, N. Y., Agricultural Society for the best walking team of any breed. I entered a pair of Clydes in a competition of a dozen pair, and won the prize of $50. Again, at our plowing match the summer following, at Mineola, where some thirty plows had entered to plow half an acre in a given time, two pairs of my Clyde horses came out first. In the horse market of this country nothing is such a hindrance to real sales as the want of size. No matter how perfectly the horse may be built, with strong body or short limbs—if he is small, he brings only a low price, and this even smaller, in proportion to his size, than the value of a larger horse. The law that like produces like, or the likeness of some ancestor, refers, of course, as much to size, as to form, color, temperament and action; and I think that the Clyde horse, weighing 1,500 or 1,600 pounds, when crossed on our native light mares, weighing 1,000 or 1,100 pounds, makes one of the most valuable breeds for farm work.

Q. Would it not be an objection to the Clydesdale horse that its cost would be entirely beyond the reach of the ordinary farmer?

A. They are now being bred in the west in large numbers, and in the New York horse markets half blood Clydes can be procured without

PERCHERON-NORMAN HORSE.

trouble nearly as cheap as the ordinary Ohio or Pennsylvania horses that have been supplying these markets for years past.

Q. What do you consider the best age and weight for a farm horse?

A. I hardly ever purchase a horse that has to do steady work at less than six or seven years of age, and for farm purposes, from 1,200 to 1,400 pounds in weight. Horses of this age and weight can be purchased in the New York markets, at this time, for about $500 per pair. The Percheron horse is also imported in large numbers into this country and is used in the West for breeding. When crossed with our common horse this makes an excellent farm animal. They are not as good walkers as the Clydesdales, and in my experience I have found them harder keepers and more subject to ailments. Their bone is larger than the Clyde horse, the legs of the latter being something similar in shape to that of a two by four-inch plank. The Percheron has become very numerous in the Western States, and seems to suit the special circumstances of the Western country exceedingly well. It is as heavy as the Clydesdale, but perhaps rather coarser in its build. The Suffolk Punch has also been imported into this country, but they are too slow for the American people. They make the very

CLEVELAND BAY HORSE.

best horses for city work, as they are capable of hauling immense loads. The Cleveland Bays have been bred extensively in the West and South, particularly in Kentucky and Virginia, for coach horses. The English Cart Horse has also been introduced into the United States, but as yet I have not heard of their success in any way. In my opinion the Highland Clyde or the Canadian horse will answer every purpose on our farms better than any other. Their weight is from 1,200 to 1,400 pounds. They are clean in the bone, easy keepers, good walkers, and have not the objection of excessive size that might be urged against the Lowland Clyde. These horses are used to a large extent in Lower Canada, Quebec and Montreal.

As there is a large demand for horses for city use, and also for exportation, the breeding of these as a business might be profitably undertaken by many more farmers than now give attention to it. A class of horses of moderate weight, but stout, clean limbed and active, is largely sought by the horse-car companies and many thousands of them are purchased every year. Foreign governments, too, are now procuring horses for their armies here in large numbers. This class of horses is bred from large mares of the kinds above described, crossed with horses having some thoroughbred blood, the progeny being able to endure severe work and having a strong constitution. The breeding of roadsters is also a very profitable part of farm business at the present time.

In this section of the country the use of mules upon farms is not nearly so general as in the South and parts of the West. But for some purposes mules are preferable to horses, as, for instance, where the work is hard, and when the team is exposed to neglect, and not fed as well as it might be. But this should not be made an excuse for neglecting them, nor for preferring mules without other and better reasons, as no other farm stock pays better for good care and treatment than the farm team.

We feed our horses in winter in about the same way that we do our cattle. When spring comes and they have to go to plowing, they are fed oats at noon time, cut feed at night and oats in the morning, a mash of bran being given them twice a week. The colts are fed with the same mixture as that given the cattle, with two or three quarts of bruised oats per day; we bruise the oats lest they might be passed undigested. Ruta Bagas or carrots mixed with meal make an excellent feed for horses; in fact, I am of the opinion that it is the very best feed for bringing a horse into good condition. It is fed in quantities of about fourteen pounds of the roots, and three to four pounds of meal mixed with a little salt. Thousands of horses are injured by feeding exclusively on grain and corn meal, which is very apt to give the colic. The usual remedy for colic is to take the horse out and walk him rapidly, rub the belly, and give injections of soap suds. These remedies are usually successful.

A caution might here be given against the common practice of giving active medicines or drugs to animals without any knowledge of what is the matter with them. No medicines of any kind should ever be given to any animal without some clear idea of its purpose, derived from intelligent study of some good veterinary work, or on the advice of some competent veterinary surgeon.

The breeding of horses as a special pursuit upon farms has been found very profitable. Men of wealth have greatly increased the value of their property, and have had the enjoyment of a pleasant and healthful occupation at the same time, in the midst of their stud. This has been frequently the case in Virginia, Kentucky and Missouri, but more especially where the names of Alexander, Harper, and several other noted breeders, and of such horses as Lexington, Longfellow, Leamington, and other remarkable sires, will always be remembered. The class of horses thus bred, however, have been used for pleasure and sport, for the turf or for driving, and for useful roadsters. The demand for such horses is not likely to become less, but, on the contrary, to increase greatly, and the steady and profitable business which has been built up will, beyond a doubt, become very much extended. The race of American trotting horses is now known and admired all over the world; our carriage horses are sought for by wealthy Europeans, and even for business purposes our light, active, but strong and serviceable draft horses are in large and increasing demand. Thus a large opening exists for enterprise in this direction, which may be profitably filled, not only by men of wealth, who invest their capital in agriculture for pleasure as well as profit, but also by those who follow the pursuit of farming for a living. The breeds above referred to are for draft and farm purposes chiefly, excepting the Cleveland Bay, which is in demand, also, for large carriage or coupé horses, and some animals of this strain have been exported for this purpose, notably several fine ones, which were purchased for the Emperor Napoleon III. when he was in the height of his good fortune. But the horses mostly desired for roadsters are of the English thoroughbred strains, and from these have been bred the race known as American trotting horses. These animals are certainly far more useful than the running horses used for sporting purposes, and come directly under notice in a work devoted to the subject of profitable farming, because they are mostly bred and reared upon farms, and the better class of farm mares, crossed by thoroughbred horses, are largely used for their production. The Morgan strains, which have been of such great service in this respect, have furnished hundreds of sires, which have been scattered all over the country, and have put thousands of dollars into farmers' pockets. Another noted instance was the horse Hambletonian, whose blood now runs in numerous strains, each of which had its source in a farm mare.

The profit of horse breeding may be easily shown by the study of the reports of the market values of horses, of which a specimen is here given, copied from a leading paper.

In these it may be found that a horse of 1,100 or 1,200 pounds sells for from twenty to thirty cents a pound live weight, while a steer brings no more than from five to six cents a pound on foot. As it costs no more to rear a colt to three years of age than to bring a steer of the same age into condition for market, when it weighs but little more than the horse, and after that age a horse more than earns his feed until he is sold, it is easily seen that there is more than four times as much money in the horse than in the steer.

DESCRIPTION.	AGE.	HANDS.	LBS.	PRICE.
Bay driver....................	6	15½	1,000	$175
Black driver...................	8	15½	1,100	350
Black driver...................	7	15½	1,100	250
Bay driver....................	7	16¼	1,300	250
Chestnut driver...............	8	15½	1,000	115
Bay driver....................	7	16	1,160	185
Draft team....................	6	16	2,500	375
Draft team....................	6	16	2,800	425
Draft team....................	8	16	2,900	450
Draft team....................	5	15¾	2,400	325
Gray mare.....................	5	15¾	1,300	185
Bay mare......................	6	16	1,400	195
Brown horse...................	7	16	1,250	160
Gray horse....................	8	16	1,400	150
Gray horse....................	5	16	1,450	210
Bay horse.....................	6	16¼	1,500	210
One car-load of farm horses, per head...				85
Six farm horses, per head.....				105
One coupé horse...............			1,300	250

It costs no more to rear a good horse than a poor one, excepting the expense of service, which may be $25 or $50, while the colt from the better horse is quite likely to bring more than the extra sum paid for the service of his sire. This fact applies to the rearing of all kinds of stock, and it should be a maxim with farmers to "always breed the best." It is a great mistake to breed from unsound animals, because these defects of unsoundness in nearly all cases descend to the progeny. There are thousands of diseased horses that are bred from diseased mares, and inherit their defects from the dams or sires. Therefore, the first requisite in breeding horses should be to use only sound, healthy mares, and to use a sound sire. Spavins and other diseases of the joints, blindness, bad temper, and many other defects, become constitutional, and are reproduced from generation to generation, and thus it is that there are so many unsound horses in existence.

The second requisite is a good mare. For a roadster or a carriage horse a large mare should be chosen; it does not matter if the bone is rather coarse if the sire is a thoroughbred, or even a well bred horse of thoroughbred lineage. It is a characteristic of a thoroughbred that the bone is hard and solid, and although fine, it has more strength than the coarser bone of the common stock; and it is also characteristic of the higher bred sire that he will confer this property upon his colts. Some time ago a few Russian horses, known as the Orloff breed, were imported into this country. These were fine specimens of sires for roadsters or trotters, and as they have been bred and kept for this purpose in Russia for many years, they would be of great value for breeding here. The Orloff horse is very compact, and has great endurance and considerable speed, with a remarkably good constitution. An excellent portrait of one of these horses is given on the opposite page.

After the breeding, the managemen of the mare is the next important point; for while the sire gives the general form and constitution to the progeny, the dam gives the disposition and temper. The mare should, therefore, be treated with good judgment, and her feeding should be generous and regular. The training and feeding of the colt must, of course, be equally well managed, for many good colts are spoiled by bad management, in spite of all the previous care in the breeding. This is also true as regards horses, for the value and profit of a horse depends quite as much upon good treatment in its use as in its breeding. Many horses are injured by carelessness in shoeing, by which the feet are ruined, and, as is well known, "no foot, no horse," for the feet of a working animal must be sound and in good condition, or the horse soon becomes entirely useless. Ill fitting harness is another frequent cause of injury to horses, by which its ability to work is greatly reduced.

The farmer who makes a special business of rearing horses must necessarily study special works on this subject, and be a close and thoughtful observer for himself. All that can be done in this work is to call attention to these special points, that they may not be overlooked.

There is considerable profit in rearing the small breed of horses known as Shetland ponies. This is a very diminutive animal, as may be seen by the engraving, which shows its relative size as compared with the Orloff stallion. They are in demand near the large cities for children's use, and usually sell for $100 each and upwards. A pair makes a very good team for a small carriage, as these ponies are strong and stout and of great bottom. The engraving represents one "in the rough," as it was imported a few years ago in a herd of about twenty. These animals are natives of the northern part of Scotland and of the Shetland Islands, a locality exposed to severe storms and having a rigorous

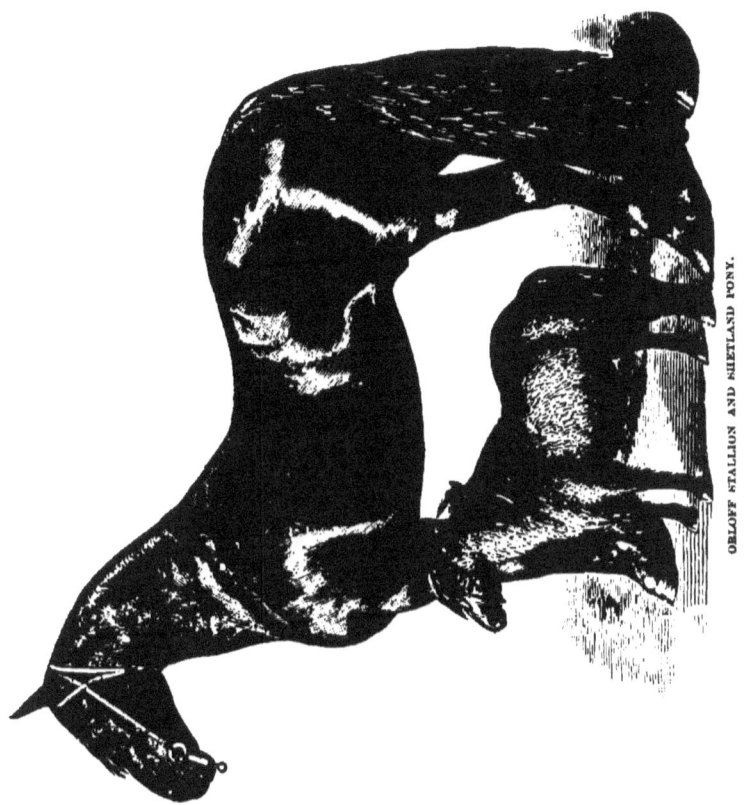

ORLOFF STALLION AND SHETLAND PONY.

climate, in which they run in herds without any shelter at any season of the year.

SHEEP.

Next to the finer breeds of cattle, my experience with sheep has probably afforded me most pleasure and profit. Although sheep keeping is not generally as profitable as breeding the finer classes of cattle, in some localities, yet it might be made more so in hilly or mountainous districts, such as Vermont, New Hampshire, the higher lands of Virginia, North Carolina and other Southern States. Great attention has been given to sheep breeding, and the finer kinds have been greatly improved by the care and skill of the breeders during some years past. Twenty-five years ago I imported a few Leicester sheep, which were then the ruling breed in England, but after a few years' experience I found they were not suited to this climate. The lambs grew to a large size and weight, but did not produce much fat. The average fleece unwashed weighed from nine to ten pounds, and after three years I found they were much given to disease and the percentage of loss was so great that I abandoned the sheep trial for several years.

I think it was in 1867 that I imported a few Cotswolds, which produced good lambs and heavier fleeces than the Leicesters, and the wool being better for combing, brought a much better price. The ram weighed when fully grown 425 lbs., and the weight of his fleece

SOUTH DOWN RAM.

was 24 lbs. The ram lambs sold for from $40 to $50 each, for breeding purposes, but like the Leicesters, they began to run down after two or three years, and I think were not suited for the climate. I had a few imported South Downs at the same time, and crossed a Cotswold ram on one of the ewes; this ewe produced a ewe lamb which I bred to a South Down ram. The produce of this cross I bred in and in until I had a flock of twenty, which I named Beacon Downs. All sheep men who saw them admired them for their compact forms, the length and fineness of wool and their early maturity, and they soon found a market among breeders. Of my three importations, the South Downs proved to be the best suited for this climate. I think one

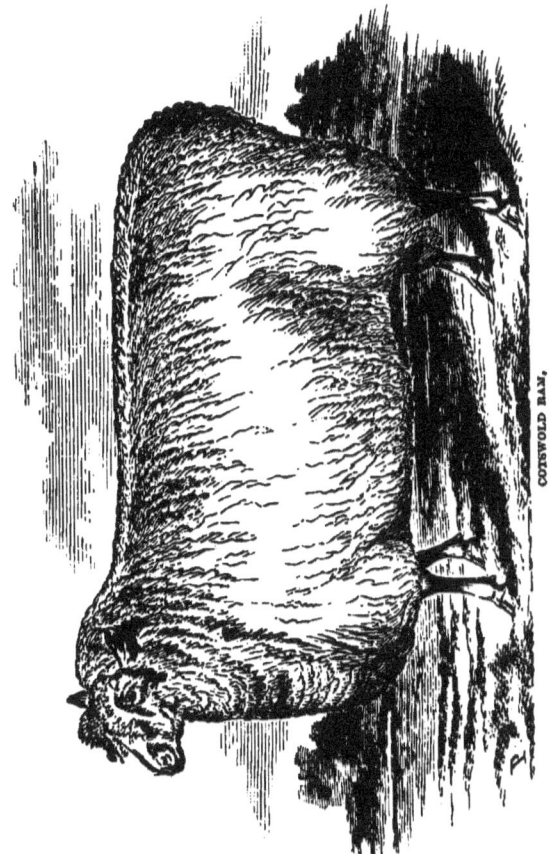

COTSWOLD RAM.

great cause of the failure of long-wool sheep in this country, is that they are often left to take care of themselves, and the rains or snows beat into their wool, and by chilling them produce lung disorders. Although in Europe there is less rain-fall than here, yet the climate is moister and cooler, and there are not so many sudden changes, which are exceedingly hurtful to sheep, especially those with open fleece. The South Down gives what is called a middle wool, which is in great demand in our markets and for the country woolen mills. The fleece is so thick that the rains cannot penetrate it, and when the sheep give themselves a shake, as they generally do, they throw the water off. They are very hardy, and thrifty feeders, and when put upon green feed or pasture they seem to fatten quicker than any other breed of sheep I know of. The lambs mature early and will bring from one to two cents per lb. more in our markets than any other breed. The ewes are very prolific and will bring generally two lambs every spring. The average of wool from my flock this spring, which is direct from Lord Walsingham's (England), was ten pounds per fleece, which is largely over the general average. The flock increased over double, losing only one lamb. I have sent South Down rams as far as Texas and Montana; and from those sent the report is that they have made a better cross than any other pure breeds they have had a trial with. If the ewes are bred early in the fall, so as to come in in midwinter, carefully fed and housed, the lambs will dress as much as thirty pounds when ten weeks old and will bring in our large cities early in the spring from twenty-five to thirty cents per pound. At this early season only a limited number could be sold, and the cost of rearing them is of course larger than at a later season.

There is a class of remarkably useful sheep which have all more or less South Down blood in them, and which have the black or dark faces and medium clothing wool of the South Down. These are generally known as the "Down" breeds. They are larger in the carcass and have more wool than the South Down, but the flesh is not so delicately flavored. As these sheep have been introduced into America and have met with general popular favor, and moreover as they well deserve it, some notice should be taken of them in this work.

SHROPSHIRE DOWN.

This sheep is not much larger than the South Down and closely resembles it in character. It differs in its more open fleece of somewhat longer and coarser wool from the South Down, and is perhaps rather more hardy and more adapted for roughing it in our less particular and considerate methods of keeping sheep. This breed has been introduced into every State of the Union, and several flocks of

SHROPSHIRE RAM.

them are kept in California. The illustration here given is a very accurate representation of this sheep.

HAMPSHIRE DOWN.

This breed is the most popular of all of this class of cross-bred sheep. Its face and legs are black and its frame is large and broad. These sheep were introduced into Virginia forty years ago and

HAMPSHIRE DOWN RAM.

although the pure race has melted away, it has left its traces widely spread among the native sheep. More recently a large number of them has been imported, and they have done well, especially for crossing on the natives for producing large early market lambs. For this purpose perhaps there is no better sheep than this. Year-old lambs have been known to dress 100 lbs. The wool is fine and longer than that of the South Down; the fleece averages about eight pounds. The wool is very close and compact, and sheds rain very well; consequently the sheep of this breed are hardy, and do not suffer from our heavy rains and snows as the long wool sheep do.

OXFORD DOWN.

The Oxford Down is a still larger sheep and has a still coarser and longer fleece than the South Down, which is a grandparent of this breed. The Oxford Down is a cross of the Hampshire Down upon the Cotswold, and while it has the dark face of the Downs, it has the long wool and more open fleece of the Cotswold. It is a very good

OXFORD DOWN RAM.

mutton sheep and does well in this country. It matures early and twenty-two-months-old wethers have weighed 300 lbs. each when fat. The rams have been known to shear twenty pounds of wool.

THE AMERICAN MERINO.

The Merino is a short or fine wooled sheep which produces large quantities of unwashed wool, and I have seen as high as thirty-four pounds taken from one ram, but when washed there was so much yolk in it that it was reduced down to eight pounds. This breed is especially a wool sheep, although nine-tenths of the American mutton is from sheep of more or less Merino blood. The Merino is well fitted for hilly or mountainous sections of the country, and are bred largely in Vermont, western New York, Pennsylvania and Ohio, from which places many thousands are shipped to Texas, the western plains and to California. Many are sent to Australia, where they are considered as the best fine wool sheep in the world. Some of the rams of this breed have been held as high as $25,000 and sold for $10,000 each, and as an instance of the effect upon the market values of farm animals of the vagaries of fashion, sheep of this same breed have since then been sold for the value of their pelts.

The American Merino originated from the Spanish Merinos, some thousands of which were imported many years ago, and by long continued careful breeding it has become the first sheep of its class in the world. Mr. Hammond and another Vermont farmer, Mr.

MERINO RAM AND EWE.

Atwood, deserve the greatest credit for establishing this breed, which is really the basis of the native sheep and wool interest of this country. The Merino is used for improving the common Mexican and Texan sheep, of which flocks of several thousands are kept all over the plains from Texas to California, and as far north as Wyoming and Montana. Its blood is more or less mingled with the forty million of sheep which now exist in this country, and its value for improving and increasing our production of wool can scarcely be estimated in figures. While I think the South Down is a better mutton sheep, yet there is no other sheep in existence but the Merino that can furnish us with the fine wool we require for our woolen manufacture. In choosing sheep the farmer must of course take this fact into account, because in most cases it is the wool which gives him the profit from his flock.

My plan of feeding sheep in winter is with cut "peas and oats" and turnips. They require little water, but water should always be kept within their reach. They require also, as all other animals do, a reasonable quantity of salt and a little sulphur occasionally. In the spring of the year I turn the sheep onto the young wheat about the 1st of May. The sheep eat the wheat leaves off close, and cause it to thicken and stool out; their droppings also serve as a top dressing and their treading firms the roots of the wheat in the soil. When the sheep are taken off the wheat, they are put on pasture, and I have received the most benefit from them when herded on rape. The rape is followed by a mustard crop, and when this is done, the land may be prepared for a crop of turnips of the softer kinds, such as Yellow Aberdeens or Tankards, which are eaten on the land by the sheep, as this is one of the best plans of bringing up poor land ready for seeding. The greatest care should, however, be taken when mustard or rape is grown, not to suffer these crops to seed and stock the soil, but to plow under the refuse before it blossoms.

Q. At about what date do you turn in the sheep on the turnip crop?

A. From the 1st to the 10th of October. I have fed a flock of fifty sheep on two acres from that time up to the end of December, or nearly three months, by giving them a little hay in racks made for that purpose in the turnip field. Those sheep I purchased at the sheep market in New York City, costing me $3.50 per head. I sold them to the butcher for $9.00 each in January, or in about four months after they were purchased, thus making $275 for the feed and care, besides leaving the land in an improved condition on account of the manure. The land was sown with oats, grasses and clover in the spring. If I had purchased the manure for this land it would have cost me fully $20, so that taking into consideration the labor in caring for the sheep, and the cultivation of the land, I may say in round numbers, that the four acres of rape and two acres of turnips gave me a net profit of considerably more than $200. They were of mixed blood, partly South Downs and partly Cotswolds—what are called Canada sheep—a large bodied, thrifty sheep, which makes the best mutton of any in America. I purchased them, as I said before, at the New York market for the purpose of feeding off this rape and the turnips, and to manure the land and prepare it for a future crop.

Sheep should be kept out of storms. It is also better not to keep over forty or fifty in a flock together. They should never be housed in a damp building, as they are very susceptible to foot-rot, and once this sets in it will work through the entire herd if not prevented. When this trouble occurs the hoof is to be pared down to remove all unsound horn and the diseased parts of the foot laid bare. These are dressed with a strong solution of sulphate of copper (blue vitriol), about an ounce in half a pint of warm water. The feet should be wrapped up in a rag smeared with a mixture of pine tar and lard melted together. Sometimes sheep become lame from being kept on gravelly or stony pasture; this is not foot-rot, and will soon be remedied by a change to softer ground. This caution as to housing the sheep of course applies only to northern climates. In the South and South-west, where the climate is milder, there would be no need for such housing, simple shelter from the rain being enough. As a guide to this we might say, that in England, where the thermometer rarely falls lower than ten degrees above zero, but where the winters are very rainy (the wet, and not the cold, being injurious), the sheep are kept out in open sheds on most farms during the entire winter. The ewes require careful watching about lambing time, as in many cases they may then need assistance. The ewe and young lamb should be separated from the flock, and put into a box stall or a pen in some convenient place, where they can be kept warm, great care being taken to remove any wool that should be on the udder, so that the young lamb can catch the teats easily without any obstruction. This may not often be necessary, but requires looking to lest it may be. The tails of the lambs should be docked when eight or nine days old. Loss often occurs when the tails are left on, as in the heat of summer on good pasture their soft droppings are apt to adhere to the tail, and in a few days the sheep will become fly-blown and maggoty, and if not relieved death will ensue. The tails are docked at about two inches from the rump. The skin is drawn back by the fingers as on the finger of a glove and a clip with a pair of sharp sheep shears divides the tail without trouble and with very little pain. A pinch of copperas will stop the bleeding. Where flocks of 100 or over are kept, they should be left to the care of an intelligent boy or man.

One of the most troublesome pests in the care of sheep is the tick, which are often on the ewes at lambing time, and will soon reach the young lambs, and it is impossible to have them grow and improve as they should do while they are infested with this insect. A good remedy is to dip the sheep in tobacco water made to about the strength and color of strong tea. Another pest to sheep and which sometimes destroys whole flocks in a miserable manner is the scab mite, which burrows in the skin and produces the disease known as scab. The wool of a scabby sheep falls off or becomes matted on the skin, in the crusts and scabs which are formed of the matter exuded by reason of the irritation caused by these pests. The remedy is to dip the sheep in strong hot tobacco water as above mentioned, with some sulphur added. The quantities are one pound of coarse tobacco, or one and one-half of the waste stems, to four gallons of boiling water, four ounces of flowers of sulphur being well stirred in. When the solution cools to about 120 degrees the sheep are dipped into it all over, except the head, and the crusts are completely broken up with some rough instrument, a corn cob being the best for the purpose. As this disease is exceedingly contagious, the mites remaining for many months upon the soil, on the fences and walls, where the sheep rub themselves, the greatest care is needed to prevent the infection of healthy sheep; and as it spreads very rapidly, the remedy should be applied at the earliest occasion for it. The sheds, also, are to be cleansed in the same manner as the sheep. Where there is any reason to suspect the presence of this troublesome pest in any sheep introduced to a healthy flock, the new comers should be dipped as a precaution. This subject is more fully referred to in the chapter on "The Pests of the Farm."

No flock can be expected to do well without a well arranged and comfortable shed and a dry yard. No other animals should ever be permitted to run with the sheep, as these inoffensive creatures cannot defend themselves, and are consequently exposed to constant attack and injury. The shed should be open to the south and well protected

BARN FOR SHEEP.

against the north; the yard should be enclosed with a dog-proof fence, and there should be an enclosed barn for feeding and housing them in severe weather, with a good floor for shearing. The accompanying engraving gives a good idea of a convenient yard, sheds and barn for this purpose.

SWINE.

Usually the keeping of hogs in any large number on the farm is not profitable. Like many other things, it is confined to sections of the country where it is made a special business. Still, it is well on most farms at least to have a few to eat up the garbage, or the offal from the dairy, and I will endeavor to state what I believe is the best method of raising them, and the kinds best suited for the purposes of the average farm. I have bred the Cheshire, Poland-China and Chester White hogs. All these breeds have large bone and a great deal of offal, and I found that they were not profitable and abandoned them. I then imported the White Suffolks, which produced more fat than any other hog I ever raised. They are small in the bone, with little offal, and are quiet and easy keepers, while the Chester Whites seem to be always looking for more feed, and are never content, and do not mature until two or three years old, and then their meat brings in our markets two or three cents per pound less than the Suffolks. I next imported Berkshires, in 1862. These were

BERKSHIRE PIG.

found to be better than any kind previously tried. They are easy keepers, make much lean meat with the fat, and mature early. I have often had them weigh, when dressed, 250 pounds at eight months old. Their hams and shoulders, when properly cured, find a ready market in all large cities, and are of such superior quality that private purchasers often order them from our farmers here six months in advance. I have made importations, about once a year, of prize Berkshires from England. In 1869 I imported fourteen hogs, a few of which I sold, to go to Missouri, for $600 each. They were exhibited at the great Pork Packers' Exhibition, at St. Louis—in 1872, I think it was—where there were some sixteen hundred entries of all breeds, from Europe, Canada and the United States, and these, with their progeny, took the first prize on boar and sow; first and second prizes on sow and litter of pigs; first prize on hogs under a year old, and prize on pigs under six months old. I mention these facts to show the superiority of the breed, because these animals were brought into competition with others of all breeds, and of course with the best specimens of them which could be procured. The Berkshire is black in both hair and skin; but in dressing, the black skin comes off with the hair, and the pork dresses perfectly white. The hair is fine and glossy, but rather thin, and is quite free from all tendency to the woolly undercoat which is so much disliked in pigs. There is a white splash on the face; the feet are white, and so is the end of the tail. These peculiar marks are all reproduced very exactly in the pure breed. The ears are pricked and very small; the face is short and dished; the neck is very short and thick; the shoulders broad; the sides are deep, and the hams broad and thick, the legs being very short and the bone light and fine. This form makes the very best ham and bacon hog, and as its habit is to make a large proportion of lean meat to the fat produced, and to produce more meat on the same feed and to do it more quickly than any other breed, and the meat being sweeter and of better quality, I must say I know of no other variety of swine that is so desirable for the farmer for hams, shoulders and bacon.

A POLAND-CHINA HOG.

Next to the Berkshire comes the Poland-China, which is quite popular in the West, where pork growing is one of the most prominent industries of the farm and consumes a considerable part of the large corn crop. This hog is mixed white and black in color, the ears are lopped, the carcass is large and fat. It therefore suits the pork packers, whose aim is fat pork for packing, rather than meaty pork for curing for sides and bacon. The importance of good breeding of swine is apparent when we consider that about ten million hogs are packed every year in the West and that the whole stock in the country is more than forty millions.

There is another black breed of swine, which has no white mark about it, and which is popular in some places. This is the Essex. It is not as good a bacon hog as the Berkshire, although it is excellent when young for light pork. When full grown it is fat, but it is not large enough for the packer's use. Among farmers who prefer white hogs, the large Yorkshire is considered as profitable, but it is a large feeder, and I think on the whole if the Berkshire were kept by farmers more extensively, both wholly, or for crossing on their present mixed stock, that the value of their swine would be doubled.

There is nothing special to be said in regard to the feeding of hogs, excepting that when young they should not be overfed. I feed a mixture of buttermilk and bran twice a day, and in the winter time they are fed cooked roots and pea meal, which is one of the best feeds that can be given. The sows are put into a pen a week or ten days before their time for farrowing, and to prevent them from eating their pigs, as they sometimes do, I give them a little salt pork, which seems to have the effect of deterring them from doing so. Perhaps if they had been given some salt previously they would not need this. There is but little bedding left in the pen at that time, and that fine and short, so that the young pigs may not be entangled in it; and they are watched closely. The pigs are left as dropped, and are then put into a box or basket, and as soon as the sow recovers they are put back in the pen, and left with her; but she requires watching, as they will often get in behind, between the sow and the wall of the pen, and get crushed. To prevent this I nail a rail or round pole a few inches from the wall, and a few inches high. The pigs are generally left with the sow untill six or eight weeks old, when they are weaned and fed with a little new milk and mush, made of oat meal and bran. I have several times put the boar to the sow the third day after she has dropped her pigs. By this there is time saved, as we can get three litters in a year, whereas if we neglected it at that time, the sow probably would not be in farrow again for three months. It is my opinion that boars should never be used longer than two years, as they become vicious and dangerous.

Q. Without taking into consideration the fancy prices at which these Berkshires have sold, how would they compare in profit with sheep?

A. I think they are not as profitable as sheep. The wool pays for keeping the sheep, and six months in the year they are on pasture, and require but very little care, while the hog has to be attended to twice daily throughout this full term, and unless we have a special market for hams and shoulders, and sides of bacon, it hardly pays to raise hogs here. But the farmer can ill afford to be without them, as they are used to root among the manure and turn it over, and generally get their living upon what would otherwise be wasted.

When pork is prepared for sale in the form of hams and bacon, it must be home cured, because then we get the profit in this work. A hog should not be fed for twelve hours before slaughtering. When it is scalded to remove the hair it is necessary to avoid over scalding, or the hair becomes set and cannot be scraped off. This of course injures it for sale to private customers or to the best dealers. I find 180 degrees to be the proper temperature for the water. The carcass should hang where it will not be frozen for twenty-four hours. Where a farmer has ten or twenty hogs to dress during the season, he will find it convenient to have a shed or place properly provided and furnished for this work, with a boiler and scalding vat.

My method of curing is as follows: When the meat has been properly cut up it is well rubbed with salt and left on the benches to drain for twenty-four hours. This removes the moisture from it. Seven and one-half pounds of salt, two and one-half pounds of brown sugar, four ounces of saltpeter, are then put in as much water as will dissolve them completely, and two ounces of cayenne pepper is added. The liquid is boiled a few minutes and skimmed and set aside to cool. Meanwhile the meat is rubbed with a mixture of the same, and is closely packed in the barrels or tubs, and the pickle is poured over it until it is covered. In six weeks it is cured and is ready for smoking. It is smoked with hickory brush wood or corn cobs, or both, one hour a day for ten days. The fire is made outside of the smoke-house and the smoke is carried in by a flue, so that it is cooled and does not warm the meat. After ten days the meat is rubbed with pepper and is ready for sale, or if to be kept should be packed in close boxes with wheat chaff or cut straw, and kept in a dry, cool place.

Hams and bacon are frequently injured by a small beetle, which lays its eggs upon the meat, and when these hatch the small worms bore into the meat and harbor near the bone. This insect is a variety of weevil, a small brown beetle, and the larvæ are small white grubs, which are commonly called skippers. It is very important that the meat should be protected against this pest, or it may be damaged so as to spoil it for sale and also injure it for use. There are several ways of doing this. One of the best and the most convenient is to rub the meat well with ground pepper, and then pack it in boxes in oat or wheat chaff or in finely cut hay; a few inches in depth should be covered over the meat, and the box closed tightly. It should be kept in a dry, cool place. The dry packing will absorb all the moisture, and prevent the meat from becoming moldy.

FARM BUILDINGS.

The styles of farm buildings will of course vary according to the necessities of the farmer, the amount of money he is willing or able to invest, or other conditions. As I have heretofore done in our conversations on other farm work, I will give my own practice in this matter, which for the special purposes required, after an experience of nearly thirty years, I have found to be the best. When wanted for other purposes than dairy farming they must be modified accordingly. In years past, when I leased farms, I always had the bad fortune to get poor buildings, and I have often had to put up sheds at my own cost. My object always has been to make a court or square surrounded on all sides with buildings, with one opening into the yard, so that it could be easily locked up at night, that if any animal should by chance get out of its pen it would be found in the yard in the morning. The homestead which I purchased three years ago was bare of buildings and open to the streets. I first graded the yard into a hollow square, sloping on all sides to the centre, where I placed the cistern or cesspool for liquid manure, as before described. On the south side of this yard, running east and west, I built my cow stable, 105 feet in length, twenty-three feet wide and sixteen-foot posts. This is divided into thirty stanchions or stalls, three and one-half feet wide, with a manger running in front. Water is supplied to the manger from a tank in the barn, and is carried along the range of stalls by an inch and a quarter iron pipe, having three faucets to let the water into the manger. Hose attachments are provided to carry the water to any point in the barn in case of fire. In front of the manger is a space of nine feet for a feeding passage, in which there is a large trough, six by three feet, for mixing bran or slops in the summer. Just behind the stalls is a trench, fifteen inches wide and eight inches deep, where all the manure falls. Behind this is a walk of five feet for the convenience of the milkers and for bedding and cleaning out the stables. This large space also gives ample room for the milk cans at milking time. On the front side of the stable, and in front of the cows, are several large windows, to give sunlight and air when desired. There are also windows facing the yard, and two large doors, by which the cows enter the stables, into which the carts are backed when carrying in bedding and taking away the manure. The smallest boy can put the thirty cows into the stable in ten minutes, as they are all trained to go into their own stalls without confusion. This training saves a great deal of trouble, and is a special point in the management of cows. The method of fastening them in the stalls is simply by means of an upright oak scantling, two by three inches, held in the bottom of the stall by a pin, and, when the cow thrusts her head through the opening above the manger, this upright stick is pushed up in place, and a piece of the same size is dropped down behind it on the top rail of the manger and holds it securely. This space has a width at the top of about two feet when open, and when closed is about eight inches wide at both top and bottom, so that the cows are fastened securely and quickly, thus doing away with chains and halters. The second floor of the barn being seven and one half feet high gives ample room for ventilation, and this floor will hold seventy-five tons of hay.

On the east side of the square, running north and south, is another stable 100 feet long. This is eight feet high, built of cedar posts and rough boards, and contains ten box stalls; a few of them, of larger size, are used for the bulls. The others are eight by ten, and are used for cows at calving times. In front is the feeding manger or trough. In front of this is a walk of four feet, where the feed is supplied to the manger. The roof is made with heavy timbers and rough boards. On this are built the stacks of corn fodder, or corn stalks, to a height of about fourteen feet. The stack is built over the sides of the stable some two feet. It is made so as to run to a sharp ridge at the top. In this way we get a stack of corn fodder 100 feet in length, sixteen feet wide and an average height of ten feet, which probably contains seventy-five or eighty tons, thus serving the purposes of a roof, and a convenient place to stack fodder during the winter. When the corn fodder is fed off, the board roof of course carries off the water.

On the side of the square facing north is the main barn for horses, running east and west. In this barn are the hay-lofts, threshing machine, room for tools, seed room, offices, etc.; here too is the horse power for two or four horses, as may be required. With this we pulp the roots, cut corn fodder, etc. On the west side of the square running north and south is another stable seventy feet long, twenty feet wide and fourteen foot posts, which contains calf boxes, sheep pens and pig pens, and at the south-west corner the dairy. By this manner of erecting the building I get a hollow square containing a quarter of an acre, which not only affords a shelter for the animals, and is convenient for harnessing, and all other barn-yard work, but it keeps the whole building under the eye of the owner. This is a very important matter, because he can take a run out, the coldest night, around the whole place of nearly 600 feet in a few minutes, and see that everything is in proper condition; whereas if the barns were scattered about, as they often are, it would take greater time to make this round of inspection, and would be attended by more exposure, for in this court there is shelter no matter how the wind blows. Another advantage in this manner of building the barns, is that the rears are all placed so that no doors open to the outside, which not only affords security against the possibility of the animals breaking loose in the night, and getting out, but also prevents the chance of tramps getting into the stables or barns, and housing for the night, which they cannot well do unless they scale the gate from the outside and force an entrance.

Q. What do you consider the best method of constructing and arranging farm buildings?

A. That is an extensive subject and admits of a great many considerations. Different kinds of stock require different accommodations, and the management of the farm calls for a large variety of buildings suitable to the particular needs of it. On grain farms a barn is required of great capacity to store the grain, and having a capacious floor for threshing and cleaning it. This method of farming, however, can scarcely be followed any more in the Eastern part of the country, because the cheap grain of the far West and the low freights have made it unprofitable; and with the system of agriculture of course the special kind of buildings must go. Live stock feeding, dairying and sheep rearing must be followed in the East, and in parts of the West, swine feeding, with corn growing; and each of these special branches of farming calls for different kinds of buildings. As to the construction of the buildings, I approve of cheap wooden structures, easily built and easily renewed. A barn or stable is necessarily always filled with combustible material, and a stone and iron barn built at great cost could not be made fire-proof and would be ruined, although it might not be consumed, if the interior was burned out, so that as far as regards danger from fire, a cheap wooden building is equally as safe as a more costly stone one; and the cheaper one can be renewed ten times for the cost of the more expensive one. I have built cattle sheds which were comfortable and convenient, something in the style of my present buildings, which cost less than $10 for each head of cattle in them.

These plain and yet substantial buildings are much safer from fire than a large structure in which hay and fodder are stored over the cattle, and in which valuable animals worth, perhaps, $50,000 are kept fastened in such a way, that if the barn takes fire they cannot possibly be saved. It is only recently that a fine herd of Jersey cattle were thus burned in a large and costly barn, from which it was impossible to get them out because of the smoke. The barn cost several thousand dollars, and I know of other barns that have cost more than twenty-five thousand and some much more than that, but which are not so convenient as sheds costing only $10 per head, and which are perfectly comfortable, and from which, in case of fire, every animal could be let loose and driven out with complete safety.

The annexed drawings show how these sheds are constructed. The first gives the outside end view, the second a section showing the interior arrangement of the stall, and the third the ground plan of the stalls. Each cow has a loose stall to herself, in which she may be left unfastened, thus avoiding the risk of being caught in the

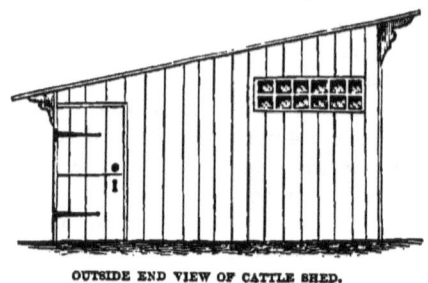

OUTSIDE END VIEW OF CATTLE SHED.

halter at any time, and getting thrown down, and in case of fire the doors may be all thrown open in a few minutes and every animal

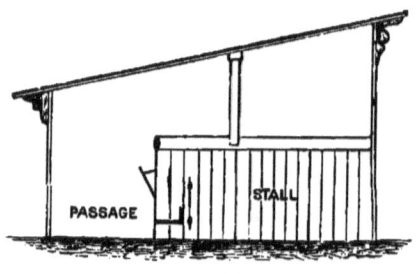

SECTION OF STALL INSIDE.

driven out to a place of safety. The shed is sixteen feet wide, giving a stall nine feet in the clear and seven feet wide, and a feeding pas-

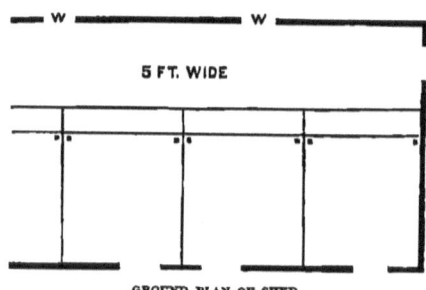

GROUND PLAN OF SHED.

sage, in front of the stalls, five feet wide. Each stall has a feeding trough with a shute through which the food can be put with a scoop, from a feeding truck, in which it is brought from the feed room, where it is prepared. A long staple of half-inch iron rod is fastened to each side, in which a steel ring and chain may be fixed, and one cow can then be fastened on each side, and two cows kept in each stall if desired. A double door is made in the front of each stall, four feet wide, and in warm weather the upper half may be left open. A long sliding window is made at each end of the shed, and, if necessary, other sliding windows are made in the rear, opening into the feeding alley. These windows provide for ample ventilation and light; and light is as necessary as fresh air for the welfare of cows. It is well to have close shutters to slide over these windows to darken the stable for the purpose of keeping out flies in the worst of the season, so that the cattle may rest comfortably in the heat of the day.

The floors of the stalls should be of earth, and graded to the rear, where a gutter should be made to carry off the drainage into the drains, which conduct it to the middle of the yard, where it is absorbed by the manure which is thrown into a heap there. Sheds of this kind can be put up for about one dollar and a half a running foot, in a plain rough fashion, and as much more money can be spent upon them as the owner's purse will allow. Paint is thrown away upon farm yard buildings, excepting for the sake of appearance. I have seen wooden buildings, unpainted, eighty years old, in which the boards had been worn but a very little, and if these had been painted once in five years the painting would have cost in all five times as much as the buildings. For painting farm buildings the common brown iron paint and raw linseed oil I think is the best; it is very durable, is fire-proof, and is not soiled by use. The color, too, is agreeable, as a contrast to the green of the trees and the fields.

HAY BARNS AND SHEDS.

Barns for storing hay and fodder are necessary where much stock is kept, and these buildings may be constructed very cheaply. High barns require heavy timber and firm framing and bracing, both to resist the winds and the pressure of the hay inside. Where land costs no more than it does in this country it is poor economy to build high barns. Lighter, broader and longer buildings can be built more cheaply and serve every useful purpose. The engravings represent two kinds of hay barns or sheds; one of large capacity for a good many head of stock; the other intended for smaller farms, and holding nearly one ton of hay to the running foot when filled to the top. The former, if thirty feet wide with sixteen-feet posts, and the self-support-ing roof here shown, will hold 3,000 pounds of hay to the running foot when filled. It has a clear space over the beams for the use of a horse fork or hay slings, and by having large doors for unloading

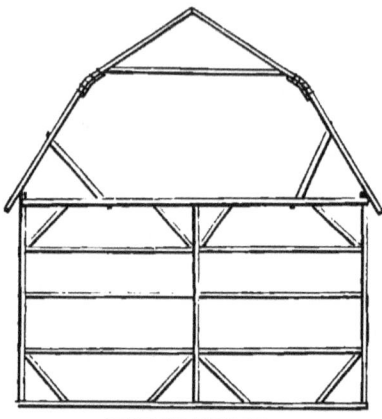

FRAME FOR HAY BARN.

1,000 pounds of hay may be unloaded with a sling at once. These slings are preferable to hay forks, as they carry a much larger load, and can be used for corn fodder as well as for hay. The engraving

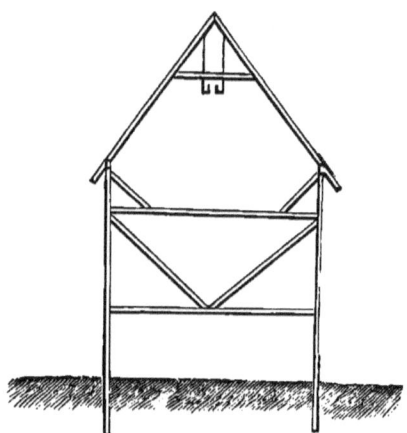

FRAME FOR HAY SHED.

shows a single bent of the frame, and by adding as many bents as may be required, the barn may be made as long as desirable. With the present useful machinery for unloading hay a barn may be made of any length, if unloading doors are provided within fifty feet of each other. This roof is a very strong one, as it cannot sag, and if properly braced and bolted to the plates, cannot spread. A three-quarter-inch iron bolt should be put through each rafter and the plate on which it rests, and a rod of the same size put through the top beam and rafter as shown to serve as a brace; a brace may be used as well, but the rod should lie close up to the brace and the nut at each end should be screwed up tight.

The smaller shed is made of posts set in the ground, twenty feet apart one way, and sixteen feet apart the other, making bents twenty feet wide, placed sixteen feet apart. Two cross girts may be bolted to the posts, which is stronger than framing them in, and two long braces should be bolted in to stiffen the building. Roof braces are spiked to each third or fourth pairs of rafters to keep these from spreading. This shed needs only a single board roof, laid closely, and a narrow batten to cover each joint, as the steep pitch sheds rain very easily.

HORSE BARNS.

Stables are used for common farm horses, but, where horses are bred, barns specially arranged for them are necessary. The use and value of farm horses are often greatly reduced by a want of proper arrangements for stabling them. Any kind of a place to crowd the poor beasts in is too often thought good enough, and the air in some stables is so bad from filthy floors that the harness is often rotted by it. A horse's lungs and eyes cannot fail to suffer in such an atmosphere, when tanned leather and carriage varnish are spoiled. No doubt a good deal of disease among horses is due to this cause. Another common fault is bad light. A horse sees on one side only with each eye, and a side light from a window strains the eyes unequally. The light should come into a stable directly in front of the horse, and it should not be too bright. If the window cannot be on the north side, it should be covered with lime-wash to mellow the light; but the stable should never be wholly dark. A stable should be airy and well ventilated, but not drafty; a draft upon a horse yet warm with work will surely injure him, and, if it does nothing worse, it will stiffen him for a few days. A few such mistakes will ruin any animal.

The feeding arrangements for a horse stable should be as follows: A hay rack above the head is objectionable, as the dust from it is apt to be breathed and cause disease of the lungs. A deep manger from a foot above the ground and three feet high, is the best for hay, and a grain box at one side of the stall serves for grain or cut feed. The grain box should be sixteen inches square at the top and sloping the same as the manger, and at least twelve inches deep. The manger should be eighteen inches in width at the top, narrowing to twelve inches at the bottom. The stall should be five feet wide. A horse cannot rest comfortably in one narrower, and if it is wider the animal may try to roll in it and get fast. The halter should not be any longer than will bring the end of it to a foot from the ground, and the loose end should run through a strong ring bolt and have a block of hard wood fastened to the end of it, so that the slack of the halter may always be taken up by the weight.

The floor of the stall is best made of concrete mixed with gas tar and rammed down hard. Such a floor will hold no moisture and always be clean. An excellent floor is made of round stone laid in a pavement, and filled between with cement well rammed, and then saturated with hot gas tar. No vermin will attack such a floor and it will always be cool for the horses' feet. For horses it is well to have a floor of wooden bars laid lengthwise and an inch apart, to provide drainage and keep the horse clean, and a drainage gutter made shallow and running lengthwise of the stable is necessary for cleanliness. Once a week the stall and gutter should be washed down with a pailful of water to cleanse and sweeten it.

A barn for a horse-breeding farm, where valuable animals are kept, should be made thirty-six feet wide, with an alley way through the middle twelve feet wide, and stalls twelve feet square on each side, opening into the alley way. A small window, protected by iron gratings, and made to swing on pivots, should be made for each stall for light and ventilation, and it should be placed six feet from the floor. A sliding door should be made in the stall into the alley for feeding, and double doors, the upper one of which should open singly, should be made to open into the alley way. It is very convenient to have feeding shutes from the floor above, to send down hay and grain into the manger and feed box. The hay shute should be a little larger below than above, so that the hay will not pack in it, and the grain shute should have a spout at the bottom leading into the feed box. The best bedding for horses is sawdust; but the dried peat, now being introduced, is equally good, and so far as its value for manure is concerned, is better than sawdust. The floor above the stalls should be laid close with matched boards.

SHEEP BARNS.

Success with sheep depends in a great measure upon having proper barns or sheds for them. Sheep culture will, no doubt, greatly increase in the course of a few years, and, as the improved breeds are more widely introduced, a better system of keeping them, with proportionately better profit, will be adopted. Few farms are well provided with accommodations for sheep, excepting where the farm is devoted to them, and even then many large flocks suffer for want of

SHEEP SHED FOR A SMALL FLOCK.

proper conveniences. This is especially injurious to the lambs, many of which are lost from accidents which might have been avoided. Sheep require pure air and dry lodging chiefly. Their fleece protects them from cold in the severest weather, and they know how to keep warm by huddling or bunching together when necessary. A close shed is therefore not healthful, because when sheep get overheated they are very apt to suffer from lung diseases, and pneumonia is one of the most fatal disorders to sheep. One night's overheating in a close shed will cause sheep to run at the nose, which is the first step towards inflammation of the lungs. A good tight roof, with an open front on the south side, placed on the north side of a dry yard, makes a sufficient shelter for a flock. For a small flock the yard and shed shown in the above engraving is recommended by Henry Stewart, the author of the "Shepherd's Manual," in that work, from which this illustration is borrowed.

A barn for a larger flock, designed by the late Hon. Geo. Geddes, of Onondaga, N. Y. (see engravings), is made with the pens eight feet high; the posts are eight feet apart and swinging doors are fixed between each pair of posts. The doors are double, one hung above the other, so that the upper or lower one, or both, can be closed when desired. The doors are hung upon pins fitted into the ends, as shown. Some of the pens may be enclosed and kept for separating ewes from the flock at lambing time. The upper part of

SHEEP BARN FOR A LARGE FLOCK.

the barn is kept for fodder, and the interior arrangement and the ground plan are here shown. In the rear of the barn, at A, is a root cellar. At C, C, is the feeding passage, over which are hay shutes to carry the hay into the rack, D, which opens into the stable by lathed bars placed up and down. The bars are not more than three inches apart, to prevent the sheep from pushing their heads

SWINGING DOOR FOR SHEEP BARN.

through and tearing the wool from the necks. A feeding trough, E, for grain or chopped roots, is under the hay rack, and is opened or closed by a falling door or shutter, which, when open, is held by cords and hooks to the sloping bottom of the hay rack. A stair-case or steps, B, leads from the feeding passage to the hay floor, and the hay should be so arranged as to leave a passage-way above. The hay floor should be of matched boards to prevent dust and chaff from dropping onto the sheep and getting into the wool.

Although abundant ventilation is provided for by the ample doors in front of the shed, it will, nevertheless, be advisable to have at least two air-shafts from the stable to the roof. These should be about four by six feet, and made of matched boards, some of which should be hung on hinges and fastened by bolts, that they may be used to pass hay down to the stable floor at times. These shutes should be two inches larger each way at the bottom than at the top, so that the hay

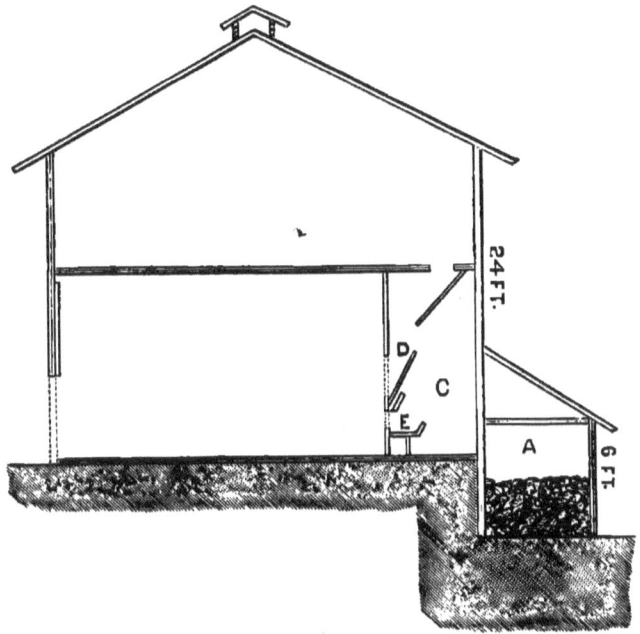

SECTIONAL VIEW OF SHEEP BARN.

will not lodge in them. The feed passage communicates with the root cellar by two or three doors, as may be convenient. With a cellar

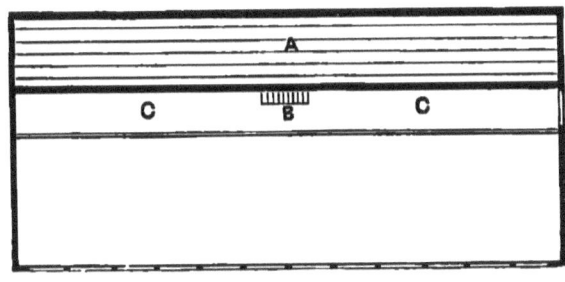

GROUND PLAN OF SHEEP BARN.

arranged as on this plan the method of preserving corn fodder by ensilage may be very easily practiced if desired.

It may be that ensilage will be found more desirable for sheep than for cows, if fed in moderation, but roots are quite free from objection of any kind, and as they can be grown, as stated in a previous chapter, quite as easily as ensilage, and require no expensive packing in a silo, no doubt roots will never wholly give way to ensilage, even for sheep. It might be well to mention that most roots are best cut in thin slices for sheep, although mangels being of a soft texture, are easily eaten when given whole.

For sheep keeping on a large scale an extensive shed arranged as here shown is convenient. When sheep are herded on the open plains or prairie, there are often losses by wolves, which pick up outlying sheep or lambs, unless the shepherd and his dogs are on the alert.

SHEDS FOR A SHEEP RANCHE.

It is safer to have the flock penned, and such a yard as this would be convenient, providing not only safety, but shelter in case of storms. For winter use some protection of this kind is indispensable. The range of sheds here shown was made for a sheep ranche in western Kansas. The walls were built of sods cut from the prairie; on the inside, the roof was supported by posts set in the ground; the roof was made of cedar poles covered with thatch of coarse marsh grass bound down with tarred rope. The side sheds were 600 feet long and the end one 300 feet; all were thirty feet wide, thus giving over an acre of ground under the roof with a yard enclosed of nearly five acres. A flock of nearly 4,000 sheep found ample accommodations in this yard and sheds during the winter. The supply of hay for occasional feeding in the winter was stacked in a long row down the centre of the yard and gave additional shelter to the sheep from driving storms. If such shelters as this were provided on the plains and exposed prairie farms, there would be very few losses in the flocks.

In all these arrangements for sheep it is necessary to avoid having any holes or open spaces into which young lambs might creep, a thing they are very apt to do, but they are not apt to get out again and of course they soon perish. Lambs are often lost in this way unless care is taken to prevent it.

PIG PENS.

Some years ago I built a range of pig pens, of which a view is here given. At first it was made seventy feet long, and I found it so convenient that it was increased by additions to 200 feet. It was nine feet high on one side, and six and one-half on the other, and sixteen feet wide.. It had a four-feet alley the whole length. The pens were

RANGE OF PIG PENS.

twelve by ten feet each, divided from each other by partitions three feet high. Each pen had a double door, the upper one used for ventilation, and the lower one to close the pen when the pigs were not allowed in the yard. At one end of the range of pens there was a boiler for cooking feed, which was distributed among the pigs along the feeding alley. As pigs are indispensable on most farms to consume the wastes, and as the profit from them and the ease of labor in attending to them depend upon the arrangement of the pens, it is very necessary that this matter should receive attention. A plank floor is required for pig pens, as the pigs would soon dig up any other kind. The floor should have a slope to the yard for the drainage, to keep them dry, for though the pig is supposed to be a filthy animal, yet none other thrive better for being kept dry and clean.

An excellent piggery, built a few years ago by Mr. F. D. Curtis, of Saratoga County, N. Y., is shown in the following engravings, the first of which represents the general view of the building and the yards. The second shows the side view; the third is the cellar, R, R, being the root bins, with a root cutter at G. The feeding box is at F; at C is the cistern; T, T, are meal bins; K is the boiler and B the stairs up to the main floor. The plan of the pens on the main floor is as follows: The first pen is for the boar in use, and has a

MR. CURTIS' PIGGERY—FRONT VIEW.

raised floor, with an outer door for the convenience of neighbors' sows brought for service. The other pens are for sows and pigs. Each is provided with an iron feed trough and with a feed shute. Each pen is provided with a guard rail for the protection of the young pigs, which is placed six inches above the floor and six inches from the wall. The floors of the pens were made water-proof in the following manner: First a floor of dry hemlock one-and-one-quarter-inch plank was laid. This was covered with a coat of hot gas tar, and a second floor was laid directly upon this tar while it was hot. Sufficient tar was laid on to fill all the cracks between the floor. The upper floor was then given a coat of hot tar and well sanded.

SIDE VIEW OF PIGGERY.

This floor was found very satisfactory, being hard, dry, quite vermin-proof, and never permitting any leakage into the cellar below.

Considering the enormous losses in swine by diseases on the large Western feeding farms, there can be no question but that the cost of

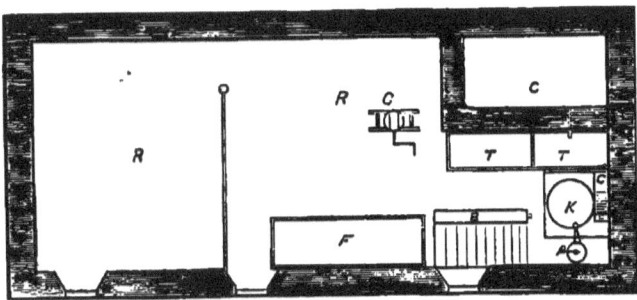

PLAN OF CELLAR OF PIGGERY.

well arranged buildings would soon be paid for in the value of the animals saved. Where losses foot up to ten million dollars in a year, it is very clear that there would be a good profit made from the use of comfortable buildings to secure shelter and cleanliness.

CATTLE BARNS.

The business of stall feeding cattle will, I am confident, greatly increase east of the great grazing plains during the coming years, along with dairying. In this respect we must follow the course of the English, Scotch and European farmers. Grain will be grown in the rich North-western Territories and in California, where land is cheap, and mixed farming is not suitable on account of the climate. Grain cannot be grown to pay in the East—and by East I mean all the States east of the Missouri River—unless stock is stall fed to make manure. Rich feeding stuffs, as oil-cakes, bran from the great Western mills, and corn from the prairie States, which can be bought more cheaply than it can be raised, must take the place of farm grown coarse grain; and fodder crops and roots will be produced in abundance for the cattle. A farm of 100 acres will have its feeding sheds where from twenty to fifty head of beeves or 200 or 300 sheep will be fattened every winter, and larger farms will feed more in proportion. I do not see how this can be helped. Calves that are now butchered or sold for a few dollars, and lean cattle from the West, will be bought up for feeding. The land can be made rich enough for profitable farming only in this way and by dairying, and every farm cannot be a dairy, because there is a limit to the demand of butter and cheese, and the great cities and foreign countries must have beef and mutton.

In this case properly arranged barns for feeding must be provided. Labor must be reduced to a minimum or the profit will be small, and labor is reduced by convenient arrangements for feeding.

One man is able to feed and care for fifty head of cattle when everything is well arranged with suitable buildings. This will cost about two cents a day for attention and care, which is about as cheap as I think it can be done. If the cattle are fed for four months, and 250 pounds only is added to the weight of each in that time, the cost for labor will be less than one cent per pound of this increase. The great profit in feeding cattle, however, is not in this increased weight, but in the increased value of the whole animal from its better quality. A fat steer can be easily made worth one cent a pound of live weight more than its cost when it was thin; thus a 1,600-pound animal will have at least $16 added to its value in this way, in addition to the value of the added weight. Those farmers who do not understand this fact lose sight of the most important part of the business.

A cattle shed should be roomy, both to give the animals plenty of fresh air, and to afford convenience in feeding them and removing the manure. The pens should be made in ranges having a feeding passage large enough for a cart to be taken through with roots, hay, straw and feed, and an alley as large for the purpose of taking out the manure. It is a good plan when there is abundance of straw for litter to fill up the pens once a day and let the manure collect for a month, or in fact for the whole feeding season, as it is kept hard trodden and is not at all disagreeable. In this case the stalls are

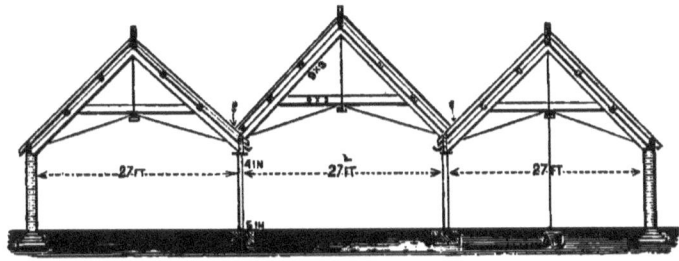

FRAME FOR CATTLE SHEDS.

enclosed and made large enough for the cattle to turn around, and the animals are left loose. This plan is very common on the large cattle farms in England. The plans here given represent one of these English cattle sheds, and may be worthy of study, as showing the system in common use there. The whole width in the clear is eighty-one feet. If the pens or stalls are made to run across the

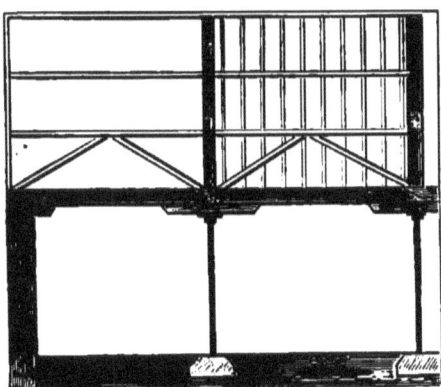

SIDE VIEW OF FRAME.

building this will afford space for five rows of pens having four passages between them, the cattle standing on the outside rows with their backs to the ends of the building. A square shed of this size will hold fifty head in five rows of ten each, and each one having a loose stall of ten by eight feet. The sides of the building will have wide double doors ten feet apart opening to the passages, and at each end there will be doors for letting the cattle in and out, and for taking out manure from the end rows of pens.

In the plan given, the roof is made with spaces between the eaves of the valleys for collecting the rain water into gutters which carry it into cisterns. About 100,000 gallons of water could be collected in four fall and winter months with our rain-fall, and this supply would be of considerable value, affording about eight gallons a day for each head. But as the water would be gathered through the whole year, if there was sufficient cistern room to save it, there would be enough to supply all the wants of the cattle for the four months of the feeding season.

The plan for the side of the building is also given. In England iron is cheaper than timber, durability and strength being considered. But as timber is cheaper here than iron, the posts shown will be made of timber. The foundations of the posts are stones bedded in the ground or blocks of concrete. The foot of each post is fitted into a cast iron socket, one inch smaller inside than the timber, the timber being cut away to fit the socket makes an even joint, and being bedded in paint preserves the wood from rotting. The floor of the whole shed may be of gravel and clay well beaten, or, for a well built shed, of concrete. An earthen floor, however, properly graded to the gutters and drains, will be sufficient when plenty of litter is furnished. Sheds of cheaper construction may be built to serve an equally good purpose, excepting so far as regards durability. A different arrangement may be made if desirable, which would greatly reduce the cost, *viz.*, the cattle may be kept loose in the shed, and fed from racks and grain troughs on each side of a drive-way. With this arrangement twice as many cattle could be kept in this shed, three drive-ways only being made, one in the centre and one at each side, leaving two large spaces for the cattle. But, as cattle feed better and make more flesh when quiet and undisturbed, it is a question if the plan of having stalls would not pay more profit, notwithstanding its larger cost. The partitions between the stalls are made of bars which are movable, so that when the cattle are taken out the bars are removed, and wagons can be driven in all over to take out the manure.

FENCES.

Another important matter to the farmer, somewhat allied to the buildings, is the fences. Conditions are so varied that this is something in which the farmer will in most cases have to be guided as circumstances may suggest. I may say, however, that I am a great foe to fences. I have torn down miles upon miles of fences, and have gained by it a great deal of the very best land. I don't believe in having any fences whatever except line fences, and highway fences. It will always pay better to hire a good boy to take care of cattle than to build fences. The kinds of fences must of course depend upon the locality. In some sections, where timber is plentiful and lumber scarce, the cheapest fence may be found to be the ordinary rail or post and rail fence; but wherever lumber can be obtained at reasonable price, I think it will be found that a board fence can be erected at less cost, besides taking up less land and presenting a much neater appearance. A solid post and three-rail fence can always be made at less cost than an ordinary worm fence, even without considering the economy of land. Live fences are now used to a great extent on the prairies, where timber is scarce. No other fence is cheaper or better than this if a little care be taken for the first four or five years in their management. The seedling plants of Honey Locust or Osage Orange can be bought at $5 per 1,000 plants, a foot high. Such plants, if set out at one foot apart and the land kept clean for a foot or so each side of the hedge, and kept carefully trimmed into the shape of a blunt wedge, will attain a height of five or six feet in five or six years, and will form a barrier, with needlelike spurs, so dense that a rat could hardly get through it; of course some temporary fence would be required till it grows up. Transplanted two-year-old plants will always be found the cheapest, even at $15 per 1,000.

Wire fences are coming into general use, both plain and barbed. Barb wire is no doubt the best, and in grazing localities is indispensable. But where valuable animals are kept there may be danger of injury, which it is better to avoid by using the plain wire. A plain wire fence may be made equally effective as one of barbed wire, by putting the posts down firmly, and bracing them sufficiently, and straining the wire tight. Ring staples with screws and nuts may be used at the end of the fences for tightening the wires, when this is needed. No less than four wires should be used. In some cases a narrow board nailed to the posts over the top wire is used with advantage, as this is more easily seen by the animals. The posts should never be more than sixteen feet apart, and twelve feet is better unless the posts are very firmly braced. Number nine galvanized steel wire is used. Such a fence, put down in the best manner, need not cost more than three cents a foot under favorable circumstances, or five cents a foot at the most.

REARING AND KEEPING POULTRY.

Poultry, like hogs, are one of the items on the farm of which, if many are kept, the cost usually overruns the profit; but the farmer cannot afford to be without eggs or chickens, and if he had to buy I fear the goodwife would come short sometimes, eggs being used in so many ways about the kitchen, and a plump fowl is so handy for a meal. In the winter time, when eggs bring fifty cents per dozen, there is a profit in fowls, but when they run down to twelve and fifteen cents, as they do for the greater part of the year, fowls do not pay for their keep, unless the farmer has a large run near his manure yard. Under special circumstances poultry may be made quite profitable. A farmer in my neighborhood keeps from six to seven hundred hens for their eggs, and although he has 300 acres of land, this is the only way in which he pays his taxes and other expenses. He plows in the woods among the trees several times from April until the end of November, and here the hens make out their living, feeding on worms and larvæ of insects. But fowls in my opinion do not often pay where grain has to be bought or produced to feed them, and they get no other food. A hen can be kept for the sum of one dollar a year for grain, where it has a good run, and where the eggs and chickens are worth two dollars per hen and the hens can be kept free from disease there will be a good profit. Where poultry raising on a large scale is practiced the incubator is used at times with success, but there are few farmers who have had any experience with it, and to such as are interested in poultry raising as a business, we would refer them to special works on the subject. I have kept the English White Dorking, but the gray variety I have never had much success with, as they seem to be more tender than the white breed. I also imported the Black Spanish, and the White Leghorn, but only kept them one season. Two years ago I got fifty Plymouth Rocks. I built a small poultry house in the fall and put them into it. They were fed morning and night with warm feed, and we had eggs all winter through, and early spring chickens large enough for broilers in May; but if I had had three times as many hens with no greater accommodations, I would doubtless not have had as many eggs, and therefore I think that every farmer should select a few of the best breed and keep only that few and tend them well, or his profit in poultry will be apt to be very light indeed.

The Plymouth Rocks I find are very satisfactory, as they are quiet and do not disturb the garden much, and mature very early, and sometimes will dress at six months old five to six lbs. and when full grown seven to eight lbs. In winter, chickens should be kept in a place where they are moderately warm, in a temperature of from forty to fifty degrees, and at that season of the year when insects are not to be obtained, they should be fed with the scraps or leavings from the kitchen, broken or crushed bones, or anything that will stand in lieu of their natural insect food.

PLYMOUTH ROCKS.

The Plymouth Rock is a large, well formed bird, with a small single comb, clean yellow legs, a large breast and bluish pencilled plumage. It resembles most in form the English Dorking of all our American fowls. It is, perhaps, the best fowl to be kept on farms, as it is a good early winter layer, a good brooder, the chicks are hardy and can be reared early, and make the best of broilers at two to three months old, thus coming in at a season when chickens bring about twenty-five cents a pound usually, and forty cents a pound at times.

One of the most profitable branches of poultry keeping is the rearing of young chickens for market. For these the earliest broods are preferable, although there is little profit in trying to rear chicks before May, unless one has a well furnished and warm poultry house, heated with a stove. Where there is a green-house or cold grapery a poultry house may be attached to it, and get the surplus heat, and in this way young chicks can be reared in January or February. It will not pay, however, on an average farm, to do this; but there are many market farms near large cities, or near summer resorts, where poultry keeping of this kind may bring in several hundred dollars a year, and this may be earned by the younger members of the family. To rear market chicks the early broods should be put in a warm coop, having a sash cover, so as to get the warmth, and another sash may cover a small yard, where the chicks may run and take exercise. On cold nights the glass cover may be protected by a sack or a straw mat. A Light Brahma hen, in a roomy coop of this kind, will take twenty chicks and rear all without the loss of one, as the brood is quite safe from accident. The food should be oat meal, cracked corn and finely chopped meat scraps, with plenty of pure water. Light Brahma chicks are exceedingly hardy, and although almost bare of feathers for several weeks will stand severe cold if kept dry. When the chicks are two months old the hen may be taken from them, and they will nestle in their coop quite comfortably alone. At ten or twelve weeks old they will weigh two to three pounds, and will sell for $1.50 a pair in good markets, and nearly as much, when half this weight, as broilers. Later chicks, ready for market when summer boarding is at its height, readily sell for twenty-five cents a pound, and a four-months-old Light Brahma cockerel, at that age, will bring a dollar. Farmers who make a special business of this have often realized $5 from each hen of a well managed flock, including the eggs sold early in the season at the usually high prices then current.

MANAGEMENT OF EARLY CHICKENS.

As in all special branches of any business, the rearing of poultry requires considerable tact and experience. And the rearing of early chickens is still more exacting in this respect. But when properly managed, either of these specialties may be made a profitable addition to the farm business under some circumstances. Grain farming and poultry keeping will not go together, but dairying and stock feeding will do very well with poultry rearing. Poultry is especially adapted for dairy farms, as fowls will consume the spare milk with equal and perhaps greater profit than pigs will. For satisfactory success, however, there are some requisites that are indispensable. It is all in the management. First a well arranged house and yard are needed; and the necessary arrangement includes the easy securing of perfect cleanliness, dryness, and thorough ventilation. Next there must be such a provision and kind of nests and fittings that vermin can find no harbor; that the hens cannot quarrel and fight and break their eggs, and so learn the bad habit of eating them. Then there must be a separate apartment for brooding hens, where they may not be annoyed by laying hens, and every provision for their feeding and comfort and security; lastly there must be a properly arranged method of protecting the young chicks as soon as they are hatched and until the whole brood is out and strong enough to go into the coop with the hen.

First let us consider the house. A very convenient one for a flock of fifty hens, which is as many as should be kept in one house and yard, is made as follows: it is twenty-five or thirty feet long, ten feet wide, eight feet high in the front and five feet in the rear, with a sloping roof. It should be divided into two apartments, one six or eight feet long, and the other eighteen or twenty feet, and separated by a tight partition, with a door in it leading from one to the other. There should be a door in each apartment, and a large window, which should face the south. The floor should be the ground, and this should be high and dry and drained, so that rain water from the roof cannot enter. The only fittings inside are the roosts, which are made in a frame of three bars four inches wide, having two cross pieces to hold them together. This frame is hinged to the rear wall, sixteen inches only from the ground and all on a level, which entirely prevents fighting to get the highest perch and prevents injury from the fowls flying down from the roosts. This frame can be raised against the wall, out of the way, when the floor is cleaned, which should be done at least every week, in a thorough manner. This will wholly prevent vermin harboring in the house and prevent much suffering for the fowls. The nests are loose boxes sixteen inches long, and twelve wide and deep; open at one side where the hen enters and having a narrow strip at the bottom three inches wide to keep the nest in its place. These nest boxes are loose and are placed on the floor around the house. When a hen sets and has settled down, the nest with the hen is removed to the setting room, and another box is put in its place. The eggs are taken from the nests at noon, and in the evening when the hens are fed. When the setting hen is settled down quietly, the brood of eggs is given to her and a card is pinned to the wall over the nest having the date on it when the hen was set. With such an arrangement as this there is no trouble, and the hens are kept quiet and docile, and this saves eggs and chickens.

The yard should be enclosed safely, and for fifty fowls should contain half an acre or 200 feet by 100. It should be divided into two parts, each to be used alternately, and while one is being used the other should be plowed up and sown with some quick growing crop, as peas, rape, turnips, oats, etc., for the fowls to feed upon and scratch among. This secures cleanliness of the ground, and a valuable provision of green food for the fowls. In this way fifty fowls can be kept enclosed all the time in perfect health and thrift and with corresponding profit. But it cannot be done in any other way. For the fences, cheap wire netting is the best and most economical.

The feeding of fowls should be regular and the food should be varied. Early morning, noon, and night, the food should be supplied and never given in excess. Over feeding surely produces disease. Fowls should never be given all they will eat. An average of one bushel of grain is sufficient for one fowl for a year, in addition to what green food is supplied in the way above mentioned, or that can be picked up in a moderate range. This is equal to about two and one-half ounces a day. A variety of grain is advisable. Wheat, barley, buckwheat, corn, and mixed meal and bran, with some boiled potatoes or milk or buttermilk, and some flesh meat occasionally, will be necessary. With such feeding, and plenty of clean fresh water twice a day, there will be no trouble from sickness, and of course sickness among the fowls will destroy all the profit.

It is a great help to have the fowls docile and easily handled. This is secured by a simple method of managing, which is as follows. And this method also has other advantage as will be seen. The hens being set in their separate apartment are fed and watered daily, and soon become used to this attendance. When the chicks begin to appear they are taken, as they come out of the shell, or with the broken shell, if necessary, from under the hen, and put in a nursing mother made as follows: A box made with double sides, filled with wool waste or cotton batting, about sixteen inches square every way inside and standing on end, has a shelf fitted in the middle. Under this shelf a tin box filled with hot water is placed to warm up the box to ninety-five degrees. The young chick is put on this shelf in a nest of sawdust, where it is kept warm and rests comfortably while the others are coming out. It is always well to set two hens on the same day, so that two broods come out at the same time. With average success from eight to ten chicks will come from each brood, and all are put into the nursing mother until the two broods are all hatched. The last two or three may be left under the hen.

The coop, which should be roomy, is prepared, and if the weather is yet cold, should be put in a glass house, or have a glass covering, and be put in a sunny, sheltered corner. At night the hen with the chicks are removed to the coop, and left in a dry, comfortable nest, made of chaff, in a corner of the coop, or upon a piece of dry bagging. The hen thus adopts all the chicks, and in the morning will be found caring for them. The hen and chicks are fed with some soaked bread or cracked wheat or coarse oatmeal for two or three days, and after that with coarse corn meal and other food. They soon become tame, and will feed out of the hand, and this tameness is encouraged afterwards, so that the fowls can be handled, and will feed out of the hand at any time. This very much eases the work, and makes it successful and profitable. The chicks should have a run out on grass or in a garden, where they will pick up myriads of insects and do no mischief; but the hen should be kept in the coop. The coop should have no fixed bottom, but a loose one of boards, which can be covered with dry earth and changed twice a week. By running over fresh ground the chicks never have the gapes. When the chicks are two months old the hens may be taken away from them, if the weather is warm, and the chicks will nestle in their coops as usual by themselves, until they are quite large and ready for sale.

In small flocks there is the most and the surest profit; but where there is a range of grass land, a poor, rough field, or one that has been run down by bad management and needs a rest, a stock of poultry, managed as above described, has often paid more profit than any other investment on the farm.

LIGHT BRAHMA FOWLS.

Light Brahmas are the most popular fowl and are even heavier than the Plymouth Rocks. When this variety is kept in the best manner, small flocks of them have been known to pay as much as four or five dollars per hen in the year. But in all poultry keeping, crowding must be avoided or the flock will suffer, and the owner will surely lose by them instead of making a gain. Overcrowding and filth are the bane of poultry, as they are the destruction of sheep or pigs, as they surely produce fatal disorders.

The Light Brahma is among poultry what the Short Horn is among beef cattle or the Jersey in the dairy. It is handsome, clean and exceedingly productive. When well kept it is not subject to disease; it lays about eighty or ninety eggs on an average in the year, and will safely rear eight chicks per hen in a flock. As a fowl may be kept for a dollar per year, the profit is large; but in farming it is never safe to calculate one's profits by arithmetic, for if a flock of fifty fowls or 100 sheep, or a herd of twenty cows, produce a certain income, it rarely follows that twice as many will double the profit. This depends strictly upon the conditions and circumstances, the conveniences, and above all upon the skill and experience of the owner.

The Light Brahma is one of the largest of fowls; a yearling cockerel will weigh ten or eleven pounds, and a pullet seven to eight; the flesh is yellow; the legs yellow; the plumage white and downy, excepting the tail feathers, and the principal wing feathers, which are black; the neck feathers are mixed with black, forming a broad collar. The legs are feathered down to the toes. The comb is small and pea formed. This is an American breed, the origin of which is now in some doubt, but in value it undoubtedly comes first among all the breeds of

SILVER SPANGLED HAMBURGS.

fowls for profitable keeping, when the requisite care is given to it; otherwise, as with every farm animal of every kind, failure is certain.

The White Dorking is an English fowl, and in that country is the most popular of all breeds of poultry. The vicinity of the town of Dorking is a noted place for rearing poultry, and is an example of what can be done in this way when a special business is made of any pursuit, and it is persevered in until experience brings success. The Dorking fowls are the oldest breed of poultry in existence, having been kept in Britain before the Romans invaded that country, but of late years they have been much improved through exhibitions and the competition of breeds. The White Dorking is smaller than the gray or colored varieties and is hardier. It is considered as the best of all the English breeds for poultry, chickens and eggs. All the Dorkings have an extra inner toe, making five in all.

The varieties of Hamburgs, of which there are Black, Golden and Silver Pencilled, Golden and Silver Spangled and White, are handsome and good fowls; they are all good layers and hardy, but are rather too small for market purposes. For family use they are desirable, when fowls are kept for ornament as well as use. The comb is flat, rose shaped and large, and terminates in a point behind. The Black Spanish is a profitable fowl as regards the production of eggs, of

BLACK SPANISH FOWLS.

which they will lay in a year one-third more than the large breeds, as the light Brahmas and others of that class. But the hens of this breed are poor brooders and rear very few chickens, so that this product, which is really the most profitable, is of very little account. These fowls have large, single, serrated combs, with large white ear lobes and cheeks, and are very tender in our climate, frequently having the combs frozen.

Of the non-brooding fowls the Leghorns are the most popular. They produce more eggs than any other breed under equal conditions, but rear very few chickens. They are small and light, and of course not so profitable for the poultry rearer as the larger fowls, excepting for the production of eggs in the winter season. They are not hardy and require careful treatment, and the chickens cannot be reared safely until the warm weather. The White Leghorn is the most popular of this class of fowls. It is very neat and handsome, and has the large comb common to all the fowls of this class.

When poultry are kept solely for eggs the Leghorns are the most satisfactory of all fowls. Their eggs are large, clear white in color, well shaped and are quite salable. These are the only fresh eggs in the market at the times when they sell at the highest price, and of course a fowl that fills the basket then is the one that produces the most profit. The greatest objection to them is their tenderness and the danger of freezing the combs, unless warmly housed. But this

WHITE LEGHORNS.

warm housing is indispensable for all fowls which are kept for profit, as hens will not lay eggs when exposed to cold, and not even the Leghorns. Before eggs are produced the fowls must be fully nourished, and a large portion of the food is consumed in maintaining the warmth of an animal of any kind. Leghorns, as all the smaller breeds of fowls, consume much less food than the larger breeds, probably not more than half as much, and although their eggs are smaller, yet so long as they are sold by count and not by weight, the smaller breeds will always be popular for the production of eggs.

The Brown Leghorn has a plumage of a bright golden bay, with black and brown intermixed, and has some resemblance in color to the Brown Red Games. Some hens of this breed have been known to continue laying eggs up to over ten years of age, and in all have produced 2,000 eggs and over in their lifetime. In addition to these varieties there are the Dominique Leghorns, a bluish pencilled sort, and the Black Leghorns.

BROWN LEGHORNS.

The crested fowls are popular with some poultry keepers, on account of the peculiar bunch of fine feathers which cover the heads. Of these there are the French and the various kinds of Polish fowls. The Houdans are a French breed, and are good layers but poor

HOUDANS.

brooders. They are black and white in color, with pencilled plumage, have large crests, and beards about the throat, and combs shaped like a deer's antlers. They have the fifth toe like the Dorkings. These birds have excellent white flesh and lay large eggs.

The Polands are of several kinds, some rather curiously varied as to plumage, as White Crested Black, White Crested White, Golden, Silver and Bearded Golden and Silver. They are good fowls for a small kind, but are most profitable when reared for sale as fancy

WHITE CRESTED BLACK POLISH.

fowls. The White Crested Black and the White Crested White are the most popular, and there is scarcely any other fowl, excepting, perhaps, some of the little bantams, which are so curious as the little chicks of these two varieties, with their peculiar crested heads.

CREVECŒURS.

The Crevecœurs, another crested breed of French origin, are all black and have beautiful plumage, with a rich greenish shade in the sunlight. They differ in no other respects from the Houdans, but in plumage and in having no fifth toe.

WYANDOTTE FOWLS.

The Wyandottes are a new breed, which as a fancy fowl have gained a good deal of popularity. They are something of the style of the Plymouth Rocks, but are spangled with white after the manner of the Silver Spangled Hamburgs. They are heavy, medium

WYANDOTTES.

sized fowls, very neat and pleasing in appearance and have a rose comb. They are said to be good layers and make good market fowls. For farmers who wish to keep a fancy fowl, for their appearance and for breeding for sale, this variety has some desirable points.

DARK BRAHMAS.

The Asiatics are all heavy bodied, thickly feathered varieties, and are chiefly valued for breeding for sale. Some of them are very handsome, as the Buff Cochin, which, when in full feather, has a very attractive appearance. The Dark Brahma approaches more closely to this class of fowls than the Light Brahma, which is a far better fowl for ordinary farm purposes. The Dark Brahma has a variegated plumage of black and white, with long, silky neck feathers of silvery

WHITE COCHINS.

white striped with black, and a small pea comb. It has a poor reputation as an egg producer, and excepting when in new and full feather is not an attractive fowl.

The White and Black Cochins are handsome varieties, large, clean

BLACK COCHINS.

and neatly formed, but they have no special value for farm purposes, as there are many better kinds to choose from. A newly introduced variety called the Langshan is so nearly like the Black Cochin that even an expert would be puzzled to distinguish between them. There is, however, a difference which appears in the flesh, the Langshans having clear white skins and flesh, while the Cochin has yellow flesh.

The various breeds known as Game fowls are kept for their beauty more than for their value otherwise. But no other fowl has sweeter flesh, or richer flavored eggs, and for use on the tables of farmers who love quality before size, the old fashioned Brown Red Game will certainly please. There are more varieties of games than any other class, no less than twelve being bred by fanciers. The viciousness of these fowls, however, debars many persons from keeping them, as a game cock will suffer no rival to live within his domain if he is able to destroy him.

BANTAMS.

The small fowls known as bantams are very pleasing as pets and for ornamental purposes, and a little bantam hen, no larger than a pigeon, with her tiny brood, makes a pretty picture upon a farm lawn, and is

JAPAN BANTAMS.

the delight of the children. There are many varieties of these, some of which have been greatly improved by an English baronet, Sir John Sebright, whose name has been given to the varieties which he has bred to perfection: as the Golden and Silver Sebrights. The eggs of these little fowls are remarkably rich in flavor, and for the table are considered the best of any fowl or bird. A very curious variety, black and white in color, has recently been brought from Japan, and sold as high as $50 the pair. The demand for them at this price has however been filled, but they still sell at large prices, compared with their size. In breeding these small fowls, every circumstance that will tend to keep them down in size is taken advantage of, and the broods are not hatched until the fall, so as to stunt the growth of the chicks as much as possible by the cold weather.

TURKEYS.

These fine fowl are found very profitable when circumstances permit special care to be given to them. As a rule the housewife succeeds best in the management of poultry, and the turkeys always fall to her share, as one of her especial perquisites. There is but one variety of turkey which is worth keeping on the farm when profit is the main pursuit. This is the Bronze variety, a cross of the wild native breed. It is not generally known that the turkey is a native American fowl, and was unknown in Europe until after its introduction from this continent. The wild turkey is now the finest variety existing, and is sometimes found weighing forty pounds, and is frequently taken of a weight of twenty pounds. The cross of this bird with the common black variety, which has been made in recent years, has given us the Bronze Turkey, and specimens of this breed have reached over forty pounds and occasionally near fifty. It is hardy, but retains its wild instincts, and loves to hide its nest, and does far better in that way. The young birds, or, as they are called, "poults," require a good deal of care in shelter from rain and cold weather, and in proper feeding. Chopped clover and young onions, coarse oat meal and cracked corn, are the best food. One visit of the male to a flock of hens is sufficient, and a hen thus attended will even lay and hatch a second brood without further service. Corn meal and oat meal scalded with hot sweet milk make the best fattening food.

WATER FOWL.

Geese deserve a passing thought, if only at those times when we recline comfortably upon the soft beds made of their feathers. They are more properly called web-footed fowl, because they can be reared as easily out of the water as with it, and perhaps better. As market fowl they are reared with good profit, and are very easily kept. Being very close graziers they require a grass field wholly to themselves;

and if they have a good pasture they will need no other food until they are put up to fatten, when twenty days' feeding with corn will put them in good condition for market. The goslings are very hardy and the goose is an excellent mother, although very stubborn in her disposition, so that once she has chosen her nest she will take no other, but will sit out her time, if with only a paving stone under her. There are two prominent varieties: the Toulouse, which is gray and is the largest of all kinds, and the Embden, which is pure white. The best time to market geese is at the Christmas holidays.

Ducks are profitable when well managed, but under other circumstances will eat three times their value of food. When the young ducklings are fed properly, and are forced, so as to be ready for market at ten to twelve weeks old, or sooner with some varieties, they

PEKIN DUCKS.

are quite profitable. There are several kinds. The Pekin is a large white variety and quite prolific, but, like all profitable farm animals, it is a great eater. The Aylesbury is also pure white, and, when fat, will weigh six pounds at four months old. It grows very rapidly when well fed. The Rouen is a gray duck, and the drake is beautifully marked with golden green, steel-blue and brown. It is a large duck, weighing eight to ten pounds when fat, and is a quick feeder. The most profitable way to rear ducks is as follows: The old ducks are kept shut up at night until they have laid their eggs, which they usually do about daylight. They are then turned out, and a wet, mucky swamp, or a green meadow with ditches in it, provides them a very desirable feeding ground. At night, when they come in, they should be fed, and at no other times. Corn, oats, barley and buckwheat are suitable food. The eggs are gathered every morning and set under hens, giving nine only to each nest. When the ducklings are hatched they are left with the hen for a day or two, and then put alone in small pens, made of a frame of boards twelve inches wide and about four feet square. They cannot escape from this, and are provided with a small covered shelter at one corner, where they may be enclosed at night. The food should be at first boiled corn meal and oat meal, with chopped lettuce and young cabbage and onions. A shallow pan covered over with coarse wire netting, so that they cannot bathe in it, should be kept furnished with clean water three times a day, and the young ducks must be fed every two hours. With this feeding they will weigh four pounds at twelve weeks old and sell for $1.50 to $2 the pair. They are then quite profitable; but every day they are kept beyond this weight reduces the profit. The old ducks may be left to forage for themselves until the winter, when they may be fed with the geese upon chopped turnips, oats and corn.

DOGS FOR THE FARM.

Perhaps the only breed of dogs that can be said to be of much service on the farm is the Scotch Collie, which has been recently introduced here in considerable numbers, and is in great demand from all sections of the country. It is not only an excellent farm dog, but is almost indispensable to the sheep or cattle raiser. I have used them on my farm for the past thirty years and can well attest the many tales of their wonderful sagacity. The cut given of my imported dog, "Sport," the winner of many prizes and one of the best dogs ever imported, will show the distinctive points of the Collie. He is broad in the forehead; ears far apart, and stand straight at the base with the tips inclined downwards when in repose, but when under orders straight up in the attitude of the closest attention. His eye is bright and has an intelligent look; face long; muzzle rather fine; head covered with fine hair; neck rather short; fore legs short but strong, hind legs much longer but generally crooked, which gives him good running power, as all dogs on the Scotch hill farms have to run a good deal. The feet are flat and they have the extra claw on the hind leg called the "Dew claw." The tail is long and bushy, and should always be curved downwards lower than the back. The color varies; in some it is black, others black and white, and others black, white and tan. There is also a rough haired Collie, much used by cattle drovers. Some of them resemble the fox in color and have sandy hair. A few years ago Queen Victoria had a number of pure black and tan Collies, which I saw at Balmoral. They were pretty, but I am of the opinion that they had been crossed with the black and tan Setter dog. This may not have been the case, but it seemed to me the only plausible explanation for the absence of that foxy look which is characteristic of all pure Collies.

In the north of England and borders of Scotland the Gordon Setter has been used as a cross and at our shows these invariably take the prize

COLLIE DOG, 'SPORT.'

against our pure Collies. But although handsomer, they are by no means so valuable for sheep as the pure Collie. The price paid for Collie pups is from $10 to $15; and trained dogs of pure breed range from $50 to $100.

In the rough haired Collie, under his outer coat of long hair he has a coat of fine, short close hair, which protects him from storms. The intelligence of the pure Collie is almost beyond belief. One of my young Collies took a great liking to the cattle, so much so that she would remain in the field all day with them, keeping all strangers out of the pasture. One Sunday not long since a neighbor went into the lot to take a look at the cows, but the dog attacked him and actually drove him out of the field. They are specially fond of children, and are usually excellent watch dogs. In driving cattle, instead of catching the tail of the animal as other dogs invariably do, they will nip the heels and draw back quickly out of danger of being kicked. They display a degree of intelligence seemingly far beyond instinct. When driving sheep, if one should turn on him, as ewes with young lambs very often will do, the Collie does not resent it, but will turn quietly aside and lie down until the sheep returns to the flock, when he will go on driving them. One of my old dogs once kept a ewe and her lamb apart in a five-acre lot from morning until evening without injury to either. The same dog, after being taken twice to bring the sheep from the pasture to the yard at five, P. M., went of his own accord every evening afterwards and brought them into the yard, fully half a mile away, part of the way through wood land, never varying more than fifteen minutes of five o'clock, at which time he delivered them in the yard.

The Collie is eminently practical in his notions and seems to enjoy nothing so much as performing his duties with the sheep or cattle, but he can be taught tricks, though I doubt if he is over fond of showing off his accomplishments in this direction. My little girl five years old can ask "Coxsie" to jump over a chair, haul her on a sled or go over a fence, which he will do, but if asked by one of the men or boys he will skulk off and lie down. When called for the cows or sheep, however, he is right up, and will leave his best meal for either duty.

Another instance which shows a peculiar phase of its natural instinct occurred in a city, where a goat was kept by a resident. This goat had, in the usual manner of these creatures, committed depredations in flower beds and upon shade trees, and the owner had been severely censured in consequence. He owned one of the rough Collie dogs, which, however, had never been trained, but which, after one lesson given by his owner, accompanied the goat in its daily rounds about the vacant lots upon which it browsed, and prevented it from injuring trees or trespassing into the gardens. The dog lay down near the goat while it fed, and as it moved kept closely behind it and brought it home safely every evening. This it did daily for years.

(Mr. H.) The Collie does seem to have almost human reason. I had a Collie pup from a breed that originally came from you, a handsome black and tan. When I got him he was about three months old. It happened that a litter of kittens arrived about the same time.

"Wattie," as we called him, observed the old cat now and then carrying her kittens from place to place, and he took it into his head to help her, but singularly enough never offered to carry any but one—a little black fellow. The cat carried her kittens, as cats do, only with some definite purpose to hide them, but Wattie seemed to have no such purpose with the black kitten he appropriated, and seemingly did so only for mischief, for he kept at it even after the black kitten had got to be a sedate, full grown puss. She never resented it, and seemed to have as much satisfaction in being carried around as Wattie had in carrying her. We got him so trained that if we ordered him to "bring the black cat," even if a hundred yards away, he bounded towards her, and taking her tenderly by the back of the neck brought her all curled up to our feet. It was a curious feature in the Collie, for he is not usually a carrying dog. Another very comical practice of Wattie's was his encouragement of tramps. If a tramp made his appearance at the gate, if Wattie happened to be around he gave him to understand by his gambols that he was safe and welcome, his practice being to run ahead of him and show him the way to the basement. One morning tramps were more than usually plentiful, and when Wattie had introduced the third one to the cook for breakfast her patience became exhausted and she remonstrated with him, exclaiming: "Goodness, beast! what do you mean? This is the third one you've brought this morning." But it was discovered that like too many of his masters, Wattie had an axe to grind in his seeming hospitality, for the tramps were in the habit of giving him a part of their breakfast. Another true trait of the Collie was possessed by Wattie. We had him trained so that we could send him to hide behind the house and return at our call a score of times in as many minutes. He undoubtedly knew the meaning of simple words, for if ordered to go and hide in the most ordinary tone of voice, without even looking at him, he never failed to do so, returning from his hiding place on being told just as promptly as a child of five or six years old would do. He was bit by a rabid dog and I had to shoot him. I don't believe I would have exchanged him for the most valuable Jersey cow in your herd.

USEFUL TABLES FOR THE FARM.

The following table of proper quantities of farm seeds for an acre of ground will often be found useful for reference. It will be observed that the quantities are somewhat more than is usual in tables of this character; but we have found that it is always safest not to risk the welfare of a crop for a little extra seed:

TABLE OF PROPER QUANTITIES OF FARM SEEDS FOR AN ACRE.

Winter Wheat, broadcast	2 to 2¼ bush.
" " drilled	1 " 1½ "
Spring Wheat, broadcast	2½ " 3 "
" " drilled	1½ " 2 "
Barley, broadcast	2 " 2½ "
" drilled	1½ " 2 "
Oats, broadcast	3 " 4 "
" drilled	2 " 2½ "
Rye, broadcast	2 "
" drilled	1 " 1¼ "
Orchard Grass (if sown alone, though it never should be sown except in mixture)	3 " 4 "
Timothy, or Herds Grass (when sown with grain in the fall, to be followed with Clover in the spring)	12 to 15 qts.
Timothy without Clover	16 " 18 "
Red Top, or Brown Top, broadcast	3 bush.
Blue Grass, broadcast	2 "
Hungarian Millet	1 "
Golden Millet	1¼ "
Red Clover, broadcast, after Timothy in the spring	10 to 12 qts.
Red Clover without other grasses in the spring	15 " 18 "
Lucern, or Alfalfa, broadcast	15 " 20 lbs.
" " " drilled	10 "
White Clover, broadcast	8 lbs.
Field Corn, in hills, small varieties	5 to 6 qts.
" " " large "	6 " 8 "
Field Corn for fodder, sown in drills 3½ feet wide and 1 foot apart	2 bush.
Oats and Peas, when sown together for fodder	2 bush. of each.
Beets and Mangels, in drills always, 30 inches apart	6 to 7 lbs.
Carrots, in drills always, 24 in. apart	2 " 3 "
Turnips and Ruta Bagas, in drills 30 inches apart	2 lbs.

TABLE OF PROPER QUANTITIES OF FARM SEEDS FOR AN ACRE.—*Continued.*

Parsnips, in drills 2 feet apart........	6 to 8 lbs.
Beans, in drills 2½ feet apart.........	2 bush.
Peas, planted alone without any mixture, in drills 3 feet apart.........	3 bush.
Potatoes, in drills 3 feet apart........	12 to 14 bush.

In the vicinity of New York rotted stable manure is usually sold by the load of 2,000 pounds; but in the Eastern States the measurement is made by the cord, containing usually two and one-half to three loads, or 5,000 to 6,000 pounds, much depending upon the condition of the manure.

Table showing the number of trees or plants that can be planted on an acre at the distances apart given:

30 x30 feet............................	48
25 x25 "	69
20 x20 "	108
19 x19 "	120
18 x18 "	134
17 x17 "	150
16 x16 "	170
15 x15 "	193
14 x14 "	222
13 x13 "	257
12 x12 "	302
11 x11 "	360
10 x10 "	435
9 x 9 "	537
8 x 8 "	680
7 x 7 "	888
6½x 6½ "	1,031
6 x 6 "	1,210
5½x5½ "	1,417
5 x 5 "	1,742
5 x 4 "	2,179
5 x 3 "	2,904
5 x 2 "	4,356
5 x 1 "	9,712
4 x 4 "	2,722
4 x 3 "	3,630
4 x 2 "	5,445
4 x 1 "	10,890
3 x 3 "	4,840
3 x 2 "	7,260
3 x 1 "	14,520
2 x 2 "	10,890
2 x 1 "	21,780
1 x 1 "	43,560

The number of hours required for the rising of cream at the different temperatures are found by actual experiment in our dairy to be as follows:

At 45 degrees, in deep pails set in ice water, as used in our dairy, all the cream will rise in... 12 hrs.
50 degrees................................. 14 "
55   "   .... 16 "
At 62 degrees, in shallow pans, in.............. 24 "
" 55   "   "   "   .... 30 "
" 50   "   "   "   .... 36 "

It is an ascertained fact, in this respect, that the sudden cooling of the milk set in deep pails in ice water is the cause of the rapid rising of the cream; if the pails are set in the air, and not in water, and are consequently cooled very slowly, the cream will not rise completely in forty-eight hours at the same low temperature.

A cord contains 128 cubic feet.
A cubic foot contains 1,728 cubic inches.
A struck bushel contains 2,150 cubic inches.
A heaped bushel contains 2,750 cubic inches.
An acre contains 43,560 square feet, or 4,840 square yards.
A square acre measures very nearly 70 yards or 210 feet on each side.
A 10-acre field is 40 rods, or 220 yards, or 660 feet, on each side.
To double the length of the side makes four times the area of a field.
A circle encloses the largest space of any figure for the same length of line. A circular cistern, therefore, is the cheapest. The following table gives the difference of

AREAS OF SQUARE AND ROUND CISTERNS.

Round.

DIAMETER.	LENGTH OF WALL.	AREA OF SURFACE.
10 feet.	31½ feet.	78½ sq. feet.
12 "	37¾ "	112 "
15 "	47 "	177 "

Square.

DIAMETER.	LENGTH OF WALL.	AREA OF SURFACE.
8 feet.	32 feet.	64 sq. feet.
10 "	40 "	100 "
12 "	48 "	144 "

Twice the diameter of a circle or a square gives four times the area in square feet; twice the diameter of a cube gives eight times the solid contents in cubic feet; half the diameter gives one-fourth of the area, or one-eighth of the cubic contents.

LEGAL BUSHELS OF VARIOUS ARTICLES IN THE FOLLOWING STATES.

	Barley.	Buckwheat.	Corn.	Corn Meal.	Onions.	Oats.	Potatoes.	Rye.	Wheat.	Turnips.	Beans.	Clover Seed.	Timothy Seed.	Salt.
Maine...................	48	48	56	50	52	30	60	..	60	60	64	..	..	..
New Hampshire...........	..	..	56	50	..	30	60	56	60	..	60	..	..	..
Vermont.................	48	48	..	..	..	32	60	56	60	..	64	60	42	70
Massachusetts............	48	48	56	50	52	32	60	56	60	..	..	..	..	..
Connecticut..............	..	45	56	..	..	28	60	56	56	..	..	..	..	..
New York................	48	48	58	..	..	32	60	56	60	..	62	60	44	..
New Jersey..............	48	50	56	..	..	30	60	56	60	..	..	64	..	..
Pennsylvania.............	47	48	56	..	..	30	56	56	60	..	..	62	..	85
Delaware................	..	..	56	..	..	..	..	..	60	..	..	..	..	..
Maryland................	48	48	56	..	57	32	60	56	60	..	62	64	45	56
District of Columbia......	47	48	56	48	57	32	56	56	60	55	62	60	45	50
Virginia.................	48	48	56	50	..	32	60	56	60	56	60	64	45	..
West Virginia............	48	52	56	48	..	32	60	56	60	60	60	60	45	..
North Carolina...........	48	50	54	46	..	30	..	56	60	..	..	64	..	..
South Carolina...........	48	56	56	50	57	33	60	56	60	..	60	60	..	50
Georgia..................	40	..	56	48	75	35	56	..	60	..	..	60	45	56
Louisiana................	32	..	56	..	..	32	..	32	60	..	..	..	..	..
Arkansas................	48	52	56	50	57	32	60	56	60	..	60	60	45	50
Tennessee................	48	50	56	50	56	32	60	56	60	..	60	..	45	..
Kentucky................	48	52	56	50	57	33	56	56	60	..	60	60	45	50
Ohio....................	48	50	56	..	50	32	60	56	60	..	60	60	45	..
Michigan................	48	48	56	..	54	32	60	56	60	58	60	60	45	56
Indiana.................	48	50	56	50	48	32	60	56	60	..	60	60	..	50
Illinois..................	48	52	56	48	57	32	60	56	60	..	60	60	..	50
Wisconsin................	48	50	56	..	..	32	60	56	60	..	..	60	..	..
Minnesota...............	48	42	56	..	..	32	60	56	60	..	..	60	..	..
Iowa....................	48	52	56	..	57	33	60	56	60	..	60	60	45	50
Missouri.................	48	52	56	..	57	32	60	56	60	..	60	60	45	50
Kansas..................	50	50	56	50	57	32	60	56	60	55	60	60	45	50
Nebraska................	48	52	56	50	57	34	60	56	60	55	60	60	45	50
California...............	50	40	52	..	..	32	..	54	60	..	..	..	..	..
Oregon..................	46	42	56	..	..	36	60	56	60	..	..	60	..	..

A ton of Timothy hay, in stack or mow, well pressed, measures 480 cubic feet, or 6x8x10 feet.

A ton of mixed Timothy and Clover measures 520 feet.
A ton of mixed meadow grasses measures 600 feet.
A ton of loose straw measures 900 feet.

STRENGTH OF ROPES.

A good rope will sustain a weight in pounds equal to the number of the square of the circumference in inches, multiplied by 200. Thus a rope 3 inches in circumference, or 1 inch in thickness, will sustain 1,800 pounds with safety. (For instance, $3 \times 3 = 9 \times 200 = 1,800$.) This would be equal to the draft strength of 12 horses.

WEIGHT OF LEAD PIPES PER FOOT.

DIAMETER.	NO. 1.	NO. 2.	NO. 3.
$\frac{1}{2}$ inch.	1 lb. 1 oz.	....	....
$\frac{3}{4}$ "	1 " 8 "	1 lb. 12 oz.	2 lbs.
1 "	2 lbs.	2 lbs. 11 "	2 " 14 oz.
$1\frac{1}{4}$ "	3 "	3 " 11 "	4 " 7 "
$1\frac{1}{2}$ "	4 "	4 " 11 "	5 " 9 "
2 "	5 " 9 oz.	7 "	8 " 5 "
$2\frac{1}{2}$ "	7 "	8 " 9 "	10 "

One foot of 1-inch round iron rod weighs.... 2.63 lbs.
" " " square " " " .... 3.36 "

For lesser sizes divide the weight by four, for half the size, and for larger, multiply by four, for twice the size.

MAN AND HORSE POWER.

An average man can draw a weight of $27\frac{1}{4}$ pounds over a pulley at the rate of 220 feet per minute.

An average horse can draw a weight of 150 pounds over a pulley for a depth of 220 feet in one minute. This is equivalent to raising 33,000 pounds one foot high in a minute, and is a standard horse-power.

To find the horse-power of a steam engine, multiply the pressure of steam per inch by the area in inches of the cylinder; multiply this product by the length of the stroke in feet, and this product by the number of strokes per minute; divide the result by 33,000. Thus, an engine working at 30 pounds pressure per inch, with a cylinder of $8\frac{3}{8}$ inches diameter, and 55 square inches area of piston, and making 100 strokes of 2 feet each per minute, is 10 horse-power (or 30×55×100×2=330,000 ÷ 33,000=10).

QUANTITY AND WEIGHT OF WATER IN SIX FEET OF PIPE OF

		POUNDS.	GALLONS.
½ inch diameter		0.5	0.06
1 " "		2.05	0.24
1½ " "		4.60	0.54
2 " "		8.18	0.96
3 " "		18.41	2.16
4 " "		32.72	3.84

(For double the diameter multiply contents 4 times.)

One barrel of cement and two barrels of sand will make mortar sufficient for 600 to 700 bricks.

One barrel of cement to 4 of sand and gravel will make 9 square yards of concrete floor 3 inches thick.

A barrel of lime with 10 bushels of sand will make mortar for 1,000 bricks.

A barrel of lime and 10 bushels of sand will make plaster for 40 square yards of surface; half a bushel of long hair, or a half more of short hair, will be required.

One hundred laths and 500 nails will cover 4½ square yards.

A hod of mortar is half a bushel.

A square yard of plastering requires three-fourths of a bushel.

Twenty-three and one-half cubic feet of sand, 17½ of clay or 18 of gravel weigh one ton.

A cubic yard of solid ground equals 1½ cubic yards when dug.

CONTENTS OF A ROUND CISTERN IN GALLONS AND NUMBER OF BRICKS REQUIRED FOR EACH FOOT IN DEPTH.

	GALLONS.	BARRELS.	BRICKS.
8 feet diameter	376	12½	292
8½ " "	424	14	308
9 " "	480	15¾	326
9½ " "	533	17½	340
10 " "	579	19	360
11 " "	690	23	418
12 " "	840	28	452
13 " "	992	33	484
14 " "	1,151	38½	520
15 " "	1,321	44	559

STONE WORK, CEMENT AND MORTAR.

One perch of stone work is 24¾ cubic feet, or 16½ square feet, 18 inches thick.

One square foot of 8-inch wall requires 16 brick.
" " " 12 " " " 24 "
" " " 16 " " " 32 "
" " " 18 " " " 36 "

CHAPTER IX.

THE PESTS OF THE FARM.

The various pests which annoy and injure the farmer include animals, insects and vegetables. In enumerating the worst of these, the difficulty is in considering what may be left out, rather than what should be put into the list, so great a legion of them are there. In considering this important part of farm knowledge, however, we may divide the subject into two parts, *viz.*: PESTS INJURIOUS TO FARM ANIMALS, and PESTS INJURIOUS TO FARM CROPS.

DOGS.

It is right to include the dog among the pests of the farm, although the fault is rather in the owner than in the animal itself. The dog, for its sagacity and its friendly and docile disposition, deserves to be well cared for, well trained, and kept in safe subjection. It is the neglected dog, of low and high degree both, which is permitted to run at large without supervision, and which consequently falls into bad company and is made vicious, that becomes the destroyer of the flock, and does more to prevent the profitable keeping of sheep on many thousands of farms than any other evil to which sheep are subject; so that a few words in regard to the proper management of dogs will be all that may be required under this head.

Every one who keeps a dog should first choose a well bred animal; second, feed it as well and as regularly as a horse or cow is fed; third, house it comfortably in a roomy and clean kennel, with a yard attached, for exercise; fourth, keep it under strict discipline, and teach it its duties; fifth, never permit it to roam at large; and, lastly, after its duties and service have been performed during the day, see that it is safely secured during the night. It would be an exceedingly happy thing for farmers if they could, by their influence, procure the passage of laws to enforce some such regulation as the last of these, and secure the destruction of every vagrant animal that might be found wandering abroad unattended and in pursuit of mischief. When this is accomplished, sheep may be left to repose in the pasture with safety, and every farmer have his flock, larger or smaller, as a source of pleasure and profit.

The dog is, unfortunately, from its habit of feeding upon carrion, very much infested with parasites, and especially with tape worms, and these disagreeable and injurious parasites are spread by dogs among sheep and cattle, and even among human beings, to an alarming extent. Among sheep these worms cause large losses every year, and thousands of these useful animals die annually from the effects of their presence in various parts of the body. This, however, will be more fully referred to under its appropriate head further on. Just here we will only repeat that to avoid this injury farm dogs should be prevented from devouring dead animals, and should be as regularly fed, upon wholesome food, as any other farm animal, as this will entirely prevent the otherwise ever-present risk of damage by reason of these parasites.

BOT FLIES.

A curious genus of two-winged fly, known as Œstrus, infest horses, cattle and sheep. The Horse Bot lays its eggs upon the hairs of the fore legs, the breast and shoulders. The presence of the eggs upon the hairs seems to annoy the horse, which bites at the part, and so removes the eggs from the hairs to the mouth, in which way they gain entrance to the stomach. Here they hatch into large stout grubs provided with strong jaws, by which they take firm hold upon the coat of the stomach, and live by sucking the purulent matter produced by the inflammation caused. In some cases these pests exist in this way by hundreds, covering the whole wall of the stomach and actually perforating it through and through, of course causing death. At other times but a few may be found, which simply cause irritation and disturbance of digestion, with attacks of colic. There seems to be no remedy but to protect the horse from the flies, by providing the fore part with a linen covering, or by carefully scraping the eggs from the hairs with a knife edge, or removing them by a wet sponge. The fly is much like a bee, buzzes about the horse's head, in its attempts to deposit its eggs, much to the animal's annoyance.

The cattle Gad Fly is a similar insect, but operates differently. It has an ovipositor which it thrusts into the skin of the animal at the loins, and deposits an egg (about July and August) at each sting. The sting is painful, as the cattle evince great terror when the fly is buzzing about them. The egg hatches in the skin, and makes its way into the flesh, where it forms a burrow and lives upon the pus which is secreted. About midwinter its presence is observed by a round soft tumor on the loins, and a small round hole in the skin at the centre of it. In the early spring the grubs may be squeezed out of their burrows, and a little later force themselves out, and fall to the ground and burrow into it, where they form pupæ, or chrysalides, and in time emerge as perfect flies. These pests should be removed from the cattle's backs and destroyed. There is no other practicable remedy. In the West the grazing cattle are so tormented by these flies, that the hides are seriously damaged for the tanners' use, to the

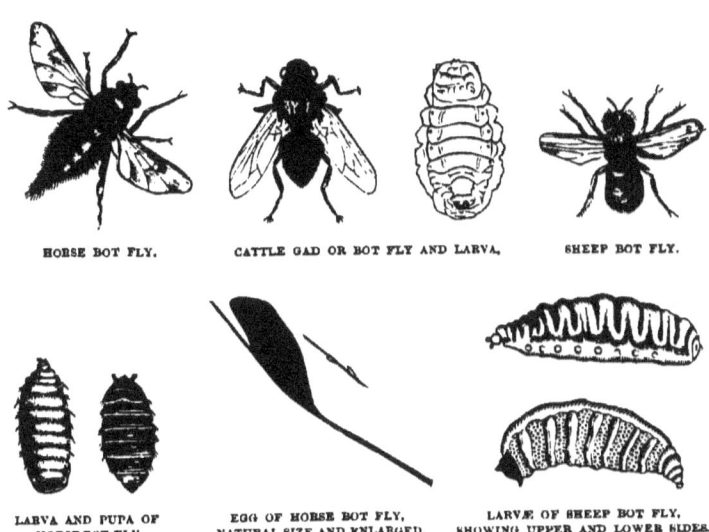

HORSE BOT FLY.   CATTLE GAD OR BOT FLY AND LARVA.   SHEEP BOT FLY.

LARVA AND PUPA OF HORSE BOT FLY.   EGG OF HORSE BOT FLY, NATURAL SIZE AND ENLARGED.   LARVÆ OF SHEEP BOT FLY, SHOWING UPPER AND LOWER SIDES.

extent at times of fifty per cent. In this case no doubt a coating of grease and tar on the backs of the cattle might be a preventive, if it could be applied.

The Sheep Bot differs from the other two in its manner of annoyance. It deposits a living larva or newly hatched egg, like that of the Flesh Blow Fly, upon the sheep's nostrils. The small grub crawls up the nostril into the nasal sinus and there attaches itself by hooks, as does the Horse Bot Fly in that animal's stomach. Unless numerous, these grubs seem to be little annoyance, but otherwise the sheep suffer greatly and exhibit great distress, pawing the ground, snorting and running about in frenzy. As with the others, remedies are only preventive, and consist in smearing the sheep's noses with a mixture of tar and grease, which remains sticky, and retains the grubs upon its surface. A few furrows plowed in the field serve as a place of security for the sheep, who instinctively push their noses into the soil and so cover them with dry, adherent dust, which cripples or kills the grubs. That these pests may be recognized when seen the accompanying engravings of them are given.

LICE, FLEAS AND OTHER PARASITES.

It is a well ascertained fact that all the parasitical vermin, both external and internal, which infest our farm animals, are greatly encouraged by that poor, low condition of health which results from want of care, poor shelter and exposure, insufficient feeding, filth, and other injurious circumstances which depress the vital force and weaken the animals. It may be, and undoubtedly is, quite true, that these pests spread from such unhealthful animals, and infest and annoy those who are stronger and more robust, but the starting point is far more often such as we have said, rather than even by contact, because these parasites do not find the necessary subsistence in the healthy secretions of robust animals, or are soon driven off by immediate precautions, while the diseased matter from the skin or membranes of unhealthy animals furnishes precisely the needed pabulum for the growth and increase of the parasites.

Without unnecessarily describing these parasites, then, we will merely mention the following as types, *viz.*, lice, fleas, tape worms, intestinal worms, liver flukes of sheep; lung and bronchial worms of young animals, as lambs, calves, and chickens (the last are known as gapes), and the dreaded scab of sheep, and mange of horses, cattle and dogs. And the first remark that may be made is that these are all easily preventible by strict sanitary precautions; thorough cleanliness of skin, stable, pasture, soil, water, food and atmosphere; and, of course, by the careful avoidance of contagion. When it is necessary to apply remedies, any kind of oil and sulphur mixed and applied to the skin will be found effective for external vermin, while linseed oil and turpentine are effective against all internal parasites.

Some of these pests, however, are so destructive, that some further notice of them would be useful. Sheep are especially tormented by parasites, which spread from one animal to another until the whole flock is infested, and the pastures even may be so infected as to be wholly useless. The first of these pests to be noticed, although not the worst, is the Tick. This is a reddish brown, leathery skinned insect, about a quarter of an inch in length. It adheres to the skin by its sharp claws and lives by sucking the blood. Sheep are sometimes, and lambs frequently, destroyed by these insects when they are numerous, and when but few in number, they greatly annoy and impoverish the animals by the pain of their punctures and the loss of blood. When sheep are shorn the Ticks leave them and go onto the lambs, which then suffer very much. At this time they may be destroyed with ease by dipping the lambs in a solution to be hereafter described. This remedy should not be neglected, as no flock will thrive when infested with Ticks. The insect produces a living pupa (see engravings), which is roundish and red in color, and nearly half as large as the Tick. The louse is also a great pest to sheep, and is destroyed by the dipping.

The worst pest of the sheep, however, is the minute Scab Mite, invisible except when dropped onto white paper, when it appears as fine dust which moves. When a lock of wool from a scabby sheep is laid upon a sheet of white paper this moving dust is seen, and this is one test of the presence of the disease in its early stages. After a time, when the mites have burrowed in the skin, and the scabs have

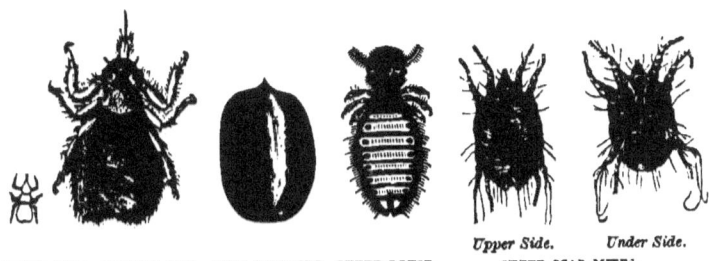

Upper Side. Under Side.

SHEEP TICK, NATURAL SIZE PUPA OF SHEEP SHEEP LOUSE. SHEEP SCAB MITES.
AND ENLARGED. TICK ENLARGED.

formed, the sheep exhibits a sorry aspect. The wool is ragged and loose, and in places is torn off by the rubbing of the sheep against fences, buildings or trees, or even upon the ground, when nothing else offers, and the body is covered in places with rough scabs or inflamed patches, with a multitude of small, watery blisters. These blisters break and exude a yellowish matter, which mats the wool and forms hard crusts, and these rapidly spread, until, by neglect, the sheep perishes in the greatest misery. It is this insect which, gathered in the wool, to which some of the scabs and crust adheres, attacks the hands of the wool sorters, and produces the disease known as the wool sorters' itch. It is akin to the Itch Mite, which produces the disease known as the itch, which so much troubles persons whose habits are the reverse of cleanly. The engravings show the character of this pest, but experience alone can give a realizing knowledge of its injuriousness. Sheep have died by thousands, and whole flocks have been lost from its ravages, when its first appearance has been neglected. One diseased sheep is sufficient to carry the disease into a flock, and so rapidly does it spread that in a few weeks thousands of sheep will be stricken with it. Even the land is infested, and at least two years are required before the soil, the fences and the buildings can be safely used for another flock.

The remedy for this pest is to dip the sheep in a strong decoction of tobacco and sulphur. Four ounces of coarse tobacco and one of sulphur are steeped in each gallon of boiling water—but are not boiled—with constant stirring. When the temperature is reduced to 120

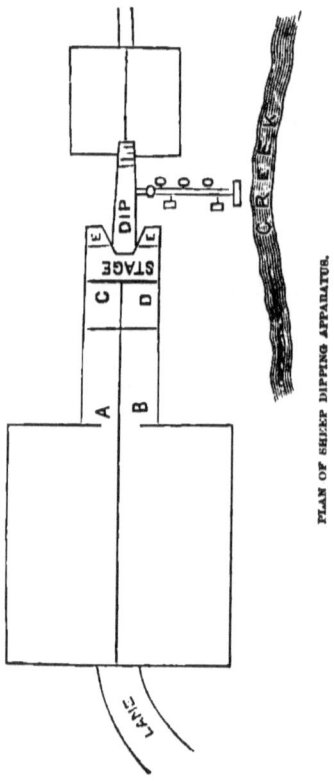

PLAN OF SHEEP DIPPING APPARATUS.

degrees each sheep is plunged into the liquid and held in it all except the head for about one minute, while the scabs are broken up by the hand or a rough cloth or hemp rubber. The sheep is then removed onto a draining floor from which the drip runs back into the dipping vat. A boiler near by is used to keep a supply of the liquid hot, to replenish and maintain the heat of the dipping vat.

The above plan represents the arrangements in use among large flocks for doing this necessary work. As it is done every year, and twice in succession, at an interval of fourteen days, which is necessary to destroy the newly hatched vermin from eggs which have escaped the first dipping, the yards and vats should be permanent structures on every sheep farm. First there is the receiving yard, to which a fenced lane is made so that the sheep can be easily driven into it. From this yard a few sheep at a time are driven into the smaller yards A, B, C, D, at the end of which is a sloping stage. At the foot of the stage are two decoy pens made of wire netting, in each of which are two sheep. The sheep seeing these decoys run to them and onto the sloping stage, from which they slip into the dipping vat. This is twenty feet long for a large flock, or smaller for a less number, and is kept filled up to a certain point so that the sheep is entirely covered as it passes through it, the head being held up to keep the liquid from being swallowed. At the end of the vat there is a barred sloping floor, up which the sheep walk to the draining yards before mentioned, from which after a time they are let out. The dipping vat is supplied by two boilers and water reservoirs to regulate the heat and the strength of the liquid; one boiler is kept for water, and the other for steeping the tobacco and sulphur. Some extensive sheep farmers make a practice of dipping the sheep twice a year, once in the fall and again after shearing, the dipping being supposed to improve the growth and quality of the wool. No doubt it has this effect because of the comfort enjoyed by the sheep from the removal of troublesome parasites.

Lice and fleas are frequently a great pest to young cattle and even horses. The origin of these is no doubt in a great measure due to vermin; rats and mice always swarm with them; swallows often stock a barn with them; while poultry that are neglected are rarely free from them. Dogs and cats carry fleas which they gather from their prey, and unless carefully freed by washing or by the use of insect powder, will soon stock a house with them. No fowls should be permitted about stables, for it has been known that horses have been so infested with vermin from them as to slowly die from the torment inflicted in this manner, which the owners have never suspected, but have attributed to other causes.

INTERNAL PARASITES—BLADDER WORMS OF SHEEP.

Our farm animals are exceedingly pestered with internal parasites, and many thousands are lost every year by diseases of which the true causes are unsuspected. Sheep, pigs, calves and lambs suffer chiefly, being from their natural weakness unable to strive successfully against the exhaustive effects of these parasites, which live upon the vital fluids of the animals, besides producing intolerable and fatal irritation in the organs in which they find their abode. The most important of these injurious parasites are tape worms, and these are more especially worthy of notice because they not unfrequently find a lodgment in the human body and produce distressing inconvenience and disease. Sheep suffer most from these parasites, one of which finds its resting place in the brain, and produces the very common disease known as "gid" or "turnside," so called because the animal appears giddy, or turns around continually towards one side in a circle, until it drops and dies in convulsions. This pest is known as the Brain Bladder

SHEEP BRAIN BLADDER WORM.

THE WORM ENLARGED, AND THE SACS OF NATURAL SIZE.

Worm, from its appearance as watery bladders in the brain of the sheep. The worm gains its entrance into the sheep's brain in the following curious manner. The mature worm inhabits the intestines of the dog, and its eggs are discharged in the dung which is dropped in the fields near fences, stones or trees or on tufts of grass, as is the habit of the dog. The sheep loves to nibble such tufts of grass, and in swallowing the herbage also swallows with it the eggs. These are very small, and when in the stomach are absorbed into the lacteal vessels and carried into the veins, and those which reach the brain remain there, forming around themselves thin envelopes like bladders, which become filled with watery fluid absorbed from the blood. In the engraving is shown the brain of a sheep having one of these bladders in it. The bladder contains a great many small sacs, one of which is also shown separately, each containing an embryo tape worm. When these bladders are numerous in the brain, they produce such disturbance of that organ as to cause the peculiar effects above described and the slow death of the animal. The disease is most prevalent in the winter, and the past season (1884) has been especially disastrous to sheep owners from this cause, which has seriously reduced the profits from their flocks. The sheep dying of this disease are cast out to be devoured by dogs, which swallow the embryo worms and so become infested. It is said that twenty-five per cent. of the dogs are carrying these worms, and if this be a fact, along with the other fact, that thousands of sheep are yearly destroyed by the ravages of dogs, it is easily seen how this pest is so abundantly spread over our fields and through our flocks, while the effective remedy is obvious.

Other species of tape worms inhabit the lungs and other organs of sheep, cattle and pigs, being found in the lungs, liver, spleen, bowels, kidneys, brain and various other parts. Thus it is seen how easily, through insufficient cooking of the meat, these parasites may be carried into the human system, and how dangerous it is to eat uncooked flesh of any kind. It is declared by competent authorities that one-sixth of the mortality in the East Indies and in Iceland is caused by these tape worms taken into the stomach in raw or partly cooked meat. Also it must be obvious to intelligent farmers that every possible precaution should be taken to prevent the spread of these dangerous parasites.

THE SWINE BLADDER WORM (THE MEASLE).

A tape worm which infests swine to a dangerous and disastrous extent is here shown. It is a small worm, and is especially noticeable because this passes between mankind and the pig, and in man produces fatal disorder of the brain in many cases. The engravings

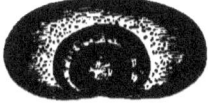

SWINE MEASLE, ENLARGED.

HEAD OF MEASLE TAPE WORM.

show the form of the head of the mature worm, and also the small bladder in which the young worm is contained, and which is found in the flesh of the infested pigs. The nature of this worm indicates the proper means of avoiding it. As it infests mankind, it is dangerous to use night soil as a fertilizer for grass or any vegetable that is eaten in a raw state, as lettuce or radishes, or to permit pigs to have access to any place where they can devour filth in which the eggs may exist. And to prevent its spread from the swine, it is necessary to be careful that pork in any form is thoroughly well cooked. The well known disease in pigs called "measles" is produced by this parasite, and measly pork is therefore exceedingly dangerous food.

THE FLUKE OF SHEEP.

The most disastrous disease among sheep is known as the liver rot. Thousands of sheep perish every year from this disease in this country, and millions have died in a year in England, where the almost constant moisture tends to encourage the pest greatly.

The pest is a species of worm (see engravings) which exists in the sheep, embedded in the liver, or free in the gall bladder and gall ducts. It is also found in other parts of the body, but it is most mischievous in the liver, because there it interferes with the distribution

LIVER FLUKES OF SHEEP.

A SHEEP WITH LIVER ROT.

of the bile, and so causes bilious disorder and fever, of which the animals die. The worm produces a large quantity of eggs, which are carried with the bile into the bowels, and ejected from these in the dung onto the grass, or into the manure heap, and from thence into grass fields. From thence some of the eggs find their way into low places, ponds or streams, and are taken into the sheep's stomach with the grass to which they adhere, or to which the young, newly hatched flukes cling, or are swallowed in the water drank from such places; or, the young flukes find their way into the bodies of snails, and these being swallowed with the water, the sheep thus become infested and diseased. The effect of the disease is to cause the eyes to appear yellow and dull, a watery swelling forms under the jaws, the fat and skin become of a yellow color, as that of a person suffering from jaundice. In time the sheep presents a wretched appearance, as is shown in the engraving; the back is bowed upwards, and the backbone appears like a sharp edge; the wool hangs in tatters, and the sheep, worn out with exhaustive diarrhœa, soon perishes. The mere avoidance of low pastures for the sheep, and the use of well water for drink, will entirely prevent the loss of sheep from this pest.

LUNG AND BRONCHIAL WORMS.

Many an owner of lambs finds them slowly pining away from some mysterious disease for which he cannot account. The skin becomes pale, as if the blood had disappeared; the young creatures waste and pine away and gradually die; and this peculiar slow death has given the common name of "pining" to this disease, which is exceedingly prevalent in districts where sheep are kept numerously.

The cause of it is the presence in the air passages of the lungs and the windpipe of countless small white worms, like fragments of thread, which, by their irritation, cause these air passages to be filled with froth and mucus, interfering with the supply of air to the lungs and gradually impoverishing the blood. Not only lambs, but young calves, pigs and chickens are also infested with similar worms, which produce the same effect, in every case, however, resulting in death, unless some remedy is found. Remedies, however, must be sought from competent sources, and beyond suggesting that sulphur or turpentine, both of which are readily absorbed into the blood and spread through the whole system, are generally used with good effect as a remedy, we confine ourselves here to what we know as regards prevention of the trouble from this pest. It is well known that when lambs and calves are pastured on fields where old sheep or poultry have run, they are sure to be affected, and that chickens that are kept among old fowls, or on ground that has been fouled by the old birds, invariably have this disease, which is known in their case as "gapes." The way of prevention, then, is obvious: never let young animals run for pasture where older ones have been kept, for the simple reason that the droppings of these animals contain the eggs of the worms which exist in their intestines, and which mature and die and are discharged, with the innumerable eggs contained in their bodies. These older animals, being more robust, are not annoyed with the worms, although in some cases these may produce diseases of which the cause is not suspected.

INTESTINAL WORMS.

Farm animals suffer exceedingly from intestinal parasites, which are so numerous as to almost defy description. There is not an organ of importance in the body which is not more or less infested with them. The liver, the kidney, the bowels, the kidney fat, the heart, are all subject to attacks by these pests; while one particular worm known as *Trichina Spiralis* (see engraving) is so common among pigs, as to have led to disputes and ill feeling between our own and foreign Governments, which have refused our pork because of this dangerous pest. The losses to agriculture on this account alone are no doubt enormous, and may be still greater, and thus seriously affect the question of "How the Farm Pays." The engravings here given show this worm as it appears when mature and filled with eggs, but greatly enlarged. In its natural state it is barely visible to the naked eye and can be seen with difficulty as an oval shaped capsule, as large as a small pin's head, embedded in the muscular tissue. In this condition it is dormant and has no further effect than to cause stiffness of the limbs at times, and it thus exists until the flesh in which it is encysted is eaten and digested, when the worms are set free and begin

   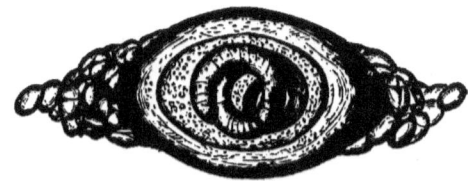

TRICHINA SPIRALIS.   THE SAME ENCYSTED, GREATLY ENLARGED.

their work of destruction. It infests rats, mice, and several other carrion or offal eating animals; but the pig, from its omnivorous habits, is specially infested by it. Pigs become infested by devouring rats, the offal of the pork packing establishments, and the dung of other swine. Some may die from the effects of the parasites, which, as they penetrate the bowels and pass into the muscular tissue, cause fever and intense pain in the limbs, with profuse diarrhœa. After a short time, if the animal does not die, the creatures form their cysts, in which they curl themselves up and begin their curious and lengthened sleep. As with other pests of this nature, prevention is the safest course, and cleanliness of feeding and lodging, with the destruction of vermin, will be sufficient to avoid it.

The pig is the prey of numerous other intestinal parasites, one of which inhabits the kidney and the fat around it. This is a small worm an inch or more in length and causes that very common disease in pigs which produces paralysis of the hind quarters. The numerous worms which are found in the bowels greatly affect the health of animals, but would be far less trouble if more care were taken to avoid impoverishment of the condition by injudicious feeding, over feeding being quite as objectionable in this respect as insufficient food. As a rule, parasites, outward and internal, trouble those animals whose poor condition causes those unhealthy secretions and products which it seems a purpose of nature that these parasites should exist to remove and destroy; and this applies to all other farm animals as well as to pigs.

THE PESTS OF THE CROPS.

The damage and loss occasioned by insects which prey upon the farmer's crops are beyond calculation. The Colorado Beetle alone must have cost the farmers a hundred million dollars in the dozen years or so since it first left its original home and came to stay with us. The Chinch Bug has frequently cost the Western farmers fifty million dollars in a single year in damage to the corn and wheat, and the Hessian Fly has occasionally cost an equal sum in one year, but is, fortunately, not so destructive as the bug. On every hand the farmer is harassed by an innumerable army, whose ravages he cannot resist, because of its numbers. But while one alone is powerless to resist, yet, by learning a lesson from his enemies and combining his forces and acting in unison, the farmer may do a good deal to save his crops from destruction.

THE COLORADO BEETLE, COMMONLY CALLED "POTATO BUG."

This insect is just now creating so much alarm in Europe that the governments are using every effort to instruct the people, old and young, in regard to its appearance and habits, so that its first accidental arrival may not pass unnoticed, and it may not escape immediate destruction. Generally the course of emigration of insect pests has been the other way, and we have received our worst insects from Europe; the course of conquest, however, in this case, seems to be reversed. This beetle is not easily mistaken. It is sluggish and slow in its movements, is roundish in form, about half an inch in length, and is marked very conspicuously with ten yellow and black lines lengthwise of its wing covers. The under or true wings are reddish, and are quite noticeable when the insect is flying. The female beetle is larger than the male, and produces about 1,200 eggs. The insect passes the winter in a mature but dormant state, in the ground, and emerges about the middle of May or 1st of June, at the season of potato planting. As soon as the first leaves of the young plants are above ground, the beetles are ready and waiting to attack them, and, unless prevented, will eat the young growth down to the ground and wholly destroy it. It is then that the beetle can be attacked most effectively. A light sprinkling of a mixture of fine flour, or ground gypsum, or fine, dry lime, with one-thousandth part by measure of Paris Green upon the young leaves, will destroy every beetle. Every female beetle—and these are far more numerous than the males—that is destroyed, of course prevents the laying of more than 1,000 eggs, and as these eggs will hatch and produce a second brood, and this a third, it follows that one female less in the spring is equivalent to many millions less in the late summer, and, of course, the next year. This fact illustrates the absolute necessity that farmers should neglect no opportunity of destroying these pests at any time and opportunity, either by hand picking the beetles early in the season, when they may be few, and using the Paris Green mixture (a mixture in water is equally effective and safer in use) upon every possible occasion. This insect attacks potatoes, egg plants and tomatoes, all species of the Solanum family, to which its natural food plant, the Horse Nettle, belongs.

THE CHINCH BUG.

This insect is not more than one-tenth of an inch in length, has the usual disagreeable odor of its family, and, like other bugs, lives by suction. It attacks wheat, corn, oats and other small grains, as well as timothy grass, and in some cases destroys meadows and leaves the ground bare. It is black, with white fore wings, and when in a mass upon a plant appears like gray dust. It usually appears on the wheat in June, and later on the corn; at times it also attacks, through the summer, all kinds of garden vegetables. It exists from Maine to beyond the Missouri River, but is most destructive in the central Mississippi Valley. Recently it has done much damage in the meadows of northern New York. It is subject to a parasitic disease, which prevails mostly in cold, wet seasons, when the insects are weakened, and at such times almost wholly disappears, but it increases very rapidly, and soon again becomes destructive, when the season is favorable to it. There is but one remedy, and this is to burn off all the stubble from the fields in the fall, or to plow it under deeply, and leave no harboring places in which the pest may survive the winter.

THE HESSIAN FLY.

This insect has at times wholly prevented the culture of wheat, in localities where this grain is a leading crop. It is a small fly which appears late in August and early in September, and lays its eggs in the early sown, young wheat, low down in the sheath, among the leaves. The eggs soon hatch and produce small maggots, which suck the sap from the tender plants, and soon cause them to fade and turn yellow. In favorable seasons the stooling of the wheat helps to overcome the damage and save the crop, but too often the plants are so weakened that they cannot resist the rigors of the winter, and in the spring nothing appears but the sere and yellow remains of what was a promising crop. If the crop survives and recovers in the spring, a second brood appears in the early summer, and attacks the stems at the upper leaves, and causes them to break down and wither, and so ruins the crop. Burning the stubble and clean culture of the fields, seem to be the only means of prevention, while the late sowing of the grain, so as to put off the appearance of the braird until after the flies have deposited their eggs elsewhere, and the liberal manuring and fertilizing of the soil to strengthen the plants, are generally effective in avoiding the pest.

THE CABBAGE BUTTERFLY.

This pest is exceedingly destructive to the cabbage crop, and sometimes by its numbers and voracity entirely ruins it. The damage is done in its larva stage, when the insect is a light green, soft caterpillar. The parent is a white winged butterfly having one or two small black dots upon each wing, and has only been known upon this side of the Atlantic for a few years, since when it has spread all over the Eastern and central portions of the country. The best preventive is to capture the butterflies with hand nets, which is easily done as they hover over the cabbages seeking places to deposit their eggs, or as they alight upon other plants to sip moisture. Poison cannot be used for obvious reasons, but a strong decoction of red peppers, or a solution of saltpetre sprinkled over the plants, will kill the caterpillars. Where the plantation is not large, hand picking can be used, and to reach the insects a long, slender pair of scissors will do the work much more rapidly than the fingers.

THE TURNIP BEETLE (JUMPING JACK).

This insignificant little pest sometimes gives great annoyance to the root grower, wholly destroying the crop, when in its seed leaves. It is a very small steel blue or black beetle, which springs very actively when it is disturbed. An effective remedy against it is to sprinkle the rows of young plants as soon as they break through the ground with fine dry air-slaked lime, fine soot or wood ashes, or to dust the rows with the strong smelling superphosphate of lime that is made with "sludge acid" or the refuse acid from petroleum refineries.

THE PEA AND BEAN WEEVILS.

The former of these beetles has been long with us; the latter is a new arrival, but is fast becoming very destructive, especially to Lima beans. Some of these beans have as many as eight beetles in them, while three or four is a common number. The pea weevil is too well known to need any remark. The only safeguard is to avoid sowing the insects with the seed. Only pure, free seed should be sown. If this could be done by general consent and determination these pests would soon disappear.

THE CORN SILK WORM.

Market farmers who make a special crop of sweet corn have been much pestered of late years with a caterpillar, or rather two of them, which begin to devour the silk of the ears, and, following it into the husk, consume the soft grain just as it becomes ready for market, in its green state. One or two inches of the tips of the ears is thus damaged, so as to render the ears unsalable. The remedy is not apparent. All that we can do here is to call attention to it, so that our readers may devise some methods to prevent the damage. Dusting the silk with fine air-slaked lime has been found to keep off the insects, and probably destroys the eggs as soon as laid, or drives away the parent moths.

THE TOBACCO AND TOMATO WORM.

This worm is a troublesome pest to the tobacco grower, and also preys upon tomato plants. It is a long, stout, green worm, having yellow angular bands on each side. Another species has white bands edged with blue. The parents are large moths of the varieties known as sphinx or hawk moths, and have long tongues, usually curled up in the manner of a watch spring, with which they penetrate to the bottom of the calyx of the flowers, upon whose nectar they feed. These moths feed upon the common "Jimson" weed (*Datura stramonium*), and tobacco growers have rid their fields of the pests by putting a few drops of solution of cobalt in the blossoms of this weed, grown for the purpose among the crop. As it is not always easy to get the seed of this plant, and as there has been some inquiry for it, we might suggest that any variety of the cultivated species of Datura, especially those having white flowers, might be sown among the crop and used as a trap for these moths. In the large tobacco fields of California flocks of turkeys are driven into the fields to devour these worms, for which these birds have a specially vigorous appetite.

THE ARMY WORM.

At times, the Army Worm commits enormous ravages upon wheat and grass. It appears suddenly in overwhelming numbers, and marching straight on, devours all before it, and leaves a barren waste behind it. Combined efforts alone, of the farmers, can avail to stop it, and these must be swift and thorough. Land rollers; loaded brush

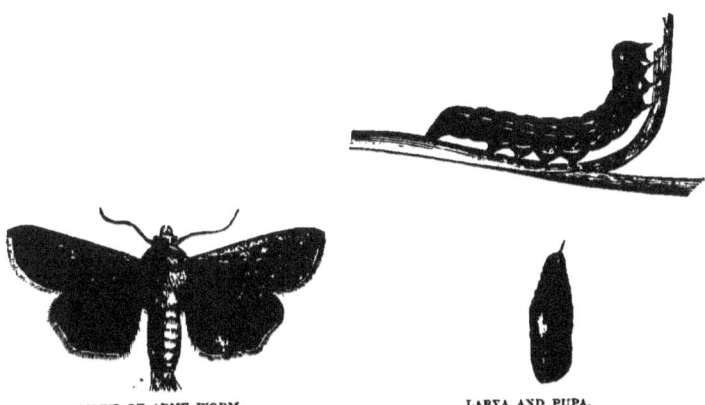

MOTH OF ARMY WORM. LARVA AND PUPA.

harrows; furrows plowed across the track of the worms ahead of them, and kept clear of the worms by drawing a log up and down so as to crush them as they gather in the ditch—all these have been used with success, when every farmer in the threatened locality has helped in the work. One man alone is powerless to stop the march of the countless horde. This worm is the larva of a small brown moth, but whence it comes in such numbers, or where it goes after having deposited its eggs to produce the myriads of worms which are its progeny, no observer has yet been able to discover. The general color of the full grown worm is dingy black, with a broad dusky stripe on the back, then a narrow black line; then a narrow white line; then a yellowish stripe; than a narrow indistinct white line; then a dusky stripe; then a narrow white line; then a yellowish stripe; then an indistinct white line. The belly is greenish. The engraving gives a very good representation of the worm, which, however, makes itself known by its numbers and its voracity in such an unmistakable manner, when it overwhelms the wheat and grass fields with its unwelcome and destructive presence, that the farmer needs no pictorial help to recognize his enemy. The chrysalis (see engraving) is a shiny brown color, of the size here given, and may be recognized by having two stiff thorns, with two fine curled hooks upon each of them; and when these are found in the soil, the appearance of the worms may be looked for.

THE FALL ARMY WORM.

Another Army Worm, which resembles the true Army Worm so much as to be taken for it even by scientific men at times, appears in the fall, and, when numerous, is a true pest. It does not confine

FALL ARMY WORM.

MOTH OF FALL ARMY WORM.

itself, as *the* Army Worm does, to grass and grain, but devours in addition purslane, turnips, garden vegetables and even evergreen trees. It differs, however, in having hairs along the back in small tufts, while the true Army Worm is smooth, without any appearance of hairs. Its destructive character, however, makes it worthy of notice among the pests of the farm.

THE CUCUMBER AND SQUASH BEETLE.

The small striped beetle, which is found harboring about cucumber and melon vines, is an insidious and injurious foe to the grower of these crops. Few suspect how much mischief this little lurking pest accomplishes. But this beetle is the cause of the mysterious wilting of the vines, " going down," the growers call it, which occurs without warning, and for which no remedy has previously been found. But if search is made about the roots of the plants a small, slender white worm, or more of them, will be found gnawing into them; and as they destroy one root, first one plant "goes down," the leaves droop and then wilt and finally die, and then another and another goes down, until the whole hill is destroyed. This small worm is the larva of the striped beetle. The past season we have found a remedy which is effective, both to entirely prevent the damage, or to arrest its course when it is begun. It is to make a mixture of one gill of kerosene oil with a solution of one pound of common yellow soap in one gallon of hot water; the whole is shaken into an emulsion, and a small quantity of it is poured about the roots in each hill.

THE SQUASH BORER.

When the leaves of a squash plant are seen to wilt, the cause may be found by searching along the vines, when a scar may be perceived near a joint. If the stem is slit with a small knife above the scar, a white grub, or two or three, may be discovered in the hollow stem. These are the Squash Borers, and are the larvæ of a yellowish moth, which is akin to the dahlia stalk borer. It does not injure the vine to thus slit it and remove the grubs, and if the joints of the vine are covered with soil, and the kerosene emulsion sprayed over the stems, these will serve as a preventive of the injury. The vines will root at the joints, and the main stem may be then wholly destroyed without stopping the growth of the plant.

THE ONION MAGGOT.

This pest, which greatly annoys onion growers, is the larva of a small fly related to the radish fly. The larva is a small white grub, which eats its way into the bulb and destroys it. The fly appears late in June, and to prevent damage by it the onion grower may dust the rows with fine lime or soot, or the strong smelling superphosphate of lime previously mentioned. This fly is closely related to the parent of the CABBAGE ROOT MAGGOT, which causes club-root in this plant. Similar precautions may be also taken for this pest. Large applications of lime or gypsum to the soil have been found useful to repel the attacks of all the different species of these root flies. Continuous growing of onions, cabbage or turnips on the same ground encourages the attacks of these pests.

CUT WORMS.

Perhaps there is no other pest that is so irritating to the farmer as the worm which comes in the night and cuts down his young corn, cabbage and peas, and cuts off the fruit stalks of the strawberries when they are loaded with the newly set fruit. No remedy seems to be completely effective against them. We have found the best remedy to dig the worms out of the soft soil around the plants, where they harbor in the day-time. All surface applications are unavailing. For large fields it seems to be the best way to plant thickly, so that enough may be left after the cut worm has been satisfied. There is a common belief that when the hot weather of July comes, the cut worms burst with the heat and die. This should be seen at first sight to be a mistake, for Nature never works in such a useless manner as that. These worms are the larvæ of various species of moths, and about July they change into the pupa or chrysalis stage, and become dormant for a time until they emerge as full grown moths.

WHITE GRUBS.

These insects, which are the larvæ of the May Beetle or June Bug, a large brown insect, which comes into houses in the evenings of early summer, do great mischief to crops. They devour the roots of grass during mild weather in the winter, and in fall and spring; they also eat the roots of strawberries, corn, cabbage and other vegetables, when they are half grown, and stop the growth. They are particularly destructive to potatoes at times, and scoop out the flesh, making large cavities in the tubers, or even leaving mere useless shells. The beetles devour the leaves of the grape vine and the Virginia Creeper. Another beetle, similar in shape and size, but having black spots on the wing covers, is equally destructive in its larva and mature stage, as the May beetle, and in the same ways. Late fall plowing exposes these grubs to their enemies—crows and skunks chiefly—which devour them in large quantities. Clean culture and thorough cultivation of the soil tend very much to keep these pests in subjection.

WIRE WORMS.

A hard, wiry, brown worm, which is not an insect, but belongs to the family of myriapods, or "thousand legs," and commonly called wire worm, is a great pest, especially to the potato grower. Although there may be some doubt still remaining, yet there is abundant reason for believing that the scabby appearance of potatoes which makes them unsalable is due to the attacks of this worm, which gnaws the skin and causes the rough scabs. This worm is exceedingly injurious to wheat and grass, and also to strawberries, eating the roots and the fruits which rest upon the ground. So far as potatoes are concerned, it appears that the use of the chemical fertilizers avoids the damage, while of all the common manures, cow manure encourages the pest the most. While there is such an easy remedy for the potato crop, which is the most injured by it, it is quite unnecessary to suggest any other.

BORERS.

A great variety of insects—flies, moths and beetles chiefly—in their larva condition, subsist upon the wood, bark or pith of trees, shrubs and herbaceous plants. The apple, quince, peach, plum, cherry, currant, raspberry, blackberry, squash and dahlia are the most infested with these pests. The remedies for the tree borers are to dress the lower part of the stem with some repellent preparation, as a mixture of cow dung, clay and strong smelling superphosphate of lime, made into a thin paste and plastered on the bark near the ground, beginning in June and continuing until late in the summer. Either the parent insects avoid the trees so protected, or the young larvæ cannot or will not penetrate the coating, and so perish. Another remedy is to dig out the grubs that have made an entrance with knife and small chisel, or to follow them up with a flexible wire in their burrows and kill them. The smaller shrubs are saved by pruning off the branches into which the borers have penetrated, while soft stemmed plants may be split, as described under the head of Squash Borers, and the grubs taken out and destroyed.

LEAF SLUGS.

Pears, plums and quinces are much troubled by a small, dark, soft bodied slug, which devours the soft substance of the leaves and reduces them to a skeleton. This checks the growth of the tree by destroying its breathing organs. There is a very simple remedy, *viz.*, to dust the leaves with fine, dry, air-slaked lime, which at once destroys, by its strong alkaline and acrid property, these moist, soft creatures.

THE APPLE WORM.

The greatest pest of the apple tree is the Codling Moth or Apple Worm. This is a grayish moth, which lays its eggs upon the blossom end of the fruit when it is set, and later, up to the time when it is half grown. The larva eats its way into the heart of the apple, around and into the core, when the fruit falls, and the insect leaves it, and goes into the ground to mature. It is the second brood which attacks the half ripened fruit and remains in it during the winter. There are several remedies: one is to gather the fallen fruit and burn it, or feed it to pigs; or to turn pigs or sheep into the orchard to consume the fallen fruit before the grubs leave it; and another is to spray the trees when the blossoms have fallen, and again as the fruit increases in size, with a mixture of one teaspoonful of Paris Green in three gallons of water, adding a little molasses to keep the mineral in suspension, and to make it adhere. This application also destroys the Canker Worms, Tent Caterpillars and other pests which infest this tree.

THE PLUM WEEVILS.

The curculio or plum weevil is so prevalent, sly and yet active, as to wholly prevent the profitable culture of plums in extensive districts. It is a small beetle, akin to the pea and bean weevil, and deposits its eggs in the young fruit, making a crescent shaped mark, which is characteristic of it. Of course the fruit drops from the tree, when the insect escapes and matures in the ground to repeat its depredations. An effective method of destroying is to jar the tree twice a day, when the beetles fall to the ground and lie quite still for a time. By spreading a sheet under the tree the insects may be caught and destroyed. Another pest of the same character is the plum gouger, which remains in the fruit, eating its way to the heart, and penetrating the soft stone, where it devours the kernel. The fruit shrivels on the tree and finally drops. From the habits of these insects, any outward application to the tree is of course useless.

PLANT LICE.

The family of insects known by the name of Aphis, or Plant Lice, is exceedingly numerous and varied. These pests attack every part of the plants—roots, stems, bark and leaves. Their power of increase is amazing, as the females are able to produce several generations, which reproduce themselves without any sexual union, so that a plant or tree once attacked by them is very soon completely overrun. Grape vine roots are attacked by one species, which render the culture of foreign varieties in the open air impossible. The orange, apple, pear, plum and cherry are infested, both upon the bark and the leaves, with myriads of various species, while some of the willows are so completely covered with them as to become a source of contagion to all sorts of trees in their neighborhood. The remedies are, for the bark lice, to wash the bark with a strong solution of concentrated potash, or with lime wash, or to scrape off the outer bark from old trees and burn it; and for the leaf lice, to syringe the trees from underneath, so as to reach the under side of the leaves, where these pests gather, with a solution of whale oil soap with one part in a hundred of kerosene oil added. Melons, cucumbers and cabbage are especially subject to these pests. For cabbage lice, a strong decoction of red peppers or sprinkling with dry, air-slaked lime has been found useful. Tobacco dust or snuff dusted on when the dew is on the leaves is a certain remedy.

THE ROSE CHAFER OR BEETLE.

An ashy brown colored beetle, commonly known as the Rose Bug, but wrongly so, for it is a beetle (all bugs are sucking insects), is exceedingly destructive to grape vines, upon which it devours the blossoms, and to cherries, the young fruit and leaves of which it consumes. It also eats into the hearts of the buds and blooms of roses; besides this it infests many other plants and vegetables, but not so injuriously. It is easily captured from vines, by holding under the insects a common empty fruit can attached to a handle for convenience, and touching them with a short rod, when they immediately fall into the vessel. A small quantity of water covered with a film of kerosene oil kills them at once. As they attack the vine first, the main army of them may be routed by an early raid upon them. A sprinkling of Paris Green in water upon the leaves of cherry trees, when the fruit is setting, will destroy a good many of them, and as the dressing remains for some time, it is quite effective.

VEGETABLE PESTS.

These include parasitic plants chiefly of a fungoid character, as blights, mildews, rust and smuts. As our knowledge of this class of pests becomes more accurate, it is learned that they generally attack trees and plants that are either constitutionally weak, or are imperfectly nourished, or are weakened by some accidental injury, through exposure to excessive cold, or too much heat, or by extreme moisture or dryness. This is seen sufficiently clearly in the cases of many plants for which our climate is too hot or dry, as the gooseberry, the English bean, peas late planted, lettuce, and others, which are subject to mildews to a degree that makes their culture extremely difficult; as well as the rusts, which attack oats and wheat when excessively hot sunshine follows a moist, cool night, with fog in the morning. Generally, we believe that the most effective preventive of these diseases (for they are really diseases) is to secure robust health to the trees and plants as far as possible, and then to use such remedies as have been found most useful in checking their spread by contagion.

Mildew consists of a white fibrous growth, the fibres separately being too fine to be visible to the eye, and this growth generally appears on the leaves, but sometimes on the fruit as well. It cannot be doubted that this outward appearance is merely the symptom of an internal disease, originating from some cause of the nature above mentioned. Rust consists of small orange-yellow or reddish oval bodies, so thickly interspersed among the white fibres of mildew as to give the leaf the appearance of being covered with red dust. Other forms of rust consist of cup shaped bodies, made up of these very small reddish ovals. Smut consists of a mass of small, brownish, round or variegated shaped spores, some being beautifully reticulated and marked when seen under the microscope. It usually occupies the place of the seed in oats and wheat, and also in corn; but in corn it also appears in masses, breaking through the stems, leaves and flowers or tassel, thus showing that the whole plant is impregnated with the disease. No doubt in most cases rust and smut are sown with the seed, either adhering to it or infecting it internally. The so-called potato rot is one of these fungoid, parasitic diseases, closely allied to the smut of grain.

But a good deal has yet to be learned in regard to the nature of these parasitic diseases, and until our knowledge is more complete it interests us more to consider what can be done to avoid them. This is generally to see that the trees and plants chiefly affected by them are maintained in vigorous health by the best cultivation, and by fertilizing with lime and potash, which are principally needed by them. And as far as the common farm crops are concerned, to avoid too frequent repetition of them upon the same fields, practicing as wide a rotation as may be possible, to avoid exhausting the soil of the most needed elements of their growth. Also by preventing the infection of healthy plants by destroying the contagion; cutting off and burning blighted limbs; rooting out rusted plants and destroying them in some effective manner, but by no means permitting them to get into the manure; by carefully destroying all smutted fodder, all diseased potato tops; and every particle of smut in the seed sown, by using the pickle referred to in the chapter on the Culture of Wheat. No doubt, too, the regular use of lime in the rotation of manuring may have a good effect in adding to the fertility of the soil and in giving greater vigor to the vegetation. Finally, knowing how infinitely small and light are the spores or seeds of these mildews, rusts and smuts, we should not be surprised to find them abundantly distributed in the air, in water and in the soil, so that we cannot wonder that any weak plant may become infected with them just at the time when it offers the most favorable conditions for their growth.

CHAPTER X.

FARM MACHINERY.

This work would be very incomplete if no notice were taken of farm machinery, for this is the age of machinery, in which head work has, in a great measure, displaced hand work, to the very great profit of the farmer. No farmer can expect to make the farm pay by hand work, as it was done a number of years ago, when the scythe, the sickle, the grain cradle, the hand rake, the flail and the hay fork were in use. He is forced now to use the mower, and the reaper which now binds the sheaves and leaves them ready for the shock; the horse rake, the threshing machine and the hay and grain elevators; and there are now thousands of farms upon which steam engines do the work of horses, or of the still earlier hand work. The farmer now must be a mechanic, and make a study of machines, as he has done of stock and feed and fertilizers.

The first implement the farmer thinks of is the plow; and when he remembers the old-fashioned plows, and compares them with the innumerable improved kinds now in use, he gets a fair idea of the advance that has been made in agricultural practice by the aid of the mechanic. No doubt this improvement will still go on until the present difficulties in the way are removed, and the fields will be plowed by steam power, just as the grain is carried to market, thousands of miles, by the same force.

One of the greatest improvements in the common plows is the use of steel, and chilled cast iron, which is even harder and more durable than steel. This improvement, together with forms better adapted to meet and overcome the resistance of the soil, has much reduced the draft of plows and eased the work. A plow that represents a type of the modern improved implements, and which deserves more extended notice in this chapter than has been already given to it, is

THE ROLAND CHILLED PLOW.
(See Illustration, page 39.)

The shape of this plow is such that the whole front of it is a sharp cutting edge; the material is harder than the hardest steel and will not rust, and is so smooth and non-adherent that it will scour itself in any soil, sticky clay and swamp muck included. The cutting edge can be taken off and ground sharp when desired; the land side inclines from the unplowed ground, and so relieves the friction; the standard cannot choke, and an arrangement of the heel enables the form of the furrow to be changed with ease, and so balances the plow that it can be held steadily with a very little exertion of the plowman.

THE SLIP SHARE.

To avoid the frequent change of shares, and the extra cost of replacing them, a reversible, self-sharpening slip point is now made. When the bottom of this point is worn, and the plow tends to run out of the ground, by reason of the rounded point, the slip point is

THE SLIP SHARE.

taken out and reversed, and thus doubles the length of its useful life. When it is wholly worn out a new point is put in in place of it, and thus the share is made to last as long as the plow, and seldom needs renewing.

THE SWIVEL PLOW.

The old-fashioned side hill plow has recently been so much improved that it is now used for level plowing with much advantage. By the adjustment of the coulter the furrow slice is cut even in going either way, and one former difficulty in its use has been avoided. These plows have not been used so freely as they deserve to be, when we consider the great advantage in their use by avoiding all dead furrows, and the perfectly level plowing of the land, from one back furrow in the centre of the field to each side, thus laying all the furrows of each half of the field in the same direction. As no "lands" are made, the harrow and the sowing of the seed or the planting may follow the plow immediately, and the seed thus be deposited in the fresh, moist soil. This makes a great saving of time, which in the spring may often be of considerable importance.

THE DOUBLE MOLD BOARD PLOW.

This plow is used for opening drills for planting potatoes and in preparing the ground for roots, so that manure may be deposited in these for the benefit of the crops. It may also be made of valuable

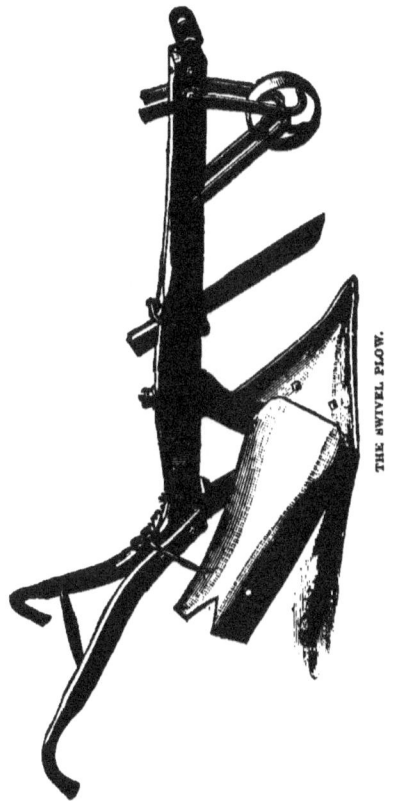

THE DOUBLE PLOW.

use in opening ditches for making drains, and every well stocked farm will find use for it.

THE SULKY PLOW AND PLOW SULKY.

The greatest present improvement in plows is the sulky or riding plow, by which the work of the plowman is wholly relieved, and he may now ride at his ease, with nothing more to do than to guide his team. The wheels are arranged so that the plow runs level; the draft is, of course, reduced to a minimum, because the weight of the plow does not rest upon the ground. It is provided with a foot lever, by which the driver can either hold the plow to its place in hard ground or wholly lift it out of it. The plow can turn a square corner without leaving the ground, and it has only one lever by which all the changes required in its work are made. With this plow a crippled

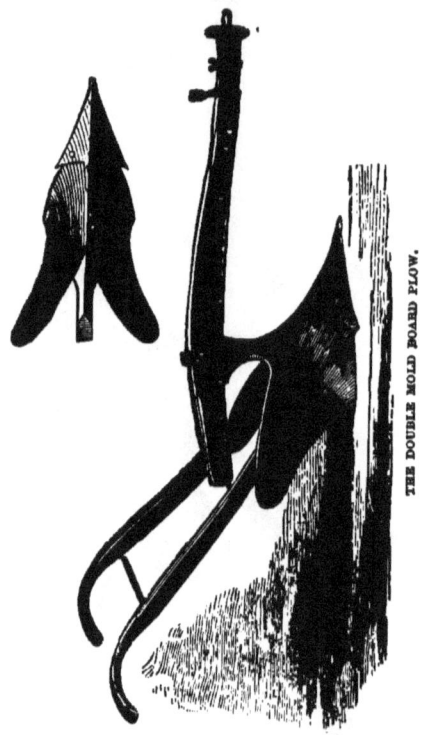

THE DOUBLE MOLD BOARD PLOW.

man, having but one leg, is able to work as well as an able-bodied man, and cases have occurred in which, on the death of a farmer, his widow and daughters have been able to work the farm and support themselves without the aid of hired labor. With mowers and reapers, riding harrows, and cultivators, there was only required the riding plow to fill the whole bill, and this is done now by more than one excellent implement of this kind. The engraving here given represents a plow sulky which can be attached to any plow in a few minutes, and so makes a sulky plow of any ordinary plow. The cost of this attachment alone is $35 only, and with the plow costs $46. It is called the Daniels Plow Sulky.

SUBSOIL PLOW.

Some soils require deeper stirring than can be given by the common plow. This deep stirring of the soil, at times, may be

THE SULKY PLOW AND PLOW SULKY.

equivalent to drainage and when practiced as a rule, by admitting the air down into the subsoil, improves its quality and gradually changes its character. By following the common plow with the subsoiler, the land may be broken up to a depth of sixteen or twenty inches, with much benefit in all soils excepting loose sandy loams.

POTATO DIGGER.

As cheapness of product is now indispensable to profit, and as the harvesting of the potato crop is a work of great labor without an

SUBSOIL PLOW.

effective implement, a potato digger that does its work well is very desirable. The improved potato digger here shown has been fully

POTATO DIGGER.

tested and has been found quite satisfactory in use. It opens the rows, raises the tubers and throws them upon each side of the row, the loose soil sifting down between the finger bars and leaving the potatoes free and clean.

THE DISC SMOOTHING HARROW.

This harrow consists of a frame six feet eight inches by six feet one inch, having four sets of rollers with fifty-eight discs, eight inches in diameter, upon them. The discs on the front rollers are set six inches apart, the discs of each set working between the others. The discs on the hind rollers are three inches apart. The cross bar in the centre is set at an angle with the frame and acts as a leveler and smoother. This harrow cuts and grinds the clods and mellows and firms the soil in an excellent manner, serving the purpose of a harrow and a roller at the same time. It is especially useful for preparing the soil for grass seeding, and also for covering seed that has been sown broadcast. An engraving of this harrow is given on page 44. We have used the Disc Smoothing Harrow for three years, and find it the most valuable implement in our garden operations. Its cost of $25 or $30 is paid ten times each season.

THE SMOOTHING HARROW.

The selection of the harrow for any special work is of great importance. For harrowing sod ground, for instance, a common heavy straight tooth harrow will undo much of the work of the plow; while for breaking up stubble ground and firming the soil preparatory to drilling the seed, it does excellent service. For use in plowed sod

THE SMOOTHING HARROW.

and for all other kinds of harrowing, the Acme harrow is probably unsurpassed, while for covering small seed, or harrowing growing crops, such as fall wheat early in the spring, and potatoes and corn immediately after the planting, and again after the plants are above the surface, the light smoothing harrow, with sloping teeth, will be found of great value.

THE ROLLER.

In the early part of this work we have frequently spoken of the roller and its indispensable usefulness. There are several kinds of this implement made. One is made of cast iron sections, having the surface covered with sharp projections which crush the clods and

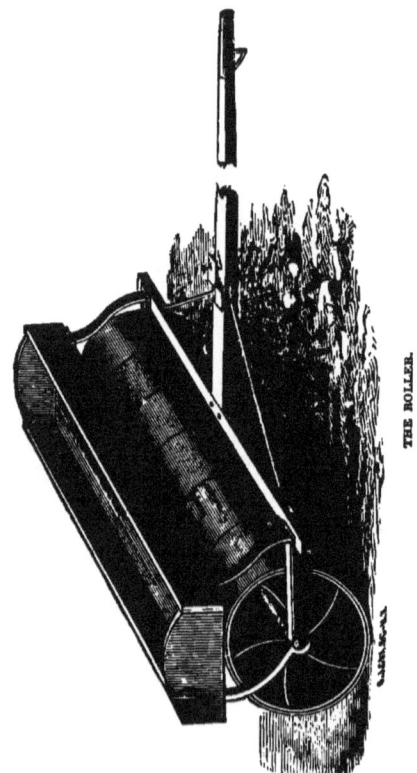

THE ROLLER.

quickly reduce them to powder. The surface is left slightly rough, which is a better condition for it than the smooth hard surface left by the common roller. It is, however, quite costly, its price being $100. The common rollers are made of cast iron sections twelve inches in length on the face, from three to six sections being used; or of wood covered sections, fitted in a draft frame and having a box on it which can be filled with stone to increase the weight. A roller of some kind, however, is indispensable, and those made with at least two sections are better than those made in one cylinder.

THE MUMBLER.

A new implement, of remarkably simple construction, but of undoubted value, is called a "mumbler." Its character is seen, at a glance, from the engraving here given. It is a smoothing harrow, a crusher, a leveler and a smoothing frame all combined in one simple

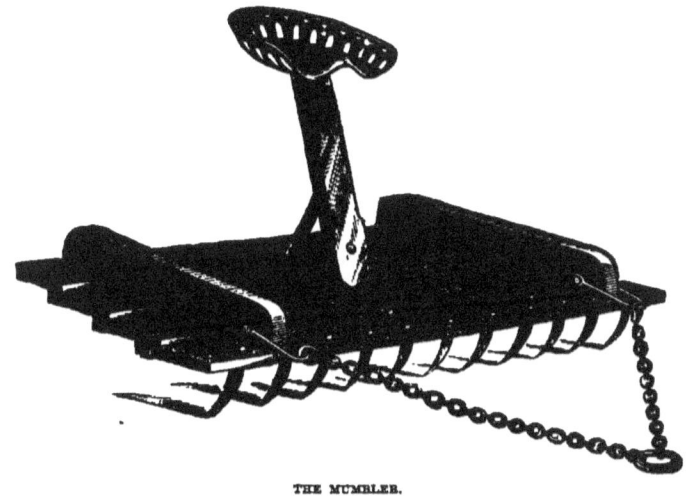

THE MUMBLER.

implement, and it is so made that, by turning it over, it serves as a sled or a stone boat, or drag for conveying tools or seed to the field. It is cheaply made, costing only $12, with draft chain and clevises.

THE MANURE SPREADER.
(See Illustration, page 70.)

The principle of the Spreader is that of a substantial cart of strong construction, mounted on broad tired wheels. The floor of the cart is a revolving apron, provided with suitable machinery geared from the axle, and when in gear moves slowly to the rear, bringing its load in contact with a swiftly revolving beater, that picks the material to pieces and scatters it evenly over the land as the cart moves along. By a simple device a fast or slow speed is given the apron to spread different quantities per acre as may be required, and the farmer may know just how much manure he is using without the trouble of measuring his field and manure pile. It handles all grades of manure on the farm, from the coarsest to the finest; also lime, ashes, muck, marl or cotton-seed, broadcast or in drills, and when in operation will do the work of ten men. It is thrown in gear by means of a single lever at left of the driver's seat, and throws itself out of gear when the load is spent. When traveling to and from a field none of its machinery is in motion.

This machine is of exceeding value for top dressing grain or grass in the spring. The broad tires carry the load over the soft ground without sinking into it and spread the manure more evenly than can possibly be done by hand, besides breaking it up fine so that the grain or grass is not smothered in places by the large unbroken lumps. Some personal experience with this machine has strongly convinced us of its great value. It can be made to spread the finest artificial fertilizers with perfect evenness, by first putting on a load of manure, setting the gears to spread as little as five or even two loads to the acre, and then scattering the proper quantity of fertilizer upon the top of the manure. As the revolving floor or apron feeds the manure down to the spreader or revolving beater, the manure and the fertilizer are thrown out together with perfect evenness. As little as 100 pounds of fertilizer per acre can be spread in this way. Two minutes is sufficient to spread a load of manure at the rate of twenty loads to the acre.

CULTIVATORS.

Cultivated or hoed crops have taken the place in our modern farm work of the old-fashioned summer fallow, in which, to reach a certain end, a whole season's use of the land was sacrificed. We have learned to do better than this, by growing what are known as cultivated crops, as corn, potatoes, beans and roots. For these crops there are several valuable implements provided. Perhaps the most useful of all these is the

PLANET JUNIOR HORSE HOE, CULTIVATOR, PLOW AND COVERER COMBINED.

The various uses of this implement are shown by the engraving here given. It is drawn by one horse, and from personal experience during several years past we can testify to its value. Being wholly of iron and steel, except the handles, it is light and durable, and the many combinations for which it may be arranged, all of which are necessary for their special uses on the farm, make it a very economical implement. For corn and root crops it has no superior. It will work

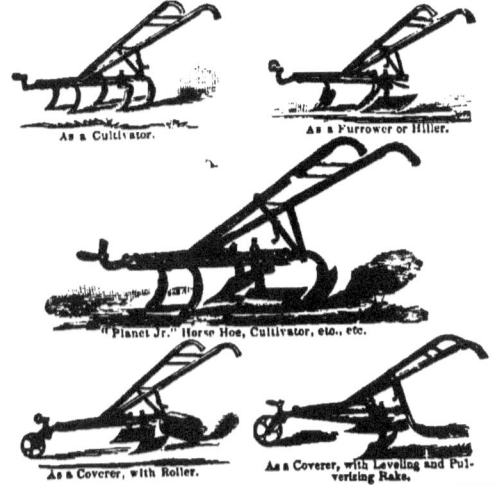

PLANET JUNIOR HORSE HOE, CULTIVATOR, PLOW AND COVERER COMBINED.

the soil level, or throw it from the rows of plants, or turn it to them, or even hill up the rows, when desired. It opens furrows for planting, covers the seed, and after the plants are up will do all the requisite work of cultivation. It can be adapted to rows of various widths.

CORN PLANTERS.

The old method of marking out corn ground both ways and dropping the seed by hand is not profitable. Machines for planting corn are now made which will plant and finish eight to twenty acres of corn in a day. Some of these in use in the West are made to drop the corn in check rows, which is the preferable method there; but where the fields are smaller and where weeds are not so abundant, corn can be grown in drills more profitably than in hills marked out both ways. For planting corn in drills, one of the most popular machines is

THE KEYSTONE CORN PLANTER.

This machine is simply constructed, so that any workman or farmer can use it without difficulty, and it will drop either in single kernels or three or four together at any desired space apart. This method of planting will produce one-fourth more grain and fodder than hill planting. The machine is provided with four dropping rings, and pinions to regulate the number of grains dropped, and the distance

THE KEYSTONE CORN PLANTER.

of the seed apart in the rows. Another good machine of a similar kind is the Albany Corn Planter. This machine will sow all kinds of seed in drills, and can also be used as a cultivator. Both of them have arrangements for applying fertilizers as well.

GRAIN DRILLS.

Drilling grain is more economical of seed, as well as of time, and does the sowing better than broadcast sowing. Drill sown grain resists the freezing and thawing of winter better than broadcast, and

GRAIN DRILL.

it can be better harrowed in the spring. Even oats are better to be drill sown, and some farmers prefer to drill them both ways, crossing the first sowing, by which the plants have more room and "tiller" better.

There are many good drills in the market, the difference between them being chiefly in the feeding arrangement. This is a very important part of the drill, because it regulates the flow of seed and secures it from interruption or stoppage. The Force Feed Grain Drill possesses this special feeding arrangement for the grain as well as for the fertilizer. It is provided with a grass seeding attachment, and also a land measurer, which shows the area of ground sown, and also the rate per acre at which the seed is sown. The drill commonly used is that with eight tubes, placed eight inches apart.

MOWERS AND REAPERS.

There are a great variety of mowers and reapers, and the modern ones are now made wholly of iron and steel. The principal differences between the leading mowers are now very slight so far as mechanical structure, draft and work are concerned, and a choice between

THE WARRIOR MOWER.

them is more a matter of taste, as regards style and appearance, than of intrinsic value. The Buckeye, the Warrior, the Champion and the Champion Haymaker are all excellent. The New Warrior is one of the most modern make, and has a high reputation for its simplicity, strength, ease of management, light draft and adaptation to all conditions of surface of the ground, and character of the grass. This machine has no gears upon the driving wheels, and the rim of the wheel is provided with lugs running lengthwise for the purpose of preventing the machine from slipping down when working on sloping ground. The cutting bar is made to tilt downwards to cut lodged grass and there are several other valuable improvements in its construction. It is made for one or two horses.

The necessities of the grain growers have greatly stimulated the inventive genius of the makers of reapers, and these machines, indis-

THE WARRIOR REAPER.

pensable on farms where even twenty acres of grain are produced, can now be procured so cheaply that every farmer who grows grain must provide himself with one of them. For the larger grain growers self-binding reapers, which not only cut the grain, but bind it into sheaves and throw these off onto the ground to make room for the next ones, are made; but upon smaller grain farms the ordinary reaper, with a self rake, which leaves the grain in gavels, is sufficient. An excellent machine of this kind is

THE WARRIOR REAPER.

This machine has a special mechanism, by which the rakes are brought completely under the control of the operator, and can be set and changed without the use of wrench or other tool while the machine is in motion, to deliver the gavel automatically, with every rake, or every second, third, fourth, fifth, sixth or seventh rake, as may be desired, or the operator may, with his foot, prevent its raking altogether, enabling him to carry gavels at the corners to make a clear track for the horse the next time around, or he can deliver the gavel with any rake he pleases, whether the same is set to deliver or not, and it can be set not to deliver the gavel, allowing the operator to discharge it at his pleasure. Unlike any other reaper, when a gavel has been delivered with the foot the one following it will be of regular size. If the operator carries the gavel on turning the corner, the next rake after removing his foot from the trip will discharge the gavel, and the following one will be of regular size. The small cost of this machine, which is $100, brings it within reach of every farmer who has a few acres to cut.

THE HAY TEDDER.

Where the hay crop is large the hay tedder cannot be dispensed with. This machine is used for stirring the hay so as to dry it thoroughly in the shortest time, and by its constant use, grass and

THE HAY TEDDER.

clover cut in the morning can be made ready for the cock at night. One of these machines will turn and spread four acres in an hour, so that the grass cut by one mower can be turned five times in the day, and by this constant turning and the light and open condition in which it is left by the machine, the hay has been cut, cured, raked and stored in the barn, all in one day.

HAY RAKES.

The horse hay rake is also one of the indispensable modern farm machines, and is one of the necessary results of the mower. There are some points about horse rakes which should be considered in making a choice, and the principal one of these is the ease of dis-

SELF-DISCHARGING HAY RAKE.

charging the load. In the self-discharging rake above shown this movement is automatic, which of course frees the hands of the operator and leaves him to give his sole attention to the driving.

THE HORSE HAY FORK AND CARRIAGE.

For putting hay and grain away in the barn rapidly, one requires the horse fork or elevator and carriage. The hay fork takes the hay from the load, and the elevator or carriage moves the load to any part of the barn, where it can be dropped. For unloading grain, or corn stalks, or fodder corn to be cut for ensilage, slings of rope are used, these being hooked onto the carrier.

THE DOUBLE HARPOON HAY FORK

is one of the most effective forks made, and is the only one that will lift loose straw in an effective or satisfactory manner. The Nellis

Harpoon Fork is made on the same principle, but has a single shaft. A very good hay carrier is known as

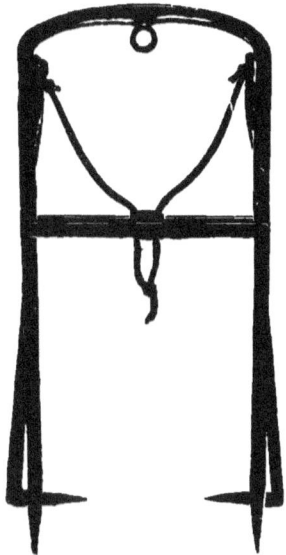

THE DOUBLE HARPOON HAY FORK.

PORTER'S HAY CARRIER.

This runs upon a track of two by three and three-quarters inch plank, which is attached to the peak of the barn by hooks; the top of the

PORTER'S HAY CARRIER.

carrier is open and passes by the hooks which hold the running track. There are several other hay carriers, which differ, however, very little from this in the method of operating. With the best hay carriers one horse is able to lift about 240 lbs. of hay at one haul. A ten-horse-power engine will lift a whole load at one haul, if room could be made to receive and handle it conveniently. A single horse will lift over a single pulley about 125 lbs. at one haul; with two pulleys the power is doubled, or very nearly.

FODDER CUTTERS.

Fodder cutters are indispensable for the profitable feeding of stock. By their aid and use coarse fodder may be so prepared and mixed with ground grain, bran or other fine feed, as to make it equally valuable as hay. This is one of the points to which the farmer will give special study, because it is useless to grow good crops unless these are expended in the most economical manner. By the use of a good fodder cutter, and ground feed of various kinds, three cows or horses can be kept where only two were kept on long fodder or hay and whole grain. For hand or light power

THE COPPER STRIP FODDER CUTTER

is an excellent machine, as it cuts easily and rapidly. For cutting

THE COPPER STRIP FODDER CUTTER.

corn stalks and for tearing them into pulp for ensilage

THE FODDER CRUSHER

has been devised. This is made on a new principle, and is probably the best machine for preparing corn stalks and other fodder for feed for stock. It is durable, not liable to get out of order and makes the fodder in good condition for the stock. There are two sizes made, differing in the size of the cylinder. In feeding the machine the

THE FODDER CRUSHER.

feeder stands at the side and feeds the fodder in crossways. By this process it is readily seen that the fodder will be broken up and torn into shreds much better than can possibly be done by a cutting box of any kind, and the fodder is left free from those sharp edges produced by the cutting process when knives are used.

THE CORN HUSKER.

Next to a corn harvester, which so far has baffled the inventive genius of mechanics, the corn husker is the greatest help to the corn grower in reducing the cost of his crop. The only one in use is

PHILLIPS' SPIRAL CORN HUSKER.

This machine does its work thoroughly—stripping every ear, large or small, soft or hard, completely of its husks and silk. The stalks being crushed, not torn in pieces, nor left stiff and hard, make much better fodder for stock and rot more quickly in the manure heap; while the husks, separated from cobs and stems, are always useful, or salable for the purpose of making mattresses, mats, paper stock, and for many other uses. Any ordinary two-horse power, such as used for threshing, is sufficient to operate this machine. It has now

PHILLIPS' SPIRAL CORN HUSKER.

been in operation several years, and is largely used. It husks about 500 bushels per day, and separates the ears in a clean state, free from the husks, and these from the stalks.

CORN SHELLERS.

A good corn sheller should deliver the corn clean and free from the chaff and cobs. For small quantities a sheller is made which does all this very well, having a fan attached to the driving wheel.

For large quantities the Cannon Corn Sheller, so called from its lengthened cylindrical form, is in general use. It has a capacity of about seventy-five bushels per hour.

FARM GRAIN MILLS.

As it costs one-tenth of the value of the grain fed to grind it, it is a profitable expenditure, where many stock are fed and where sufficient power is available, to use a grain mill at home. A mill occupies very little space and can usually be run on stormy days when outdoor work is suspended. There are a large variety of farm mills made, but it is advisable to choose one of these with a view to its

GRIFFING'S CORN SHELLER.

durability and solidity, as grinding is hard work. The Farmer's Iron Frame Mill is made especially for farm work, and is simple, strong and durable, as all farm machinery should be. With two-horse power it is able to grind ten or more bushels per hour, and the cutters can be regulated to grind fine or coarse as may be desired. But in all cases and for all kinds of stock, the finer the feed is ground,

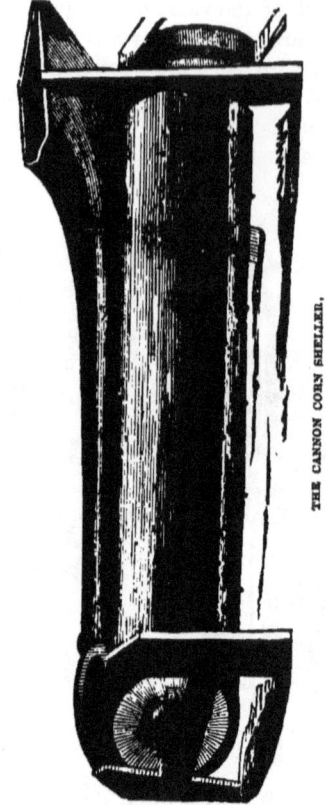

THE CANNON CORN SHELLER.

the better it will be as regards the welfare and profit of the animals; the fine feed is easily digested and therefore goes further in use than when coarsely ground.

FARM CARTS.

Carts are in general use upon English farms, and doubtless they might be made available upon American farms to a much larger extent than they now are. The great advantages of carts are, the ease with which they are turned about in a small space; the rapidity with which they are unloaded by tipping; the fact that but one horse is required, and that by the use of an extra man in driving the force employed in loading may by kept busy without waste of time in waiting for the return of the empty vehicles. Carts are exceedingly useful for bringing in roots, corn fodder and other loads from the fields, which can be dumped very quickly, also for carrying out manure. When cattle are fed upon soiling crops and the feed is brought in from the field, it is frequently a great saving of time to take back

THE FARMER'S IRON FRAME MILL.

to the field a load of manure instead of going empty. Farm carts should always have wide tires, four or five inches at least, and should be made as light as is consistent with strength and durability. The cost of a good cart is from $50 to $70. At times light hand carts are very useful for distributing feed in the stables, and where twenty or thirty head only are kept, the three-wheeled hand cart will be found to save much time and labor.

THE FRUIT EVAPORATOR.

The improved process of drying fruit which is known as "evaporating," has added another to the many profitable domestic employments of the farm. Evaporated fruits are so much better in quality than the ordinary dried fruit, that they bring four times as much in the market and yet cost less in labor to produce. This fact of course shows that the demand is much greater than the supply. The most convenient machine for this purpose is that here shown, viz., The American Fruit Evaporator.

Its manner of use is clearly indicated by the engraving. The fruit being first prepared and sliced, is laid upon wire frames, and is carried

THE AMERICAN FRUIT EVAPORATOR.

gradually through the drier, in which it is exposed to the hot air from the heater below. This heating is really a process of ripening and develops the sugar of the fruit, so that fruit prepared by this process is sweeter than any other, and even unripe fruit may be passed through it, and come out fit for use and sale. The machines are made of small sizes for family use and as low in price as $25.

FARM ENGINES.

The use of steam on the farm for such purposes as cutting fodder, pumping water, grinding grain and threshing is now quite common, and, as the economy and simplicity of this power is better understood, it is certain that its use will be very much extended. The heavier work, such as plowing, harrowing, and especially the deep grubbing of heavy clay and gravelly hard pan soils, will no doubt, before long, be done by steam power, and this more effective work will greatly help to make the farm pay. For as horse power is much cheaper than human power, so steam is cheaper than horses, and it has the advantage that when it is not at work it has not to be fed, nor is an engine subject to disease which shortens the useful life of a horse so much.

A recent experience in the use of plowing by steam both in Kansas and in Dakota holds out the most sanguine hopes that in such localities and under such conditions as prevail there, steam engines will yet be used for plowing with economy and advantage. The requirements are large fields, fairly level ground, and such suitable plows as may be best fitted for the work. The engine here repre-

ECLIPSE PORTABLE ENGINE.

sented is the one which has been used in both these cases. It has drawn a gang of eight plows, cutting a furrow four inches deep in raw prairie soil, at a cost of one dollar per acre, and plowing twenty-five acres in ten hours. The saving in cost, although very important, is not so great an item as the rapidity with which the work can be pushed forward in the short seasons, and another great advantage is that a very large force of men and animals are not required to be kept over during a slack season, so that they may be available when work presses for a short time only.

A portable engine is much more useful than a stationary one, as it can be taken to its work, for forcing water to the buildings, clearing land of stone or stumps, threshing in the field, hauling loads, etc., and for use in the barn can be drawn into its place, where it will stand and work without any costly bedding in permanent masonry. In procuring a steam engine the mistake is almost invariably made of getting too light and small a one, and in a short time this has to be discarded for the larger one, which should have been procured at first. A safe rule in this respect is, where a three-horse engine is thought to be sufficient a five-horse power should be chosen, and for all larger ones a ten-horse engine will be found the most economical even at the rather larger cost.

CHAPTER XI.

DIRECTIONS FOR THE FARM CULTURE OF VEGETABLES AND FRUITS.

BY PETER HENDERSON.

Principal Market Garden Crops.

It seems appropriate that a short chapter on the cultivation of vegetables and fruits should be introduced into this work, not only for the information of the farmer himself, for his own private use, but also for the advantage it may be to him in localities where he can dispose of such products at a much greater profit than he can dispose of ordinary farm produce. There are tens of thousands of farmers adjacent to the smaller towns and villages, hotels, watering places and summer boarding houses, where the want at the table, of fresh vegetables and small fruits, is most conspicuous. In many such places it is unquestionable that, if the farmer would devote a few acres to the cultivation of fruits or vegetables, or both, the chances are more than equal that they would be found much more profitable than ten times the amount of land cultivated in ordinary farm crops; for most land that will grow a good crop of corn or potatoes will, under proper tillage, yield a good crop of either fruits or vegetables. However, I will say, that whenever choice can be made, the land used for such purpose should be as level as possible, and be of the nature of what is known as sandy loam; that is, a dark colored, rather sandy soil, overlaying a sub-soil of sand or gravel. All soils that have adhesive clay for their sub-soils are not so well suited for vegetables, besides requiring at least double the amount of labor for cultivation. Above all things necessary for success in growing either vegetables or fruits, is manure. It may be laid down as a settled fact that, unless manure can be obtained in quantity sufficient, the work is not likely to be half as remunerative as where plenty of it can be had. The quantity of manure used per acre by market gardeners around our large cities is not less than 100 tons per acre *each year*, and if barn-yard manure is not accessible, concentrated manure, such as bone dust or superphosphates, should be harrowed in the land after plowing at the rate of not less than two tons per acre, if no other manure is used. For fuller instructions on this subject see chapter on "Manures, and their Modes of Application," in this work.

Such large quantities of manure per acre will, no doubt, be appalling to the average farmer, as it is no unusual thing for a farm of fifty acres to get no more than we market gardeners put on a single acre; but every one who has had experience in growing vegetables or fruits knows that the only true way to make the business profitable is to use manure to the extent here advised. It is safe to say that the average profits to the market gardener in the vicinity of our large cities, where he pays sometimes as high as $100 per acre annually for rent, is at least $300 per acre. The usual amount of ground cultivated by market gardeners is ten acres, and they think it is a poor year when their profits from that amount of land do not average $3,000, and that, too, when nearly all the products are sold at wholesale to middlemen, in large quantities, and which, before reaching the consumer, costs him at least double the original price paid. The farmer, in most cases, growing vegetables or fruits, has a great advantage in selling direct to the consumer, and the small amount of land necessary for growing these crops will cost him comparatively little, so that, with proper attention, I think there is every inducement for many farmers to add this profitable branch to their farm operations. A case in point, which has been communicated to me by a friend, is as follows: His farm adjoined a village of 2,000 inhabitants. He had one year a large surplus of strawberries and sweet corn, and had many applications for the fruit and the corn by the village people. He conceived the idea of employing a man with a cart to supply this unexpected demand in the village, and sold the whole of these products at such prices as paid a clear profit of $175 per acre, which was about five times as much as the average value of the farm crops. In addition, the sale of the strawberries created a large demand for cream, which was equally profitable. No doubt this example could be followed in the neighborhood of nearly every village in the country.

I will give in detail brief, and as clear directions, for the culture of the leading varieties of both vegetables and fruits, as an experience of nearly forty years in the business may enable me to do. Any one, however, who may desire a more lengthy and elaborate treatise on the subject, I would refer to my work, written especially for market gardeners, entitled "GARDENING FOR PROFIT."

The following list of vegetables and fruits, whose culture we describe, are such only as are likely to be wanted for the purpose alluded to, supplying smaller towns and villages, hotels and summer boarding houses.

All references made to quantities of seeds, number of plants, or amount of profits, are by the acre. I simply do this as a matter of convenience, taking the acre as a standard, although cultivators will of course understand that in application any amount of land can be used in the same proportion.

ASPARAGUS.

This is perhaps one of the most profitable vegetables that is cultivated. The reason for this is the fact that because it requires two or three years before it gives a full crop, cultivators are usually so impatient, or are compelled by necessity, that they will plant only such crops as give them a return the first season. That being the

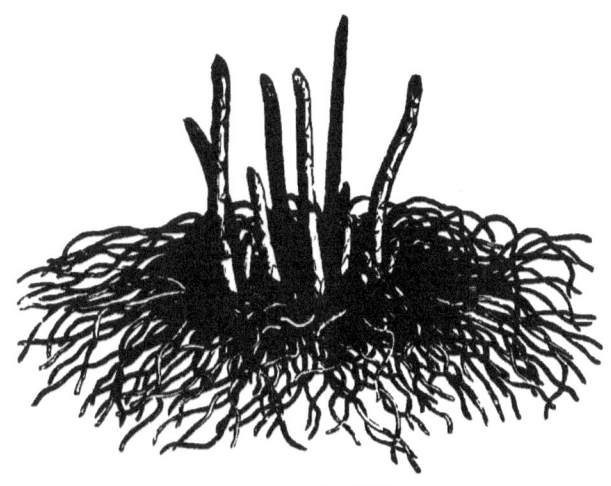

A STOOL OF ASPARAGUS.

case, comparatively few plant asparagus, and hence the supply is rarely equal to the demand. It is a plant of the easiest culture, only requiring, as nearly all vegetables do, a deep soil and liberal manuring. The usual method has been to transplant the Asparagus into beds five feet wide, with three rows planted in each bed, one in the middle and one on each side, a foot distant, thus bringing the rows one foot apart, with alleys two feet wide between the beds; the plants being set in the rows nine inches apart. In planting, a line is set, and an opening made a little slanting to the depth of six or eight inches, according to the size of the plants. The plants are then laid against the side of this trench at a distance of nine or ten inches, care being taken to firm the roots well with the foot. The plants should be covered with about three inches of soil, and immediately after planting the beds should be touched over with a rake, or, if on a large scale, the brush harrow, which will destroy the weeds. This raking or harrowing should be continued at intervals of six or eight days until the plants start to grow, when the hoe or cultivator may be applied between the rows and alleys, but the weeds that come up close to the plants must of necessity be taken away with the hands.

ASPARAGUS BUNCHED FOR MARKET.

Another method, and which probably would be simpler for the farmer to pursue, is to line out just as for turnips or mangels, the lines being three feet apart, in which the Asparagus seed should be sown about the first week in April by a seed drill, using at the rate of six pounds to the acre. This would be less expensive than the roots, both in labor and seed. In the beginning, in most cases it would probably not be well to plant more than one-fourth of an acre, but to be sure of getting a "stand," not less than two pounds of seed should be used for a quarter of an acre, the seed for which would cost about $1, while the plants for that amount of land would cost at least $10, and there is more labor in planting the roots. The advantage in using the plants, however, is that a year's time would probably be gained, as the plants are usually from one to two years old when planted. If the asparagus crop is to be grown from seed in this way it is all important that the ground should be kept clean.

It is no use putting in the crop unless provision is made for keeping down the weeds. Otherwise they would inevitably be destroyed, as it is a plant of comparatively feeble growth for a month or two. The seeds will come up thickly in the rows, and should then be hoed out to a distance of six inches between the plants. If the ground has been put in proper condition by plowing, harrowing and manuring a partial crop will be got the third year from the time of sowing, and a full crop the fourth year. After that, the Asparagus bed, with a top dressing of two or three inches of manure every fall, will last for a lifetime. I have seen beds that have been in culture for over thirty years without abating an iota of their vigor. Asparagus, when old enough to give a full crop, in the vicinity of New York brings annually about $500 per acre, the labor costing, at the extreme figure, not over $100 per annum, so that a clear profit of $400 per acre can be made each year. The kind now grown is what is known as Colossal, which should be grown to the exclusion of all others. It is generally known that the part used of the Asparagus is the young bud or shoot coming up, which is cut off when it is five or six inches above the ground. It varies in thickness from half an inch to an inch and a half, and is tied in bunches usually weighing about one pound each when sold in the market.

BEAN—BUSH, KIDNEY OR SNAP.

This vegetable is so well known by every one who grows any vegetables at all, that but little instruction in its culture is necessary. It may be grown on poor soil, although it will always be more tender when quickly grown on rich or highly manured land. The bush bean is a tropical plant, and hence should not be sown until the ground becomes warm. A good rule is to sow it about the date of corn planting, in rows eighteen inches to two feet apart, the seed being dropped in the drills at about two inches apart and the soil drawn over them with the foot, as that is the best way to cover seeds of this size. Like all crops, after planting, they should not be allowed to remain over a week before the hoe or rake is applied to keep down the weeds. We cannot too often insist on the necessity of this for every crop, as the work of an hour with a rake five or six days after planting or sowing, so as to break the crust on the soil, and destroy the embryo weeds, will be more effective than ten hours' labor if this is neglected until three weeks after. It will be understood, that this crop is used almost always in the pod in a green, unripe state, and is rarely ever used as a shell bean. To ensure a succession of bush beans throughout the season they should be sown at intervals of ten days from the first week in May (or time of corn planting) until the first week in August. They are a fairly profitable crop, but not so much so as some others, as their culture is so simple and easy. The best varieties for cultivation are the Early Valentine and the Golden Wax.

BEAN (LIMA).

This is the best known and the best of all the running or pole beans, although there are quite a number of kinds in cultivation. They are rather more tender than the bush beans, and a very common mistake is to plant them too early, in which case they are almost certain to rot. In the latitude of New York they should not be planted sooner than the middle of May, and will come just as quick into bearing if planted then, as ten days earlier, besides the chance of loss by the chilling of the seed. They should be planted in hills from three to four feet apart and five or six seeds in each hill. The seeds should be planted about two inches deep, and are better placed edgewise, with the eye downwards. In each hill should be placed a pole seven or eight feet high, for the bean to climb on, as it is no use to grow it unless it has some such support. This variety is used in a green state, shelled just as peas are used, although they are occasionally dried and used in winter, or when good samples are dried they can be sold to the seed stores at well paying prices.

BEET.

When grown for table use this root should be sown in drills about one foot apart, if to be worked by hoe or by hand cultivator, or two feet apart if to be worked by horse cultivator. We always prefer to sow the seed by hand in drills about two or three inches deep, treading in the seed with the foot, as there is hardly any other seed so easily dried up and its growing properties destroyed as this. When sown by hand twenty pounds of seed to the acre is required; or, by seed drill, half that quantity. When grown for table use in the vicinity of our large cities, beets are usually a very profitable crop, generally yielding a clear profit of about $300 per acre. Upon the first introduction of Egyptian beet, a few years ago, the crop sold for $1,500 per acre in the New York market, as it was ten days earlier than any other variety. After sowing and treading in the seed, the row is covered up and the ground again firmed by being beaten down with the back of a spade, or rolled. The first crop is usually sown about the middle of April, and about the first week in May the plants will have shown through the ground sufficiently to define the rows, and should then be cultivated between to stir the soil and keep down the weeds. After they have attained a height of three or four inches they should be thinned out, so that the plants are left four to five inches apart in the rows; these thinnings are often used as spinach, and usually will pay for all

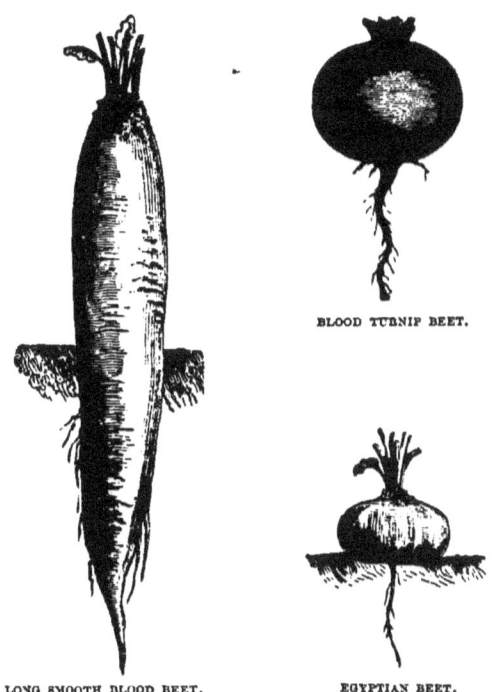

BLOOD TURNIP BEET.

LONG SMOOTH BLOOD BEET.   EGYPTIAN BEET.

the labor of thinning. The earliest kind is that known as Egyptian, which is a round variety of a deep crimson color. The next in earliness is the Blood Turnip, which comes in some ten days later than the Egyptian. Another variety, known as Long Smooth, makes a root about three inches in diameter and eight or nine inches in length, is equally tender as the other two kinds, although not quite so early, and is the kind usually grown for winter use. For the best manner of keeping in winter, see chapter in this work on "Roots for Farm Stock."

CABBAGE AND CAULIFLOWER.

As these are usually the most profitable of all vegetable crops, I give full extracts on their culture taken from my new essay on that subject, published in 1883:

Manure for the early cabbage crop should always be spread on broadcast, and in quantity not less then 100 cart loads or seventy-five tons to the acre, which will leave it, when spread, about two or three inches in thickness. It is quite rare that much choice can be made in stable manure, but when such is the case equal portions of cow and horse manure is preferable, not that there is much difference in value, weight for weight, but that it is advantageous to have the manure of the cow stable mixed with that of the horse so as to prevent the violent heating of the horse manure, which, if not repeatedly turned, will generate heat so as to cause it to "fire fang" or burn, which renders it comparatively useless. Always bear in mind that the more thoroughly rotted and disintegrated manure can be had, the better will be the results. When manure is thoroughly rotted and short, no matter for what crop, it may be turned in by the plow just as it is spread on the land; but if long, it is necessary to draw it into the furrow ahead of the plow so that it is completely covered in. After plowing in the manure and before the ground is harrowed, our best growers in the vicinity of New York sow from 400 to 500 pounds of guano or bone dust, and harrow it in deeply, smooth over with the back of the harrow, after which the bed is ready to receive the plants.

In the vicinity of New York, and, in fact, now wherever the business of market gardening is intelligently followed, the best

VARIETIES OF CABBAGE

for *early* crop are recognized to be the "Early Jersey Wakefield" and "Henderson's Early Summer" for general culture, and to describe others of the scores named would be only confusing. The "Jersey Wakefield" is the earliest and is a little the smallest, and is planted usually twenty-eight inches between the rows and sixteen inches between the plants, thus requiring from 10,000 to 12,000 plants per acre. The "Early Summer" grows a little larger, and should be planted thirty inches apart and eighteeen inches between plants, requiring from 8,000 to 10,000 per acre. The reason for placing the rows so wide apart and the plants so close in the rows is to admit of a row of lettuce, spinach or radishes between the rows of cabbage. All of these vegetables mature quickly, and can be cut out before the cabbage grows enough to interfere with them, and it is necessary that this double crop should be taken off the land so as to help pay for the manure that is so lavishly used, but which is absolutely necessary to produce a good crop of cabbages. Where early cabbage is grown alone (and for the farmer, whose labor is scarce, they had better be grown alone), then it would be better to plant about two or two and a half feet each way, so that cross cultivation can be done; and also in cases where manure in sufficient quantities is not attainable, they are better thus planted when manure has to be applied in the hill. If applied in the hill, a good shovelful of stable manure should be used to each, mixing it well with the soil, but raising the "hill," so called, no higher than the general surface. The

RAISING OF CABBAGE PLANTS

for the early crop is a very important point, though when small quantities are wanted they had better be bought from those who make a business of growing them. The great majority of plants for early

EARLY WAKEFIELD CABBAGE.

crop are sown by the New York market gardeners between the 15th and 20th of September, that is, when the "Early Wakefield" is used; but the "Early Summer" should not be sown until the 25th to the 30th of September. Careful attention is given to have the sowings made as near as possible to these dates, for if earlier, many of the plants will go to seed—particularly the "Early Summer" variety. Again, if much later than the dates last given, the season will be too far advanced and the plants would not be strong enough to keep over winter in the cold frames.

A case occurred some years ago in Philadelphia where a market gardener sowed "Early York" cabbage on the 5th of September; nearly every plant ran to seed. The gardener sued the seedsman for damages, got nonsuited, as he deserved, as the seedsman had no difficulty in showing that other gardeners who had purchased this same seed, and who had sown it at the proper time (in that latitude, 20th September), had no such bad results.

In about thirty days from the time cabbage seed is sown in September, the plants are of the right size to "prick out," or trans-

HENDERSON'S EARLY SUMMER CABBAGE.

plant into the cold frames. The plant must be planted down to the first leaf, the root well firmed with the dibber—about 500 is the number allowed for a three by six feet sash. The cold frame, as most gardeners know, is simply two boards run parallel six feet apart, the back board being ten inches and the front one seven or eight inches. We generally have all our cabbage plants transplanted here from the seed-bed to the cold frames by 1st November, and it seldom happens that we have the weather cold enough to have the sashes put on before the end of November. We are repeatedly asked the question,

WHAT DEGREE OF FROST CABBAGE PLANTS WILL STAND

in the frames before being covered with the sash. Much depends on the condition of the plants; it sometimes happens that after the transplanting is finished in October (we usually *begin* the transplanting in the frames about the 15th) that we have a continuation of comparatively warm weather, which induces a quick and soft growth in the plants, which, of course, renders them very susceptible of injury from frost. When in that condition, we have seen them injured, when the thermometer only marked twenty-seven above zero or but five degrees of frost; while if gradually hardened by being exposed to chilly nights, they would receive no injury, even when the thermometer marks ten or twelve above zero. This will be well understood when we remember that in midwinter, when covered with sash alone, they sustain a cold often for days together of ten degrees *below* zero, but then of course they have been gradually inured to it. In sections of the country where the thermometer falls to fifteen or twenty degrees below zero, it will be necessary to use straw mats or shutters over the glass. At all times, from the time of putting sashes on in fall until taking them off in spring (which is usually from 15th March to April 1st), abundant ventilation should be given, so as to render them as hardy as possible. The sure indication that they are in the "frost proof" condition is when the leaves show a bluish color, which they get when they have been gradually hardened off. Although the most of the Jersey market gardeners still use the cold frames for growing the bulk of their early cabbage crop, yet of late years the system of spring sowing and transplanting, and sometimes even without transplanting, is also used to a considerable extent. This is usually done by sowing the seeds thickly (about one ounce to three sashes) in hot-bed or green-house about February 1st and transplanting into a slight hot-bed about March 1st, placing about 600 or 700 in a three by six feet sash. The hot-beds must, of course, be carefully protected by straw mats from frost, and with the proper attention to ventilation and watering, fine plants can be obtained by April 1st. We ourselves have grown nearly a quarter of a million plants each spring in this manner for years with most satisfactory results. Another plan is to sow the cabbage seed in *cold* frames from 15th February to March 1st, or even later for second early. By this method one ounce of seed is enough for five or six sashes, and it had better be sown in rows at six inches apart, as thus sown the air gets better around the plants, making them stronger. When the seed is sown in the cold frames in this way, it is absolutely necessary that the frost should be excluded by covering the glass with straw mats and shutters, for, of course, unless kept above the point of freezing, the plants cannot grow. The cold frames to be used for this purpose should be placed in the warmest and most sheltered place possible, the soil should be light and well enriched with *short* manure, nicely dug, leveled and raked for the reception of the seed. If sown in drills, they should be about two inches deep; if sown broadcast, it is best to "chip" the ground all over with a steel rake so as to sink the seed to the depth of an inch or so, but in both cases do not omit to firm the soil by patting the surface over with the back of the spade. All these directions for spring sown plants are given for the latitude of New York, where operations of planting cabbage plants in the open ground is usually begun about 25th March and finished by the middle of April. For it must be always borne in mind that cabbage, being a hardy plant, when wanted for an early crop, its setting out in spring should be done in any section as soon as the land is dry enough to work. As a guide, we may say that whenever spring crops of rye, wheat or oats can be sown, cabbage may safely be planted in the open field, for if plants have been properly hardened they will not be injured after being planted out, even by eight or ten degrees of frost.

The conditions in the different Southern States are so varied that it is not easy to give directions. It may be taken, however, as a general rule, that in any section of the country, where the thermometer does not fall *lower* than fifteen *above* zero, cabbage plants should be sown about 1st October, left (without covering) in the seed-beds all winter, and transplanted to the open ground as soon as it is fit to work in spring, say February or March. In some sections, where the fall weather continues fine into November, transplanting is done in that month where the crop is to mature. After planting in the field, no crop takes so kindly to

HOEING OR CULTIVATING

as cabbage. In ten days after the planting is finished, cultivation should begin. If the cabbages have been set two or two and a half feet apart each way, then the horse cultivator is the best pulverizer, but if a crop has been sown or planted between the rows of cabbage, then a hand or wheel hoe can only be used—we ourselves now use the wheel hoe exclusively and find it a saving of three-fourths in labor, with the work better done.

The price at which early cabbage is sold now varies so much at different dates, and in different parts of the country, that it is impossible to give anything like accurate figures, the range being all the way from $2 to $12 per 100. Perhaps $4 would be a fair average for "Wakefield" and $5 for "Early Summer," so that counting 11,000 as the average per acre of the former and 9,000 of the latter, we have respectively $440 per acre for "Wakefield" and $450 for "Early

Summer." These are the wholesale prices for large markets, like New York. In smaller cities, where the product is sold direct to the consumer, one-third more would likely be obtained.

LATE CABBAGE

are such as mature during the months of September, October and November, the seed for which is sown in open ground in May or June. Perhaps the best date for sowing for general crop is about 1st of June. We always prefer to sow cabbage seed for this purpose in rows ten or twelve inches apart, treading in the seed with the feet after sowing and before covering; we then level with a rake lengthwise with the rows and roll or beat down with the back of a spade, so as to exclude the air from the soil and from the seed. Sown in this way cabbage seed will come strongly up in the driest weather, and is less likely to be injured by the black flea than if it made a feeble growth. As the ground used for late cabbage only yields one crop, unless manure is cheap and abundant, it will not often pay to use it in the profusion required for the early cabbage, so that it is usual to manure in the hill, as is done for early crop, if with stable manure, but when that is not attainable, some concentrated fertilizer such as bone dust or guano should be used, using a good handful for each hill, but being careful of course to mix it well with the soil for about nine or ten inches deep and wide. In this way about 300 pounds per acre will be needed, when 6,000 or 7,000 plants are set on an acre. In our practice, we find nothing better than pure bone dust and guano mixed together. For further information on this subject, see chapter on "Manures and Modes of Application," in this work.

In

TRANSPLANTING CABBAGE

from the seed-bed to the open field in summer, the work is usually done in a dry and hot season—end of June or July—and here again we give our oft-repeated warning of the absolute necessity of having every plant properly firmed. If the planting is well done with the dibber, it may be enough, but it is often not well done, and as a measure of safety it is always best to turn back on the rows after planting and press alongside of each plant with the foot. This is quickly done, and it besides rests the planter, so that he can with greater vigor start on the next row. In some sections of the country, particularly in the New England States, six or eight cabbage seeds are planted in the hills, and when of the height of two or three inches are thinned out to one plant in each hill. This we think not only a slower method, but is otherwise objectionable, inasmuch as it compels the manure to be placed for three or four weeks in the ground before the plant can take it up, to say nothing of the three or four weeks' culture necessary to be done before the seedlings in the hill get to the size of the plants when set out. The cultivation of late cabbage

HENDERSON'S SELECTED LATE FLAT DUTCH.

SAVOY CABBAGE.

GREEN CURLED SCOTCH KALE.

is, in all respects, similar to that of early, except as it is usually planted alone; the work is done entirely by the horse cultivator, the rows and plants in the rows, being according to the kind, from twenty-four to thirty inches apart. There are a great number of kinds offered in the different seed lists, but experienced cultivators confine themselves to but very few kinds. These we give in the order in which they are most approved: "Henderson's Selected Late Flat Dutch," "American Drumhead," and "Marblehead Mammoth." The late cabbage sell all the way from $2 to $10 per 100; but it is always a safe crop for the farmer, because if he is unable to sell the cabbage for table use, they will pay even at $2 per 100 as a food for sheep or cattle.

In addition to these the "American Drumhead Savoy" is grown to a considerable extent, and it is really surprising that it is not grown to the exclusion of nearly all other sorts, as it attains nearly as much weight of crop, and is much more tender and finer in flavor. The "Green Scotch" and "Brown German Kale" belong to the cabbage family, but do not form heads. The curled leaves of the whole plant can be used, and are, like the "Savoy," much finer in flavor than the plain head cabbages, particularly after having been subjected to the frost in fall. There are various methods of

KEEPING CABBAGES IN WINTER.

It is best to leave them out as late as possible, so that they can be lifted before being frozen in. In this latitude, they can be safely left out until third week in November. They are then dug or pulled up, according to the nature of the soil, and turned upside down—the roots up, the heads down—just where they have been growing, and the heads placed closely together in beds, six or eight feet wide, with alleys of about same width between, care being taken to have the ground leveled so that the cabbages will set evenly together. They can be left in this way for three or four weeks, or as long as the ground remains so that it can be dug in the alleys between the beds, the soil from which is thrown in on the beds of cabbage, so that when finished they have a covering of six or seven inches of soil, or sufficient to cover the roots completely up. Sometimes they are covered up immediately on being lifted, by plowing a furrow, shoveling it out wide enough to receive the heads, then plowing so as to cover up, and so on till beds six or eight feet wide are thus formed. This plan is the quickest, but it has the disadvantage, if the season proves mild, of having the cabbages covered up too soon by the soil, and hence more danger of decay. After the ground is frozen, stable litter, straw or leaves, to the depth of three or four inches, should be thrown over the cabbage beds, so as to prevent excessive freezing, and to facilitate the getting at the cabbages in hard weather.

INSECTS.

The insects that attack the cabbage tribe are various, and for some of them we regret to say that we are almost helpless in arresting their ravages. Young cabbage plants in fall, or in hot-beds in spring, are often troubled with the *aphis*, or, as it is popularly known, the "green fly" or "green louse." This is easily destroyed by having the plants dusted over once or twice with tobacco dust. This same insect, of a blue color, is often disastrous to the growing crop in the field, and on its first appearance, tobacco dust should be applied, as, of course, if the cabbage are headed up it could not be used. Another insect which attacks them in these stages, is a species of slug, or small caterpillar—a green, glutinous insect, about one-fourth or one-half inch in length. This is not quite so easily destroyed as the other, but will also succumb to a mixture of one part white hellebore to four parts lime dust, sprinkled on thick enough to slightly whiten the plants. This same remedy we found to be the most efficacious in preventing the ravages of the black flea, or "jumping jack," that is often so destructive to cabbage plants sown or planted in open ground during May and June, but in this case its application may have to be repeated daily often for two weeks.

Another most troublesome insect is the cabbage caterpillar, which attacks the crop often when just beginning to head. This is the larvæ of a species of small white butterfly, which deposits its eggs on the crop in May or June. When fields of cabbage are isolated, or where neighbors can be found to act in unison, the best plan is to catch the butterflies with an insect-catching net as soon as they show themselves. This is the most effective and quickest way to get rid of them. However, if that has been neglected, the caterpillar can be destroyed by dusting white hellebore on the cabbages, but, of course, this cannot be done when the heads are matured enough to be ready to use, as the hellebore is to some extent poisonous, though used when the plants are about half grown it will do no harm, as the rains will have washed it sufficiently off by the time they head up. The insects here described are not, probably, all that afflict the cabbage crop. A letter just received from a gentleman in Montgomery, Ala., says that the young cabbage plants in that region are often swept in twenty-four hours by a small green worm—a species of slug or caterpillar, no doubt. The remedy for all such is white hellebore powder, which had better be dusted on the plants once a week as a *preventive*, before the insect makes its appearance. In fact, all remedies against insects are best used as preventives, or at least, on the very first appearance of the pest. But the insect enemies which attack the *roots* of the cabbage are not so easy to destroy. In fact, with the wire worm and cabbage maggot we are almost helpless, as far as my experience has gone. For the latter, which is the worst enemy, a remedy has recently been recommended to me, which, as yet, I have had no opportunity to test. It is to make a hole with the dibber, five or six inches deep, close to the root of each plant, and drop into it nine or ten drops of bi-sulphide of carbon, closing up the hole again. Last year the cabbage and cauliflower in our "trial grounds" were attacked by the cabbage maggot at the roots early in May. A small handful of Peruvian Guano was at once strewn around each plant and hoed in around the roots. This at once started an unusual vigor of growth, which sustained the plants until they matured excellent heads. Understand, the Guano did not injure the insect, it only enabled the cabbage to outgrow its attack. For the destruction of the insect which causes the excrescence known as "club root" in cabbage a heavy dressing of lime in fall and spring will check it to a great extent. In fact, on lands adjacent to the shores of New York Bay, where the soil is mixed with oyster shell, "club root" is rarely seen, cabbage having been grown on some fields successively for fifty years without a trace of it being seen, showing that the insect that causes the "club root" cannot exist in contact with lime; for it is found on lands where there is no oyster shell deposit, a quarter of a mile distant, and cabbages cannot be grown two years in succession on the same land, unless heavily dressed with lime, and even then it is always deemed safest never to plant cabbages two years in succession on the same ground; for while such crops as onions show but little benefit by rotation with other crops, cabbages, perhaps more than anything else, are benefited by such alternation; and when it can be done, nothing is better than to let the cabbage crop be alternated with grasses, such as German millet, timothy or clover, or a crop of oats or rye. This is the method pursued by many of the Long Island market gardeners, who grow for the New York market, where their lands are cheap enough to allow them to do so; but the gardeners of Hudson County, New Jersey, which is in sight of New York City, whose lands now are limited in area, and for which an average of $50 per acre rent is paid per annum, cannot well afford to let their lands lay thus comparatively idle, and in consequence do not now raise as fine crops as the lands thus "rested" by the grass or grain crops.

If the land for the cabbage crop is of a kind suitable to grow a good crop of corn or potatoes, and is tilled or fertilized in the manner advised, it is rare indeed that a crop will fail to head, if the plants are in good condition, and have been properly planted, unless they are attacked by the maggot or "club root." In our trial grounds, where over a hundred different stocks of cabbage are tested each year, we have found that every kind of cabbage tested, early or late, have produced solid heads, showing *that when the conditions are right all kinds of cabbages will head up and produce a crop.* A circumstance came under our notice, in the summer of 1882, which well illustrates the necessity for care in planting. We had sold, some time in February, a large lot of our "Early Summer" cabbage seed to two market gardeners in Rochester, N. Y. The orders were filled from the same bag of seed. Some time about the end of June one of the men wrote, saying that he had evidently got some spurious kind of cabbage from us, as his neighbor was marketing his crop, while in his field of ten acres he had not a head fit to cut, nor was there any appearance of their ever doing so, he thought. Investigation showed that no maggot, "club root" or other insect was affecting the roots; the land was nearly identical with that which had made a successful crop, and had been equally well manured and cultivated. So the only probable solution of the matter was that the plants in the case of failure had been *loosely planted* and had failed to make a prompt start, as in the other case, where the planting had been properly done, so that while the one lot advanced without a check, the growth of the other lot was arrested. This was undoubtedly the case, for there could be no cause for the difference unless on some such hypothesis. But there was a fortunate sequel to the case. It luckily happened that a heavy rain storm occurred while the cabbages were yet in this unheaded condition. This started, as it were, a second growth, which resulted in their forming splendid heads by August 1st, at a time when cabbages were scarce, which, luckily for the owner, brought a much higher price than had they matured at the proper season, in June or July. The result was fortunate for us, who had sold the seed, for had not rain come so opportunely, the crop might never have headed up, and it would then have been hard to have convinced the man that he had not been furnished with spurious seed. What has been advised for cabbage crops, either early or late, is exactly the culture necessary for a crop of

CAULIFLOWER.

Cauliflower being a plant of more delicate constitution than cabbage, it requires to be more carefully handled; for instance, where the cabbage plants in the cold frames will keep safely over winter in this latitude, with no covering but the glass sash, cauliflower plants require the use of straw mats over the sashes, as the plant is much more easily hurt by frost. In fact, it is better never to keep the plants through the winter; those sown in February, and transplanted into cold frames in March, and planted in the open ground in April, as recommended for spring sown early cabbage, being better. The plants, however, must be started early enough so that they can be set out not later than middle of April, for if not rooted well before warm weather sets in, they will either "button"—that is, form small, stunted flowers—or else fail entirely to head up. Cauliflower delights in a cool atmospnere, and never does well when the season is hot and dry, unless complete irrigation can be given when the plant is about half grown. If this can be done the crop is certain. We have grown in this manner nearly an acre for many years, the crop selling for an average of $1,200 per acre annually, and that was before we had introduced the now famous

VARIETY

known as "Henderson's Early Snowball," which is ahead of all other kinds in its certainty to make a crop. The next in succession to this is the "Early Erfurt," which is again succeeded by the "Early Paris,"

HENDERSON'S EARLY SNOWBALL CAULIFLOWER.

but neither of these in any respect is equal to the "Snowball." For late crop the varieties known as "Algiers, and Erfurt," are the kinds usually grown. The plants are obtained by sowing at the same dates as for late cabbages. It is planted three feet each way and cultivated exactly as late cabbages, and often sells as high as $25 per 100 in November and December. We are of the opinion, however, that the "Snowball," of which twice the number can be grown per acre, will prove a more profitable crop even for late than the "Algiers," as it is always more certain to form heads. It is not once in twenty years that a variety of vegetables or fruit makes such an advance in earliness and quality as this "Snowball" cauliflower, and we have much satisfaction in the knowledge that we were the first to bring it into cultivation, about five years ago. It is now grown to almost the entire exclusion of all other early kinds of cauliflower in this country, and hundreds have succeeded both North and South in raising a crop from this variety, who had previously completely failed with all other kinds. In cauliflowers, as in cabbages, it is folly to attempt the experiment of many kinds. Long experience has taught us that two or three of each, for early and second early, is all-sufficient. Although our seed catalogues enumerate scores of kinds, gardeners, who know what they are about, fight shy of all except those whose merit has been proved beyond any question of a doubt. For this reason, we only give the names of such as we *know* to be the best.

CARROT.

The cultivation of this vegetable is almost identical with that given for the beet, excepting that the crop may be thinned out a little closer;

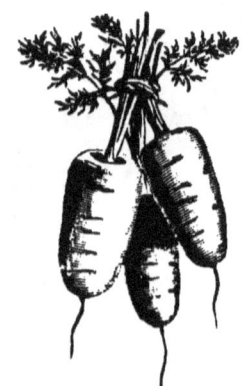

DANVERS CARROT.   EARLY SCARLET SHORT HORN CARROT.

that is, carrots may be allowed to stand at a distance of three or four inches apart, while the beet requires five or six inches. This is a particularly safe crop for the farmer, and he can never go far wrong in growing plenty of it, as it is a hardier root than beet, and can be left until late in the fall and dug at leisure times, but always before there is danger of its being frozen in; and will always sell at a fair price even as feed for horses and cattle, rarely bringing in our markets less than $1.00 per barrel. The average crop on suitable soils is about 300 barrels to the acre. The carrot crop has one advantage over many others—if the ground is fairly good, it may be grown without manure, particularly on lands that have been broken for potatoes or corn the year previous. I might say here that the seed of the carrot, being

HALF LONG STUMP CARROT.

very small, is easily affected by drought, and great care should be taken to firm it in the soil well, and I would ask the reader, if he has not already been thoroughly imbued with the importance of firming seeds, to read the chapter given in this work on the "Use of the Feet in Sowing and Planting." The kind used for table purposes is the Early Horn, a short, beautifully colored, dark orange variety. For a second crop the Half Long is grown. That used for farm culture is known as Long Orange, or the Danvers. The quantity of seed required, if sown by drill, is four to six pounds per acre; if sown by hand, eight to twelve pounds per acre. When sold at retail for table use it is equally profitable as beets, but comparatively few carrots are wanted in the summer months.

CELERY.

Celery is annually becoming of more and more importance as a vegetable crop. Thousands of acres of it are grown in the neighborhood of all our large cities; of late, in the vicinity of New York, the demand has been in excess of the supply, and the extraordinary circumstance of a vegetable of this description being sent from Michigan to New York occurred last year. The soil and climate of Michigan seem to be particularly suited to the growth of Celery, and the samples sent to New York exceeded anything grown in the neighborhood, and brought a price sufficient to justify the heavy freight from that great distance. Celery requires rich soil and heavy manuring to have it of the best quality; although on land that has not been used for it before, such as following after potatoes or corn, fine crops may be raised, if the ground is in good heart, without extra manuring. As a little more requires to be said on the culture of this crop than a good many other vegetables, I insert the following from my Horticultural Essays, published in 1882, which contains, in my opinion, about all the information necessary on the subject.

ON THE GROWING AND PRESERVING OF CELERY FOR WINTER.

The seeds are sown on a well pulverized, rich border, in the open ground, as early in the season as the ground can be worked. (For instructions in sowing, see article headed "Use of the Feet in Sowing and Planting.") The bed is kept clear of weeds until July, when the plants are set out for the crop. But as the seedling plants are rather troublesome to raise, when for private use only, and as they can usually be purchased cheaper than they can be raised on a small scale, it is scarcely worth while to sow the seed. But when wanted in quantity, the plants should always be raised by the grower, as Celery plants are not only difficult to transplant, but are usually too expensive to buy when the crop is grown to sell. The European plan is to make a trench six or eight inches deep in which to plant Celery; but our violent rain storms in summer soon showed us that this plan was not a good one here, so we set about planting on the level surface of the ground, just as we do with all vegetables. Celery requires an abundance of manure, which, as usual with all other crops, must be well mixed and incorporated with the soil before the Celery is set out. When the ground is well prepared, we stretch a line to the distance required, and beat it slightly with a spade, so that it leaves a mark to show where to place the plants. These are set out at distances of six inches between the plants, and usually four feet between the rows, when the Celery is to be "banked" up for early or fall use; but when grown for winter use, from two to three feet between the rows is sufficient. Great care must be taken, in putting out the Celery, to see that the plant is set just to the depth of the roots; if much deeper, the "heart" might be too much covered up, which would impede the growth. It is also important that the soil be well packed to the roots in planting, and this we do by returning on each row, after planting, and pressing the soil against each plant firmly with the feet; and if the operation can be done in the evening, and the plants copiously watered, no further attention will be required.

Planting may be done any time from the 25th of June to the second week in August. After planting, nothing is to be done but keep the crop clear of weeds until September; by that time the handling process is to be begun, which consists in drawing the earth to each side of the Celery, and pressing it tightly to it, so as to give the leaves an upward growth preparatory to blanching for use. Supposing this handling process is done by the middle of September, by the first week in October it is ready for "banking up," which is done by digging the soil from between the rows, and laying or banking it up with the spade on each side of the row of Celery. After being so banked up in October, it will be ready for use in three or four weeks, if wanted at that time. But if, as in most cases, it is needed for winter use only, and is to be put away in trenches, or in the cellar, as will hereafter be described, all that it requires is the operation of "handling." If the celery is to be left in the open ground where it was grown, then a heavy bank must be made on each side of the rows, and as cold weather approaches—say in this latitude by the middle of November—an additional covering of at least a foot of leaves or litter must be closely packed against the bank, to protect it from frost; but it is not safe to leave it in the banks where it grows, in any section of the country where the temperature gets lower than ten degrees above zero.

Perhaps the best way to keep Celery for family use is in a cool cellar. This can be done by storing it in narrow boxes, of a depth a little less than the height of the Celery. A few inches of sand or soil are placed in the bottom of the box, and the Celery is packed upright, the roots being placed on the sand at the bottom; but no sand or anything else must be put between the stalks of the Celery, all that is needed being the damp sand on the bottom of the box, the meaning of which is, that before Celery will blanch or whiten, it must first start at the root; hence the necessity of placing the roots on an inch or so of damp sand. Boxes thus packed and placed in a cool cellar in November, will be blanched fit for use during January, February and March, though for succession it will be better to put it in the boxes, from the open ground, at three different times, say October 25th, November 10th and November 20th. Or if the boxes are not at hand, the Celery may be put away on the floor of the cellar, in strips of eight or nine inches wide, divided by boards of a width equal to the height of the Celery. That is, if the Celery is two feet high, the boards separating it must be about the same height. The reason for dividing the Celery in these narrow strips by boards is to prevent heating, which would take place if placed together in too thick masses. The dates above given apply, of course, to the latitude of New York; if further south, do the work later; if further north, earlier. If one has no suitable cellar, the Celery can be very readily preserved in the manner followed by market gardeners. Thus, after it has been "handled" or straightened up, as before described, what is intended for use by Christmas should be dug up about October 25th; that to be used in January and February, by November 10th; and that for March use, by November 20th, which latter date is as late as it can be risked here. Although it will stand quite a sharp frost, the weather by the end of November is often severe enough to kill it, or so freeze it in the ground that it cannot be dug up. The ground in which it is to be preserved for winter use must be as dry as possible, and so arranged that no water can remain in the trench. Dig a trench as narrow as possible (it should not be wider than ten inches), and of a depth equal to the height of the Celery; that is, if the plant of Celery be eighteen inches high, the trench should be dug eighteen inches deep. The Celery is then packed exactly in the manner described for storing in boxes to be placed in the cellar; that is, stand it as near upright as possible, and pack as closely together as can be done without bruising it; no soil or sand must be put between the stalks. As the weather becomes cold, the trenches should be gradually covered with leaves or litter to the thickness of six or eight inches, which will be enough to prevent severe freezing, and enable the roots to be taken out easily when wanted. Another method now practiced by the market gardeners of New Jersey is as follows: before the approach of very cold weather —say the middle of December— the Celery in the trenches is pressed somewhat closely together by passing a spade down deeply alongside of the trench on each side, but about three or four inches from the Celery. It is best done by two men, so that they press against each other, thus firming the top of the Celery in the trench until it is compact enough to sustain a weight of three or four inches of soil, which is taken from the sides of the trench and spread over the Celery.

VARIETIES OF CELERY.

This earth covering keeps it rather fresher than the covering of litter, though on the approach of cold weather the earth covering is not sufficient, and a covering of six or seven inches of leaves must yet be placed over the earth covering.

From 200 to 500 roots are usually required for use by an ordinary family. The varieties we recommend are the Golden Dwarf, Sandringham, White Walnut, and London Red. The red is as yet but little used

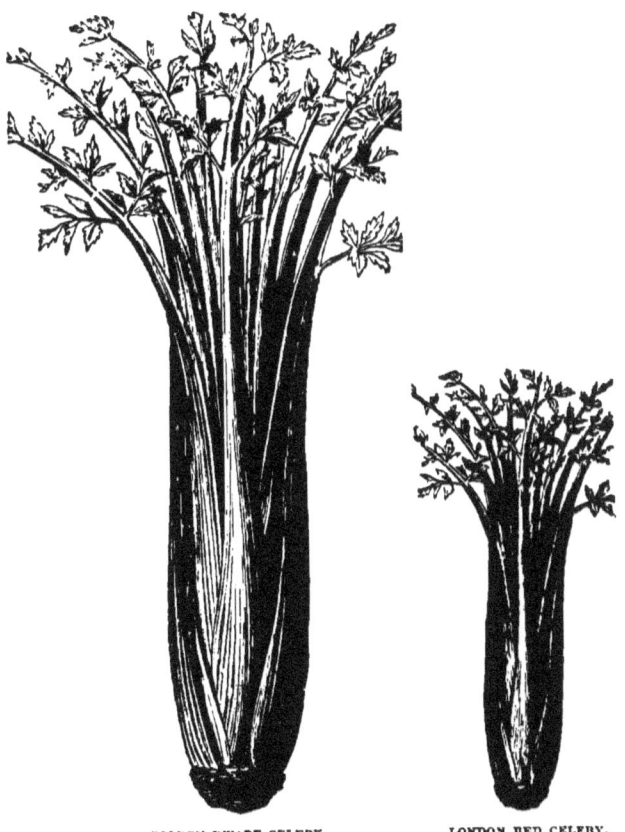

GOLDEN DWARF CELERY.   LONDON RED CELERY.

in this country, though the flavor is better, and the plant altogether hardier than the white. A new variety, known as the Parsley leaved, has just been introduced, which will be very useful for table decoration, as well as for all purposes for which Celery is used, as it is equally as good as any of the others.

We are often asked for the cause of and remedy for Celery rusting or burning. The cause, we think, is the condition of the weather, which destroys the tender fibres, or what are called the working roots of the plant, for we find it is usually worse in seasons of extreme drought or moisture, particularly in warm weather.

We know of no remedy, nor do we believe there is any. We may say, however, that it is less liable to appear on new, fresh soils, that are free from acids or sourness, than on old soils that have been surfeited with manure, and have had no rest.

Although, under ordinary conditions, if proper varieties of Celery are used, the crop should never be pithy or hollow, yet we have found that now and then even the most solid kinds of Celery have become more or less hollow when planted in soft, loose soils, such as reclaimed peat bogs, where the soil is mostly composed of leaf mould. In fact, on heavy or clayey soils the Celery will be considerably heavier than on lighter soils.

THE WHITE PLUME CELERY.

Since writing the above, we have this season, 1883, been fortunate in originating a new kind of celery known as the "White Plume," a name given to it from its resemblance in structure to an ostrich plume. It has a most beautiful pinnated leaf cut in segments, and in all respects, as regards quality, is unsurpassed by any of the very best kinds. The great advantage which it possesses, is a peculiarity in its nature that is going to do away with nearly all the labor that we have heretofore had in banking or trenching celery. When the plant attains its full growth, the stems and all the inner leaves are white, and all that is necessary to do in order to blanch it, is to draw or hoe the soil up close against each root with the hands and again plow or hoe it up, and the work is done, so that the celery will come out in as fine a blanched state as other kinds will do, even when banked up, with a spade, two feet in height. This banking up with the spade is always a slow process, and very difficult to learn, unless with large practice, and has been the drawback more than anything else against the cultivation of celery. This new kind will do away with all this labor and expense, and will open a new era in celery culture, so that anybody can grow it just as easily as they can grow a head of cabbage. The only disadvantage attending this new celery is that from its whiteness and consequent tender nature it will not keep later than the middle of February, but for fall and early winter use there is no kind that will answer the purpose so well.

As the greatest demand for celery is at the Thanksgiving and Christmas holidays, this only drawback is of little account. For general use we advise that three-fourths of this variety be grown, the other

fourth being London Red and Golden Dwarf. The White Plume should therefore for this reason always be used as the first crop, the green kinds, whose culture we have just described, being used for second crops. One great disadvantage with the older kinds is that the work of banking up of two or three feet required to be done, may in the event of severe rain storms be made completely useless, as these banks become saturated with the rain and washed down and the whole work has to be gone over again, but with this new kind, no banks being necessary, all such danger is avoided. About 30,000 of this new kind of celery (planted three feet in the rows and six inches between the plants) can be grown on an acre. At the very lowest price of $2 per 100 roots, $600 would be the gross receipts. Estimating $200 for manure and labor, we have a net profit of $400 per acre, but in many parts of the country celery is sold at twice and sometimes three times this price.

CRESS (WATER).

I allude to this vegetable here, not to recommend its culture to the farmer unless under special favorable conditions. The special conditions required for it may, however, occasionally be found, and in such cases, by a little attention, it may be made an exceedingly profitable crop. Many a farmer in the vicinity of large cities may realize more profit from this plant on his farm, with but little labor, than he could from months of hard work in his corn or potato field. The following brief instructions will be found to be all that is required for the culture of this vegetable, where the proper conditions are present. Suppose there is a stream running through the farm one to three feet deep and three to twelve feet wide, with level banks. A simple plan of cultivation is to make excavations at right angles with the stream, forming sunken beds six or eight feet wide and about eight inches deep, with alleys raised between of the same width, so that the beds can be flooded by the stream, the plants of the Water Cress being planted in the sunken beds at eight or ten inches apart each way. Where the beds cannot be drained dry, the slips or cuttings are made into small balls with clay, and these are dropped into the water; they settle to the bottom, and the slips quickly take root. The advantage of having the beds made at right angles to the stream is that, in the event of freshets, the crop is less liable to be washed out. It is not easy to determine the value of an acre of Water Cress, as so much depends on the thickness of its growth; yet I think it safe to say that, whenever sold in any of our large markets, such as New York, Boston, Philadelphia or Chicago, it would rarely fail, at present prices, to bring less than $1,000 per acre, and one great advantage of it is that it is so light in proportion to its value that from $100 to $150 worth can be easily placed in a single wagon load. For full particulars on this subject I would again refer to my work, "Gardening for Profit."

CORN (SWEET).

It may seem presumption in me to instruct the farmer how to grow corn; but as their methods of growing this special variety of corn for table use are probably not as well known as for the field varieties, I will here give them. All the varieties of sweet corn may either be sown in rows four and one-half feet apart and about six or eight inches between the seeds, or planted in hills at distances of three or

TOM THUMB SWEET CORN.

EVERGREEN SUGAR CORN.

four feet each way, according to the variety of corn or richness of the soil. The smaller and earlier varieties, as the Tom Thumb and Early Minnesota, may be planted in hills two feet apart each way. The taller the variety or the richer the soil, the greater should be the distance apart. Such later varieties as Egyptian and Evergreen require to be planted at least three feet apart, or even more, on very rich soil. We make our first plantings in this latitude about the middle of May, and continue successive plantings every two weeks until the last week in July. In more southern latitudes, or in warm, light soils at the north, planting is begun a month earlier and continued a month later. I have repeatedly sold it in the New York markets, realizing as high as $200 per acre, and this, too, at the first wholesale price, the consumer paying about twice as much. An ordinary yield is about 11,000 ears to an acre. In such cases, however, it was either an early crop or a very late one, bringing two or three dollars per 100 ears, while the intervening crops, which came in competition with the full market, often sold as low as seventy-five cents per 100 ears. The importance, then, will be seen, of striking the market at such seasons when the article will be scarce. The quantity of seed required per acre is from six to eight quarts.

CUCUMBER.

This vegetable is best suited for warm, rich, sandy, loam ground. It should not be planted until there is a prospect for settled warm weather—in the vicinity of New York about the middle of May—and in hills four feet apart each way. The hills should previously be prepared by thoroughly mixing in a shovel full of well rotted stable manure. In the absence of manure, a small handful of bone dust, or some well known superphosphate, may be used instead. In each hill

IMPROVED WHITE SPINE CUCUMBER.

should be planted from eight to ten seeds. When all danger from insects is passed, and the plants are well started, they are thinned out to three or four to each hill. The fruit should be gathered while green, as, if left to ripen on the vines, it very soon destroys their productiveness. Quite a number of farmers in the vicinity of New York have of late years grown cucumbers for pickling very largely, some devoting as much as twenty acres to this purpose. When grown for pickling they are usually not sown until the middle of July, the ground used being such as has been sown with rye, oats or clover. They are planted in hills about four feet apart, and manured as for table use, and it is claimed that they give an average profit over all expenses of $75 per acre. The kind used for table use is that known as the Improved White Spine; that used for pickling is the Green Prolific. Care should be taken not to get these varieties reversed, or the pickling variety will be found of little use for the table, while the White Spine would be too large for pickling. Quantity of seed required for cucumbers in hills, about two pounds per acre. An experienced grower gives the following information in regard to this crop:

"The culture of cucumbers for pickling is very profitable under some circumstances. These are when the grower is near a large city, or has facilities for disposing of his product in a fresh state to factories in which the vegetables are pickled either in salt or vinegar, or when he has facilities for preserving them himself for sale in distant markets, as in manufacturing towns, lumbering or mining villages and camps, or to dealers in ship stores, or even to village stores, where the pickles can be retailed during the winter season. As there is a large and regular demand for pickles, there are many places where factories can be established for their manufacture with success and profit, and more conveniently in conjunction with the business of cider making, with a view to providing a supply of pure vinegar; canning and drying vegetables and fruits; making jellies, and even adding to all these an outfit for making sorghum syrup and sugar from the cane. A factory of this kind could find work the whole year round, and would require only a very moderate capital for its furnishing, because the same building and much of the apparatus would serve for all these purposes, and some only would be required for each special use. But a pickle factory should be erected in a good apple country, where fruit for cider could be procured very cheaply.

"The culture of the cucumbers is very simple. Although this vegetable consists almost wholly of water, yet it requires rich soil, or at least a liberal quantity of manure, to force the growth so quickly as to secure the requisite tenderness and succulence. A light, sandy, warm soil is the best. This is plowed deeply, because the roots of all the gourd tribe spread widely and love a loose soil, in which they can find adequate moisture and warmth. For the pickling varieties, of which the Green Prolific is the best and is almost universally grown, the ground is marked out four feet apart each way, a deep furrow being made so as to leave room for a good shovelful of rich compost at each crossing. This is worked in with the spade or hoe and the ground leveled. Five or six seeds are dropped in each hill, about one pound of seed being required for one acre. When the plants are up they are thinned out to three to each hill. When the seed is sown a broadcast dressing of 300 or 400 pounds of Peruvian guano per acre may be given with great advantage, as this fertilizer seems to have a specially good effect on this crop; superphosphate of lime is the next best, and fine bone flour comes next. With this preparation and 400 pounds of guano per acre, costing $15, we have grown over 300,000 cucumbers to the acre, which is double the average crop and equal to about 100 to each hill. The excess in this case was clearly due to the fertilizer, as the product was more than doubled by it, so that the expenditure of $15 repaid nearly $200 in increase of crop, as the cucumbers were sold at $1.50 per 1,000. Some attention is required to secure a good yield. The ground must be kept loose by frequent cultivation until the vines cover the ground. The main vines must be pinched at the ends to keep them within bounds and to encourage the outgrowth of side branches, which are the most prolific of fruit. The main branches bear chiefly male or staminate flowers, which are barren of fruit, and the side branches bear the pistillate or productive flowers; so that the great secret in growing this crop, as well as all kinds of cucumbers, melons and squashes, consists in this shortening in of the main vine and the encouragement of the laterals. The fruit is gathered every morning as soon as it has reached a proper size, which is from two to three inches. These cucumbers are never cut, but are always preserved and pickled whole. The chief labor is in preventing damage by lice and the small cucumber beetle; for the former we find the best remedy to be to pluck off the first infested leaves, by which the otherwise rapid spread of this pest is prevented. For the other pest dusting with finely ground gypsum is the best and usual remedy."

EGG PLANT.

This vegetable is not likely to be much wanted in country towns, although it is used to a considerable extent at the watering places in

NEW YORK IMPROVED EGG PLANT.

hotels and boarding houses. It is not worth while for the farmer, for all he would be likely to want of this crop, to go to the trouble of raising his own plants, as it is rather a difficult process, and requires warm hot beds to start them in during the early spring months. He can purchase the plants cheaper than he can raise them. The nature of this vegetable is very much similar to that of the tomato, being a very tender plant, and should never be set out, in the latitude of New York, sooner than the 15th of May. It should be planted at distances of four feet apart each way. It will begin to produce its fruits by the middle of July and continues fruiting until September. It is not unusual for single plants to produce ten or twelve large fruits, enough to fill a bushel basket. They are usually retailed in our markets at $1.50 per dozen fruits.

LETTUCE.

This is, perhaps, one of the most universally cultivated of all vegetables, and from its tractable nature and freedom from nearly all insect diseases, it is easily managed by every one. For main crop the seed is usually sown by market gardeners in the open ground, about the middle of September, and transplanted to cold frames as soon as

BLACK SEEDED SIMPSON LETTUCE.

large enough to handle, being wintered over in the same manner as early cabbage, which see. But when sown in dry, well sheltered spots and covered with leaves or litter late in the fall, lettuce plants will be safe through the winter without glass covering, particularly in southern sections. We have often seen plants in sheltered places, even in New Jersey, coming out in the spring perfectly fresh, simply by having sown the seed in the open ground in the middle of September. These plants that are sown in September, it will be understood, are for the early spring crop, to be planted in April in the open ground. For such as are wanted for successive crops sowings may be made in the open ground as early as the season opens, say 15th of April, until July, and, as it is somewhat difficult to transplant in hot weather, the best way is to sow it in drills twelve inches apart, and thin out the plants in the rows so that they will stand eight or ten inches apart. The crop in this way is exceedingly easy to handle; all that is necessary to do is to hoe it once, so as to keep down the weeds. It is a plant of comparatively tender growth, and unless care is taken to promptly destroy all weeds it may be quickly choked up so as to be worthless. The kinds best to use are those known as Black Seeded

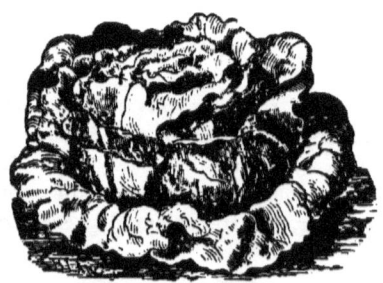

SALAMANDER LETTUCE.

Simpson and Salamander; the one is a curled leaved variety, the other is plain or smooth leaved, and forms a solid head. Many of the German gardeners in the vicinity of New York make an excellent living on half an acre of land by this process of sowing lettuce, which they sell at not more than one cent per head; but as they get four crops in a season, and the plants are set about one foot each way, half an acre four times cropped will sell for upwards of $800, even at one cent per head. When lettuce is sold at retail direct to the consumer, it is fair to presume that, in most places, it will bring two or three times that amount.

MELON (MUSK).

I have often wondered that a delicious fruit, so easily grown as melons, is so little cultivated by farmers who have often acres upon acres of land of which they make but little or no use. Melons will thrive best in a rich, light soil, although there is no necessity for heavy manuring on soils where a good crop of corn or potatoes, which has been well manured, has been grown the previous year. Usually a shovelful of rotted manure or compost is put in each hill, and the best growers use also a small handful of guano or superphosphate in

MUSK MELONS.   335

addition. A clover sod, plowed in, is especially favorable for this crop. The main point in melon growing is to push the crop forward as quickly as possible, so as to catch the high prices which rule then. A well known melon grower of Hackensack, N. J., where this crop is

HACKENSACK MUSK MELON.

largely produced, mentioned an instance where one farmer admitted having lost the whole of his late crop of melons by a frost, which would have been avoided by the expenditure of $25 or $30 in guano, used at the planting, as this would have pushed the crop forward

MONTREAL MARKET MUSK MELON.

several days and have saved it. For this reason, a dressing of guano in the hill should always be used. They, like cucumbers, should be planted in hills, but somewhat wider, from five to six feet apart each way, according to the richness of the soil. Ten or twelve seeds are planted in each hill early in May, and when well up the plants are thinned out to three or four of the most promising. It is a crop that can be as easily raised as a crop of corn, and when sold at wholesale, it is safe to say, will pay a profit of at least $100 per acre. The variety most preferred for this section is that known as Hackensack, which is grown by the thousands of acres for the New York market. The flesh is of a greenish-yellow color, and is of the most delicious flavor. Another variety is the Surprise, equally good in all respects, the flesh being of a salmon or pink color. This variety, however, is not so popular in the markets as the green-fleshed sorts. The most successful growers greatly increase the yield of this crop by a system of pinching the main vine, so as to encourage the lateral shoots, upon which the fruit is borne. A large grower in the vicinity of Hackensack, N. J., a noted locality in this respect, gives the following details of the culture:

Melons are a special crop which needs particular care and culture. In some localities they are grown for market in great quantities. It is said that, on one evening last summer, 160 two-horse wagon loads, each of about 1,000 melons, crossed by one ferry from a suburb of New York City. And this was by no means an extra occasion. The melon season lasts from July into October, so that some idea may be gained from this of the magnitude of this business. The crop is a very profitable one when skillfully cultivated, and often realizes $500 to $1,000 an acre, and more rarely even as high as $1,500, when the melons are the first in the market and bring the highest price of the season. But as with other products, these large profits are only realized by those growers whose long experience and skill give them more than usual advantages. The methods, however, are no secret, and any one who will follow them may just as easily meet with the same success.

The most suitable soil for melons is a rich, warm, deep, sandy loam having a southern or south-western exposure. The latter is preferable, as it gets the last rays of the sun and the soil is thus warmed up for the night, and, being sheltered from eastern and northern winds, retains this warmth until the morning. This may make several days' difference in the ripening of the crop, which may be equivalent to $300 or $400 an acre in the value of the fruit. The best fertilizer is well decayed stable manure and night soil in equal parts, with a moderate addition of Peruvian guano applied in the hill. The manner of culture is as follows: The soil is plowed in the fall or early in the spring and is cross-plowed the first days of May, about twenty loads per acre of manure being plowed under. The ground is then well harrowed and furrowed out six feet apart each way. A full shovelful of mixed fine manure and night soil is used in each hill, being well mixed with the soil; a liberal dusting of guano or superphosphate of lime is then scattered about the hill and six or eight seeds are planted. The first planting is early in May; other plantings may be continued through June. The hill is raised two or three inches above the surface, and is made about two feet broad and quite flat. When the plants appear above the surface they require protection from cut worms, which would otherwise cut the stems and destroy them; and as the rough leaves appear the weaker plants are thinned out and three only left. A good method of protecting the plants against the cut worms is to make a ring of thick paper, about a foot in diameter and three inches broad, and place this around them, so as to form an obstacle over which they cannot climb. The after cultivation consists of deep plowing at intervals at least twice and frequent cultivation, until the vines begin to run, when the terminal buds are pinched off to cause the growth of the lateral branches. The main vine produces chiefly male and barren flowers, and if this is left to run the laterals would not push out and there would be little or no fruit. The lateral vines bear the female or perfect flowers, and to encourage the growth of these is one of the secrets of melon culture upon which the profits depend. The same peculiarity of growth is found in all the gourd tribe, and applies to squash, cucumbers and water melons, as well as to musk melons.

The pests of the melon are lice, the striped beetle, and the squash bug. The lice appear on the under side of the leaves and are difficult to get at, so that the simplest and most effective remedy is to pinch off the affected leaves or the part of the vine and carry it away and burn it. If left undisturbed the lice from one hill will quickly spread over several square rods and completely destroy the crop. The striped beetle is the worst enemy to deal with. It lays its eggs on the stem at the ground, and the small grubs work their way to the root and feed upon it. The first indication of their presence is the wilting of the leaves—"going down" of the vines, the growers call it —and vine after vine thus goes down, until at times the larger part of the crop may be destroyed when the melons are half grown. The remedy for this pest is to apply strong tobacco water around the stem on the first appearance of the small striped beetle and repeat it in a few days, and to repeat it again as soon as the wilting of the first leaf is noticed. The fruit begins to "net" about two weeks before it ripens, and the indications of ripeness are the fragrant scent, the softness of the blossom end of the melon, and the cracking and easy parting of the stem.

MELON (WATER).

Water melons require the same soil as musk melons for their best development, and thrive best in warm latitudes. Unless the soil is especially warm and sandy they do not usually give as good ressult in the Northern and Middle States as the musk melon, and are now, essentially, for market purposes, a plant of the South and South-

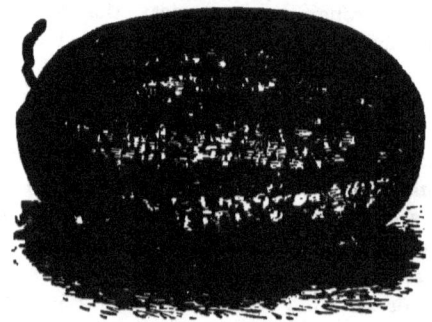

PHINNEY'S EARLY WATER MELON.

western States, where hundreds of thousands of them are annually grown for our Northern markets. The culture is exactly the same as for musk melons, except that the hills should be just double the distance apart, namely, nine to ten feet. Of varieties, the Black Spanish, Ice Cream and Phinney's Early are the favorites for this section, and the Georgia or Rattlesnake variety in the Southern States.

OKRA, OR GUMBO.

This vegetable is extensively grown in the Southern States. Its long pods, when young, are used in soups, stews, etc., and are very nutritious. It is easily cultivated and grows freely, bearing abundantly in any garden soil. It is sown at the usual time of all tender vegetables, in May, in drills, two inches deep and three feet apart, the seeds being dropped at two to three inches apart.

ONION.

It is the generally received opinion that onions grow best in old ground. This we think is an error; it is not because the ground is "old," or has been long cultivated, that the onions do better there,

Soils Suitable for Onions. 339

but because such lands, from their long culture, are usually better pulverized; and experience has shown us repeatedly that when new soil has been equally well pulverized and fertilized, an equally good crop is obtained, and usually a cleaner crop, more exempt from rust or mildew. As a matter of fact, the finest crop of onions we ever beheld was on sandy swamp land, which had been first thoroughly drained and broken up. In fact, new soils, particularly when broken up from pasture land—turned over early enough in the fall so that the sod is rotted completely—make excellent land for onion crops, as they are usually free from weeds. Such land, however, must be well

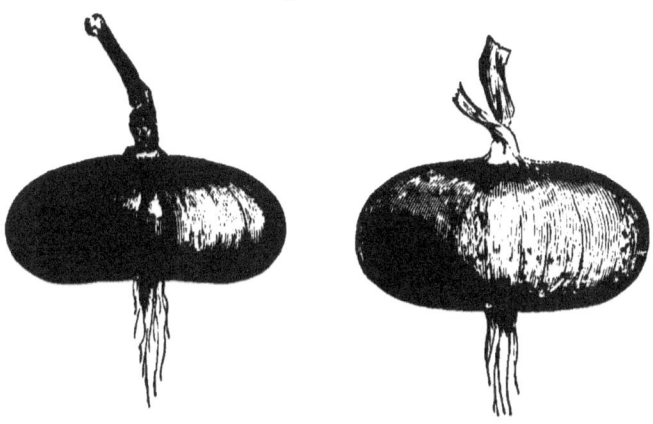

EARLY FLAT RED ONION.   YELLOW DUTCH ONION.

pulverized, by the use of the plow, harrow and smoothing harrow, or good results may not follow. Much depends on the quality of such soil. If rather sandy loam, it will, of course, be much easier to pulverize than if stiff or clayey loam, and such soil, in our experience, is always preferable for most crops. Such soils, also, are nearly always free from under water, rarely requiring artificial drainage, if the land is level, and it always should be selected as level as possible for the onion crop, as when land slopes to any great extent, much damage is often done by washing out, the onion roots being near the surface, and consequently cannot resist floods as crops that root deeper.

Many onion growers, who make a specialty of the business, find it is economical to alternate the crop with a green crop such as German millet, which can be cut for hay in July, the "stubble" plowed down in August, giving a fresh fibrous soil, *clear of weeds*, for the onion crop to be sown next spring. It is not claimed that the alternation of a green crop with the onions is a necessity, as it is well known that the onion is one of the very few crops that does not seem benefited by alternating; but it is claimed that it gives almost entire freedom from weeds, as, after a crop of millet which has been cut before its seed ripens, few troublesome weeds will come up the next year.

MANURES.

I have always held the opinion that when well rotted stable manure, whether from horses or cows, can be procured, at a cost not exceeding $3 per ton delivered on the ground, it is cheaper and better than any kind of concentrated fertilizer. It should be plowed in at the rate of thirty tons per acre. The concentrated fertilizers in the

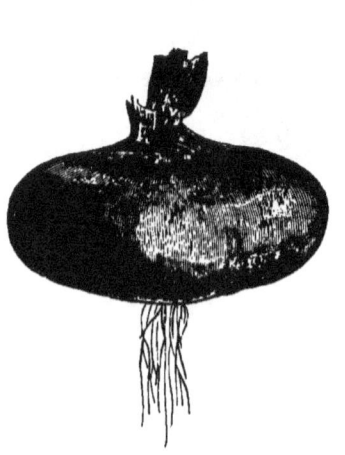

WHITE PORTUGAL ONION.

YELLOW DANVERS ONION.

market are now so numerous, that it would be invidious to specify particular brands. We ourselves, except in using occasionally the "Blood and Bone Fertilizer," which we have proved to be excellent, use only pure Ground Bone and Peruvian Guano, which, for onions, we prefer to mix together in equal parts, sowing it on the land after plowing, at the rate of at least one ton per acre of the mixture (when no stable manure has been used), after sowing to be harrowed in, as described in "Preparing the Ground."

One of the most valuable manures for the onion crop are the droppings from the chicken or pigeon house, which, when mixed with twice their weight of lime, coal or wood ashes, so as to disintegrate and pulverize, may be sown on the land after plowing, to be harrowed in, at the rate of three or four tons per acre of the mixture. Night soil, when mixed with dry muck, coal ashes, charcoal dust, lime or lime rubbish as absorbents, and spread on after plowing at the rate of six or eight tons per acre, and harrowed deeply in, will never fail to produce a heavy crop of onions in any suitable soil.

There are many other manures that will answer the purpose, often to be had in special localities, such as the refuse hops and "grains" from breweries, which should be used in the same manner and quantities as stable manure. While fish guano, whalebone shavings,

WETHERSFIELD RED ONION.   GIANT ROCCA ONION.

or shavings from horn, when pulverized so as to be in proper condition to be taken up by the plants, are nearly equal in value to ground bone. Wood ashes alone, spread on at the rate of five or six tons per acre, will usually give excellent results.

It is well ever to keep the fact in mind, that it will always be more profitable to fertilize one acre of onions well than two imperfectly. If thirty tons of stable manure or one and one-half tons of concentrated fertilizer are used to an acre, the net profits are almost certain to be larger than if that quantity had been spread over two acres; for in all probability nearly as much weight of crop would be got from the one well manured acre than from the two that had been done imperfectly, besides the saving of seed and labor in cultivating two acres instead of one. In

PREPARING THE GROUND

for the reception of the seed (if it has been plowed the fall previous), plowing should be begun as soon as the land is dry enough to work, first having spread over the land well rotted stable manure, at the rate of thirty tons to the acre. This should be lightly turned under, plowing not more than five or six inches deep, and covering the manure so that it will be three or four inches under the surface. For this reason, the manure must be well rotted, otherwise it cannot be well covered by the plow. If concentrated fertilizers are to be used, it is best to plow the land up roughly, sow the fertilizer at the rate of one to two tons per acre, according to its

SOUTHPORT YELLOW GLOBE ONION.

SOUTHPORT WHITE GLOBE ONION.

fertilizing properties; then harrow thoroughly, so that it is regularly incorporated with the soil. After harrowing with an ordinary toothed harrow, the surface should be further leveled with some kind of a "smoothing" harrow, either Meeker's Smoothing Disc Harrow, or some sort of chain harrow. The former we like best, as the revolving discs pulverize the soil, to a depth of three inches, much better than it can be done by raking, and the smoothing board, which follows in the wake of the revolving wheels, makes the surface, if free from stones, smooth as a board—far better than it can be done by raking.

The ground being thus prepared, the next thing is the sowing of the seed (about six pounds being used per acre). This, of course, nowadays, is done always by the seed drilling machine, of which there are a dozen or more in the market, nearly all of which do the work well. In our business at the present date, we sell the Planet, Jr., and Mathew's, giving the preference in the order in which they are named. In sowing the first row, a line must be stretched so as to have that line straight, after which the sower can readily regulate the other lines. The favorite distance for onion rows to be placed apart is fifteen inches, though they are sometimes sown as close as twelve inches, leaving out every ninth row for an alley, thus forming them into beds of eight rows each. Where there is reason to believe weeds may be troublesome, this plan of forming in beds has the advantage of the alley (twenty-four inches wide) to throw the weeds. We so firmly believe in the value of firming in the seeds after sowing, that we advise, in addition to the closing and firming of the seeds by the drill, to use a roller besides, particularly if the land is light, or where the soil has not been sufficiently firmed down. There is no crop where the adage of "a stitch in time" is so applicable as in the onion crop; so that just as soon as the lines can be seen, which will be in ten or twelve days after sowing, apply the scuffle hoe between the rows. There are a great many styles of hand cultivators, many of which are exceedingly useful, after the onions get strong enough after weeding, but for the first hoeing, after the seed shows the lines, use the scuffle hoe or some onion wheel hoe. The distance at which onions should stand in the rows is from one to two inches, and if the crop is sown evenly and thinly few require to be taken out. In hoeing, whether it is weeds or onions that are to be removed, one thing should never be lost sight of—that when this operation is done, every inch of the surface should be broken; this is best done after the machine, by using a wooden lawn rake, all over the land, lightly raking across the rows. It is one of the most common mistakes, when weeding or hoeing, if the laborer sees no weeds, to pass over such portions without breaking the crust. By this neglect, not only is it likely that he passes another crop of weeds in embryo under the unbroken crust, but the portion unbroken loses the stirring so necessary for the well-being of the crop. In our long experience in garden operations, we have had more trouble to keep our workmen up to the mark in this matter than in any other; and I never fail when I discover a man in such negligence to set him back over his work until he does it properly, and if he again fails to do so, promptly dismiss him.

The onion crop is usually fit to harvest in this section from 5th to 20th of August; that is, when the seed has been sown in early spring, which should be not later than May 1st, if possible, and if by April 1st all the better. If the seed is sown too late, it may delay the time of ripening, which may result in a complete loss of the crop; for if the bulbs are not ripened by August, there is danger, if September is wet, that they will not ripen at all; hence the great necessity of early seeding in spring. If the onion crop is growing very strong, it will facilitate the ripening process by bending the leaves down with the back of a wooden rake, or some such implement, so as to "knee" them, as it is called, at the neck of the bulb; this checks the flow of sap and tends to ripen the bulb.

After the tops of the onions become yellow and wither up, they should then be pulled without unnecessary delay, for if continued wet weather should occur and delay the pulling too long, a secondary growth of the roots may be developed, which would injure the crop seriously. After pulling, lay the bulbs in convenient rows, so as to cover the ground, but not to lay on each other. By turning them every day or two, in six or eight days they will be usually dry enough to be carted to their storage quarters, where the shriveled tops are cut off, and the onions stored on slatted shelves, to the depth of six or eight inches, in some dry and airy place. It is of importance to have the bottom of the shelves slatted, so as to leave spaces an inch or so apart, that air can be admitted at the bottom as well as the top of the heap. The shelves, when all the space at hand is to be made available, may be constructed one above another. But if to be kept through the winter, they must be protected in some building capable of resisting severe frost, or covered with hay or straw, as a protection against extreme cold. For although the onion will stand a moderate degree of frost, yet any long continuation of a zero temperature would injure. When frozen they should never be handled, as in that condition they are easily blemished and would rot. When kept in barrels holes should be bored in the sides, and they should be left unheaded until shipping so as to permit the escape of any moisture that may be generated.

For the

INSECTS AND OTHER ENEMIES

that attack the onion crop, I am much afraid there are few, if any, effective remedies. Every year's experience with the enemies that attack plants in the open field convinces me that with very few of them can we successfully cope. The remedy, if remedy it is, for rust, smut, or other mildew parasites, must, in my opinion, be a preventive one; that is, whenever practicable, use new land, or renew the old land by a green crop, such as rye, timothy or millet, in all sections subject to these diseases. The same plan had better be adopted in all sections where the onion maggot, or other insects, attack the crop. The theory for this practice is that it is believed that nearly all plants affected by insects or disease, have such *peculiar to themselves*, and that the germs lay in the soil ready to fasten on the *same* crop, if planted without intermission on the same ground, while if a season intervenes, the larva or germ has nothing congenial to feed on, and is, in consequence, destroyed. In practice, we usually find that cultivated land "rested" for a season by a grass crop gives always a cleaner and healthier crop to whatever vegetable following it.

THE PRODUCT

of the average onion crop varies very much, ranging from 300 to 900 bushels per acre, the mean being about 600 bushels per acre. The price is variable, like all perishable commodities, ranging from fifty cents per bushel, the price at which they usually wholesale in the New York market in fall, to $1 or $1.50 per bushel for winter and spring prices. The estimate, then, of profit per acre may be given about as follows:

Manure, per acre	$72 00
Plowing, weeding and harvesting crop, per acre	100 00
6 lbs. seed, average, $2 per lb	12 00
Rent or interest on land, per acre	9 00
Marketing crop, per acre	7 00
	$200 00
600 bushels per acre, at 50c	$300 00
Cost	200 00
Profit,	$100 00

This estimate is a moderate one, for if the crop is sold in spring, the chances are that the profit may be two or three times as much.

ONIONS SOLD GREEN.

All the foregoing relates to the onion crop ripened, but in all large cities immense quantities of onions are sold in the green state, many of them before they have half attained their growth. To get the earliest crop of onions in this condition, the onion sets are used, which are small onions from the size of a pea to size of three-quarters of an inch diameter, but the smaller the better, as they make a crop nearly as quick and never run to seed, while the large ones occasionally do. Onion sets must all be planted by hand, in rows made by the garden marker at about nine inches apart, the sets being planted from two to three inches apart; they are most conveniently planted in beds of eight rows each, leaving a space of eighteen inches for an alleyway. The green onions are tied in bunches of eight or ten each, and often sell at eight and ten cents per bunch. The crop is usually begun to be marketed by the middle of June, and is sold off by middle of July. This garden crop of onions is usually heavier manured and requires more labor than the field crop, but its market value is often three times that of the field crop. Onions are also sold in this way when grown from seed, but of course this matures two or three weeks later and is not usually so remunerative as the green crop from the sets.

POTATO ONIONS

are increased by the bulb as it grows, splitting into six, eight or ten sections, which form the crop from which the "set" or root for next season's planting is obtained. These are planted in early spring, in rows one foot apart, the onions three or four inches between, and like the onions raised from sets, are generally sold green, as in that state they are very tender, while in the dry state they are less desirable than the ordinary onion.

TOP ONIONS,

so called, are propagated by the peculiar property of this variety of onion producing a cluster of small bulblets on the onion stalk, an excrescence of bulblets is formed instead of flowers and seeds. In all respects its culture is the same as the Potato Onion, only that, as the bulbs are smaller, they can be planted closer.

SHALLOTS,

a vegetable nearly allied to the Potato Onion, only that it never forms an individual bulb, but always grows in clusters, is planted in the fall, same distance apart as the Potato Onion, and starts to grow on the first opening of spring, so that the crop is usually marketed in May.

VARIETIES OF THE ONIONS.

We here give a short description and illustration of the leading varieties of onions. The seeds of onions have heretofore been raised mainly in Connecticut, Massachusetts, Rhode Island and Michigan, but of late years, large quantities have been raised in California. A prejudice against that raised in California originated in consequence of the first lots raised there being from inferior stocks, but latter experience has shown us beyond question, that, when the quality of the stock from which the seed was raised has been the same as used in the Eastern States, the crop has been in all respects equal. In our "trial grounds," where upwards of fifty stocks of onions are tested annually, we find that the California raised seed is in no way inferior to that raised in Connecticut or Massachusetts. Onion seed loses its germinating power sooner than almost any other seed, and, unless the sample is very fine indeed, it is of little use the second year. This is the reason for the great disparity in the price of seeds, for as the onion seed crop is a very uncertain one, and from its germinating qualities being limited so that no stock can be held over, the price in different seasons fluctuates from $1 to $5 per pound.

FIRST EARLY. EXTRA EARLY FLAT RED, a thin, and a good keeper, rather light colored onion, but earliest of all.

LARGE RED WETHERSFIELD. One of the favorite sorts for general crop, and a good keeper and yielder.

YELLOW GLOBE DANVERS. A half globe shaped stock, one of the best yielders and a splendid keeper.

EARLY RED GLOBE. One of the earliest of Globe varieties, smaller than the *large* Red Globe.

LARGE RED GLOBE. Later and larger than above, but a favorite market sort, and a perfect globe shape.

SOUTHPORT LARGE WHITE GLOBE. One of the best, and a favorite sort in New York markets, always bringing the highest price.

SOUTHPORT LARGE YELLOW GLOBE. Similar to the white globe, except in color, and a good keeper.

WHITE PORTUGAL, or SILVER SKIN. One of the leading sorts of white flat onion, a most excellent keeper and good yielder.

YELLOW DUTCH. A flat yellow onion, good yielder, but not so desirable as the other yellow sorts on account of its color and shape. This and the *Flat* Yellow Danvers are very similar. One of the heaviest croppers.

Italian varieties well adapted for growing in the Southern States:
QUEEN. The earliest of all onions, small, flat, white and mild flavor.
NEAPOLITAN MARZAJOLE, an early white flat onion, fine flavor.
LARGE WHITE ITALIAN TRIPOLI, grows to a large size, later than either the preceding.
LARGE RED ITALIAN TRIPOLI, similar to the preceding, except in color.
GIANT ROCCA. A very large growing globe shaped variety of a reddish brown color; flavor mild and sweet.

PARSNIP.

This is a crop used almost exclusively in winter, and is probably not often wanted for the market which the average farmer could

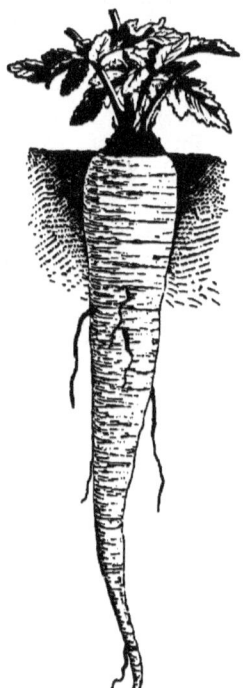

LONG SMOOTH PARSNIP.

supply. It is, however, the most valuable of all roots for farm feeding, and can always be turned to good use in this way, if in no other. Moreover, it is very convenient, as it may be left in the ground all winter without injury, and used in the spring. Still, it is a vegetable well worth growing for private use. Its culture is almost identical with that of carrots. It is sown as early in the spring as the weather will permit, in drills fifteen inches apart, if the culture is by hand, or two feet, if by horse cultivator. The seeds are covered half an inch deep, being careful to firm them in the soil with the foot, as they are very light. When well up thin out to five or six inches apart in the rows. Unlike carrots they are improved by frost, and it is usual to dig up in the fall only what are wanted for winter use, leaving the rest in the ground until spring, to be dug up as required.

PARSLEY

is only used for soups, and but very little of it is wanted, unless for this purpose or for garnishing or flavoring. As the seeds germinate very slowly, three or four weeks will be required for it to make its

DOUBLE CURLED PARSLEY.

appearance. It should be sown early in the spring, thickly, in rows one foot apart and half an inch deep. For winter use it is kept in boxes in a light cellar or sitting-room. The variety most in use is that known as Double Curled.

PEAS.

For table use this is really more a crop for the farm than the garden, as they require more space than market gardeners near large cities, paying high prices for land, can well afford to spare. Consequently, peas are grown mainly by farmers, and where pickers can be obtained at the proper season, they are often found to be a very paying crop. For early varieties sow in drills three inches deep and three feet apart, requiring two and one-half bushels to the acre. The land need not

HENDERSON'S FIRST OF ALL PEAS.

be very rich for peas, and they will follow very well after corn or potatoes, if the ground is in good heart, without manure. The variety most favored for market purposes is that sent out in 1883, known as "Henderson's First of All," which matures about five or six days earlier than any other sort we have ever tried. Daniel O'Rourke is another popular variety, very similar to the above, but, as we have said, five or six days later. A recent introduction is the sort known as American Wonder. It is very dwarf, and can be grown

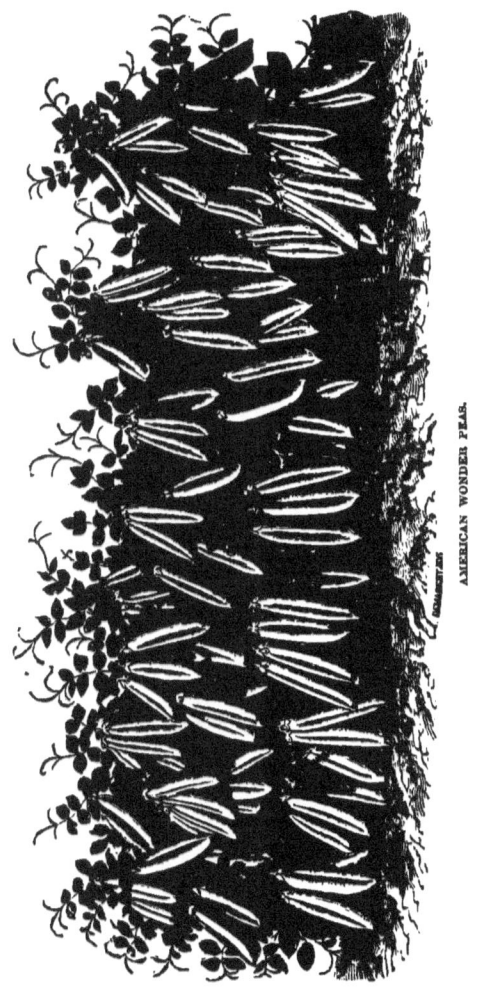

AMERICAN WONDER PEAS.

in rows about two feet apart, producing a heavy crop of the very finest quality. The profit of the pea crop is very variable. Occasionally, when the market is glutted, they will hardly pay the price of picking. Again, when the crop comes in at the proper season, they will often pay a profit of $150 to $200 per acre. In sowing peas the seed should be dropped in the drill from half an inch to an inch apart.

POTATO.

The culture of the potato as a garden crop in no way differs from that of the field—which see in chapter under that head. The only necessity for referring to it here is the advice we can give in using the earlier kinds, when used as an early market vegetable. For this purpose there are no varieties better than those known as the Early Rose and Beauty of Hebron, which, when grown in warm situations under favorable culture, will often prove a profitable crop for early market. There are, however, so many new varieties being introduced every year, that it is quite probable these standard kinds may soon be superseded. These new kinds should be tested in a small way as they appear.

RHUBARB.

Like asparagus, this is a vegetable that does not require to be renewed each season, having a perennial root, and, when once well set in the ground will remain without replanting for at least eight or ten years; but it is better to take up the roots when five years old,

RHUBARB.

and divide them and make a new plantation. The quickest way, perhaps, if a small quantity is wanted, is to procure the roots, which should be set out in hills about three feet apart each way. It is one of the grossest feeding plants of all vegetables, and requires, for perfection, a large amount of manure to be incorporated every year with the soil in each hill. If a large quantity is wanted it is best sown in drills three feet apart and thinned out to about one foot apart in the rows when a few inches high. When the plants of rhubarb become large they can be taken up in the fall, placed in the cellar, or in some place safe from frost. The roots are simply taken up with the soil adhering to them, and packed closely together in a corner of the cellar. As a matter of course this forcing process is done at the expense of the root, which is of no further use. The shoots will grow in the dark just as well as in the light, and in this condition are very tender. A couple of dozen roots of rhubarb will be sufficient for the use of a moderate sized family during the entire winter months. When grown in this blanched condition it is a most desirable article for table use, coming, as it does, at a season when fresh fruit is scarce and a change is agreeable.

RADISH.

This vegetable does best when sown in a light, sandy loam. Heavy or clayey soils not only delay maturity, but produce crops much inferior both in appearance and flavor. For a successive supply sow

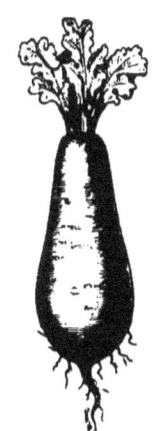

EARLY SCARLET RADISH.   WHITE OLIVE-SHAPED RADISH.

from the middle of April until the middle of September at intervals of two or three weeks. They can either be sown broadcast or in drills. When sown broadcast about twenty pounds of seed is required per acre; if in drills, eight to ten pounds. The varieties mostly grown are the Scarlet Turnip, and the Long Scarlet Short Top, the one being round and the other long. It is a profitable crop, and one which the market gardeners always depend on to get their first money

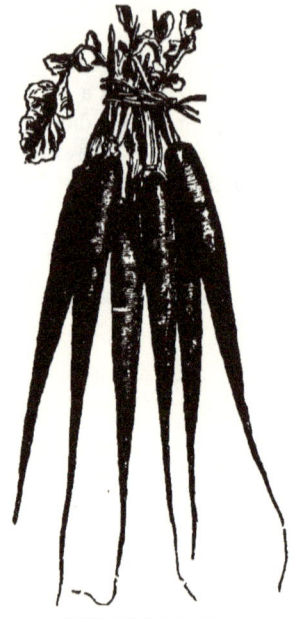

LONG SCARLET RADISH.

from, after the dull winter months, as it matures usually in this latitude from the middle to the end of May, and generally yields a profit over all expenses of $100 per acre.

SPINACH.

This is one of the easiest managed crops, although it is one of the most important in our market gardens. The main crop is sown in drills just as we sow beets or radishes, the drills being one foot apart. The first crop—that intended to stand through the winter and to be used the succeeding spring—is sown in September, and if it keeps well during the winter it rarely fails to become very profitable. In exposed places it is usually covered with straw or marsh hay during the winter, which prevents it from being cut by the frost, but in sheltered fields there is no necessity for its being covered. This covering is only necessary in the latitude of New York. South of Philadelphia it is rarely done.

It is also grown in the summer as an early crop, sown the same way as is done in the fall, about the middle of April, when it comes in before cabbages or other greens, about the end of May. The spring crop is not usually so profitable as the winter crop, but there is hardly anything that requires so little labor and produces so much weight. The kinds now in use are the Savoy Leaved and the Round Leaved. The quantity of seed used is from ten to twelve pounds per acre. Spinach is now grown in Norfolk, Va., and other Southern localities, for Northern markets, bringing about $300 or $400 per acre, or twice as much as that grown in the North.

SQUASH.

Squashes are of luxuriant and vigorous growth, and, although they will grow rapidly in almost any soil, they will repay generous treatment. Like all vegetables of this class, it is useless to sow until the weather has become settled and warm, say the 15th of May.

BUSH SCALLOP SQUASH.

Light soils are best suited to its growth, and it is most economical of manure to prepare the hills for the seed in the ordinary manner by incorporating two or three shovelfuls with the soil in each hill. For what is known as the Bush varieties, a distance of three or four feet each way is required, and for running sorts from six to eight feet. Eight to ten seeds should be sown in each hill, thinning out, after they have attained their rough leaves, to three or four of the strongest plants. When only a limited quantity of this vegetable is wanted, as will be understood by most farmers, they can be grown in the hills of corn, where they will mature without interfering with the latter crop, although I myself do not like this system of feeding two crops on the land at the same time, believing that it will always be better to allot the land for each particular crop, as I think the saving of labor and better yield more than compensate for the extra land and manure. The favorite kinds for summer use, of the bush varieties, are White Bush Scallop and Yellow Bush Scallop; for winter use the Hubbard and Yokohama are preferred. A special point in the management of this crop is the pinching in of the main vines to force out a growth of lateral branches. These bear the fruits, as in all of

HUBBARD SQUASH.

the gourd tribe of plants, to which this, as well as melons and cucumbers, belongs. When the main vine has reached a length of three feet the terminal bud is pinched off with the finger and thumb. The same kind of pruning is done with the laterals to prevent the vines spreading too far and to encourage the growth of fruit.

TOMATO.

The tomato is now one of the most important of all garden vegetables, tens of thousands of acres of it being grown for canning purposes. When the plants are to be raised, the seed should be sown in March in a hot-bed or greenhouse. Or they may be sown in a box and kept inside the window of a room where the night temperature is not less than sixty-five degrees. They should be sown in drills five inches apart, and half an inch deep. When the plants are two or three inches high, they should be set out in the same temperature, or planted in small flower pots, allowing one plant to each pot, or in soap or similar boxes, cut to a depth of three inches, and planted in them at three inches apart each way. They are sometimes transplanted a second time into larger pots or into hot-beds, at five inches apart, by which process the plants are rendered more sturdy and branching. By the middle of May in this latitude the plants may be set in the open ground. They are planted for early crops on light sandy ground in hills three feet apart. A good shovelful of rotten manure is mixed in each hill. On heavy soils, which are not suited for an early crop, they should be planted four feet apart. It is

ACME TOMATO.

not absolutely essential that manure should be used for a tomato crop. If the ground is in good heart following a corn crop, potato or root crop that has been well manured, it will usually be sufficient to carry them through. In fact, if the ground is too rich they will grow to

PERFECTION TOMATO.

leaves and branches instead of fruit. It is only when wanted for a very early crop, in a light sandy soil in some sheltered place, that the recommendation, to use manure in the hills, applies. When it is not convenient for the grower to raise his own plants they can be had at very low rates from a dealer, as the tomato plant is probably more easily raised than any other vegetable plant we grow. The most popular kinds for market use are the Perfection and the Acme. The Trophy was long a favorite, but is not now considered so desirable as some of its newer competitors. Tomatoes for canning purposes are usually grown in immense quantities, and by farmers rather than gardeners. The profit over all expenses is generally not less than $50 per acre, and occasionally when the crop is heavy as high as $100 per acre. When grown for table use, in particularly favored positions as to soil and shelter, and sold in the markets, a profit of $300 per acre is not unusual.

TURNIP.

Although this vegetable has been treated in the chapter of this work devoted to "root crops," yet its culture for a table vegetable is somewhat different, and it may be well to allude to it here. Turnips do best on highly enriched and light sandy or gravelly soils. Com-

PURPLE TOP STRAP LEAF TURNIP.

mence sowing the earlier varieties in April, in drills from twelve to fifteen inches apart, if hand cultivation is used; if by horse cultivator, two feet apart. Thin out as soon as the plants are large enough to handle to six or nine inches in the rows. For a succession of crops sow at intervals of a fortnight until the last week in July, from which time until the end of August sowings may be made of the fall or main crops. Turnips may be preserved until spring by cutting off the tops at one inch from the bulb, and placing the roots in a cellar or pit during the winter. For further particulars see chapter entitled "Root Crops for Farm Stock." The quantity of seed required, which should be put in by the drill, is about one pound to the acre. The favorite kinds for early table use are the White Egg and Purple Top

Strap Leaf; for winter use, the Yellow Aberdeen and Purple Top Ruta Baga. Wherever the soil is suitable for early turnips, and will produce them in a clean condition, without being affected with the maggot, they are a safer and more profitable crop to grow than beets; but it is only in special localities where this cleanliness of crop can be had, and hence the profit to the fortunate owner of such soils. They

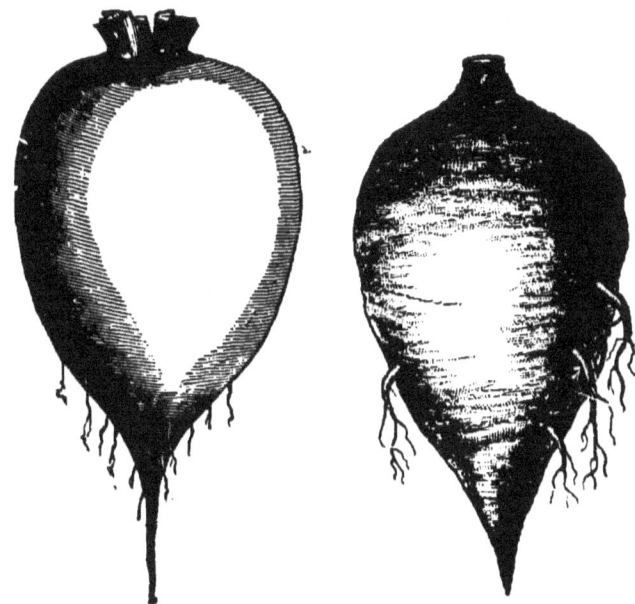

WHITE EGG TURNIP.   PURPLE TOP RUTA BAGA.

are largely grown in the vicinity of New York on Long Island, in locations near the sea, where they seem to be exempt from the maggot and wire worm. It is no uncommon thing for them to pay a profit of $500 per acre when these special conditions can be obtained. The turnip fly or flea, which damages and sometimes destroys the first sowings, may be driven off by dusting fine lime or wood ashes along the rows as soon as the young plants appear above the ground.

QUANTITIES OF SEED.

The following table will give the quantity of vegetable seeds required to sow an acre:

   Beans, dwarf, in drills....................2 bushels.
   Beans, pole, in drills.................10 to 12 quarts.
   Beets, in drills.......................5 to 6 pounds.

QUANTITIES OF SEED.—*Continued*.

Cabbage, in beds to transplant.............½ pound.
Carrot, in drills......................3 to 4 pounds.
Corn, in hills......................8 to 10 quarts.
Corn (for soiling).....................3 bushels.
Cucumber, in hills........ ....2 to 3 pounds.
Melon, musk, in hills.................2 to 3 pounds.
Melon, water, in hills.................4 to 5 pounds.
Onion, in drills....................5 to 6 pounds.
Onion (sets), in drills................6 to 12 bushels.
Parsnip, in drills...... ....5 to 6 pounds.
Peas, in drills......................2 to 3 bushels.
Radish, in drills...................9 to 10 pounds.
Spinach, in drills..................10 to 12 pounds.
Squash (bush varieties), in hills. ......5 to 6 pounds.
Squash (running varieties), in hills.....3 to 4 pounds.
Tomato (to transplant)....................¼ pound.
Turnip, in drills....................1 to 2 pounds.

Where drills are referred to the seed should be put in with seed drill.

Table showing the quantities of seeds required for a given number of plants, number of hills or length of drill:

Asparagus, 1 ounce...................60 feet of drill.
Beet, 1 ounce......................50 feet of drill.
Beans, dwarf, 1 quart................100 feet of drill.
Beans, pole, 1 quart......................150 hills.
Carrot, 1 ounce ....150 feet of drill.
Cucumber, 1 ounce.........................50 hills.
Corn, 1 quart............................200 hills.
Melon, water, 1 ounce.....................30 hills.
Melon, musk, 1 ounce......................60 hills.
Onion, 1 ounce.....................100 feet of drill.
Onion, sets, 1 quart..................40 feet of drill.
Parsley, 1 ounce....................150 feet of drill.
Parsnip, 1 ounce....................200 feet of drill.
Peas, 1 quart.......................75 feet of drill.
Radish, 1 ounce....................100 feet of drill.
Spinach, 1 ounce....................100 feet of drill.
Squash, early, 1 ounce ....50 hills.
Turnip, 1 ounce....................150 feet of drill.
Cabbage, 1 ounce......................1,500 plants.
Cauliflower, 1 ounce..................1,000 plants.
Celery, 1 ounce.......................2,000 plants.
Egg Plant, 1 ounce....................1,000 plants.
Lettuce, 1 ounce......................3,000 plants.
Tomato, 1 ounce.......................1,500 plants.

CHAPTER XII.

PRINCIPAL SMALL FRUIT CROPS.

As with vegetables, so there are many fruits that can be cultivated with but little trouble on the farm, particularly the kinds known as small fruits, which consist of strawberries, blackberries, raspberries, currants and grapes. The larger fruits, apples, pears, peaches, cherries, plums and quinces, may also be grown in limited quantities with advantage.

STRAWBERRIES.

This fruit is perhaps the most important of all, as there is hardly a town where this fruit cannot be sold at remunerative rates. For, as is the case with fresh vegetables, the want of fresh fruits at our summer hotels and boarding houses is rarely sufficiently supplied. As strawberries occupy the most important place, we will here describe their culture at greater length than will be necessary with most of the others, and for that purpose I will insert in full my essay on that subject written in 1882, which I am happy to know has already been the means of causing hundreds to grow this delicious fruit with success never before attained.

STRAWBERRY CULTURE.

Strawberries will grow on almost any soil, but it is all-important that it be well drained, either naturally or artificially; in fact, this is true for the well-being of nearly all plants, as few plants do well on soils where the water does not freely pass off.

Thorough culture requires that the soil should be first dug or plowed, then spread over with at least three inches of thoroughly rotted stable manure, which should be dug or plowed under, so far as practicable, to mix it with the soil. If stable manure cannot be had, artificial manure, such as ground bone dust, etc., should be sown on the dug or plowed ground, thick enough to nearly cover it, then harrowed or chopped in with a fork, so that it is well mixed with the soil to at least six inches in depth. This, then, is the preliminary work before planting, to ensure a crop the next season after planting—in nine or ten months. The plants must be such as are layered in pots, and the sooner they are planted out after the 15th of July the better, although, if not then convenient, they will produce a crop the next season even if planted as late as the middle of September; but the sooner they are planted, the larger will be the crop. They may be set from *pot layers* either in beds of four rows each, fifteen inches apart, and fifteen inches between the plants, leaving two feet between the beds for pathway; or be set out in rows two feet apart, the plants in the rows fifteen inches apart; and if the plants are properly set out (care being taken to firm the soil around the plant, which is best done by pressing the soil against each plant with the foot), not one plant in a thousand of strawberry plants that have been grown in pots will fail to grow. For the first three or four weeks after planting nothing need be done except to hoe the beds, so that all weeds are kept down. Be careful to do this once in every ten days; for if the weeds once get a start it will treble the labor of keeping the ground clean. In about a month after planting they will begin to throw out runners, all of which *must be pinched or cut off as they appear*, so that by the end of the growing season (1st of November) each plant will have formed a complete bush one foot or more in diameter, having the necessary matured "crowns" for next June's fruit. By the middle of December the entire beds of strawberry plants should be covered up with salt meadow hay (straw, leaves or anything similar will do as well) to the depth of two or three inches, entirely covering up the plants and soil, so that nothing is seen but the hay. By April the plants so protected will show indications of growth, when the hay around each plant is pushed a little aside to assist it in getting through the covering, so that by May the fully developed plant shows on the clean surface of the hay. This "mulching," as it is called, is indispensable to the best culture, as it protects the plants from cold in winter, keeps the fruit clean, keeps the roots cool by shading them from the hot sun in June, and at the same time saves nearly all further labor after being once put on, as few weeds can push through it. By this method we prefer to plant new beds every year, though, if desired, the beds once planted may be fruited for two or three years, as by the old plans; but the fruit the first season will always be the largest in size, if not greatest in number. Another advantage of this system is that, where space is limited, there is quite time enough to get a crop of potatoes, pease, beans, lettuce, radishes, or, in fact, any summer crop, off the ground first *before* planting the strawberries, thus taking two crops from the ground in one year, if desired, and there is also plenty of time to crop the ground with cabbage, cauliflower, celery, or other fall crop, *after* the crop of strawberries has been gathered. The plan of getting the pot layers of strawberries is very simple. Just as soon as the fruit is gathered, if the beds are well forked up between the rows, the runners or young plants will begin to grow, and in two weeks will be fit to layer in pots. The pots, which should be from two to three inches in diameter, are filled with the soil in which the strawberries are growing, and "plunged" or sunk to the level of the surface; the strawberry layer is then laid on the pot, being held in place with a small stone. The stone not only serves to keep the plant in its place, so that its roots will strike into the pot, but it also serves to mark where each pot is; for, being sunk to the level of the surface, rains wash the soil around the pots, so that they could not well be seen unless marked by the stone. In ten or twelve days after the strawberry layers have been put down the pots will be filled with roots. They are then cut from the parent plant, placed closely together, and shaded and watered for a few days before being planted out. Some plant them out at once when taken up, but, unless the weather is suitable, some loss may occur by this method; by the other plan, however, of hardening them for a few days, not one in a thousand will fail. Strawberries for field culture are usually planted from the ordinary layers, either in August and September in the fall, or in March, April or May in the spring. They are usually planted in rows, two to three feet apart, and nine to twelve inches between the plants. In planting, every plant should be well firmed, or great loss is almost certain to ensue, as the strawberry is a plant always difficult to transplant. They are usually worked by a horse cultivator, and generally two or three crops are taken before the beds are plowed under; but the first crop given (which is in the second year after planting) is always the best. The same care must be taken in planting by pot layers; the ground must be kept clear of weeds, and the runners pinched or cut off to make fruiting crowns. By the usual field method of culture, it will be seen that there is a loss of one season in about three; for in the year of planting no fruit, of course, is produced, and for this reason we incline to the belief that, if a portion were set aside to produce early plants, so that pot layers could be set out by the 15th of July, a full crop of the finest fruit could be had every season, and with less cost, we think; for the only labor after planting is to keep the ground clean and pinch off the runners, from July to October, with the certainty of getting a full crop next June, or in less than a year from the time of planting, while by planting by ordinary layers, if planted in August, we have three months of fall culture, and six or seven months of the next summer's culture, before a crop is produced. Again, if the crop is continued to fruit the second or third year, every one who has had experience with the nature of the plant, knows that the labor of keeping the plants free from weeds is enormous; while by the pot layering method of taking a fresh crop each year, all such labor is dispensed with.

Although it is difficult to give any list of kinds of strawberries that will do well under all conditions, yet, taking the suburbs of New York as a standard (which, with its great variety of soil, is likely to be as good as any other), we find that the best six kinds, having the greatest combination of good qualities, that we can select from a collection of fifty leading sorts, are the following, which we name in the order of their excellence:

THE HENDERSON.—This new strawberry originated with Mr. George Seymour, South Norwalk, Conn., who named it in our honor. It is doubtful if there is another strawberry in cultivation having such a combination of good qualities as the "Henderson." The fruit is of

HENDERSON STRAWBERRY.

the largest size, rich, glossy crimson in color, looking as if varnished, early and exceedingly productive, but its excelling merit is its exquisite flavor and aroma. Whether for family or market use the "Henderson" is certain to become a standard sort, and its strong and healthy growth will adapt it to almost every soil. It is a perfect flowered variety, and, therefore, will never fail to set its fruit. By the pot layer system this vigorous and productive strawberry, planted in August, is certain to give a full crop of fruit in June of the next year, or in ten months from time of planting. It is sold for the first time this year—1884.

JERSEY QUEEN.—This variety was sold for the first time in the fall of 1881, and is, perhaps, one of the very best strawberries so far introduced. The size is immense, often measuring six inches in circumference. Shape, roundish conical; color, a beautiful scarlet crimson; perfectly solid, and of excellent flavor. It is an

enormous bearer, many plants averaging a quart of first quality fruit. It is one of the latest strawberries, the crop in this vicinity being in perfection about the 25th of June, while the average crop of strawberries is at its best by the 15th of June in the locality of New York.

BIDWELL.—One of the earliest, abundantly productive, medium size, excellent flavor, and light scarlet in color. Plants set out from pot layers on August 5th, 1880, had fruit ripe June 5th, 1881, ten months from date of planting. The plants averaged one quart of fruit each.

SHARPLESS.—With the exception of Jersey Queen, the largest and one of the heaviest berries of this collection. It is of fine flavor, a good bearer, and has now become a standard sort.

JUCUNDA.—This is an old, well known sort, possessing so many good qualities, that we place it as one of the best six in preference to scores of others of later origin. It is of full average size, wonderfully productive, of great beauty of color and form, and excellent flavor; but its distinctive value is in its ripening, extending from the earliest to the latest of the crop, the first berries being ripe here about June 4th, and extending unto July 4th.

DOWNING.—One of the best of the older sorts. It combines all the best qualities, being large, early, rich in color and flavor, and abundantly productive.

GLOSSY CONE.—Although this has been grown by the raiser, Mr. Durand, for several years, it was issued last season for the first time. In a test of fifty kinds in our grounds, we found it the earliest of all, and very prolific, of good size, fine flavor, and altogether has a combination of good qualities rarely found in any *early* strawberry. Its only fault is, that it is rather a weak grower, and requires a rich and rather heavy soil to develop its best qualities.

Strawberries rarely sell at less than an average of $8 per 100 quarts, and when retailed to the consumer, average one-third more. As about 20,000 plants are grown on an acre, and an average crop under

BIDWELL STRAWBERRY. SHARPLESS STRAWBERRY.

good culture will give at least 5,000 quarts per acre, the crop, when sold even at lowest rates, is a very profitable one. But it is a crop that must be promptly attended to in hoeing and weeding. It never can be made profitable under slipshod culture, for, from the nature of the plant, it cannot defend itself against weeds, and if neglected will quickly get overwhelmed and destroyed. Thousands of acres of strawberries are planted annually, which, from the want of prompt work at the proper time, are allowed to be destroyed by weeds. At a small cost in labor at the proper time, such crops might have paid a clear profit of $300 per acre.

BLACKBERRIES.

Although blackberries are found in a wild state in almost all sections of the country, yet the varieties are so much inferior to the cultivated kinds, that it is poor economy to depend on them for a supply, no matter how abundant they may be. Cultivated blackberries comprise varieties which are not only double the size of the wild kinds, but have the advantage of ripening in succession throughout the season, from the middle of July until the last of September. To have blackberries in perfection, the soil should have the same thorough culture and manuring that we recommend for all vegetables and fruits, for it should always be kept in mind that the richer the soil and the better the cultivation, the larger the fruit will be, and hence the greater the return in quantity for the space cultivated. The distance apart to plant blackberries may be, if in rows five feet, with the plants two feet apart in the rows. Or, if in separate hills they may be set five feet apart each way. In either case they should be supported by strong stakes driven into the ground, having a height of from four to five feet, to which the canes

WILSON BLACKBERRY.   KITTATINNY BLACKBERRY.

or shoots should be tied. They may be set either in the fall or in the spring. If in the fall a covering of four or five inches of rotted manure or leaves should be spread over the roots, to prevent them from being frozen too much. The plants of blackberries set out either in fall or spring will not give fruit the first season, but if a good growth has been made they will give a full crop the next year. That is, if planted, for instance, about the middle of April, 1884 (or the previous fall), by the middle of July in 1885 a full crop should be obtained. After the fruit has been picked, the old canes or shoots should be cut out to give the new ones a chance to grow. As the new shoots are very vigorous, when they reach a height of four feet or at most five feet they should be checked by pinching the tops off. This will cause an abundance of side shoots to start, which are to be pinched when about a foot long. This treatment increases the productiveness of the plants and keeps the fruit within easy reach for gathering. The bushes should be carefully tied to the stakes. Of the varieties, that known as Wilson's Early comes in a week before any of the others. It is a deep black, large and of excellent quality, being destitute of that hard centre so peculiar to wild sorts. The Kittatinny comes next in succession. It is an immensely large berry of fine flavor, of a deep shining black color—one of the very best. It is somewhat given to rust, which may be checked by removing all the rusted young shoots as they appear. The next is the old Lawton variety, which is hardly as good as either of the others, but has the merit of coming in after they are nearly done fruiting. Any one growing strawberries to supply a local demand must of necessity have such fruits as blackberries to succeed them, as the season advances, and in most localities they will be found equally profitable as strawberries, although perhaps for local demand they could not be sold in as large quantities.

RASPBERRIES.

The culture of the raspberry is almost identical with that of the blackberry, except that they may be planted one-third closer, and that in some sections the raspberry is not quite so hardy, and it is better

to take the precaution of laying the shoots down close to the ground in the fall, being careful not to break them, and covering them up with corn stalks, straw, leaves or litter. This should not be done, however, until the weather is quite cold, say, in the latitude of New

York, the first week in December. The covering may be from three to six inches thick, and should not be removed in the spring until the middle of April, as, if removed too soon, the shoots, which would then

THE GREGG RASPBERRY.

be beginning to start, might be hurt by the late spring frosts. Raspberries are of three colors—red, black and yellow. Of the red, Cuthbert, Hansell and Hudson River Antwerp are the favorites. Of the black varieties, the Gregg is of the largest size, an enormous pro-

THE HANSELL RASPBERRY.

ducer, of excellent flavor, and should, perhaps, be grown to the exclusion of all others of the "black caps." A yellow variety, known as "Caroline," is of rich orange color, entirely hardy and of excellent flavor. Another yellow kind, known as "Brinkle's Orange," is of the most delicious flavor, but it is not hardy unless in well sheltered spots. It is somewhat curious, when the true reason is not known, that this variety is more hardy in Canada than in the United States, the reason being that it is protected by the deep and long continued snow through the colder Canadian winter. Cultivated varieties of Raspberries, like blackberries, are so much superior to the wild kinds, that it will be found, wherever raspberries are wanted, their culture will well repay the trouble. About the same quantity of raspberries are usually in demand as of blackberries. A new variety of red raspberry, called "Hansell," promises to become one of the best standard varieties. (See engraving.)

CURRANTS.

The currant is but little used except for pies and for preserving purposes. There is perhaps no other small fruit that will give more weight of crop for the space it occupies than the currant. However, as it is only used for these special purposes, and is but little used to eat as dessert, in an uncooked state, comparatively few are required. The plants should be set out in the garden in rows about four feet apart, and three feet between the plants; for market purposes these distances may be increased one-half. The young shoots require to be pruned in the fall, cutting off about one-third of their growth, and thinning out the old shoots when they become too thick. They are all trained in bush form to a height of three or four feet. The best red varieties grown are known as the Red Dutch and the Cherry. Of the white kinds, that known as the White Dutch is the best. It is of a yellowish white color. This variety is sweeter than the reds, and for that reason is better for dessert purposes. Black currants are but little grown, and then exclusively for jams and jellies. They should be cultivated in the same way as the whites and reds, although they are an entirely different plant, belonging to a different species.

GOOSEBERRIES.

The gooseberry is but little grown in this climate, as our summer is entirely too hot for it, and it is rarely seen in good condition, as it ripens just in the heat of summer, when the weather is the hottest, thus forcing it unnaturally to maturity, so that the fine flavor obtained in milder climates such as Great Britain is never found here. For that reason it is not much grown, except to be used in a green state for pies or tarts, and is in but little demand. Many of the English varieties are offered for sale here, but they are so subject to mildew, that they rarely do any good. Of the native varieties, that known as the Downing is of a greenish white color when ripe, and of very

HOUGHTON'S SEEDLING GOOSEBERRY.

fair quality. We have also a red native seedling known as Houghton's, which is of average size and flavor. The culture is same as that of the currant.

GRAPES.

Although grape vines can be grown in almost any soil, yet if a position can be obtained on a sloping bank, facing south or southeast, running at an angle of ten or fifteen degrees, where the soil is stony or shaly, they will be found usually to do better than when planted on level lands, particularly if they can be manured. All the finest vineyards in Germany and France are so located, and the fruit is always better flavored and freer from mildew and other diseases than when on the level. However, such conditions are not always to be obtained, and the vines of course are not so easily worked as when planted on the level. There is now so much advance made in our hardy native varieties of grapes, that those who have not had opportunities of seeing them will be surprised to find the vast improvement that has been made in this delicious fruit within the last ten or fifteen years. We have now grapes of the finest flavor of all colors, ranging through all the shades of green, amber, red and black, ripening in succession from the middle of August until the middle of October. Immense areas are now being planted with the kinds which have proved most profitable for market purposes, and as they can be safely shipped to almost any distance, there is no need of being dependent upon a local market. There is much misconception as to the age at which a grape vine should be planted. It is the general impression that they should always be three or four years old. This is a popular error, for no matter how large the vine is, it will never fruit to any extent the same season it is planted, and the

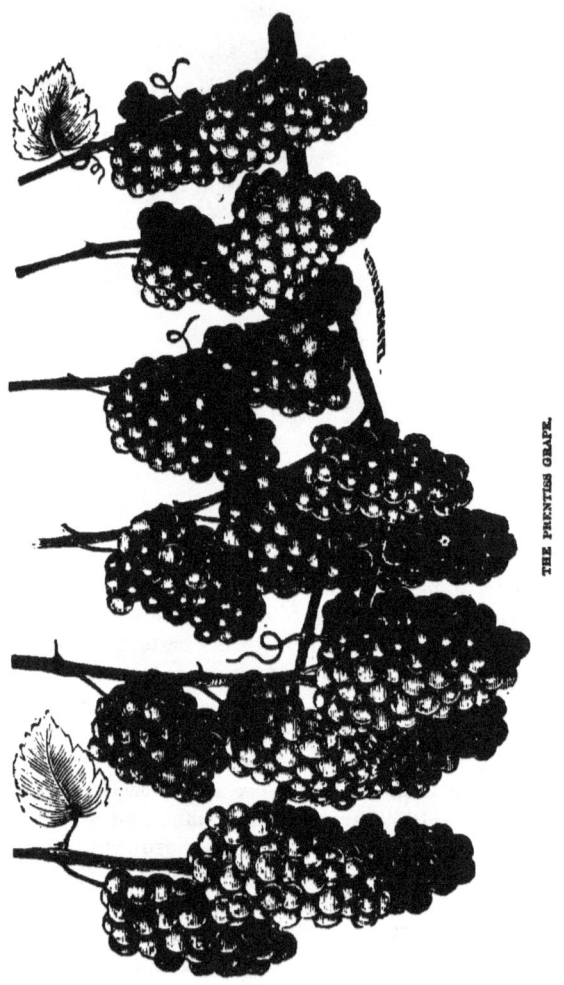

THE PRENTISS GRAPE.

larger it is, the more it will suffer in being lifted and transplanted. Therefore I always recommend purchasers to buy young plants, which not only can be bought at one-third the price of two or three year old ones, but are infinitely better, even at the same price. If a trellis is made for them they should be planted at a distance of six feet apart. The trellis may be any height from six to twenty feet, as desired. If planted in vineyard style in the open field, without trellises, they may be set six feet between the rows and three or four feet between the plants, and tied up to strong stakes.

The first year after planting, if with vineyard culture, they should be cut down, and only one shoot left to reach to the top of the five or six foot stake. If it has grown strongly and ripened well, that shoot will give a few bunches the second year and may be pruned close, so as to resemble a walking stick, but, with the lateral shoots cut back to one eye only—that is, the main shoot is allowed to stand, and the side shoots or laterals are trimmed to one bud or eye. This is what is called the Spur System, and will be found to be the most convenient for the inexperienced cultivator. There are special modes of pruning, which are best shown by illustration, and for such as require fuller information on this subject, I will refer to my work, "Gardening for Pleasure," where the subject of pruning is fully treated. The six kinds which we would recommend for general culture are the following:

MOORE'S EARLY.—This variety has large and compact bunches; berries large, black and covered with a rich bloom; excellent flavor, and is one of the earliest, ripening about the 1st of September, or a week before Concord.

PRENTISS.—Is of greenish white color, sometimes tinted with rose; of medium size for a white grape, flavor almost equal to the best hot-house grapes; is immensely productive, and sold in the New York markets last year for twenty-five cents per pound, while Concord and other older varieties sold at six cents per pound; ripens middle of September.

WILDER.—Has berries of medium size; color reddish bronze; berry of exquisite flavor, ripening middle of September.

SALEM.—Has large bunches; color, white, tinted with pink; of medium size; delicate flavor; ripening about 1st of October.

BRIGHTON.—Color reddish bronze, bunch and berries of average size, flavor excellent; a most abundant bearer, and one of the very best. Ripens about the 1st of October.

CONCORD, the last we name, is one of the best known of all the sorts. It is much inferior in flavor, but it has the valuable quality of never failing to bear abundant crops, and is indispensable in any collection, and if but one grape is grown this should be chosen.

ORCHARD FRUITS.

Unlike the "small fruits," such as strawberries and raspberries, when once planted in suitable soil, the large fruits will last a life-time, and as many of them are several years before they come into bearing, any error made in the selection of kinds is a serious one. Whenever practicable, therefore, the purchase of trees for the orchard should be made direct from nurserymen whose reputation is beyond question. Many thousands of farmers in nearly every section of the country have been victims of the irresponsible tree peddlers, who, whether from ignorance or design, have palmed upon the unfortunate patrons apples, pears, peaches and plums which after years of anxious waiting for have proved entirely worthless. No doubt there are honest and trustworthy tree agents; but these bear such a small proportion to those who are otherwise, that the safest plan, for the uninitiated farmer, as I have before said, is to make his purchases direct from his nearest reliable nurseryman, keeping always the point in view, that it is best to buy *north* of his latitude.

It is not safe to leave the selection of kinds exclusively in the hands of the nurseryman, for no matter how respectable he may be, there is always a temptation to send out such kinds as he may happen to have a surplus stock of. For that reason I will in all cases, as has been done with all crops throughout this work, give a list of what in my experience are the safest kinds to use for general planting.

The soil and its preparation for the orchard are also vital matters. For most fruits a deep and rather sandy loam is best, but, as in all other crops, it is useless to plant trees unless the soil is free from water, and if draining is necessary it must be thoroughly done. (See article on draining.) A limestone gravelly soil is best for apples, pears succeed best upon good clay loams, plums require a rather moist soil for the best results, and peaches must have a warm light sandy loam with a somewhat heavier subsoil, but well drained, either naturally or artificially. The location of an orchard is quite important. Apples and peaches do best upon hilly or rolling ground, while pears and plums do well in low lands. A western exposure, and in some cases a northern slope, is preferable to any other, for all fruits. A southern slope is the worst of all, as the trees in such a case are forced by the sun's warmth into a too early growth, and often suffer from late spring frosts, which destroy the blossom, while the more backward trees upon western or northern slopes are uninjured. The advantage of a western slope is that it escapes the morning sun, which is sometimes injurious after a cold frosty night, while it enjoys the last of the evening sun and so gets a large share of warmth which remains during the night.

The preparation of the soil and the manner of planting the trees are of the utmost importance, and should be thoroughly well done. A rich soil is not required. If the land is able to produce a good crop of corn, potatoes or clover, it is rich enough; if made too rich the trees are apt to make too much wood, or a weak, rank growth, which must be cut away by pruning, and thus really exhaust the tree and put off its bearing period for some considerable time. The following details will suggest a proper method for the average conditions. The planter of course must study his particular case and make a judicious application of these suggestions. The land should be well plowed in the fall or late summer, as deeply as possible; deep plowing in this case is beneficial, when it might be otherwise for an ordinary crop. The next thing to be done is to prepare a sufficient quantity of good compost of rotted leaves, sod, scrapings of the barn-yard, lime, wood ashes and some rotted manure. These are well mixed and put into a heap ready for use. The trees are then ordered to be delivered at a special time, and for safety, and the proper guidance of the nurseryman, full and accurate directions should be given for shipping. The orders should be sent so as to give the nurseryman ample time to ship the trees. The next work is to stake out the ground, and dig the holes, two feet deep, and large enough to give the roots ample spread, say four feet wide. The top soil should be thrown on one side by itself. The compost is then hauled onto the ground, and a liberal quantity of it is thrown into the hole and spread, and partly mixed with the earth in it, being left slightly raised in the centre for the tree to rest upon. Everything is now in readiness for the trees. When these arrive, they should be unpacked and sorted at once, and each variety laid in the wagon by itself. Each variety should be planted separately in a row or block. The wagon is then taken to the field. The planter, who has a boy to assist him, takes a tree, sets it firmly upon the earth in the hole so that it is a little deeper than it has been in the nursery, and while the assistant holds it, he spreads the roots and carefully works the soil among them so that they are in as natural a position as possible. This is very important and should be well done. After this, the rest of the top soil is thrown in and well trodden with the feet. Then the subsoil is put in with a little of the compost mixed with it and thoroughly well firmed with the feet, but left in a slight mound, so as to turn water from the stem. After all the trees have been thus planted, each one should be properly pruned, the young wood being cut back one-third and the head properly shaped. Fall planting, which is generally preferable, should be done from the 15th October to the 15th November, and spring planting as soon as the ground is free from frost and dry enough to work.

The after treatment of a young orchard should be as follows: For the first three years such crops as potatoes, beans or turnips, that are cultivated and manured, may be grown, but no others, both to manure the ground, destroy weeds and for the sake of the cultivation, the trees being hoed as the rest of the crop. Afterwards the ground may be sown to clover, but not to grass, as a sod is injurious to a young orchard, although it may be permitted in an established one.

APPLES.

Apples being a crop that can be shipped from any distance, unless they are known to do well in a locality, had better not be grown largely, as, if the locality is not suited to their growth, they are not likely to be satisfactory. However, as the trees cost but little, a hundred or two is a necessity for the farmer, if only for his own use. They should be planted at about thirty feet apart each way. The kinds best suited for most localities are, for early, Early Harvest, Sour Bough and Red Astrachan; for fall, Twenty Ounce Pippin and Fall Pippin; for winter, Baldwin, Greening, Rambo, King and Northern Spy. The caution may be given, that even if a hundred acres should be planted, only a few varieties should be chosen. As a guide to the choice of varieties for a northern locality it might be mentioned that at the exhibition of fruits held in November, 1883, by the London Horticultural Society, the following varieties were sent from Nova Scotia, *viz.*: Ribstone Pippin, Baldwin, Rhode Island Greening, Newtown Pippin, Hubbardston's, Tallman's, King's and Blue Pearmain. All these were remarkable for their quality and size, indicating that these kinds are especially suitable for a cold climate.

PEARS.

Pears, like apples, are adapted to certain localities, although, as a rule, they are usually a more certain crop in most sections, and when the dwarf varieties are planted they come into bearing more quickly than apples do. When standard pears, so called, only were grown, it required a life-time to get them into bearing; but the dwarf kinds, which are grafted on the quince stock, will fruit in two or three years after planting. The dwarf varieties can be planted at ten feet apart each way, while the standard sorts require about the same distance as apples, thirty feet apart each way. It is a convenient way, and saves room, to plant dwarfs between the standards alternately; when the standards come into bearing the dwarfs may be cut out. The best varieties are Manning's Elizabeth, Clapp's Favorite, Tyson, Bartlett, Duchess, Seckel, Flemish Beauty and Lawrence. These are all excellent, and give a succession from July to midwinter. These varieties are named in the order of their ripening. The late kinds are kept in a cool cellar, free from frost, and ripened in a warm room as they may be wanted.

PEACHES.

Peaches are not likely to do well unless the locality specially suits them, and should not therefore be grown in large quantities, unless in sections that are known to be adapted to them. When the soil does suit, however, they are often one of the most valuable crops of the farm, as they mature much more rapidly than either apples or pears, and the finer sorts never fail to sell at a good price in the markets of our large cities. The soil best suited for a peach orchard is a dry sandy or gravelly loam. The tree is short-lived in most sections, and attains its best fruiting condition when from five to ten years old. The great difficulty in growing peaches is a disease known as yellows. It has been found that liberal dressings of lime to the soil tends to prevent this disease and lengthen the life of the tree. In the best peach growing districts cultivators are well satisfied if they get three crops in five years, because contingencies, such as early frosts, may occasionally destroy the whole crop in certain districts, while others are exempt, this exemption being due, in nearly every case, to the well chosen selection of a western or northern slope upon which to plant the orchards. The distance apart may be from twelve to twenty feet; if the soil is very rich, the greater distance. The best kinds known in the markets are Crawford's Early, Crawford's Late, Honest John, Stump the World, Yellow Rareripe, Morris White, Troth's Early and Alexander.

PLUM.

The cultivation of the plum is rendered exceedingly difficult in almost all sections of the country by the attacks of what is known as the Curculio or Plum Weevil. All proposed remedies have been applied without any permanent satisfactory results, excepting the old-fashioned plan, which has been in use for over fifty years, of jarring the tree and shaking down the insects and catching them in sheets. If this is done as soon as the fruit is formed, and energetically persisted in every other day until ripe, the crop may be saved; but if neglected, the chances in most places are that the crop will be destroyed. It is claimed, also, that when plum trees are planted in the poultry yard they are rarely affected by the Curculio, as the fowls pick up the insects in the larvæ state. No doubt this may be effective to a certain extent; but it is not as safe as the jarring of the trees. There are sections of the country, particularly about Newburgh, N. Y., where this pest does not seem to have got a foothold, and that district supplies plums mainly for the New York market, and must be immensely profitable from the prices obtained. It would be well for farmers having heavy clay lands to plant a few trees as an experiment, or on lands where they can be planted near the banks of a running stream, as it seems that in such localities they are less liable to be troubled with the insect. The trees should be set out at distances of from fifteen to twenty feet each way. The most approved kinds are Golden Drop, Green Gage, Purple Favorite, Washington, Lombard and German Prune. The Damson is also a good kind for preserving, as is also the Wild Goose Plum. This is an exceedingly hardy tree, and bears so profusely as to always furnish a crop in spite of the Curculio.

CHERRY.

The cherry, like the peach, bears in two or three years after planting, and continues annually to enlarge its growth and productiveness. It is a long-lived tree and often attains a great size. It grows freely on almost any soil, preferring, however, one that is deep and loamy. It should be planted at distances of from fifteen to twenty feet apart. The varieties are Black Tartarian, a purplish black color; American Amber, yellow or amber colored; May Duke and Early Richmond. Cherry trees are very subject to a disease known as black knot, by which they are greatly disfigured, and, at length, destroyed. The remedy is to cut out every branch which shows the first sign of the disease as soon as it appears and burn the cuttings. A liberal dressing of wood ashes and lime has been found a preventive.

QUINCE.

This fruit is only grown for use in preserves. It requires little attention, and for that reason it is often much neglected, and when so neglected makes a very unsightly tree. A little pruning, however, rounds up its form and brings it to a symmetrical shape. In that condition it is an ornamental tree when in blossom or fruit, and the fruit is more regularly distributed over the tree. The kinds are the apple shaped or orange, a round variety of a golden yellow color. Pear shaped, of a greenish yellow color, is larger than the former, and is considered to be better flavored when used in preserves. The Champion is a popular new variety, which ripens later than either of the others. The quince does best upon a low marsh soil, and when well grown is a very profitable market fruit. The trees, or rather bushes, being small and dwarf, may be planted ten feet apart.

INDEX.

(Illustrations are marked by an *.)

A.

	PAGE.
Abortion in cattle	105
Acme harrow for spreading manure	17
*Acme harrow, value of	44
Acre, seeds for an	241
Acre, plants in an	241
Age for breeding heifers	174
Agricultural colleges	11
Alderney cattle	156
*Alfalfa, culture of	87
Apple worm	271
Apple, culture of	376
Area of cisterns, square and round	246
*Army worm	267
*Arrangement of dairy stables	205
*Asparagus, culture of	303
Asparagus, profits of	305
Ayrshire cows, profitable for milk	146
*Ayrshire cattle	157
Ayrshire cow, points of	164

B.

*Bantam fowls	237
*Barns	209
Barley, cultivation of	80

	PAGE.
*Barrack for hay	134
*Barn for sheep	200
Beans, field cultivation of	81
*Bean harvester	82
Bean, varieties of	305
Beets, sugar, composition of	144
*Beets, cultivation of	306
*Berkshire swine	201
*Bermuda grass, its value for hay	119
*Blackberry, culture of the	366
*Black Spanish fowls	231
*Bloat in cattle	100
Bloat in cattle, remedy for	101
Borers	271
*Bot flies, varieties of	252
*Blue grass, Kentucky	131
Bone dust, value of	26
Bone from glue factories	31
*Brahma, light, fowls	229
*Brahma, dark, fowls	235
Breeding age for heifers	174
Buckwheat as green manure	36
Buckwheat, cultivation of	83
Buckwheat, varieties of	84
*Buildings for the farm	204
Buildings, poultry house	227
Bushel, weight of	247
Business of farming, training for	9
Butter, feeding cows for	169
*Butter, churning and management of	179
*Butter workers	180, 181
*Butter box for shipping	182

C.

*Cabbage, cultivation of, for market	308
Cabbage as a fodder crop	77
Cabbage, insect pests of	265
Calf, management of	171

	PAGE.
Calf, five months old, in milking	173
Calf, lung worm of the	261
*Caps, hay	137
*Carrots, culture of	64, 320
Carts for farm use	296
Cattle, danger of choking	51
Cattle, feeding potatoes to	54
Cattle, advantage of currying	104
Cattle, abortion in	105
*Cattle, Jersey	146
Cattle, Alderney	156
*Cattle, Ayrshire	157
*Cattle, Dutch or Holstein	158
Cattle, Devon	158
*Cattle, Scotch polled	159
*Cattle, Hereford	160
*Cattle, Short Horn	161
Cattle, Polled Norfolk	159
Cattle, Swiss	162
Cattle, Texas	163
Cattle, young, care of	170
*Cattle, shed for	208, 220
*Cattle, bot flies	253
*Cauliflower, cultivation of	319
*Celery, culture of	322
Centrifugal separator	182
Characteristics of good and bad soils	13
Cherry, culture of	378
Chickens, early, rearing of	226
Chickens, gape worm of	261
Choice of a farm	18
*Choking in cattle, remedy for	54
*Churns and churning	179
Churning, temperature of cream for	181
Cisterns, contents of	246, 249
Clay land, retains manure	16
Clay land, how drained	22
*Cleveland Bay Horse	186
Climate, effect of, on crops	14

	PAGE.
Clover as green manure	36
Clover as green fodder	92, 137
*Clover, mammoth	115
Clover, Japan	126
Clover as a special crop	131
Clover hay, how made	136
*Clydesdale Horse	184
*Cochin fowls	236
*Collie dog	241
Collie dog, sagacity of	242
Colorado beetle	263
Compost, how much per acre	17
*Corn, Chester Co. Mammoth	53
*Corn, Golden Beauty	53
Corn, time for cutting	70
Corn for fodder	97
*Corn marker	98
Corn silk worm	266
*Corn planter	286
*Corn husking machine	293
*Corn shellers	295
*Corn, sweet, cultivation of	329
Cost of cultivating ten acres	78
Cow-peas, for fodder	95
Cows that have made fourteen pounds of butter in a week	150
Cows, the best for the dairy	167
Cows, feed and care of	169
Cows, kicking, how to manage	177
Cows, how to milk	176
*Cow milker	178
Cream, proper temperature for raising	246
Cream, how managed for churning	179
*Crevecœur fowls	234
*Crops, pests of	263
Cucumber beetle	268
Cucumber, culture of	330
Cultivating	45
*Cultivator, Planet, Jr	45, 285
*Culture of vegetables and fruits	301

Currants, culture of	370
Cut worms	269

D.

Dairy, the best cow for	167
*Dairy, management of	176, 182
Dairy, construction of	183
Dairy, stable for a	205
Devon cattle	158
Devon cow, points of	165
*Disc harrow	44
Disease, potato	57
Diseases, scab in sheep	199
Diseases, foot rot in sheep	199
*Dogs for the farm, Collie	241
Dogs as farm pests	251
*Double mould board plow	278
Drainage, cost of	21
*Drains, construction of	23
*Drill for grain	286
*Ducks, rearing of, and varieties	239
Dutch cattle for milk	146
*Dutch cow	158
Dutch cow, points of	165

E.

*Egg plant, culture of	332
*Engines for the farm	299
Ensilage discussed	140
Ensilage not safe feed	141
Ensilage, F. D. Curtis' opinion of	142
Ensilage *versus* roots	144
*Ergot in grasses causes abortion	108
*Ergot in rye	108
Escutcheon, significance of	173
Essex swine	203

	PAGE.
Exhaustion of land a fallacy	18
Exhaustion of land only temporary	22

F.

Farm, how to choose a	18
Feeding fowls	227
Feeding potatoes	54
Feeding roots	99
Feeding soiling crops	100
Feeding cows for milk and butter	169
Feeding horses	187
Feet, use of, in sowing	47
Fences	222
Fertilizers, effect of, not permanent	27
Fertilizers, preparation of, for use	28
Fertilizers, quantity per acre	28
Fertilizers, special, objected to	30
Fertilizing by feeding stock	37
Firming the soil	47
Fortunes made on rented land	18
Fodder corn, culture of	77, 98
Fodder corn, composition of	144
Fodder crops	85
Fodder crops, feeding	100
Fodder for the South	120
Fodder cutters, etc	292
Fowls, rearing	224
*Fowls, Plymouth Rocks	224
Fowls, management of early chickens	226
Fowls, feeding	227
*Fowls, Brahma	229, 235
*Fowls, Hamburgs	230
*Fowls, Black Spanish	231
*Fowls, Leghorns	232
*Fowls, Houdans	233
*Fowls, Poland	234
*Fowls, Crevecœurs	234

*Fowls, Wyandotte	235
*Fowls, Cochin	236
*Fowls, bantams	237
*Fowls, water	239
Fowls, turkeys	238
*Foxtail meadow grass	111
Fruit culture	361
*Fruit dryer	298
Fruit, orchard varieties of	374

G.

*Gooseberry, culture of the	370
*Grain drill	286
*Grapes, culture of	371
Grapes, varieties of	373
Grass seed per acre	93
*Grass, Orchard	110
*Grass, Ergot in	108
Grass, management of	110
Grass, mixed	112
*Grass, meadow foxtail	111
*Grass, red top	113
*Grass, Italian rye grass	113
*Grass, sweet vernal	114
*Grass, hard fescue	114
*Grass, sheep's fescue	114
*Grass, meadow fescue	115
Grass seed, how to sow	114
*Grass, Bermuda	119
*Grass, Southern crab	121
*Grass, crow's foot and barn yard	122
*Grass, Guinea	124
*Grass, Johnson	125
*Grass, Rhode Island bent	128
Grass seeds sown alone	129
*Grass, June	131
*Grass, Kentucky blue	132

	PAGE.
*Grass, fowl meadow	133
Grass lands, when manured	17
Green manuring	35
Grubs, white	270
Guano, value of	26
*Guinea grass	124
*Guernsey cattle	153

H.

*Hamburg fowls	230
Harrow, for spreading manure	17
*Harrow, chain	41
*Harrow, Acme	42
*Harrow, disc	44, 281
*Harrow, smoothing and brush	68, 281
Harrowing	38, 41
Harrowing sod	76
Hay, cutting and curing	134
Hay, clover, how made	136
*Hay caps, how made	137
*Hay, barns and sheds	210
*Hay making machines	287
Hedges for fences	223
Heifers, age to breed	174
*Hereford cattle	160
Hereford cow, points of	165
Hillsides, effect of, on crops	15
Hillsides, grasses for	128
*Holstein cattle	146, *158
Holstein cow, points of	164
Homestead, Mr. Crozier's	205
Hops, refuse, value of	29
*Horses for the farm	184
Horses, how fed	187
Horses, profit of breeding	188
Horses, market prices of	189
*Horses, Russian	191

Horses, how to breed	190
Horses, barns for	211
Horse-power, what it is	248
*Horse, bot flies of	253
*Houdan fowls	233
House for poultry	227
Hungarian grass	96

I.

*Implements, seed drill	61
*Wheat Cultivator	71
*Bean Harvester	82
*Corn Marker	98
*Harrows	281
*Plows	275
*Roller	282
*Mumbler	283
*Manure Spreader	70, 284
*Cultivators	285
*Corn Planters	286
*Grain Drill	286
*Mowers and Reapers	287
*Hay Tedder	289
*Hay Rakes	290
*Hay Forks, etc.	291
*Fodder Cutters	292
*Corn Husker	293
Insects, potato beetle	57
*Army Worm	75, 267
*Sheep Tick	199, 235
*Bot Flies	253
Lice, Fleas, etc.	254
*Louse of Sheep	255
*Scab of Sheep	256
*Potato Beetle	263
Chinch Bug	264
Hessian Fly	264
Cabbage Butterfly	265

Insects, Turnip Beetle... 265
       Pea Weevils.. 266
       Corn Worm... 266
       Tobacco Worm.. 266
       Cucumber Beetle... 268
       Squash Borer... 269
       Onion Maggot.. 269
       Cut Worms... 270
       White Grubs... 270
       Borers... 271
       Apple Worms.. 271
       Leaf Slugs... 271
       Plum Weevils.. 272
       Plant Lice... 272
       Rose "Bug".. 273
Insects injuring cabbages... 315
Insects attacking onions.. 344
*Intestinal worms... 261
*Italian rye grass... 113

J.

*Japan clover.. 126
Japanese bantams.. 237
*Jersey cattle... 146
Jersey cow, yield of... 148
*Jersey bull, portrait of... 149
Jersey, points of.. 163
Jersey calf, precocity of... 173
Jersey cattle, highest price for.. 174
Jersey cross, how improved... 175
Johnson grass in the South... 125
Johnson grass in Florida... 127
June grass.. 131

K.

*Kale, Scotch, cultivation of... 314
*Kentucky blue grass... 132

L.

	PAGE.
Lambs, lung worms of	261
Leaf slugs	271
*Leghorn fowls	232
Leicester sheep	192
*Lettuce, culture of	333
Lice, plant	272
*Light Brahma fowls	229
Lime, value of	32
Lime, how applied	23
Live stock of the farm	146
*Liver rot in sheep	260
*Louse of the sheep	255
Lucern, for soiling	86
*Lucern, culture of	87
Lung worms of calves, lambs, etc.	261

M.

*Machinery for the farm	275
*Machines, various farm	275
*Manure Spreader	70
*Corn Shellers	295
*Portable Engines	299
*For making hay	287
*Bean harvester	82
*Corn Marker	98
*Corn Planter	286
*Corn Husker	293
*Cultivators	285
*Fodder Cutters	292
*Grain Drill	286
*Hay Forks and Elevator	291
*Hay Tedder	289
*Hay Rake	290
*Mower and Reaper	287
*Mumbler	283

	PAGE.
*Machines, Plows	275
*Roller	282
Management of calves	171
Management of dairy	176
Management of horses	190
Management of a brood mare	191
*Mangels, culture of	59
Mangels, composition of	144
Manure retained in the soil	16
Manure, how much per acre	17, 29, 52, 302
Manure, when applied to grass	17
Manure, spreading	17, 69
Manure, comparative value of	26
Manure, green, value of	35
Manure for wheat	69
Manure, top dressing with, after hay	135
Manure, weight of a cord of	244
*Manure spreader	70, 283
Manure for onions	340
Manuring grass lands	17
Mare, management of breeding	191
Market prices of horses	189
Market garden crops	301
*Marker for corn	98
Masonry, measures for	249
Measures	246
*Melon, culture of the	334
*Merino, American, Sheep	197
Mildews	274
Milk, the best cows for	146
Milk, how to	176
*Milk tube	177
Milk, how managed	178
Millet for fodder	95
Millet, pearl, cultivation of	96
*Mill for farm use	297
Mixed farming the safest	19
Molds and mildews	274
*Mower and reaper	287, 288

INDEX. 393

	PAGE.
Muck, swamp, value of	29
Muck, swamp, how used	33
*Mumbler, the	283

N.

Necessity for personal work	9
*Norman horses	184

O.

Oats, culture of	76
Oats, yield of, per acre	76
Oats, weight of seed	79
Oats, rust in	80
Oats, with peas, for soiling	93
Okra, cultivation of	338
Onion maggot	260
Onion, cultivation of	338
Onion, varieties of	339
Onion, manures for	340
Onion, insects attacking	344
Onion, profits of	345
Onion, varieties of	347
Orchard fruits, culture of	374
Orchard Grass, for soiling	93
Orchard Grass, feeding value	99
*Orchard Grass, description of	110
Orchard, selection of soil for an	374
Oxford Down Sheep	194

P.

*Parasites of sheep	255
*Parsley, culture of	349
*Parsnip, culture of	64, 348

	PAGE.
Pasturing sheep on wheat	73
Peaches, culture of	377
Pears, culture of	376
Pea Weevil	265
Peas and oats for soiling	85
*Peas, culture of	350
*Pekin Ducks	239
*Pens for pigs	217
*Percheron Horses	185
Permanent grass, how procured	130
Peruvian Guano, value of	26
*Pests of the farm	251
*Pits for storing roots	66
*Piggery of F. D. Curtis	218
Planet, Jr., Cultivator	45, 285
Plants, cabbage, growing of	309
Plant lice	272
Plaster, value of, etc	34
*Plow, Roland chilled, and others	275
Plowing	38
Plowing in seed, advantage of	70
*Plows	39, 277
*Plows, slip point for	276
*Plows, subsoil	40, 280
*Plow sulky	277
*Plow swivel	277
Plum Weevils	272
Plum, culture of the	377
*Plymouth Rock fowls	224
Points of cattle	163
*Poland China swine	202
*Poland fowls	234
Ponies, Shetland, breeding of	190
Pork, method of curing	203
Potatoes, culture of	53
Potatoes, feeding to stock	54
Potato rot, remedy for	57
Potato bugs	263
Potato, sweet, culture of	58

	PAGE.
Potato, digger for	280
Potato, garden culture of	352
Poudrette, value of	29
Poultry, rearing and keeping	224
Poultry house	227
Power of horse and man	248
Preparing fertilizers for use	28
Preparing land for tillage	52
Prickly Comfrey	85
*Probang for choking cattle	54
Profit from ten acres of land	78
Profit from Mr. Crozier's dairy	152
Profit from a pure bred bull	168
Profit of breeding horses	188
Profit of market gardening	302
Profit of growing onions	345

Q.

Quantity of fertilizers per acre	28
Quantity of feed for a cow	103
Quantity of mixed grass seed per acre	112
Quantity of seeds to the acre	244, 359
Quince, culture of	379

R.

*Radish, culture of	353
*Raspberry, culture of	368
Rearing of poultry	224
Record of Mr. Crozier's herd	151
Record of Guernsey Cows	154
*Red Top grass	113
Refuse hops, value of, for manure	29
*Rhode Island bent grass	128
Restoring worn soils	18
*Rhubarb, culture of	352

	PAGE.
Roads, the value of good	21
*Roller, use of	46, 282
Roots compared with ensilage	144
Root crops, soils for	15
Root crops for feeding	59, 99
*Root crops, harvesting and storing	65
Ropes, strength of	248
Rose bug	273
Rotation of crops	52, 74
Rotten bone, value of, as a fertilizer	31
Rust on wheat	75
*Ruta Bagas, culture of	62
Rye as green manure	35
Rye, cultivation of	80
Rye for soiling or feeding green	86
*Rye, Ergot in	108

S.

Sagacity of Collie dog	242
Salt, value of	29, 34
Salt, value of, upon hay	134
Salt, quantity of, for butter	179
Saunders, Wm., Report on Grasses	125
*Scab in sheep	255
*Scotch Kale, cultivation of	314
*Scotch Polled Cow	159
Science of agriculture as compared with practice	12
Seed, choice of	53
Seed, plowing in	70
Seed, wheat, weight of	74
Seed, best, the cheapest	78
Seed, oats, weight of	79
Seed, mixed grasses	112
Seed, mixed, how sown	129
Seed, quantity to the acre	244, 359
Sewage, utilization of	138
Shallots, culture of	346

	PAGE.
*Share, slip point for plows	276
Sheep, experience with	191
*Sheep, South Down	192
*Sheep, Cotswold	193
*Sheep, Shropshire Down	194
Sheep, Beacon Down	192
*Sheep, Hampshire	195
*Sheep, Oxford Down	196
Sheep, Leicester	192
*Sheep, American Merino	197
Sheep, feeding in winter	198
Sheep, foot rot in	199
*Sheep, barns and sheds for	213
*Sheep, bot flies	253
*Sheep, dipping for scab	256
*Sheep, insect parasites of	255
*Sheep louse	255
Sheep, pasturing on wheat	73
*Sheep ticks	199, 255
*Sheep, bladder worms of	257
*Sheep, fluke worm	260
*Sheep, liver rot in	260
*Shetland ponies	190
*Shipping box for butter	182
*Short Horn cattle	161
*Short Horn fat heifer	162
Short Horn Cow, points of	166
*Slip share for plows	276
Small fruit culture	361
*Smoothing harrow	68, 281
Smut in wheat	75
Sod, value of a	26
Soil, characteristics of	15
Soil, a good or bad	13
Soil, how to restore	18
Soil, good, how known	18
Soil, what it needs	32
Soiling and fodder crops	85
Soiling crops, feeding of	100

	PAGE.
Soiling, cost and profit of	103
Soiling, peas and oats for	85
Sowing seed	48
Spinach, culture of	354
*Spreading manure, machine for	70
Squash borer	269
Squash, culture of	355
Steam engines for the farm	299
Steam engine, power of	248
*Stone drains	23
Straw, bean, value of	83
Strawberry, culture of	361
Strength of ropes	248
*Subsoil plows	40, 280
Success, how a young man met with	10
Sugar beets, composition of	144
*Sulky plow	277
Summer feeding cattle	102
Swamp lands	15
Swamp muck, value and use of	29, 33
Sweet potatoes	58
Swine, breeding of	201
*Swine, internal parasites	259
*Swine, Berkshire	201
*Swine, Poland China	202
Swine, Essex	202
Swine, management of	203
Swine, Large Yorkshire	203
*Swine, pens for	217
Swiss cattle	162
*Swivel plow	277

T.

Tables of weights and measures	244
*Tape worms of sheep and swine	258
Temperature, effect of	30
Temperature for setting milk	178, 181

	PAGE.
Temperature for churning	181
Timothy grass, feeding value	100, 117
Timothy and clover, culture of	116
*Tomato, culture of	356
Top dressing grass lands	139
Training for farming	9
*Trichina spiralis of swine	262
*Trochar and canula	100
Turnip beetle	265
Turnip, culture of	59, 77, 358
*Turnip, Cow Horn, value of	63
Turnip, feeding sheep on	198
*Turnip, varieties of	358
Turkeys, rearing of	238

V.

Value of manures	26
Vegetable pests of crops	273
Vegetable culture	302
*Vegetables, varieties of	303
Vetches for fodder	85

W.

Water Cress, culture of	328
Water fowls	239
*Water melon, culture of	338
Weevils, plum	272
Weight of Clyde Horses	185
Weight of a cord of manure	244
Weight of bushels	247
Weight of lead pipes	248
Weight of water in pipes	249
Weights and measures	244

	PAGE.
Wheat, culture of	68
Wheat, manure for	69
Wheat after a root crop	71
*Wheat, cultivator for	71
Wheat, effect of late sowing	72
Wheat, pasturing with sheep	73
Wheat, seed	74
Wheat, remedy for rust and smut	75
Wheat, rust and smut	274
Wire fences	223
Wire worms	270
*Worms, intestinal	261
*Wooden drains	24
*Wyandotte fowls	235

Y.

Yards for poultry	227
Yield of Jersey Cow	148
Yield of remarkable Jersey Cows	150
Yield of Guernsey Cows	154
Young cattle, care of	170

GARDENING FOR PROFIT.

—BY—

PETER HENDERSON.

To such as are intending to begin the business of Market Gardening, we offer for their instruction our work, "Gardening for Profit," published first in 1866, and a new edition in 1873. "Gardening for Profit" has had a larger sale, probably, than any work ever published on the subject of Horticulture. Upward of 100,000 copies have been sold, and we have hundreds of grateful testimonials from those who have been benefited by its teachings. The subjects of its contents are:

The Men Fitted for the Business.—Amount of Capital Required and Working Force per Acre.—Profits of Market Gardening.—The Market Gardens near London.—Location, Situation and Laying Out.—Soils, Drainage and Preparation.—Manures.—Implements.—The Uses and Management of Cold Frames.—The Formation and Management of Hot-beds.—Forcing Pits and Green-houses.—Seeds and Seed Raising.—How, When and Where to Sow Seeds.—Transplanting.—Packing of Vegetables for Shipping.—Preservation of Vegetables in Winter.—Insects.—Vegetables; their Variety and Cultivation.—Monthly Calendar of Operations.

Sent post-paid, on receipt of $1.50.

PETER HENDERSON & CO.,
35 & 37 Cortlandt St., New York.

PRACTICAL FLORICULTURE.

—BY—

PETER HENDERSON.

The first edition was published in 1868, the second edition in 1873, and the third edition in December, 1878. It was written to teach how flowers and plants can best be " grown for profit." The success of this book has been fully as marked as that of "Gardening for Profit," when we consider that it only refers to a business exclusively a luxury. Upward of *thirty thousand* copies of this work have been sold, and it has been the means of establishing thousands of persons in an agreeable, and, in a majority of cases, profitable business. Its contents embrace:

Aspect and Soil.—Laying out the Lawn and Flower Garden.—Designs for Ornamental Grounds.—Planting of Flower Beds.—Soils for Potting.—Temperature and Moisture.—The Potting of Plants.—Cold Frames; Winter Protection.—Construction of Hot-beds.—Green-house Structures.—Green-houses attached to Dwellings.—Modes of Heating.—Base Burning Water Heater.—Propagation of Plants by Seeds.—What Varieties come True from Seed.—Propagation of Plants by Cuttings.—How Plants and Flowers are Grown.—Propagation of Lilies.—Culture of the Rose.—Culture of the Verbena.—Culture of the Tuberose.—Orchid Culture—Holland Bulbs.—Cape Bulbs; Varieties and Culture.—Culture of Winter-Flowering Plants.—Construction of Bouquets, Baskets, etc.—Wire Designs for Cut Flowers.—Hanging Baskets.—Parlor and Window Gardening.—Wardian Cases, Ferneries, etc.—Formation of Rockwork.—Insects.—Are Plants injurious to Health?—Nature's Law of Colors.—Packing Plants.—Plants by Mail.—The Profits of Floriculture.—How to Become a Florist.—Short Descriptions of Soft-Wooded or Bedding Plants of the Leading Kinds.—What Flowers will Grow in the Shade.—Green-house and Stove or Hot-house Plants.—Annuals, Hardy Herbaceous, Perennial and Biennial Plants, Ornamental Shrubs and Climbers.—Culture of Grape Vines under Glass.—Diary of Operations for Each Day in the Year.

Sent post-paid, on receipt of $1.50.

PETER HENDERSON & CO.,

35 & 37 Cortlandt St., New York.

GARDENING FOR PLEASURE.

— BY —

PETER HENDERSON.

This book was written by Mr. Henderson in 1875, to meet the wants of those desiring information on gardening for their private use, and who had no desire to make it a business. It is flattering to state that the demand for this book, for the time it has been issued, has been greater than either of its predecessors. Its scope of subjects is naturally greater than either "Gardening for Profit" or "Practical Floriculture," as it embraces directions for the propagation and culture of fruit, flowers and vegetables. Its contents include:

Soil and Location.—Drainage.—Preparation of the Ground.—Walks.—Manures.—How to Use Concentrated Fertilizers.—Special Fertilizers for Particular Plants.—The Lawn.—Design for Garden.—Planting of Lawns and Flower Beds.—Fall or Holland Bulbs.—Propagation of Plants by Seeds.—Propagation of Plants by Cuttings.—Propagating by Layering.—About Grafting and Budding.—How Grafting and Budding are Done.—Treatment of Tropical Bulbs, Seeds, etc.—The Potting of Plants.—Winter Flowering Plants.—Unhealthy Plants; the Remedy.—Plants Suited for Summer Decoration.—Hanging Baskets.—Window Gardening.—Parlor Gardening, or the Cultivation of Plants in Rooms.—Wardian Cases.—Ferneries.—Jardinieres.—Winter-Forcing the Lily of the Valley.—Green-houses attached to Dwellings.—A Detached Green-house or Grapery.—Heating by Hot Water.—Green-house Pits without Artificial Heat.—Combined Cellar and Green-house.—Hot-beds.—Shrubs.—Climbers and Trees.—Hardy Herbaceous Perennials.—Annual Flowering Plants.—Flowers which will Grow in the Shade.—Insects.—Mildew.—Frozen Plants.—Mulching.—Are Plants in Rooms Injurious to Health?—Shading.—The Laws of Color in Flowers.—Pruning.—Hardy Grapes.—Cold Grapery.—The Hot-house or Forcing Grapery.—The Strawberry.—Cottage Gardening; a Digression.—The Vegetable Garden.—Garden Implements.—Monthly Calendar of Operations.

Sent post-paid, on receipt of $1.50.

PETER HENDERSON & CO.,
35 & 37 Cortlandt St., New York.

GARDEN AND FARM TOPICS.

Published in January, 1884. Contains portrait of Peter Henderson and embraces within its scope the following subjects:

Popular Bulbs and their Culture.—Window Gardening, and Care of Plants in Rooms.—Propagation of Plants.—Rose Growing in Winter.—Green-house Structures, and Modes of Heating.—Formation and Renovation of Lawns.—Onion Growing.—How to Raise Cabbage and Cauliflower.—On the Growing and Preserving of Celery.—The New Celery "White Plume."—Strawberry Culture.—Root Crops for Farm Stock.—Culture of Alfalfa or Lucern.—Manures and their Modes of Application.—Market Gardening around New York.—The Use of the Feet in Sowing and Planting.—Popular Errors and Scientific Dogmas in Horticulture.—Humbugs in Horticulture.—Draining.

Sent post-paid, on receipt of $1.50.

HENDERSON'S HAND-BOOK OF PLANTS.
— BY —
PETER HENDERSON.

This new work is designed to fill a want that many amateur and professional Horticulturists have often felt, the need of a concise yet comprehensive Dictionary of Plants. The work above named, written and compiled with great care, we think will fully meet such a want.

The scope of the work embraces the Botanical Name, Derivation, Linnæan and Natural orders of Botany of all the Leading Genera of Ornamental and Useful Plants, up to the present time (comprising every plant of importance relating to the mechanic arts, as well as to the green-house and vegetable garden), with concise instructions for propagation and culture. A valuable feature of the book, particularly to amateurs, is the great care that has been given to obtain all known local or common names; and a comprehensive glossary of Botanical and Technical terms is also given, which will be found of great value even to the experienced Horticulturist.

As a book of reference, HENDERSON'S HAND-BOOK OF PLANTS will take the place, for all practical purposes, of the expensive and voluminous European works of this kind, as it has been written with a view to meet the wants of those engaged in Horticulture in this country. Instructions for the culture of many important plants have been given at length.

HENDERSON'S HAND-BOOK OF PLANTS is a large octavo volume of 412 pages, printed on fine white paper, and handsomely bound in cloth.

We will forward the book, post-paid, by mail, on receipt of $3.00; or we will send it, as well as any or all of our other books, as a *Premium* on orders for *Seeds* or *Plants* selected from our Catalogue of "EVERYTHING FOR THE GARDEN." Full information as to how these Book Premiums may be obtained will be found in the Catalogue, which we shall be pleased to send to any address free of charge.

PETER HENDERSON & CO.,
35 & 37 Cortlandt St., New York.

SPECIAL NOTICE.

All purchasers of this book, *"How the Farm Pays,"* are entitled to receive our Descriptive Catalogue of Farm and Garden Seeds, Implements and Fertilizers, *free of charge.* The catalogue, ready Jan. 1st, 1885, is a large, finely illustrated book of 132 pages, containing beautiful colored plates. Any one desiring it, however, must fill in their name and address below, *detach this sheet,* and return to us, when the catalogue will be mailed.

PETER HENDERSON & CO.,
35 & 37 Cortlandt Street,
NEW YORK.

P. H. & Co.—Please mail Catalogue as per above offer to

Name............

Town............

County

State............

www.ingramcontent.com/pod-product-compliance
Lightning Source LLC
Chambersburg PA
CBHW051246300426
44114CB00011B/905